Microsoft® SharePoint® 2007 For Dummies®

Cheat Sheet

W9-BAR-161

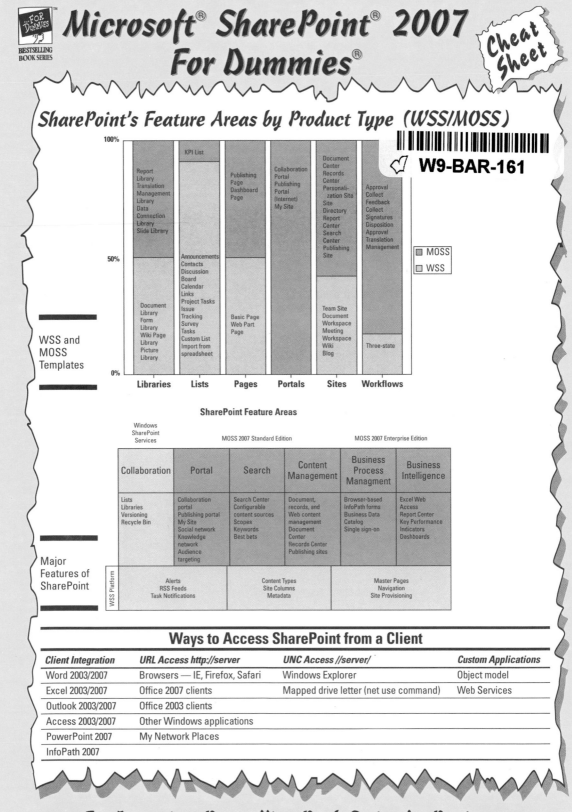

SharePoint's Feature Areas by Product Type (WSS/MOSS)

WSS and MOSS Templates

Libraries:
- Report Library
- Translation Management Library
- Data Connection Library
- Slide Library
- Document Library
- Form Library
- Wiki Page Library
- Picture Library

Lists:
- KPI List
- Announcements
- Contacts
- Discussion Board
- Calendar
- Links
- Project Tasks
- Issue Tracking
- Survey
- Tasks
- Custom List
- Import from spreadsheet

Pages:
- Publishing Page
- Dashboard Page
- Basic Page
- Web Part Page

Portals:
- Collaboration Portal
- Publishing Portal (Internet)
- My Site

Sites:
- Document Center
- Records Center
- Personalization Site
- Site Directory
- Report Center
- Search Center
- Publishing Site
- Team Site
- Document Workspace
- Meeting Workspace
- Wiki
- Blog

Workflows:
- Approval
- Collect Feedback
- Collect Signatures
- Disposition Approval
- Translation Management
- Three-state

Legend: ■ MOSS □ WSS

SharePoint Feature Areas

Major Features of SharePoint

Windows SharePoint Services	MOSS 2007 Standard Edition			MOSS 2007 Enterprise Edition	
Collaboration	Portal	Search	Content Management	Business Process Managment	Business Intelligence
Lists Libraries Versioning Recycle Bin	Collaboration portal Publishing portal My Site Social network Knowledge network Audience targeting	Search Center Configurable content sources Scopes Keywords Best bets	Document, records, and Web content management Document Center Records Center Publishing sites	Browser-based InfoPath forms Business Data Catalog Single sign-on	Excel Web Access Report Center Key Performance Indicators Dashboards
WSS Platform	Alerts RSS Feeds Task Notifications		Content Types Site Columns Metadata		Master Pages Navigation Site Provisioning

Ways to Access SharePoint from a Client

Client Integration	URL Access http://server	UNC Access //server/	Custom Applications
Word 2003/2007	Browsers — IE, Firefox, Safari	Windows Explorer	Object model
Excel 2003/2007	Office 2007 clients	Mapped drive letter (net use command)	Web Services
Outlook 2003/2007	Office 2003 clients		
Access 2003/2007	Other Windows applications		
PowerPoint 2007	My Network Places		
InfoPath 2007			

For Dummies: Bestselling Book Series for Beginners

Microsoft® SharePoint® 2007 For Dummies®

Cheat Sheet

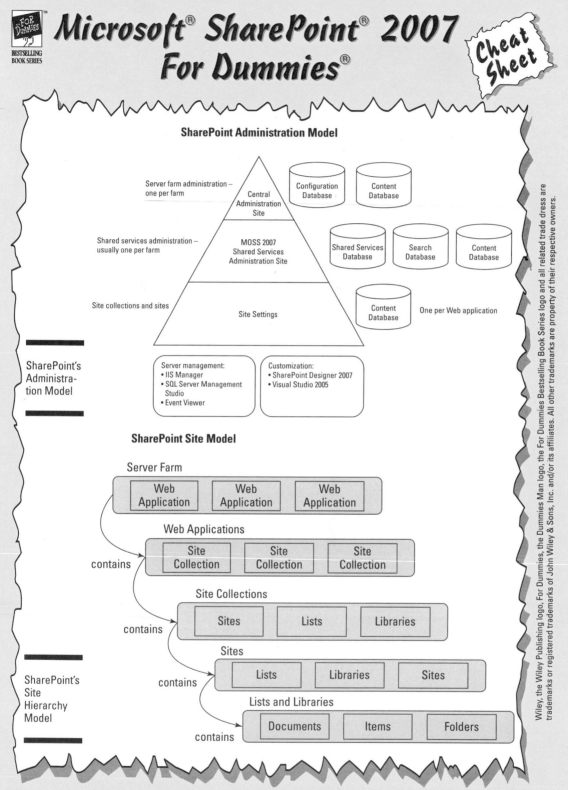

SharePoint Administration Model

Server farm administration – one per farm

Central Administration Site

Configuration Database

Content Database

Shared services administration – usually one per farm

MOSS 2007 Shared Services Administration Site

Shared Services Database

Search Database

Content Database

Site collections and sites

Site Settings

Content Database

One per Web application

SharePoint's Administration Model

Server management:
- IIS Manager
- SQL Server Management Studio
- Event Viewer

Customization:
- SharePoint Designer 2007
- Visual Studio 2005

SharePoint Site Model

Server Farm

Web Application · Web Application · Web Application

contains

Web Applications

Site Collection · Site Collection · Site Collection

contains

Site Collections

Sites · Lists · Libraries

contains

Sites

Lists · Libraries · Sites

contains

Lists and Libraries

Documents · Items · Folders

contains

SharePoint's Site Hierarchy Model

For Dummies: Bestselling Book Series for Beginners

Microsoft® SharePoint® 2007 FOR DUMMIES®

by Vanessa Williams

Wiley Publishing, Inc.

Microsoft® SharePoint® 2007 For Dummies®

Published by
Wiley Publishing, Inc.
111 River Street
Hoboken, NJ 07030-5774

www.wiley.com

Copyright © 2007 by Wiley Publishing, Inc., Indianapolis, Indiana

Published by Wiley Publishing, Inc., Indianapolis, Indiana

Published simultaneously in Canada

For general information on our other products and services, please contact our Customer Care Department within the U.S. at 800-762-2974, outside the U.S. at 317-572-3993, or fax 317-572-4002.

For technical support, please visit www.wiley.com/techsupport.

Wiley also publishes its books in a variety of electronic formats. Some content that appears in print may not be available in electronic books.

Library of Congress Control Number: 2006939595

ISBN: 978-0-470-09941-4

Manufactured in the United States of America

10 9 8 7 6 5 4

WILEY

About the Author

Vanessa Williams is an author and consultant specializing in SharePoint technologies. She helps organizations, technology professionals, and end users find meaningful uses for technologies, such as SharePoint, Office 2007, Visual Studio, and the .NET Framework.

Vanessa grew up in Indianapolis, where she graduated from the Kelley School of Business at Indiana University with a Bachelor of Science degree in Business Management and Computer Information Systems. She still lives in Indy, about three miles south of downtown in the wonderful Garfield Park South neighborhood.

In her spare time, Vanessa likes to read books about sociology, religion, spirituality, and current affairs. She enjoys hiking, traveling, and spending time with her family, including her two dogs Rosie and Buffy. She also enjoys staying current on enterprise technologies and consumer electronics.

Vanessa loves to talk about SharePoint. You can contact her via her Web site at www.sharepointgrrl.com.

Author's Acknowledgments

In the time that's passed since I wrote *SharePoint 2003 For Dummies* (Wiley), I now have two dogs and another cat. I couldn't have finished this book if I didn't have Buffy (Dog # 1) to lick my toes and Rosie (Dog # 2) to play tug-of-war with. The cat lies on my desk while I'm trying to work. I could do without the cat.

The number of people (and animals) it takes to produce a book is mind-numbing. I came in contact with a brave few this time around. I know them mostly by their assigned color and the initials they used to sign their editorial comments. Many thanks to pgl (pink), Jen (green), and kc (red). I'll never forget our time together in SharePoint purgatory.

I must also thank all the poor souls who've had to endure my SharePoint-babble while writing this book — over breakfast with Mel, over far too many coffees with Denis, over e-mail with Katie, and over dinner with Mel. I promise to stop talking about SharePoint eventually.

Finally, I need to thank all the readers. You bought the first SharePoint book and sent wonderful feedback. You took me with you to your server rooms, board rooms, and rest rooms. I hope to have that privilege again.

Publisher's Acknowledgments

We're proud of this book; please send us your comments through our online registration form located at www.dummies.com/register.

Some of the people who helped bring this book to market include the following:

Acquisitions, Editorial, and Media Development

Project Editor: Paul Levesque

Acquisitions Editor: Katie Feltman

Copy Editor: Jennifer Riggs

Technical Editor: Ken Cox

Editorial Manager: Leah Cameron

Media Development Manager: Laura VanWinkle

Editorial Assistant: Amanda Foxworth

Sr. Editorial Assistant: Cherie Case

Cartoons: Rich Tennant (www.the5thwave.com)

Composition Services

Project Coordinator: Adrienne Martinez

Layout and Graphics: Stephanie D. Jumper, Barbara Moore, Laura Pence, Heather Ryan, Erin Zeltner

Proofreader: John Greenough

Indexer: Aptara

Anniversary Logo Design: Richard Pacifico

Publishing and Editorial for Technology Dummies

    Richard Swadley, Vice President and Executive Group Publisher

    Andy Cummings, Vice President and Publisher

    Mary Bednarek, Executive Acquisitions Director

    Mary C. Corder, Editorial Director

Publishing for Consumer Dummies

    Diane Graves Steele, Vice President and Publisher

    Joyce Pepple, Acquisitions Director

Composition Services

    Gerry Fahey, Vice President of Production Services

    Debbie Stailey, Director of Composition Services

Contents at a Glance

Table of Contents

Introduction

SharePoint is nothing new. Heck, it's been around since 2001. As fast as technology changes, SharePoint should be ancient history by now. Quite to the contrary, SharePoint has finally found its legs after all these years.

ShareWhat, you say? SharePoint is the server-side connective tissue that binds the slippery client-side outputs of office workers into a manageable, searchable, and accessible information environment. Gone are the days when workers just organized their files in electronic folders and had to call the help desk every time something was deleted accidentally. SharePoint provides a self-service environment where office workers can take control of information — how it's organized, who gets access to it, and how it's displayed.

Don't feel bad if you don't know SharePoint from Shinola. You aren't alone. Many obstacles are along the path to a successful SharePoint implementation. This book uses plain English to get you started on your SharePoint journey so that nothing trips you up along the way.

Coming Out of the Shadows

Since SharePoint was first released in 2001, Microsoft has made steady progress on the product's features. The first few releases of SharePoint consisted primarily of the ability to dynamically generate team Web sites. These sites hosted document libraries, tasks lists, and calendars to enable a small team of users to manage documents and collaborate on a project. The initial product was called SharePoint Team Services but was changed in 2003 to Windows SharePoint Services (WSS).

The building blocks — lists, libraries, and user-customizable Web pages — used by WSS to create team sites turned out to be very versatile and could be used for more than just team collaboration. Many companies started creating SharePoint sites to solve all kinds of business problems, such as managing help desk tickets and automating expense check requests.

Microsoft created a more expensive add-on product, SharePoint Portal Server, that added the ability to create portals and search across team sites. The portal allowed companies to provide centralized access to all their team sites.

Despite SharePoint's usefulness, the product's adoption was nichey and sporadic. Also, there was (and still is) significant confusion in the marketplace about what SharePoint is and what it does. When Microsoft sat down to consider the product's future after the 2003 release, they saw an opportunity to more tightly integrate the product with the Office clients that virtually all office workers already have on their desktops. Increased integration with Office 2007 catapulted SharePoint onto center stage.

Microsoft used a host of existing and newly created products to develop the 2007 release of SharePoint. Like pieces of a puzzle, the following product opportunities came together to create a better SharePoint:

- ✔ **ASP.NET 2.0:** The release of ASP.NET 2.0 provided the foundational layer that was missing in previous versions of SharePoint. By using ASP.NET 2.0, Microsoft was able to focus on building a better SharePoint without spending so much time on low-level services. Some of the ASP.NET 2.0 features used or extended by SharePoint include the Web Parts framework, personalization, pluggable authentication, and master pages. WSS 3.0 is truly a testimony to what you can build with ASP.NET 2.0!

- ✔ **Content Management Server 2002:** Like chocolate and peanut butter, many companies, including Microsoft, realized that Content Management Server could be used to support SharePoint. Instead of having a separate server, Microsoft decided to roll Web content management into SharePoint.

- ✔ **Office 2007:** Microsoft realized that companies need a compelling reason to upgrade to Office 2007. Adding more features to Word and Excel doesn't cut it any more. In addition to completely redesigning the look and feel of most Office clients for the Office 2007 release, Microsoft added many new features that are available only via a server infrastructure. SharePoint is a major player in providing the Office 2007 server infrastructure.

- ✔ **Search:** In 2006, Google went after the desktop, and Microsoft went after search. Microsoft introduced a family of search products that target the Web, desktop, and enterprise with the expressly stated intent of taking Google head-on. SharePoint is the key element that delivers enterprise search.

- ✔ **Windows Workflow Foundation (WF):** The release of WF with version 3.0 of the .NET Framework brings a workflow engine to SharePoint, Office 2007, and all applications that run on Windows. Workflows make it possible to step through a process, such as submitting a document for approval. Building a separate workflow engine decouples workflow capabilities from specific server products. Instead of having only a few products with workflow, all products can have workflow. SharePoint extends WF and provides several out-of-the-box workflow implementations that businesses can use to automate business processes without writing custom code.

By taking advantage of these products along with the new goals of winning search while keeping its talons securely fastened to the business desktop, Microsoft completely re-architected SharePoint into a layer of technologies that consists of these two primary products:

- ✔ **Windows SharePoint Services (WSS) version 3.0** is the foundational product that provides a set of building blocks for creating SharePoint applications. The two primary usage scenarios for WSS are still document management and collaboration. The third usage scenario is a platform for creating applications with SharePoint.

- ✔ **Microsoft Office SharePoint Server (MOSS) 2007** is the server-side infrastructure that turns Office 2007 clients into generators and consumers of content for SharePoint applications. MOSS 2007 is the successor to SharePoint Portal Server 2003. Although MOSS supports the creation of portals, Microsoft has expanded it to include many enterprise-level services, such as business intelligence and business process integration. MOSS 2007 is an example of an application created using WSS as a platform.

At this point, I could give you the obligatory laundry list of SharePoint's features. Even if I did that, you still wouldn't understand how to use SharePoint. Instead, this book focuses on using SharePoint's out-of-the box application building blocks to get up and running solving problems relevant to your business.

Who Should Read This Book

Now that SharePoint is no longer the red-headed stepchild of Microsoft's server family, an increasing amount of buzz surrounds it. Whether you're brand new to SharePoint or you're looking to get acquainted with SharePoint's new features, this book is for you.

To help you cut through the hype, this book tells you everything you need to know to start using WSS or MOSS 2007 in your business today. If you're unsure about which SharePoint product to implement, I give you the breakdown of where WSS features end and MOSS 2007 picks up.

You'll get guidance for planning your project and ideas for ways you might use SharePoint in your organization. I don't go into the details of performing upgrades in this book, although I do explain how to set up and configure a SharePoint infrastructure.

This book isn't really intended for end-users unless you're curious about SharePoint's configuration options. Instead, I suggest my book *Office 2007 and SharePoint Productivity For Dummies* (Wiley). Also, I don't cover customizing SharePoint in this book. I suggest you see my book *SharePoint Designer 2007 For Dummies* where I show you how to create custom sites and solutions for SharePoint that don't require you to write code.

How to Use This Book

I know you don't want to read this book cover to cover, and you don't have to. Your role in SharePoint's implementation makes some topics more relevant than others. If you want to zero in on a particular topic, you can use the table of contents and index to focus on that coverage. Part II focuses almost exclusively on Windows SharePoint Services, whereas Parts III and IV lean more toward MOSS 2007 coverage. I compiled a list of topics that I know many of you are interested in:

- ✔ Setting up, configuring, deploying, and administering SharePoint — see Chapters 1, 2, 3, 18, and 19.

- ✔ Understanding the basics of SharePoint sites, including how to create, configure, and secure them — see Chapters 4, 5, and 6.

- ✔ Understanding how to add and manage content in SharePoint — see Chapters 7 and 8.

- ✔ Figuring out how end users interact with SharePoint — see Chapters 9 and 10.

- ✔ Setting up your portal and people directory in MOSS 2007 — see Chapters 11, 12, and 13.

- ✔ Configuring and understanding SharePoint's search features — see Chapter 14.

- ✔ Diving into SharePoint's options for document and records management — see Chapter 15.

- ✔ Using SharePoint to manage and publish content to portals and Internet-facing sites and exploring your options for customizing SharePoint's look and feel — see Chapter 16.

- ✔ Getting introduced to SharePoint's features for integrating enterprise applications into SharePoint, creating business intelligence (BI) dashboards and reports, and displaying Excel spreadsheets in SharePoint — see Chapter 17.

You'll get the most out of this book if you work through the examples when you read the text. You may also find it helpful to have access to both a WSS server and a MOSS 2007 server so you can see the differences between the products.

I run both servers on a single physical machine using Virtual Server 2005. As long as you have a fast processor along with plenty of RAM and disk space, you should be fine using a virtual server for a testing environment.

Foolish Assumptions

While writing this book, I had to make a few assumptions about you — the reader. Don't worry, I didn't take you for the pocket protector type with a dozen servers in your bedroom. But I wouldn't be surprised to find a hipster PDA and a pile of Mountain Dew cans.

In order to work the examples in this book, you need access to a working SharePoint installation with either WSS version 3 or MOSS 2007. If you don't already have a SharePoint server, I walk you through how to install SharePoint in Chapter 2. I'm assuming you know your way around a Windows server and have basic networking skills. You certainly don't need to be certified or know how to build a server.

I also assume that you're working inside a Windows network that's running Active Directory (AD). You don't have to run AD to perform most of the examples in this book. The examples in this book haven't been tested when accessing SharePoint from the Internet.

SharePoint is a server-based technology, so you have to know the name of your server in order to access SharePoint's resources. Because I don't know what the names of your servers are, I have to assume that you know the server names and URL paths to your SharePoint server. While I walk you through all the various ways you can access SharePoint (it isn't just the browser, you know — see Chapter 6), you have to substitute your server and path names to access the resources in your SharePoint deployment.

How This Book Is Organized

This book groups related SharePoint topics together in parts. Each part covers a different aspect of implementing or using SharePoint.

Part 1: Setting Up SharePoint

In this part, you get your first lessons in SharePoint-speak. I walk you through setting up SharePoint servers and configuring the high-level infrastructure that holds your business content. You probably want to read Chapter 1, but you can browse Chapters 2 and 3 if you already have a functioning SharePoint server.

Part II: Exploring SharePoint's Building Blocks

Part II walks you through all the foundational elements used to create solutions in SharePoint. Chapters 4, 5, and 6 address issues related to creating, navigating, and securing a site infrastructure. Chapters 7 and 8 get into the meat and potatoes of solving business problems with two of SharePoint's most useful features: data and business process management.

Part III: Improving Information Worker Collaboration and Productivity

In Part III, I start to look at some of the ways that end users interact with SharePoint in their native habitat, Windows client applications. Chapter 9 focuses on accessing SharePoint through Office 2007 clients, other Windows applications, and alternatives to using Web browsers. In Chapter 10, I explore using e-mail to send information to and receiving information from SharePoint. Chapters 11–14 deal primarily with MOSS 2007 features, including portals, user profiles, personalization, and enterprise search.

Part IV: Enterprise Applications for SharePoint

In this part, I cover some of the more advanced features of MOSS 2007. Chapter 15 explains the document management features offered by WSS and how MOSS 2007 expands on those with advanced document management and records management features. Chapter 16 explores Web content publishing, along with opportunities for customizing SharePoint's look and feel. I explain the opportunities for data integration and creating business intelligence dashboards in Chapter 17.

Part V: Administering SharePoint

The chapters in this part follow up on the material covered in Chapters 2 and 3 by explaining SharePoint's server farm administration features. You'll see how to monitor your server farm and perform a backup.

Part VI: The Part of Tens

When it comes to SharePoint, a single resource is never enough. In Chapter 20, I share with you my top ten list of resources for staying up to speed on all things SharePoint. And because making the business case is vital to all successful SharePoint implementations, I offer you ten positive outcomes that you might aspire to achieve with your SharePoint implementation.

Icons Used in This Book

You'll find a handful of icons in this book, and here's what they mean:

Tips point out a handy shortcut or help you understand something important to SharePoint.

This icon marks something to remember, such as how you handle a particularly tricky part of SharePoint configuration.

This icon means that what follows is technical, insider stuff. You don't have to read it if you don't want to, but if you want to become a SharePoint pro (and who doesn't?), take a look.

Although the Warning icon appears rarely, when you need to be wary of a problem or common pitfall, this icon lets you know.

Where to Go from Here

Alright, you're all set and ready to jump into Chapter 1. You don't have to start there; you can jump in anywhere you like — the book was written to allow you to do just that. But if you want to get the full story from the beginning, jump to Chapter 1 first — that's where all the action starts. (If you already have a SharePoint server up and running, you might want to jump ahead to Chapter 4, where you can get your hands dirty with some site content.)

Part I

Setting Up SharePoint

The 5th Wave   By Rich Tennant

"Okay, well, I think we all get the gist of where Jerry was going with the site map."

In this part . . .

Discover SharePoint's features and how they fit into your existing technology environment. I show you how to get up and running with your very own SharePoint server. Because installing SharePoint is only half the battle, I also get you started on the necessary next steps you'll need to carry out before you can hang that Open sign on your SharePoint deployment.

Chapter 1

Getting to Know SharePoint

*I*f you believe everything you read on the Internet (and who doesn't?), you know that SharePoint is either an over-hyped Microsoft product with no real business value or it's the next Messiah in information and knowledge management. So, which is it? Only you can answer that question.

SharePoint's usefulness in your organization is determined by whether SharePoint has a role in your existing information systems environment. To determine SharePoint's role, you really have to understand what SharePoint is and what it does. However, simply having this knowledge doesn't guarantee you a successful SharePoint implementation. However, it does give you a strong foundation, which is what this chapter is all about.

Understanding SharePoint Technology

SharePoint is a family of technologies from Microsoft that provides a server infrastructure to support the needs of information workers and their employers. These needs include collaboration, knowing who's online, document storage, and the ability to inform and be informed. The companies that hire information workers need to audit, monitor, organize, retain, and protect information.

SharePoint makes it possible for companies to engage all their information workers through the tools people are using already — Office clients (such as Word and Excel), Internet browsers (such as Internet Explorer), and e-mail clients (such as Outlook). Obviously, SharePoint works best with Office 2007. Whether you're using Office 2007 or OpenOffice, SharePoint gives employers a means to connect with workers where they work — at their desktops.

By reaching workers where they work, companies can use SharePoint as a key component for implementing new strategic initiatives and internal communications plans. Beyond sending blast e-mails and convening one-time town hall meetings, companies can use SharePoint to integrate information about campaigns, achievement of performance objectives, and company news into workers' daily routines. Sound like information overload? It need not be. SharePoint makes it easy to target content so that people see only the information that's relevant to achieving their objectives.

With SharePoint, companies can create a managed information environment that isn't centrally managed. Yes, it's secure, protected, and audited, but workers make decisions about how information is organized. If workers change their minds about the organizing structure, it can be changed easily. By evaluating the ways that employees set up their work environments in SharePoint — where they store documents, the properties they affix to documents, and with whom they're collaborating — the information environment created in SharePoint can provide companies with valuable feedback. When's the last time your information environment told you how many Word documents pertained to a particular customer account or product? You can get that kind of information from SharePoint.

SharePoint also provides workers with the ability to connect with each other. Instead of sending files back and forth via e-mail, workers can set up information environments that make it easy to collaborate on documents or share a calendar.

SharePoint uses a Web site infrastructure to deliver the bulk of its features. Users can use a Web browser or familiar Office clients, such as Word and Excel, to access SharePoint's features. Office clients enable information workers to use familiar tools in new ways, which reduces training and support costs and increases solution development opportunities. SharePoint offers organizations a much faster return on investment because SharePoint fits neatly into most companies' existing technology infrastructures.

SharePoint isn't a new technology. The ability to provision team sites for use with Office clients was first introduced in May 2001 (as shown in Figure 1-1) with a product called SharePoint Team Services. *SharePoint Portal Server 2001,* a product for connecting team sites, was released in June 2001. With each subsequent release, more and more features were added. Windows SharePoint Services (WSS) version 3, which was released in November 2006, represents a major re-architecting of the product.

Starting with the 2003 release, WSS became a component of the Windows Server operating system. The portal product, SharePoint Portal Server 2003, released alongside Office 2003. The latest release, Microsoft Office SharePoint Server (MOSS) 2007, is now officially part of the Microsoft Office suite of products.

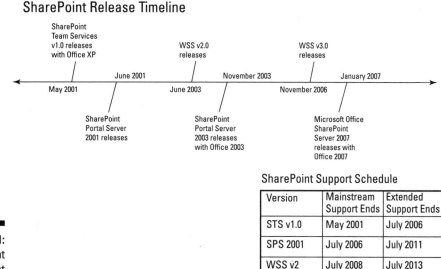

SharePoint Release Timeline

SharePoint
Team Services
v1.0 releases
with Office XP

WSS v2.0
releases

WSS v3.0
releases

June 2001   November 2003   January 2007

May 2001   June 2003   November 2006

SharePoint
Portal Server
2001 releases

SharePoint
Portal Server
2003 releases
with Office 2003

Microsoft Office
SharePoint
Server 2007
releases with
Office 2007

SharePoint Support Schedule

Version	Mainstream Support Ends	Extended Support Ends
STS v1.0	May 2001	July 2006
SPS 2001	July 2006	July 2011
WSS v2	July 2008	July 2013
SPS 2003	Nov 2009	January 2014
MOSS 2007	April 2012	April 2017

Figure 1-1:
SharePoint
product
release
timeline.

In the days of client/server applications, an application commonly consisted of a relatively short stack of technologies. A Windows application might be written in a programming language, such as Visual Basic, that accesses a database on a database server. As long as you had network connectivity and your database was up and running, probability was high that you could use the application. More importantly, installing, supporting, maintaining, and troubleshooting the application was relatively easy.

In the same way that today's information workers don't work in isolation, neither can SharePoint. To support the needs of workers and their employers, SharePoint requires a relatively high stack of technologies. Understanding SharePoint's technologies in broad terms is important because this knowledge helps you do the following:

✔ **Identify opportunities for reuse and customization:** When you gain an understanding of the technologies SharePoint uses, you can leverage some of your existing infrastructure. You don't have to start at square one. Also, you can extend SharePoint to find new ways to use the infrastructure.

✔ **Troubleshoot SharePoint:** You'll encounter many points of failure in SharePoint — and discover that many aren't actually part of the SharePoint software proper. By understanding how SharePoint works and which technologies SharePoint uses, you can develop a systematic approach to troubleshooting.

✔ **Understand the skills necessary to implement and support SharePoint:** SharePoint requires a lot of skills, and it's not likely that you have all of them. I know I sure don't. You have to make arrangements to acquire the skills you don't have in-house.

The SharePoint family of technologies consists of several products. In this book, I focus on the two primary SharePoint products: Windows SharePoint Services (WSS) and Microsoft Office SharePoint Server 2007 (MOSS). Each of these products has a different role in the stack of SharePoint technologies.

See the section, "Licensing SharePoint," later in this chapter, for a complete rundown of all the products available in the SharePoint family.

Laying the foundation

The core product in the family of SharePoint technologies is Windows SharePoint Services (WSS). Because WSS is the foundational product, no other product in the SharePoint family is possible without it.

WSS is a full-blown ASP.NET 2.0 Web application, which means it runs hosted inside ASP.NET. When you install WSS, you have to install ASP.NET and everything it requires to run, including the following:

✔ **Internet Information Services (IIS) version 6 or 7:** This is Microsoft's Web server, which is used to host SharePoint. Most typical SharePoint usage scenarios can configure IIS from within SharePoint. You don't have to manage IIS directly very often.

✔ **.NET Framework version 2.0 and 3.0:** This is a set of software that installs ASP.NET and Windows Workflow Foundation (WF). After you enable ASP.NET 2.0 on the server, you don't have to do anything else to configure .NET.

✔ **SQL Server 2000 or later:** This is Microsoft's database management system. SharePoint can create all the databases it needs, or you can create them yourself. You're responsible for managing backups of your data.

✔ **Windows Server 2003 or later:** This is Microsoft's server operating system. Monitor the servers that host SharePoint just like you would any server.

I walk you through installing these technologies on your server in Chapter 2. Figure 1-2 shows the stack of technologies required to run WSS. Note that these are logical servers. Your implementation may include several physical servers.

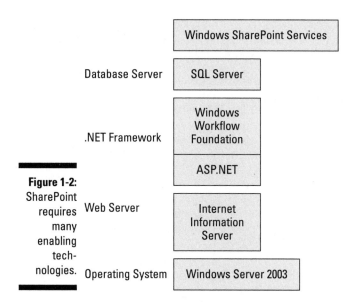

ASP.NET is the Microsoft platform for building Web applications. A Web application is more sophisticated than a Web site, which may only display information. Web applications can provide services, such as electronic commerce. Much of the ability to customize and extend SharePoint comes from ASP.NET 2.0.

You can think of the technologies listed in Figure 1-2 as SharePoint's enabling technologies. SharePoint requires these technologies in order to function properly. SharePoint integrates with many other technologies to provide extra functionality, such as Microsoft Exchange Server. See Chapter 9 for more information on such technologies.

WSS provides the core set of services consumed by all products in the SharePoint family, especially MOSS 2007. These services include the following:

- ✔ **Data storage and content management:** WSS provides lists and libraries as structures for storing data. Lists are primarily used to store tabular data, whereas libraries store files. WSS provides a robust set of services for managing the data and files stored in lists and libraries, services that allow you to do the following:

    - • Associate metadata with list items and files (see Chapter 7).

    - • Create versions of list items and files (see Chapter 15).

    - • Check out files for editing (see Chapter 15).

    - • Index sites, lists, and libraries for searching purposes (see Chapter 14).

What's in a name?

When someone says SharePoint, what does he mean? Is he referring to a specific SharePoint product or the whole kit and caboodle? The only way to know for sure is to ask him. Although, don't be surprised if you don't get a straight answer. With SharePoint, you inevitably encounter an abundance of hype, misunderstanding, and uncertainty. Generally speaking, when someone says SharePoint, I find he usually means whichever SharePoint product is most relevant given the context of the discussion, or he's just referring to the SharePoint technologies. Many people genuinely don't know.

Although I hate to add to the confusion, I find that constantly referring to a specific SharePoint product, such as WSS or MOSS 2007, is equally confusing. Because most people don't know the difference between the two products, I usually just use the term SharePoint. In most cases, WSS can be used in many of the same ways as MOSS, so referring to them generically usually is technically correct. For example, both WSS and MOSS have document management features. (The MOSS features just expand on those found in WSS.) Similarly, MOSS has some very specific built-in features for business intelligence. However, that doesn't mean that you couldn't use WSS for business intelligence.

In this book, I try to be specific about which product I'm referring to, especially when I'm talking about MOSS 2007. I often use the generic term *SharePoint* any time I'm referring to WSS or any feature that's available in both products.

- Manage content approval (see Chapter 15).

- Use list items and libraries in a business process (See Chapter 8)

WSS includes many specialized kinds of lists and libraries that you can use to perform certain tasks. See Chapter 4 for a complete run-down of the lists and libraries you encounter in SharePoint.

✔ **Web platform and site model:** All SharePoint's features are delivered via a hierarchy of Web sites. It takes only a few mouse clicks to generate sites with SharePoint's site provisioning model (see Chapter 4). SharePoint generates a full-featured Web site based on an XML configuration file. (WSS includes many of these configuration files that allow you to create a variety of SharePoint sites to suit the needs of your business. You can also customize the files or create your own.)

Because SharePoint is an ASP.NET Web application, SharePoint is an excellent platform for delivering Web applications that include a Web part framework, navigation, and dynamic form and page generation. SharePoint gives you a viable alternative to building ASP.NET Web applications from scratch.

✔ **Security:** SharePoint provides a security-trimmed user interface so that users see only the options they have permissions for. SharePoint uses groups and roles for granting access to secure content, and virtually everything in SharePoint is securable. The most common authentication scenario for SharePoint is Active Directory, although SharePoint supports custom authentication schemes (such as forms-based authentication) as well. See Chapter 6 for more details on SharePoint's security features.

✔ **Management:** SharePoint provides a multi-tiered administration model that makes it possible to isolate technical administrators from sensitive content. Administrators can't see the files and other content that information workers save in SharePoint sites. Additional administration features include auditing, monitoring, and backing up and restoring tools. SharePoint provides specialized administration Web sites. All administrative features are also accessible from the command line and via code. Chapter 18 walks you through accessing the SharePoint administrative features.

✔ **Services:** A number of services are provided by SharePoint that support SharePoint's other core services. These include notification services, such as RSS feeds, alerts, and inbound e-mail (see Chapter 10). WSS indexes all list, library, and site content so these items can be searched (see Chapter 14). SharePoint also provides migration tools to assist with deploying SharePoint.

✔ **Application programming interfaces (APIs):** SharePoint has a powerful object model and Web services. Everything you can do from the SharePoint user interface uses SharePoint APIs; thus, you can write code to access all SharePoint's features. SharePoint makes available numerous before-and-after events that make it possible to customize SharePoint's default behavior.

Kicking it up a notch

Given that WSS is an application platform, it makes sense that Microsoft has released several products that are built upon that application platform. MOSS 2007 is one such product; it's essentially a WSS application.

As a WSS application, MOSS consumes WSS resources and extends WSS to provide completely new features. Similar to how WSS consists of a set of services, MOSS adds the following services:

✔ **Core services** are the foundational features that enable MOSS 2007 applications. Core services of MOSS 2007 include personalization, search, business data catalog, and Excel Services. MOSS 2007's core services are *shared services* because they're shared across an entire SharePoint deployment.

✔ **Application Services** are the building blocks for creating applications in MOSS 2007. Examples include dashboards, workflows, and user profiles. These services are mixed and matched to provide a myriad of MOSS 2007 applications.

MOSS combines the services of WSS, along with its own core services and application services to create MOSS 2007 applications (see Figure 1-3). MOSS 2007 includes the following SharePoint applications right out of the box:

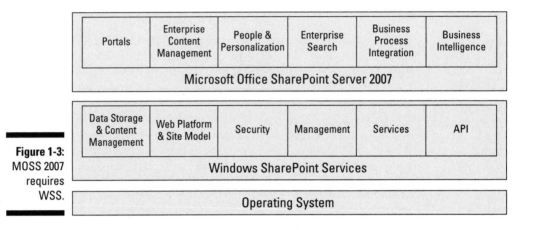

Figure 1-3:
MOSS 2007
requires
WSS.

✔ **Portals** are an essential user interface feature of SharePoint and are used to aggregate content, highlight featured content, and provide access to other SharePoint resources (see Chapter 11).

✔ **Enterprise content management** consists of document and records management (see Chapter 15) as well as Web content management (see Chapter 16). WSS also provides document management, but MOSS adds to those features with information management policies and document information panels. I like to think of Web content management as MOSS's publishing feature. Web content management makes it possible to publish content to a site that's intended to be read by many people.

✔ **People and personalization** encompasses all the features related to managing user profiles, targeting content to audiences, and personalizing portal content. See Chapters 12 and 13.

✔ **Enterprise search** provides the ability to index all content within SharePoint and content outside SharePoint. Search is configurable so that you can manage the relevancy of results delivered to users. See Chapter 14.

✔ **Business process integration** provides the ability to integrate data from outside sources with SharePoint (see Chapter 17). MOSS can render InfoPath forms in the browser to automate business forms (see Chapter 8).

✔ **Business intelligence** provides support for reports, dashboards, and Excel Services (see Chapter 17). Excel Services creates server-side versions of Excel spreadsheets and renders them in a Web page.

Chances are your company doesn't rely on just one of these applications. In reality, you combine features from each application to meet your business's needs. For example, your SharePoint implementation might be 75 percent document management and 25 percent business intelligence. Conversely, you might build your own SharePoint application by using the building blocks of WSS. If Microsoft's Office developers can do it, so can you!

Licensing SharePoint

Figuring out which features go with which product is challenging. In this section, I explain the official products in the SharePoint family and what it takes to license them. Pricing varies depending on the kind of licensing agreement you have with Microsoft.

All SharePoint deployments require Windows Server 2003. WSS version 3 is part of Windows Server 2003, so you don't have to buy separate licenses for WSS. You can download WSS from the Microsoft Web site.

MOSS 2007 products are available for purchase only through volume licensing agreements; you can't buy them via retail channels. Microsoft offers several types of volume licensing agreements. The pricing associated with each agreement varies depending on the number of desktops in your organization, the benefits you receive, and whether you pay up-front or a certain amount each year. See the Microsoft Products Licensing Advisor at `www.microsoft.com/licensing/mpla` for assistance with choosing a licensing agreement.

Properly licensing MOSS 2007 requires a combination of server licenses and Client Access Licenses (CALs). A *server license* allows you to run the software, such as MOSS 2007, on your server. Clients need a *CAL* to access the server's features. Two types of CALs are used for MOSS 2007:

- **Base CAL** allows clients to access the portal, personalization, search, and enterprise content management features of MOSS 2007.

- **Enterprise CAL** allows clients to access the business intelligence and business process integration features of MOSS 2007 (such as the Report Center, Business Data Catalog, Excel Services, and InfoPath Forms Services).

If you want users to access the features provided by the Enterprise CAL, you must also purchase a Base CAL. You need to provide an Enterprise CAL to only those clients who need to access the advanced services.

You have the option to buy a separate CAL for each user or device. Talk with your software acquisition professional for advice on which approach best suits your organization.

Several additional SharePoint products go beyond MOSS 2007:

- ✔ **MOSS 2007 for Search Standard Edition:** This server license offers small- to medium-sized businesses all the features of Office SharePoint Server Search. The number of indexed documents is limited to 500,000.

- ✔ **MOSS 2007 for Search Enterprise Edition:** This server has no limit to the number of documents that can be indexed with this edition.

- ✔ **MOSS 2007 for Internet Sites:** This server license entitles you to use MOSS 2007 for Internet-facing Web sites that are accessed by non-employees. No separate CALs are required.

In addition to Windows Server 2003, you may need to implement the following:

- ✔ **Microsoft SQL Server:** All SharePoint content is stored in a back-end database. WSS installs with an internal database; however, you likely want to use SQL Server 2000 with service pack 4 or higher or SQL Server 2005 with service pack 1 or higher.

- ✔ **Microsoft Internet Security and Acceleration (ISA) Server:** To ensure that remote users are accessing SharePoint in the most secure fashion, implement ISA Server or a similar product. ISA Server has automatic configuration tools for protecting SharePoint.

- ✔ **Microsoft ForeFront Security for SharePoint:** ForeFront protects your SharePoint server from malware, viruses, and enables compliance with content policies, such as prohibiting the use of profanity in documents saved to document libraries. If you choose not to use ForeFront, you need some kind of anti-virus solution.

- ✔ **Microsoft Exchange Server:** Microsoft's premiere e-mail and collaboration platform integrates with SharePoint search. Although Exchange and SharePoint play nicely together, you can use any e-mail server to send e-mail to SharePoint.

- ✔ **Office Live Communications Server:** Enables presence information that lets users know who's online and instant messaging in SharePoint with Communications Server.

- ✔ **Office 2007 Groove Server:** Access SharePoint resources during real-time collaboration sessions with Groove Server.

Obviously, Microsoft wants you to run out and upgrade all your desktops to Office 2007. And while you're at it, you might as well install Vista, too. The truth of the matter is that, although your users will certainly have the best experience with Office 2007, you can work just fine with Office 2003. You can use previous versions of Office and even non-Office applications with SharePoint. See Chapter 9.

To customize SharePoint, you need either SharePoint Designer 2007 or Visual Studio 2005.

SharePoint's Role in Your Company

Although understanding the technologies that enable SharePoint and SharePoint's features is important, I believe that understanding how SharePoint fits into your existing information systems environment is even more valuable than understanding all the SharePoint features. Just because SharePoint can be used for a certain purpose, doesn't mean that your organization will find it useful. I believe that understanding SharePoint's role in your organization is key to making the business case for implementing SharePoint.

An information systems environment is the mix of software, hardware, and manual processes within a company. In some cases, deciding to use SharePoint is easy because SharePoint solves an obvious problem. For example, you can use SharePoint to automate business processes by using electronic forms. However, I find that most companies intuitively think they need SharePoint but can't quite figure out the arguments for why.

All the information found in an organization's information systems environment are the company's *information assets.* Typically, we think of assets as tangible items of value, such as equipment and land. Information (such as how well the company is performing and who the company's top five competitors are) may be intangible, but I think most people agree they're of value to the business.

Most organizations have many disparate repositories for storing their information assets. Some repositories are easier to manage than others. Listed here are some information assets and where they're commonly stored:

- **General business transactions** are stored in custom and off-the-shelf, line-of-business applications.
- **Department-specific transactions** are stored in departmental software applications and tools.
- **Documents, spreadsheets, and images** are stored in a user's My Documents folder and network shares.
- **Directions, instructions, and reference materials** are stored in three-ring binders.
- **Cheat sheets and calendars** are stored on cork boards.
- **Archived files** are stored on CDs and storage boxes.
- **Protected documents** are stored as PDF files.
- **Links to resources on the Web** are stored in a user's Favorites folder.
- **Posts from syndicated blogs and Web sites** are stored in feed readers.
- **Musings** on life, love, and what's for lunch are stored in blogs.
- **Ideas and actionable items** from meetings and brainstorming sessions are stored on notepads, sticky notes, and easel paper.

✔ **Sanitized product and company information** is stored on Web sites.

✔ **Meeting invitations, announcements, and discussion threads** are stored in e-mail Inboxes.

✔ **Phone numbers and job titles** are stored in a directory, such as Exchange Server.

✔ **Know-how** is stored in the heads of employees.

In most organizations, Information Technology (IT) departments are charged with creating an information systems environment for managing all these information assets. Databases are a common repository used to manage information assets. *Databases* place a structure on information assets that makes them easier to manage. Even physical assets, such as vehicles and buildings, are often tracked in databases.

Not all information assets lend themselves well to the kind of structure required by most databases. These information assets are often saved to folders on file servers. Because there's no way to enforce an organization scheme in file folders, the folders quickly erode into a dumping ground.

Whether you need to manage access to a set of disparate structured assets or gain more control over less structured assets, SharePoint creates an environment that equalizes the different properties of information assets.

Accessing structured assets with SharePoint

Structured assets are often found in the formal systems of organizations that use databases to store their data. Because they use databases, it's relatively easy to query and aggregate data from these systems. Line-of-business applications are good examples of repositories for structured assets. Systems for managing structured assets are usually supported by IT staff and have the following characteristics:

✔ **Formal:** They're the "official" systems of the company, and everyone in the company can rattle off their names and what they're used for.

✔ **Mature:** Because it takes a long time to implement structured systems, they tend to be predictable and stable. Despite what businesses say about being innovative and thinking outside the box, an information systems environment isn't the place most organizations want to find surprises.

✔ **Scope:** A large number of people often use structured systems. These are often the systems for which permission is requested as a matter of course when someone is hired.

The problem with structured assets isn't managing the assets; the problem is managing *access* to the assets. What makes structured assets so easy to manage also makes them difficult to access. It's challenging to teach executives how to log into a system and run reports or to show a large group of end users how to navigate menus and access a single process, such as entering a purchase order. SharePoint makes it possible to more finely control the access to structured assets in the following ways:

✔ **Customize access to structured applications:** Instead of granting large numbers of users access to enterprise applications when they only need limited access, you can provide alternative access in SharePoint. For example, if someone needs to look up lists of data, query the customer database, or look up a part number, you can make that data available via SharePoint.

✔ **Supplement structured applications:** You can supplement structured applications by automating business processes. Oftentimes, an enterprise application encompasses only part of a business process, not the whole thing. For example, most software has purchase order or expense report processing. Oftentimes, the request is manual or in e-mail and must be signed by a manager. You can initiate the process in SharePoint and then queue the transactions in your primary system.

✔ **Link structured data to unstructured data:** Commonly, Word documents and spreadsheets support a business transaction. You can link documents stored in a document repository to transactions in your structured systems.

✔ **Limit access:** Create a data catalog in SharePoint to access data for the purposes of querying and report building.

✔ **Consolidate assets:** Many times, you need to present an aggregated view of structured data that comes from multiple sources. SharePoint makes it possible to provide a consolidated view from multiple back-end sources.

Managing unstructured assets with SharePoint

Unlike structured assets, less structured assets (such as Word documents) usually aren't stored in databases. They're often stored on file servers and removable media, such as CDs. Other less structured assets (such as e-mails and blog posts) may be stored in databases, but the information conveyed by the e-mail or blog post isn't managed. Instead, the mail server acts like a file server, and the e-mail acts like a file.

The problem with files is that they're hard to manage and control. End users can easily store them on thumb drives and send them as e-mail attachments. Despite IT's attempts to control files with policies and backups, files are slippery.

Contrary to what IT staff want to believe, less structured information assets are stored in more places than just file servers, such as the following:

- My Documents folder
- Favorites folder
- RSS feed readers
- Blog sites
- Web sites
- Inboxes and other mail folders
- Filing cabinets
- Off-site storages

Table 1-1 lists some of the less structured assets you can expect to find.

Table 1-1	Common Information Assets
Type of Asset	*Examples*
Word documents	Policy manuals, forms, memos, letters, procedures, white papers, press releases, contracts, plans, and strategies
Excel spreadsheets	Return on investment, accounting schedules, forecasts, analysis, mailing lists, schedules, and directories
PowerPoint presentations	Sales demonstrations, training materials, and new hire orientations
Access databases	Departmental databases for tracking contacts and resources
E-mails	Meeting requests, discussion threads, notifications and announcements
PDF files	Archived and protected documents and brochures
Images	Company outings, products, and Web content
HTML pages	Departmental Web sites, self-service portals, and secure areas of public Web sites

Although repositories for storing structured assets are formal, mature, and of a wide scope, the environment for less structured assets is often more difficult to control. Although businesses don't want their employees' sales presentations to be boring, stuffy, and staid, they do want the environment in which these documents are created to be manageable. By creating a manageable environment for less structured information, SharePoint confers the following benefits to less structured assets:

- ✔ **Structure:** SharePoint stores everything in a database. As a result, users can create properties that describe their documents. These properties can be used to better organize documents. Some of the information found in documents is better suited for storage in a database table. Rather than storing the document in SharePoint, users can store the document's data in the database.

- ✔ **Standardization:** SharePoint allows you to define the kinds of documents and other information (or *content types*) stored in the database. When someone attempts to add documents, SharePoint prompts the user for the set of properties associated with that content type. Using content types ensures that the same properties are captured.

- ✔ **Share:** SharePoint makes the information available in documents accessible to larger numbers of people. Oftentimes, the only way to distribute documents now is with an e-mail attachment.

- ✔ **Archive:** SharePoint allows you to define policies that determine for how long a document must be archived.

- ✔ **Backup and restore:** By keeping less structured assets in a common repository, SharePoint makes it possible to back up and restore these assets.

- ✔ **Secure:** Creating a secure environment means more than just restricting unauthorized access. SharePoint makes it possible to extend those restrictions beyond the managed information environment by preventing unauthorized distribution of assets.

- ✔ **Audit:** Part and parcel of securing assets is the ability to audit their access. SharePoint makes it possible to monitor the information environment for less structured assets in ways previously not possible.

- ✔ **Summarize, analyze, and mine data:** By applying properties to less structured assets, SharePoint makes it possible to query and search these assets like structured assets.

- ✔ **Legitimize:** By bringing in social tools (such as blogging, RSS, Web, and search) inside the information systems environment, SharePoint acknowledges the valuable role these tools play. Organizations don't operate in a vacuum. SharePoint extends access to the external environment in a controlled and measured way that encourages productive and purposeful uses of these resources.

SharePoint as the hub

With the significant investment companies have made already in people and technology, how can SharePoint possibly have a role in this already crowded information systems environment? With IT staff overburdened already, it's little wonder at the lack of enthusiasm in implementing yet another system.

Despite all the technological advances, the big budgets, and the far-reaching plans, many end users and members of the business community find themselves increasingly alienated from their company's information environments. Most end users can tell you that something is clearly missing. SharePoint aims to be the missing link in a company's information systems environment by acting as the hub, as shown in Figure 1-4. As the hub, SharePoint is an integral player in providing users access to information assets.

Whereas your current information environment uses file shares, e-mail Inboxes, and databases as storage repositories for information assets, SharePoint provides its own set of repositories for creating manageable information environments. These organizing containers are organized in a hierarchy. Organizing them in a hierarchy creates parent-child relationships between containers, which makes it possible for the settings in a higher-level container to apply to a lower-level container — a process called *inheritance*. Using a hierarchy also makes it possible for administrative tasks to be delegated to administrators of lower-level containers. For example, a higher-level administrator might choose to enable a set of features so lower-level administrators can disable those features if they want to.

Whether containers are administered by IT staff, power users, or information workers depends on how the company chooses to make administrative assignments. The containers that are often managed by IT include these:

- ✔ **Server farm:** Like most server software, SharePoint often requires multiple servers — dubbed a *server farm* — to work productively. Although it's possible to have multiple server farms, most companies only ever need one. IT is responsible for deploying the server farm and managing its health. I walk you through setting up SharePoint in a single-server or server farm configuration in Chapter 2.

  Some editions of SharePoint (those based on MOSS 2007) have an additional component — the Shared Services Provider (SSP). The SSP is responsible for providing services that are required across the entire server farm, regardless of how many servers you have. Each server farm usually only has one SSP. See Chapter 2 for details on setting up the SSP.

  SharePoint provides special administrative interfaces — Central Administration and Shared Services Administration — for managing the server farm and SSP, respectively.

✔ **Web applications:** Web applications are most often used to create an information environment for a single company. If the company is especially large, IT may choose to create separate Web applications to separate the company's divisions. For example, if the company has an operation in the United States and one in the United Kingdom, IT would likely create separate Web applications for each. Also, if the company wants to provide an information environment that will be accessed by the public, such as vendors or customers, they may choose to separate that content into its own Web application. I'm sure you guessed that you can apply some rules for when you should create separate Web applications. I discuss rules for creating Web applications and how to create Web applications in Chapter 3.

✔ **Site collections:** Each Web application contains at least one site collection. A site collection can be used to create an information environment for a single company, or there may be separate site collections for each division within the company. Similar to Web applications, there are rules for how site collections are created (see Chapter 3). A site collection contains at least one top-level SharePoint site, which is used to store and display information. Site collections are usually created by IT staff, but their content is often administered by a member of the business staff.

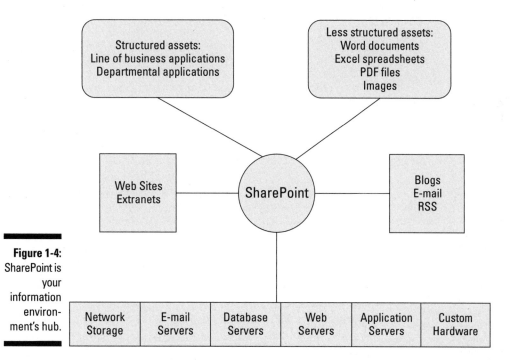

Figure 1-4: SharePoint is your information environment's hub.

The containers that are often created and managed by business users include the following:

- ✔ **Sites:** SharePoint sites are usually created for a specific purpose, such as coordinating a project team or providing an information environment for a department. It's common for companies to create sites for each of the departments within their organization. SharePoint provides a special kind of site, called *portals,* which is intended for providing information to larger groups of people. For example, the top-level site in a site collection is often a portal. Sites can contain additional sites as well as lists and libraries. Each site has its own administrative interfaces for managing permissions, navigation, and appearance. I discuss sites in Chapter 4.

  SharePoint sites can inherit permissions, navigation, and appearance settings from their parent site.

- ✔ **Lists:** SharePoint provides a number of predefined lists that can be used to store data, such as tasks, events, and announcements. You can create your own custom lists to store data that's specific to your business. By default, list data appears in a tabular format, but SharePoint provides additional view formats. You can easily customize how much data appears on the screen and whether the data is sorted, filtered, and grouped. You can even create master/detail displays of data. SharePoint automatically generates Web pages to add, edit, and display the data you store in lists.

- ✔ **Libraries:** SharePoint sites can contain any number of libraries for storing files. The most common SharePoint library is the document library, although you can also use libraries to store electronic forms, pictures, and PowerPoint slides. You can create new file properties for the files you save in SharePoint libraries. SharePoint automatically prompts users to enter values for the properties when they upload files. Users can open files from and save files to SharePoint libraries from their usual desktop applications, such as Word and Excel.

From SharePoint's perspective, all the information assets that you store and manage in SharePoint are *content.* All the Word documents, Excel spreadsheets, and PowerPoint slideshows that users upload to libraries are content. All the tasks, announcements, and other data that users enter into lists are content. Even the Web pages that are displayed in a portal are content. The sites, lists, and libraries that you create to display, organize, and store content are *content structures.*

SharePoint's content structures are more than just passive storage containers. To have a managed information environment, SharePoint provides a framework of features that includes workflows, content types, versioning, content approval, and permissions management. I introduce lists and libraries in Chapter 4. You can read more about SharePoint's content management features in later chapters.

Selling SharePoint

When you make new discoveries about SharePoint's capabilities, don't be surprised if everyone else doesn't fall in line. You have to see SharePoint to believe its technologies. That's why I think it's so important to ask for a hunting license. Only by taking on a few projects and showing SharePoint's value can you start to get people on board.

When you prepare your case for selling SharePoint, keep the following in mind:

- ✔ **Remember your audiences.** Be ready to present your business case to multiple stakeholders many times over your project's life cycle. You won't just sell SharePoint once. Consider the different perspectives of executive management, operations, technical staff, and end users when you prepare your case. Each of these stakeholders has a different set of criteria for evaluating SharePoint.

- ✔ **Get buy-in.** If you know ahead of time that a particular individual or department is a roadblock, court them early and often. If possible, get them to take a stake early in the planning phases and don't let people or departments drop out of this process at any time.

- ✔ **Know your politics.** Be aware of the formal and informal power structures in your company. If you think that politics might hinder your project's success, consider using a consultant. Management is often more willing to listen to a third party than to an employee.

  A common roadblock to implementing SharePoint is the Not Invented Here syndrome. All companies have people who are entrenched in using a current process or product that they refuse to relinquish. If that solution was hand rolled — as in the case of a home grown portal solution — it can be especially brutal to convince people to embrace SharePoint.

- ✔ **Show business value.** You have to show your stakeholders how this project adds value to the business. Again, remember your audience. To executive management, business value often means financial return. Operations may see value in a project that streamlines business processes, whereas ease of use may appeal to a line worker.

Finally, you may very well come to the conclusion that SharePoint isn't right for your business. If you have trouble getting people to cooperate with you, that's a red flag. You may need to wait until the winds of change come through. Of course, you're a shoo-in if you can figure out how to make the IT manager think SharePoint was his idea.

Getting Started with SharePoint

Having a set of objectives in mind is important when you start implementing SharePoint. Developing a list of objectives helps you define the scope for your SharePoint project. Don't think of your project in terms of "implementing SharePoint." Instead, state your project in terms of whatever it is that you're *doing* with SharePoint. Here are some good examples of SharePoint project objectives:

- ✔ Create secure, version-controlled document repositories for departments, teams, and task forces.
- ✔ Move contacts, calendars, and announcements into an easily accessible site.
- ✔ Automate the process for submitting business expense forms.
- ✔ Track documents, events, and tasks related to projects.

Any of these goals are easily achievable with WSS. I suggest that you attack each of these as a separate phase of your project. Also, narrow the scope to a particular team or department. Instead of trying to implement all these goals for your entire organization, pick a single group to act as the pilot. For example, start using document repositories with the Marketing department.

I suggest you start with projects similar to the ones in the preceding list. Even though document management and team sites are basic features of SharePoint, many companies are overwhelmed quickly by them. Plan on spending anywhere from 3–12 months training and supporting users on SharePoint's basic features.

MOSS 2007's My Site feature is a great way to get users introduced to using SharePoint. If you know you want to implement MOSS 2007, I suggest training users on My Site first. Each member of the SharePoint portal is the administrator of his or her own My Site personal site. This is a great way to get folks up to speed on administering SharePoint sites.

After you're confident that most people know how to save files to a library and work with lists, I suggest you move on to the basic features of MOSS 2007. Example projects include the following:

- ✔ Creating a collaboration portal that aggregates content from SharePoint team and departmental sites.
- ✔ Implementing a document review or approval procedure for documents saved in team or departmental repositories.
- ✔ Archiving documents, e-mail, and other content to a protected records management repository.
- ✔ Adding file shares and other content to be searched from within SharePoint.

Advanced uses of MOSS 2007 include the following:

- ✓ Integrating data from back-end business databases in lists and libraries being used by teams and departments.

- ✓ Creating executive dashboards that display the company's progress on key performance metrics.

- ✓ Converting all manual forms to browser-based electronic forms.

If you want to read about specific companies that have successfully implemented SharePoint, you can visit the Office Solutions Showcase at `www.microsoft.com/office/showcase`.

Choosing SharePoint projects

Deciding where to start with SharePoint is daunting. Most people go with what's easy only to find themselves quickly overwhelmed by too many "easy" projects. Instead of going with whatever jumps out at you, I suggest you sit down and make a list of candidate projects. A *candidate project* is any problem that you think you can solve by using SharePoint. Identifying SharePoint's role in your existing information systems environment is a good place to start. Specifically, you can look for holes in the IS environment or situations where you need to create links between different kinds of information. For example, any time you encounter a spreadsheet that's being used by multiple people, you probably have a good use for SharePoint.

After you create a list of candidate projects, I suggest you do the following:

- ✓ **Identify the reward level** of candidate projects on a scale of 0–100. You can define reward based on your organization's values, such as exposure, usefulness, impact, and profile of the project.

- ✓ **Assign the risk level** of candidate projects on a scale of 0–100. Identify risks, such as difficulty, obstacles, political issues, and probability of success.

- ✓ **Plot the values for reward and risk level on a chart** with the numerical values you assign.

You can make your approach to creating the reward and risk values as scientific as you want. You can best guess the values or come up with an approach that assigns weights to the underlying characteristics of reward and risk. You can even use financial analysis, such as internal rate of return and net present value, to assist with your analysis.

I like to plot the values on a scatter chart in Excel with the X-axis values in reverse order. The graph provides a visual representation of which projects you should tackle, as shown in Figure 1-5. The quadrants in the graph help you prioritize your projects, as I describe here:

- ✔ **Quadrant I: Low reward, high risk.** These aren't the projects you want to start with.

- ✔ **Quadrant II: Low reward, low risk.** You can test the waters with this low-hanging fruit. Implement several of these projects so the rewards pile up.

- ✔ **Quadrant III: High reward, low risk.** Implement one or two projects from this quadrant and increase your star power.

- ✔ **Quadrant IV: High reward, high risk.** You're betting the farm with these projects. If you're unsuccessful, you could be putting the entire SharePoint implementation at risk. Make sure you have some success to show from other projects before tackling these.

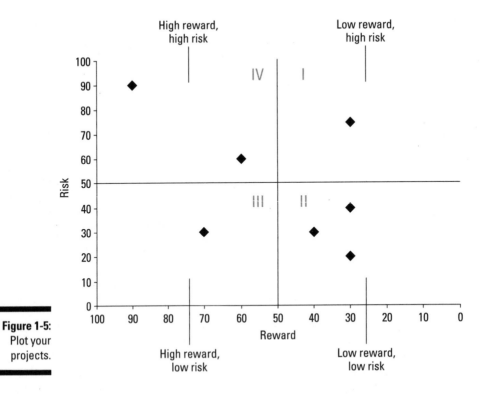

Figure 1-5:
Plot your
projects.

Getting a hunting license

Because every business is different, every SharePoint implementation looks slightly different. Only you can determine what those gaps are in your information systems environment for SharePoint to fill. When it comes time to decide which SharePoint features, if any, you should implement and in what order, I suggest you start out by asking for a hunting license. In other words, look around your business for opportunities to evaluate SharePoint.

I've given some suggestions throughout this chapter for ways that you can use SharePoint in your business. Even if you know very little about SharePoint, here are a few rules of thumb for how you can bring your existing information assets into SharePoint:

- **Spreadsheets** are the easiest candidates for implementing into SharePoint because SharePoint has so many options. Spreadsheets that have columns and rows of data are prime candidates to become lists in SharePoint. Spreadsheets that display schedules, analysis, and charts are often better displayed as Web content in Excel Services. In both cases, end users can continue to open the file in Excel and update it.

  Another obvious use for spreadsheets is to store them in document libraries. Although this is better than using a regular file share, it doesn't start to unlock the information stored *inside* the spreadsheet. Instead of just storing everything as a file in a library, see if the file's contents are valuable to the organization as a whole.

- **Word documents** most often make their way into document libraries. This makes sense if you need to take advantage of collaboration tools, such as version control, approval routing, and archival policies. You can also convert Word documents to Web pages. When documents are used as forms, consider converting them to InfoPath forms. Tables displayed inside documents are prime candidates to become SharePoint lists. Documents that describe tasks or business processes may be the blueprints for creating a workflow. Documents intended for consumption by a large number of people should make their way to the portal's Document Center.

- **PowerPoint presentations** can be stored in document libraries. Individual slides can be stored in a slide library to create a reusable collection of templates and slides for building presentations.

- **Access databases** can be replaced with custom lists and workflows in SharePoint.

- **Visio diagrams** can be stored in document libraries or saved as Web pages and displayed in SharePoint sites.

- **E-mails** can be replaced with announcements, calendars, and tasks lists in SharePoint. Instead of sending attachments, users can send URLs to resources stored in SharePoint.

✔ **Image files** can be stored in picture libraries. Users can create Web pages to display the images for everyone to see. Images used for production of Web sites and other media can be checked in and version controlled in libraries.

✔ **Paper documents** can be scanned and stored in libraries. Paper forms can be converted to InfoPath forms.

✔ **Know-how** is what gets done, who does what, when something is done, why it's done that way, how it gets done, and where it gets done that only the people who do a job seem to know. A person's job- related know-how is an information asset that can be stored in SharePoint. By using SharePoint to trigger workflows, store contacts, track tasks, schedule events, and keep lists, an employee's know-how can become a reusable information asset.

SharePoint's document libraries can be used to store any kind of file, including audio, video, and cad/cam files. The primary limitation of using document libraries is the file sizes uploaded to the library.

Preparing for SharePoint

Ideally, you've already made your business case, and you've created a list of projects and prioritized how you want to proceed. Many planning tasks are involved in implementing SharePoint. When you start planning your project, it's helpful to consider the many roles that are required to implement SharePoint:

✔ **Technical people** are responsible for installing SharePoint on the servers and monitoring its health. This also includes database administrators who create databases and schedule backups.

✔ **Solution builders** are people with any kind of background who are responsible for using technology to solve business problems. Sometimes solution builders belong to IT staff, but they may also be power users. Solution builders may use tools like SharePoint Designer to customize solutions.

✔ **Developers** write code for extending SharePoint or creating custom solutions.

✔ **Designers** are responsible for SharePoint's look and feel. This could be as simple as changing the color scheme to completely branding SharePoint to be consistent with internal policy.

✔ **Subject matter experts** are most often your business personnel who understand how your business functions. You may also need to bring in specialized experts to assist with certain aspects of your project.

There are many additional roles. Some are part and parcel to projects. For example, you obviously need a project manager. It's probably also a good idea to have a project champion and sponsor to help sell the project throughout your organization. Consider involving Legal to make sure you cover all your bases as it relates to privacy and terms-of-use agreements.

I like to think of a SharePoint project as using three distinct types of planning. Each of the following types maps to a group of users who perform the planning:

- **Technical people** must plan your server topology and server farm.
- **Subject matter experts and solution builders** are responsible for identifying the kind of content that must be stored, displayed, and managed and coming up with the appropriate site hierarchy and building blocks. Designers are also involved to help manage the look and feel.
- **Solution builders and software developers** are responsible for planning ways to use SharePoint as an application platform.

I discuss each of these planning tasks required in the rest of this section.

Planning the server farm topology

Technical people are responsible for figuring out your server farm topology. Only in rare circumstances is SharePoint deployed to a single server. In most cases, SharePoint requires at least two servers.

Planning the server farm topology requires tasks such as these:

- Matching the topology to the project's requirements.
- Determining the requirements for capacity, performance, and availability.
- Deciding how many servers are required of each kind of server role.
- Figuring out how the servers are configured within the existing network topology to prevent unauthorized access.
- Providing access to authorized and anonymous third parties as required by the project.
- Determining strategies for upgrading and migrating content from previous versions of SharePoint and other server applications.
- Identifying requirements for multilingual sites.
- Provisioning databases for use by the server farm.
- Making sure you have the proper licensing to match requirements.
- Creating a backup and restore strategy.
- Creating an ongoing administration plan.

Technical folks are also responsible for planning for the deployment of the server farm. This requires coordination with other planners to ensure that the deployment occurs in accordance with requirements.

If you don't have the internal staff to complete this phase of planning, don't worry. You have two options:

- **Hiring consultants:** You can hire a third party to come in and take care of the technical stuff for you. Depending on the size and complexity of your project, it could take as little as a day to get you up and running. This option works best for companies who already have an existing IT infrastructure but don't have the time or the skill set to bring up a server farm.

- **Hosting:** If you don't have the internal staff to support a SharePoint farm, hosting may be a good alternative. With a hosted solution, a third party allows you to access SharePoint on their servers. Hosting is a great way to get up and running with SharePoint in a very short period of time and for the lowest amount of up-front cash outlay.

   Several kinds of hosting options are available. You can find companies who host only WSS and those who also host MOSS 2007. You must decide whether you want to use a shared server or a dedicated server. With a shared server, your SharePoint installation lives alongside other people's SharePoint sites on the same server. For the highest amount of security and availability, you can use a dedicated server that only your company accesses. Obviously, a shared solution is less costly than a dedicated solution. If you go with a dedicated server, most companies let you bring the server in-house whenever you get ready.

Planning for content and usage

Deciding what gets stored in SharePoint and how SharePoint is used in your organization is the meat and potatoes of your planning. I'm assuming that you're just planning on implementing the baseline collaboration and document management features of WSS. In my opinion, this is where you should start unless you have no intention of using any of these features. These features are the underpinning for nearly every application of SharePoint you can dream up. For that reason, I think it's vitally important that your organization master these uses before you start getting too advanced. Anything beyond this project, I consider a SharePoint application.

It's at this planning level that you need to do the following:

- Figure out which sites to create and how to organize them in a site hierarchy.
- Decide whether to allow inbound e-mail.

✔ Decide how users will access SharePoint with which kinds of clients.

✔ Decide how to filter content so users see views that are personalized to their needs.

✔ Determine who gets access to what and who has responsibility for the various tasks required to maintain SharePoint.

✔ Determine who's responsible for creating new sites as well as adding new users and maintaining them.

✔ Decide how users are authenticated to SharePoint.

✔ Determine how SharePoint provides people information such as names and contact information.

✔ Decide who creates and maintains content structures, such as lists libraries.

✔ Identify content and its organization.

✔ Decide who administers all this stuff and keeps it up and running.

A vital piece to your success in this planning stage requires that you provide adequate training and support. This doesn't mean just to end users or just to technical people. Both groups need training and support. Technical people need to understand how to set up, configure, and administer SharePoint. When it comes to the day-to-day use, you have to decide whether the help desk is responsible for providing this support.

Planning for applications

Planning on using SharePoint to solve a specific business problem is the icing on the cake. The planning process for specific applications depends on how you plan to use SharePoint in your organization. Regardless of how you plan to use SharePoint in your business, here are some common planning steps:

1. **Identify the project's goals.**

2. **Identify the SharePoint features that are relevant to achieving your project's goals.**

3. **Identify the configuration information you need to set up SharePoint.**

4. **Identify the skills required to implement the features and address any skill gaps.**

5. **Create a development process for creating SharePoint applications.**

    In most cases, implementing an application in SharePoint requires some kind of development or design work. You need to identify the tools that are required to complete the task — most often you use SharePoint Designer 2007, InfoPath 2007, and Visual Studio 2005. Make sure you have the skills or the outsourcing capabilities.

Chapter 2

Installing SharePoint

SharePoint is enterprise-quality software. As such, SharePoint installation is a significant undertaking. If your organization has more than a few dozen people using SharePoint, you probably need to plan on implementing a server farm.

In this chapter, I walk you through setting up a standalone evaluation server so you can walk through the examples in this book. Later in this chapter, I discuss creating a production-quality SharePoint server farm.

Installing SharePoint

Just so you know the real lay of the land out there, installing SharePoint means making your way through eight (count 'em, eight) high-level steps in order to get SharePoint set up. Not only that, to progress through these steps, you're going to need the cooperation of many people. (Do you know who your friends are?) Note that these steps just cover the installation of SharePoint. After you complete these steps, you have a functioning SharePoint installation — nice job! — but you can't afford to rest on your laurels yet. You still have to implement SharePoint.

But first, here's my list of eight high-level steps you'll be facing:

1. **Planning your installation.**

   The planning process requires you to identify how many users you have and how you expect them to use SharePoint. You have to think about how critical SharePoint is for your organization so you can plan how much redundancy to put into your installation. I discuss planning in Chapter 1, and provide planning hints throughout the book.

2. **Building and preparing your servers.**

   Microsoft recommends that you use at least two servers for SharePoint. You may find you need to use three or four servers to provide the level of redundancy and availability that your organization requires. I walk you through server requirements — and how to prepare your servers for SharePoint — later in this chapter.

3. **Installing SharePoint on your servers and running the SharePoint Configuration Wizard on each server.**

   You must install SharePoint on each server and run a wizard to configure SharePoint on the server. I walk you through this process later in this chapter.

4. **Enabling SharePoint services on your servers.**

   The services you run on your server determine the server's role in your SharePoint installation. For example, you may have one server dedicated to serving Web pages and another to running databases. I show you how to enable services later in this chapter.

5. **Creating Web applications for administrative and content sites.**

   You must create Web applications to store the Web pages for SharePoint's administrative sites and for the content sites that your end users will access. You determine the number of Web applications to create based on your planning exercises in Step 1. I walk you through creating Web applications for administrative sites later in this chapter and cover creating Web applications for content sites in depth in Chapter 3.

6. **Creating the Shared Services Provider (SSP) for Microsoft Office SharePoint Server 2007 (MOSS).**

   If you're installing MOSS 2007, you must enable a special feature in MOSS called *Shared Services Provider.* The SSP makes it possible to share the SharePoint services across servers. I explain SSP later in this chapter.

7. **Configuring content sites and site collections.**

   You have to create *containers* — structures such as sites — to store your site's content. A small-to-medium size company may have only one content site and site collection. A larger organization may choose to create separate site collections for each division in the company. I discuss site collections in Chapter 3.

8. **Completing post-installation steps.**

   A number of services must be configured and administrative tasks must be completed before your SharePoint installation is fully operational. I discuss these steps in detail at the end of this chapter.

Which SharePoint to install?

Deciding which SharePoint product you want to install is an important outcome of your planning process. Whether you decide to implement Windows SharePoint Services version 3 (WSS) or Microsoft Office SharePoint Server 2007 (MOSS) affects all your downstream installation tasks. The decision also affects the range of features that are available to your organization.

When deciding which server application to install, I suggest you start with a list of features crucial to your enterprise. MOSS 2007 has more features than WSS. If you need the features in MOSS, the decision is obvious. If you're on the fence, I suggest you evaluate both products before you decide. There's no sense in implementing MOSS when you only need WSS.

Creating an Evaluation Server

For evaluation purposes, you may choose to install SharePoint on a single server. You can even use SharePoint in a very limited capacity in production on a single server — although, admittedly, that's rather unlikely. (For the sake of argument, though, imagine using SharePoint for a single department — in that situation, a single-server installation may be appropriate.) In this section, I'm going to walk you through a single-server installation, which enables you to get up and running so you can evaluate SharePoint.

There's no upgrade path from a single-server installation to a multiple-server installation. If you plan to start out with a single server and add servers down the road, then you want to follow the instructions in the "Installing SharePoint for the Real World" section. If you only plan to create a single-server installation for evaluation purposes, then you can follow the steps in this section.

You can use the steps in this section to install either Windows SharePoint Services or Microsoft Office SharePoint Server 2007. The installations are very similar for a single-server installation.

Note: The examples in this book work with either a single server or multiple server installation.

Hardware requirements

Your server needs to meet these minimum hardware requirements in order to install SharePoint:

- ✔ Dual-processor computer with at least 2.5 GHz processors.
- ✔ Minimum 1GB of RAM, but 2GB of RAM is recommended.

If you intend to run SharePoint on multiple servers, you may need to beef up hardware on each server. Microsoft recommends 4GB for MOSS 2007 application servers. Hardware requirements for the database server depend on which edition of SQL Server you install. For more details, see the topic "Determine hardware and software requirements" in the MOSS 2007 TechNet library at the following site:

```
http://technet2.microsoft.com/Office/en-us/library/
396ee7ae-6dc6-4d48-8448-54a0033f39781033.mspx
```

You can also run SharePoint on a Virtual Server 2005 virtual machine. Just make sure your hardware meets the minimum requirements to run Virtual Server and has enough memory to allocate for the virtual machine (at least 1GB).

Preparing your server

As with any server application, you need to prepare your server before you begin installation of SharePoint. You should start with a *clean* server — a server with a freshly installed Windows Server 2003 operating system — otherwise, you may have unexpected results. Also make sure, before you start, that your server meets the minimum hardware requirements (as described in the preceding section).

Windows SharePoint Services version 3 and Microsoft Office SharePoint Server 2007 take advantage of many new technologies. These technologies have been retrofitted to work with technologies already existing at the time of SharePoint's release. At the time of SharePoint's release, the latest release of Windows Server is Windows Server 2003 R2. Version 3.0 of the .NET Framework was released around the time as SharePoint. SharePoint needs both version 2.0 and version 3.0 of .NET. In order for SharePoint to work with these technologies, a number of prerequisite technologies must be installed.

The following instructions assume you're going to install SharePoint on a server running Windows Server 2003. The next version of Windows Server after the 2003 version is code-named Windows Server Longhorn. Longhorn Server, as it is often called, likely has the official name "Windows Server 2007." This version of Windows Server likely has all the prerequisites you need to install SharePoint. Therefore, your only preparation step is to install Windows Server 2007 on the server.

Windows SharePoint Services version 3 is likely installed by default with Windows Server 2007. If you're planning on using WSS version 3, it will be installed already, and you'll only need to configure WSS.

Preparing a Windows Server 2003 server for SharePoint installation requires many steps. If you've never configured a Windows server, then you may need to get someone with technical experience to help you. The details of all thirty-plus tasks required to prepare a Windows Server 2003 server to install SharePoint are beyond the scope of this book, but here's a high-level overview of the procedure:

1. **Install Windows Server 2003 with Service Pack 1 on a clean server.**

   You can use any edition of Windows Server 2003 *except* Web Edition. You could install SharePoint on a domain controller, but it's generally not recommended.

2. **Using the Manage Your Server window, add the Application Server role to your Windows Server 2003.**

   The Manage Your Server window usually appears automatically when you log on to a server running Windows 2003. You can open the Manage Your Server window by choosing All Programs⇨Administrative Tools⇨ Manage Your Server.

   In the Manage Your Server window, you click the Add or Remove a Role link to launch the Configure Your Server Wizard. Then you step through the wizard to add the Application Server role to your server. The wizard installs Internet Information Services (IIS) on your server, which turns it into a Web server. The Application Server role appears in the Manage Your Server window, as shown in Figure 2-1.

   You may also want to add the Mail Server role to the server if you intend to use e-mail features with SharePoint. (I discuss configuring SharePoint to work with e-mail in Chapter 10.)

3. **Download and install version 3.0 of the .NET Framework.**

   You can download the .NET Framework from Microsoft's Web site, at the following URL:

   ```
   www.microsoft.com/downloads/details.aspx?FamilyId=
        10CC340B-F857-4A14-83F5-
        25634C3BF043&displaylang=en
   ```

   Alternatively, you can search for the keywords .NET 3.0 on Microsoft's Web site to find a link to the .NET Framework 3.0 Redistributable Package.

4. **Enable ASP.NET 2.0 in the IIS Manager.**

   Version 2.0 of ASP.NET installs with the .NET Framework. You must enable IIS to use ASP.NET. Choose Start⇨All Programs⇨Administrative Tools⇨Internet Information Services (IIS) Manager. Enable ASP.NET 2.0 in the Web Service Extensions folder, as shown in Figure 2-2.

With these preparations in place, your Windows Server is ready to install WSS version 3 or MOSS 2007. You can download WSS version 3 free from Microsoft's Web site:

```
www.microsoft.com/technet/windowsserver/sharepoint/
        download.mspx
```

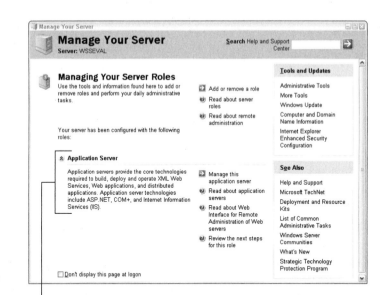

Figure 2-1:
Add the
Application
Server role
to your
server.

Application Server

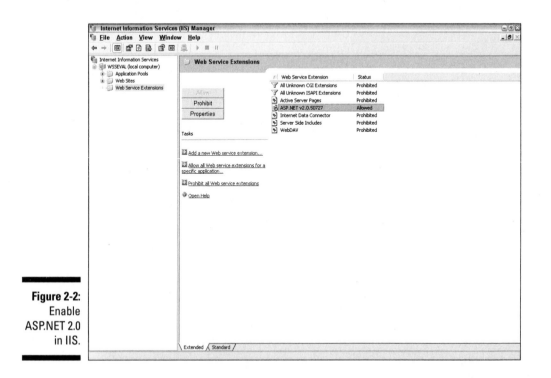

Figure 2-2:
Enable
ASP.NET 2.0
in IIS.

MOSS 2007 is only available through volume licensing, as I describe in
Chapter 1. Please see Chapter 1 to make sure you understand the licensing

requirements for WSS and MOSS 2007. The installation steps are very similar. (To help you decide which application to install, see Chapter 1.)

To install Windows SharePoint Services or Microsoft Office SharePoint Server 2007 on a single server, follow these steps:

1. **Double-click the** `Setup.exe` **file to start the installation.**

   If you download Windows SharePoint Services from Microsoft's Web site, you can double-click the `SharePoint.exe` file that downloads from their site.

2. **If you're installing MOSS 2007, enter your Product Key and click the Continue button.**

3. **Read the licensing agreement and select the check box if you accept the terms of the agreement. Click the Continue button.**

4. **Click the Basic button on the Choose the Installation You Want page, as shown in Figure 2-3.**

   The installer installs SharePoint according to the option you choose:

   - A Basic installation automatically installs a database server and SharePoint databases. You must run a configuration wizard to complete the installation.

   - The Advanced installation option allows you to specify which role the server plays when you deploy SharePoint using multiple servers. (You can see an advanced installation in action in the section "Installing SharePoint for the Real World," later in this chapter.)

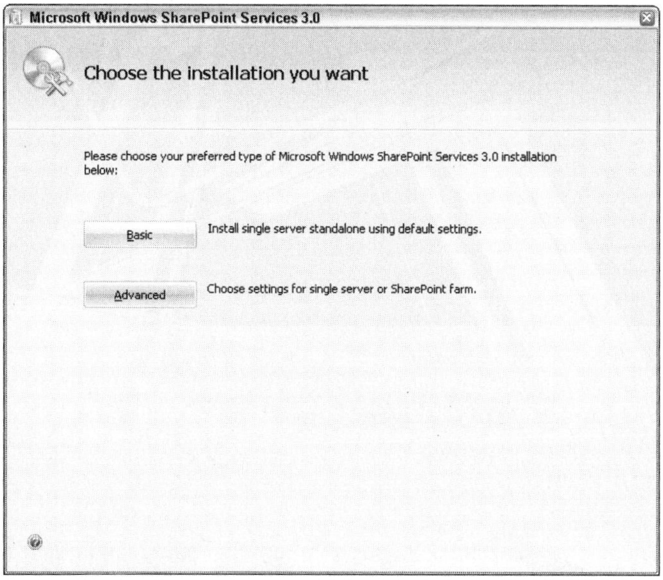

Figure 2-3:
Choose
Basic
installation.

5. **In the setup window — after the installation process completes — select the Run the SharePoint Products and Technologies Configuration Wizard check box and then click the Close button.**

   The Installation wizard closes, and the Configuration wizard opens.

6. **Click Next to start the Configuration wizard.**

   The wizard displays a dialog box notifying you that it must stop several services before starting the wizard.

7. **Click Yes to confirm that the wizard can stop SharePoint services.**

   The wizard steps through ten tasks that automatically configure SharePoint, such as creating databases and sample content.

8. **After the configuration is complete, click the Finish button to exit the wizard.**

   The home page of your SharePoint Web application appears in the browser. Figure 2-4 shows the home page from a Windows SharePoint Services basic installation.

   If the wizard is unable to complete a task, the wizard displays a list of reasons why it failed.

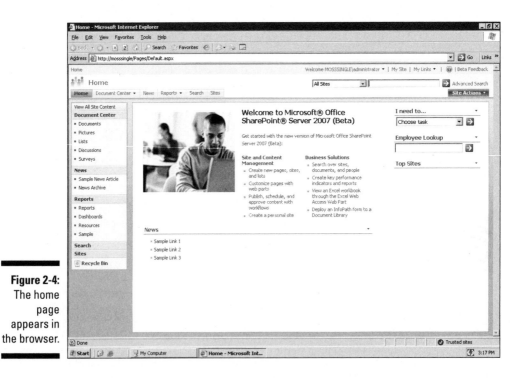

Figure 2-4:
The home page appears in the browser.

You see several prompts when SharePoint opens in the browser for the first time. I explain these prompts and how to deal with them in the next section.

Several configuration and administrative tasks must still be completed before you can start using SharePoint. See the last section in this chapter for a rundown.

Accessing SharePoint's Administrative Pages

Administrators most often access SharePoint using a browser application such as Internet Explorer. When you install SharePoint, the application creates administrative Web sites that you use to administer SharePoint. Before you can access SharePoint via the browser, however, you have to follow a few steps to configure your browser. These steps are also necessary for your end users to access SharePoint using Internet Explorer at their desktops.

Browsers, such as Internet Explorer, are mostly used for accessing content from the Internet. As such, they're configured by default to strictly limit the extent to which you can interact with the Web sites. When you want to use internal sites, such as SharePoint, you must configure Internet Explorer so that it isn't so strict.

In order to access SharePoint with Internet Explorer, you must do three things, in this order:

1. **Add SharePoint's Web applications to the list of trusted sites in Internet Explorer.**

2. **Verify that the security level is set at the proper level for the Trusted Sites zone.**

3. **Configure your browser to bypass a proxy server.**

If you're using a browser other than Internet Explorer, check your browser's documentation to determine whether you need to complete any steps to access SharePoint.

Internet Explorer uses security zones to organize Web sites as well as apply security levels to said sites. By default, all Web sites are in the Internet zone, which has a medium level of security. Although you can access SharePoint from this zone, you receive more prompts when doing so. For this reason, I recommend that you add SharePoint to the Trusted Sites zone. Sites in the Trusted Sites zone have a low level of security — which means you don't have to jump through so many hoops to gain access to them.

To add SharePoint to the Trusted Sites zone in SharePoint, follow these steps:

1. **Choose Tools↪Internet Options in Internet Explorer.**

   The Options dialog box appears onscreen.

2. **Click the Security tab.**

3. **Click the Trusted Sites icon.**

4. **Click the Sites button.**

   A list of trusted Web sites appears.

5. **Clear the check box next to Require server verification (https:) for all sites in this zone.**

   You can enable encryption using a technology called Secure Sockets Layer (SSL) which would require users to access sites using the HTTPS protocol. A server or network administrator can determine the best approach for encryption. See the topic "Plan for and design security" in the SharePoint TechNet library for more information. You can access the library at this site:

   ```
   http://technet2.microsoft.com/Office/en-us/library/
           396ee7ae-6dc6-4d48-8448-54a0033f39781033.
           mspx?mfr=true
   ```

6. **Type or paste the URL for the SharePoint site in the Add This Web Site to the Zone field.**

7. **Click Add.**

   The site appears in the list of trusted Web sites, as shown in Figure 2-5.

8. **Click the Close button to close the dialog box and then click OK to close the Options dialog box.**

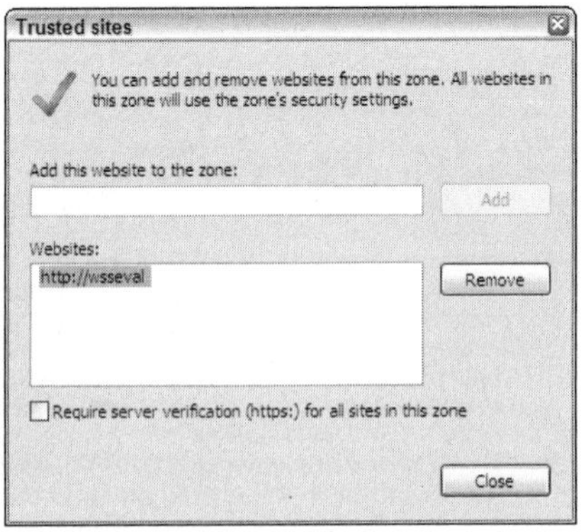

Figure 2-5:
Add
SharePoint
to the list
of trusted
sites.

If you're opening SharePoint on a computer running Windows Server 2003, you'll likely encounter a message from Internet Explorer's Enhanced Security Configuration. On servers, Internet Explorer is locked down even more than on clients. When you attempt to access SharePoint on a server, you're immediately prompted to add the site to the Trusted Sites zone. Don't ignore this prompt! You must add the site to the Trusted Sites zone; if you don't, you'll be denied access. Click the Add button on the Warning dialog box.

You may also want to configure Internet Explorer so that it doesn't prompt you for a username and password. Instead, Internet Explorer can use the username and password that you use to log into the network. The upcoming steps show you how you can set this value as part of the security level for the Trusted Sites zone.

1. **Choose Tools⇨Internet Options in Internet Explorer.**

   The Options dialog box makes another appearance.

2. **Click the Security tab and then click the Trusted Sites icon.**

3. **Click the Custom Level button.**

   The Security Settings dialog box opens.

4. **Scroll down to the User Authentication section and select the Automatic Logon with Current Username and Password radio button.**

5. **Click OK to close the dialog box and then click OK on the Options dialog box.**

If your company uses a proxy server to access the Internet, you may need to configure Internet Explorer to bypass the server for local addresses. Otherwise, the browser attempts to detect the settings, which can slow down access to SharePoint.

If you don't use a proxy server, you won't need to bother with these steps.

To configure Internet Explorer to bypass the server for local addresses

1. **Choose Tools⇨Internet Options in Internet Explorer.**

2. **Click the Connections tab.**

3. **Click the LAN Settings button.**

   The Local Area Network (LAN) Settings dialog box appears.

4. **Place a check mark next to Use a proxy server for your LAN.**

5. **Select the Bypass Proxy Server for Local Addresses check box, as shown in Figure 2-6.**

6. **Click OK and then click OK again to close the Options dialog box.**

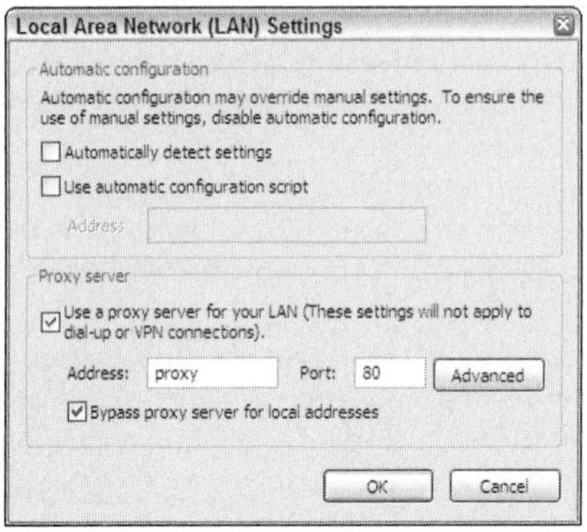

Figure 2-6:
Configure
Internet
Explorer to
bypass a
proxy
server.

Installing SharePoint for the Real World

Unless your organization is especially small, you can't get away with running SharePoint on a single server. Instead, you have to use multiple servers. When you use multiple servers to run an application, it's called a *server farm*. You don't have to start with a large farm because you can scale up by adding more servers as your needs require.

A server farm consists of multiple servers that work together to provide the SharePoint experience. Companies often find it necessary to span services across multiple servers to provide the performance and availability their organization requires.

Server farms are made up of physical servers that run logical services. The *physical* servers are the computer hardware that you can touch. The *logical* services are the applications that run on the physical servers. In many cases, your physical servers pull double and triple duty by running multiple logical services.

A minimum SharePoint installation usually has the following two physical servers:

- A *front-end* server that serves Web pages and other SharePoint services such as search and Excel Services.

- A *back-end* server where the database is stored. All the content displayed in SharePoint's Web pages is stored in databases.

The distinction between physical servers and logical services is important. SharePoint requires a dozen or so logical services to run. That doesn't mean you need a dozen servers. Some of these services run on front-end servers, and others run on back-end servers. (A server's designation as front-end or back-end is based on the logical services it provides. A *back-end server* provides some kind of service that the front-end server requires in order to function. A *front-end server* provides services directly to end users.)

Table 2-1 lists the logical services that need to be deployed and configured as part of a SharePoint installation.

Table 2-1	Logical SharePoint Servers
SharePoint Product Logical Server Name	*What It Does*
MOSS	Microsoft Single Sign-on Service Office Document Conversions Launcher Service Office Document Conversions Load Balancer Service Office SharePoint Server Search Office Source Engine
WSS	Windows SharePoint Services Administration Windows SharePoint Services Incoming E-Mail Windows SharePoint Services Search Windows SharePoint Services Timer Windows SharePoint Services Tracing Windows SharePoint Services VSS Writer Windows SharePoint Services Web Application

Logical services are installed on one or more physical servers. The logical services running on a physical server determines the role of the server in the server farm. For example, the server running the database is often called the *database server.* A database server is back-end because it provides data to front-end Web servers. Typically, an installation has at least two physical servers — an application server and a database server. The application server hosts all of SharePoint's applications and serves Web pages to end users. Table 2-2 lists the physical servers often used.

Table 2-2	Physical Servers Used in SharePoint	
Physical Server Name	*Server Type*	*What It Does*
Application Server	Front-end	Runs Office SharePoint Server 2007 services such as Excel Services and indexing.
Database Server	Back-end	Provides content from databases using SQL Server 2005 or SQL Server 2000.
Web Server	Front-end	Serves up Web pages by using Internet Information Services (IIS).

Note that you can have multiple front-end and back-end servers. You can run each logical service on its own server. You can have multiple instances of a service across servers. For example, you may need to have two or three Web servers and two or three database servers.

The number and kind of servers you deploy depend on many factors including the number of users, the volume of data, and your requirements for performance and availability. If you have lots of users accessing a relatively low volume of data, then you may decide to add Web servers. Alternatively, if your deployment is data heavy, then you may deploy additional database servers. If you're making extensive usage of Excel Services or InfoPath Forms Services, you may need to deploy separate application servers to host those services.

Creating the server farm

When you create a server farm, you usually build your back-end servers before you build your front-end servers. For example, you install your databases on your database server before you install your front-end servers. Regardless of how you divvy up the servers, the first step in any server farm installation is planning. You need to plan how many servers you need and what services are going to be installed on each.

Here's the general procedure for creating a SharePoint server farm:

1. **Plan your server farm.**

    You must determine your server topology before you start installing software. (A *topology* is a fancy word that defines how many servers you're planning to deploy.) If you're unsure, you could start with the minimum two servers and scale up as needs require.

2. **Procure all the hardware and software required based on your plan.**

3. **Prepare each of your servers for installation.**

    You want to start with clean servers running Windows Server 2003 with Service Pack 1. (Refer to the section, "Creating an Evaluation Server," earlier in this chapter, for an overview of what you install to prepare for the SharePoint installation.)

4. **Create service accounts for installing and running SharePoint.**

    You need security accounts to install and configure SharePoint. The accounts you provide are used by SharePoint's services to run on the server.

You may be tempted to just use your administrator account for all these accounts. A word to the wise: Don't yield to such temptation; in some instances, the installation adds permissions to the account. Instead, you should create separate accounts for the various services you need to run. MOSS 2007 requires more accounts than WSS because there are more services in MOSS.

You can read Microsoft's recommendation on service accounts at the TechNet library. Better yet, leave it to your network or security adminis-trator to figure out which accounts to create. See the SharePoint TechNet Library topic "Plan for administrative and service accounts" for more information. For MOSS 2007, you can find the topic at this site:

```
http://technet2.microsoft.com/Office/en-us/library/
        396ee7ae-6dc6-4d48-8448-54a0033f39781033.mspx
```

The WSS documentation is at this site:

```
http://technet2.microsoft.com/Office/en-us/library/
        89e4c579-5720-45e0-917e-abeb95266c3e1033.mspx
```

Don't confuse security accounts for services with accounts for user access. Service accounts are most often domain accounts that afford the service some level of administrative access to the server, database, and SharePoint. Generally speaking, no one's going to log on to SharePoint or the server using a service account. That's what makes them service accounts — they're used only by services. You can read about granting users access to SharePoint in Chapter 6.

5. **Install SQL Server 2005 or SQL Server 2000 on your back-end data-base servers.**

The SharePoint installation installs the databases on the database server, so you must have your database servers installed first. Note that your back-end database server may actually be a cluster of database servers, depending on how you choose to configure. You likely want to include your database administrator in this process. Your database administrator may also choose to create the SharePoint databases in advance.

If you're using SQL Server 2005, be sure to run the SQL Server Surface Area Configuration tool and then enable TCP/IP and named pipes for local and remote connections.

Refer to your planning documentation to determine additional SQL Server services that you may need to install, such as Reporting Services and Analysis Services.

6. **Install SharePoint on each of your front-end servers.**

Use the Advanced installation option on the Choose the Installation You Want page. On the Server Type tab, select the Complete option to install all SharePoint components on the front-end server, as shown in Figure 2-7. By installing all components, you can run the server as both a Web and an application server. If you want to run the server only as a Web server, select the Web Front End option. Windows SharePoint Services only includes options for Web Front End and Stand-alone. There are no other applications to install on the server for WSS. MOSS installs ser-vices such as InfoPath Forms Services and Excel Services. You can use the Stand-alone option to install SharePoint on a single server.

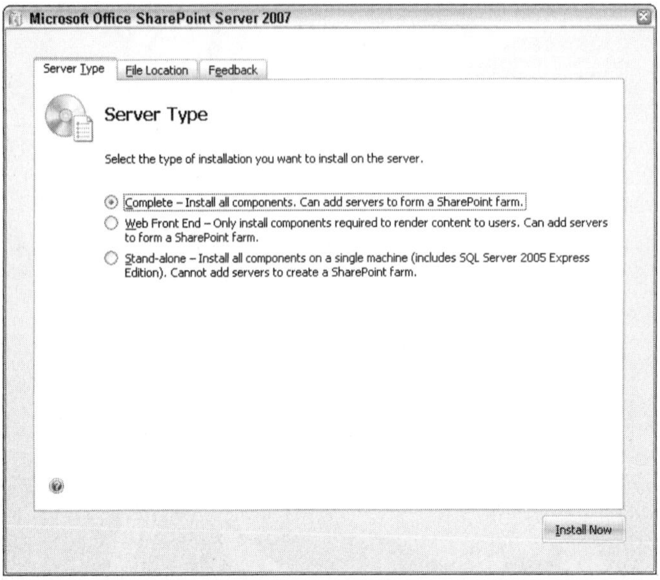

Figure 2-7:
Choose the
server type
to create a
server farm.

7. **Run the SharePoint Products and Technologies Configuration Wizard to complete the installation.**

   You have the option to run the configuration wizard after the installation wizard completes. You can run the wizard any time by choosing Start➪ Administrative Tools➪SharePoint Products and Technologies Configuration Wizard.

   Use the wizard to create a new server farm or connect to an existing farm. When you run the wizard on the first front-end server on your farm, choose to create a new server farm, as shown in Figure 2-8. When you add front-end servers, choose to connect to the existing farm.

   The configuration wizard installs the database, Office SharePoint services, and the SharePoint Central Administration Web site. You must specify the name of the database server so the wizard knows where to create the database.

   The first front-end server you create must host the SharePoint Central Administration Web Application. Central Administration launches after the configuration wizard completes.

8. **Using the Central Administration Web site, enable and disable the services you want to run on each application and front-end servers.**

   You configure all the settings for the SharePoint server farm using the Central Administration Web site. I explain more about the Central Administration Web site in Chapter 18. In Chapter 3, I discuss the configuration options for site collections.

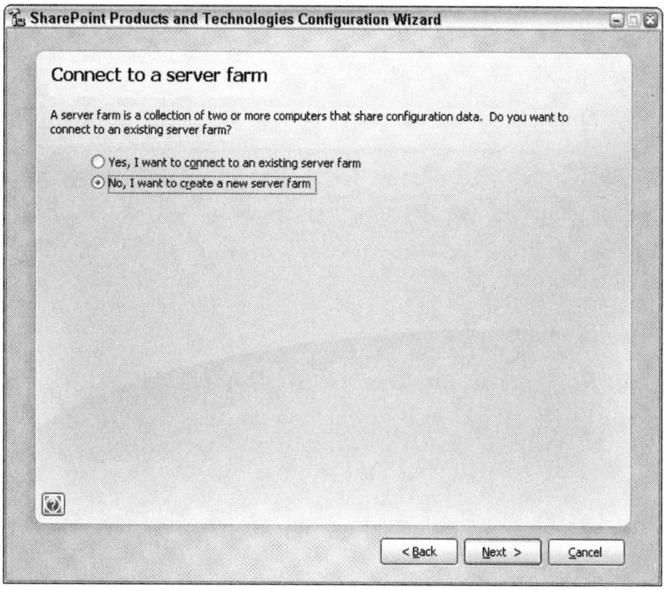

Figure 2-8:
Create a
new server
farm.

The preceding steps walk you through the basic steps to install SharePoint. But installing SharePoint isn't the same as *deploying* SharePoint. To complete your deployment, you must go through many more steps.

Configuring SharePoint Services

The SharePoint Products and Technologies Configuration Wizard creates the database and gets your servers ready for serving SharePoint. Before you can actually start using SharePoint, however, you have to configure which services you want to run on hardware in your server farm.

The following two services must be configured first for MOSS 2007:

- ✔ **Office SharePoint Server Search:** This service provides search and indexing features to your SharePoint implementation. You must implement the service on at least one front-end server.

- ✔ **Windows SharePoint Services Web Application:** This service must run on any front-end server that you intend to use as a Web server that would serve up the Web pages for your SharePoint server.

For Windows SharePoint Server version 3 installations, you need only to start the Windows SharePoint Services Search service.

To start a new service, follow these steps:

1. **Browse to the Central Administration Web site.**

   The Central Administration site is hosted on the first machine on which you installed SharePoint. On that machine, choose Start⇨All Programs⇨ Administrative Tools⇨SharePoint 3.0 Central Administration.

   You can access Central Administration from any machine on your network. You need to know the URL to access Central Administration, which you can find by launching Central Administration on the Web server. See Chapter 18 for more information on using Central Administration.

2. **Click the Operations tab on the Central Administration home page.**

3. **Click the Servers in Farm link in the Topology and Services section.**

   The Servers in Farm page appears.

   The Servers in Farm page lists all the servers in your server farm. Use this page to manage all the servers in your server farm.

4. **Click the server you want to start services on.**

   The Services on Server: *Servername* page appears, displaying a table of services that you may start or stop for the server you select.

   For example, click your front-end MOSS 2007 Web server if you want to start services such as Office SharePoint Server Search or Windows SharePoint Services Web Application.

5. **Click the Start or Stop hyperlink on the line of the service that you want to start or stop.**

   Figure 2-9 shows how to start the Windows SharePoint Services Web Application. MOSS 2007 displays a list of server roles, as Figure 2-9 shows, from which you can select. Selecting a role highlights the service you should enable on the server. If you're using a stand-alone server, you can't choose a role for the server.

6. **Configure the service if required.**

   Some services, such as the Office SharePoint Server Search, require additional configuration information before the service can start. See Chapter 14 for more information on configuring SharePoint search.

You can view a list of all services running on the servers in your server farm on the Servers in Farm page, as shown in Figure 2-10. Follow the first three preceding steps to access the Servers in Farm page.

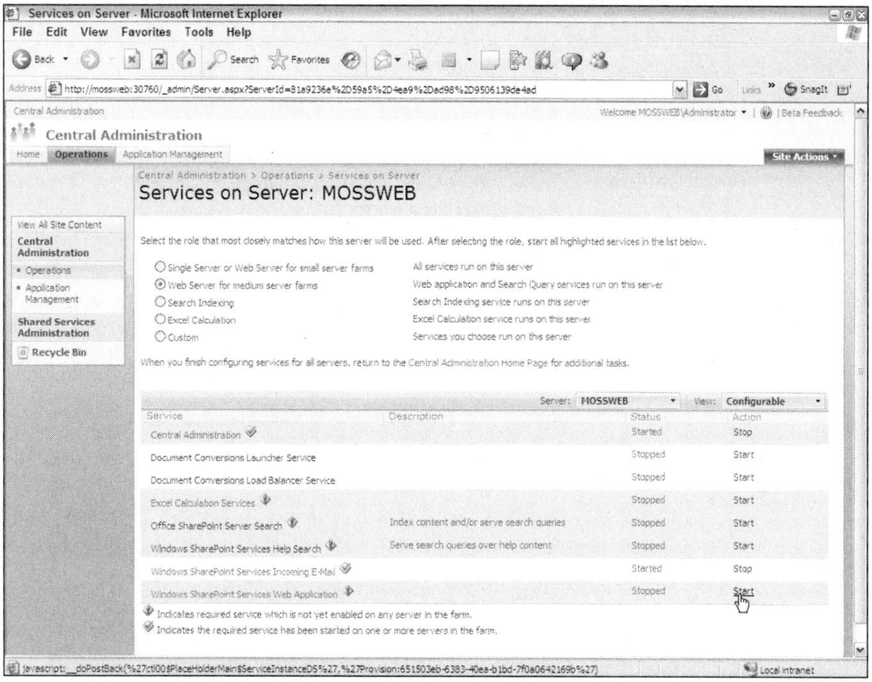

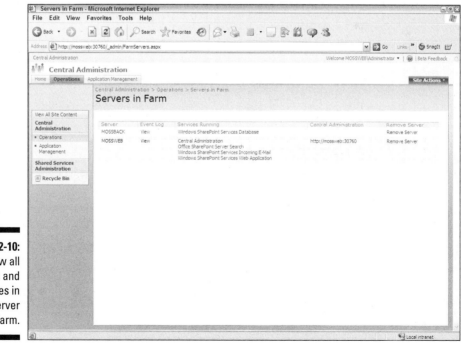

Figure 2-9:
Start
services for
your server.

Figure 2-10:
View all
servers and
services in
your server
farm.

Creating a Shared Services Provider

MOSS 2007 requires that you create and configure a Shared Services Provider (SSP). SSP enables the servers in your server farm to share services with each other. Most of the great features that you want to use in MOSS 2007, such as personalization, Excel Services, and the Business Data Catalog, are hosted by the Shared Services Provider. You usually only need one SSP per server farm, but it is possible to have more than one. See Chapter 18 for more information on the services provided by SSP.

Before you can create the SSP, you must create a Web application for the SSP administration site in Internet Information Services (IIS). See Chapter 3 for more details on working with Web applications in SharePoint. To create the new Web application for the SSP administration site, follow these steps:

1. **Browse to the Central Administration Web site.**

2. **Click the Application Management tab on the Central Administration home page.**

3. **Click the Create or Extend Web Application link in the SharePoint Web Application Management section.**

4. **Click the Create a New Web Application link.**

    The Create a New Web Application page appears.

5. **Accept the default settings in the IIS Web site and the Security Configuration sections of the page.**

    Check with your network administrator to ensure that your domain uses a standard security configuration. You may need to adjust these settings.

    In the Description field, you may choose to rename the administration site to something more descriptive, such as `SharePoint - SSP Admin`. The description you type appears in IIS Manager.

6. **Accept the default settings for Load Balanced URL and Application Pool sections.**

    You may want to change the application pool name to match the description you enter in Step 5.

7. **In the User name and Password fields, enter the service account for the application pool to use.**

    The service account used by the application pool has complete access to all site content. Microsoft recommends that you use a unique domain account for each application pool you create. The application pool account shouldn't have administrative rights on your servers. See your security administrator for assistance with properly configuring domain accounts.

8. **In the Reset Internet Information Services section, indicate whether to restart IIS automatically or manually.**

   In order for the new Web application to be accessible, IIS must be restarted. You can elect to have SharePoint automatically restart IIS on all servers in the server farm, or you can restart the servers yourself. You might choose to restart the servers manually to minimize the disruption on users who may be accessing those servers.

9. **Verify that the correct database server name appears in the Database Name and Authentication section.**

   You may want to change the name of the database to a friendlier name, such as WSS_Content_SSPAdmin. This makes it easier to identify the database's purpose.

10. **Accept the default database authentication method of Windows authentication unless your database is configured to use SQL authentication.**

11. **Accept the default value for the Search Server section.**

   If you're using a stand-alone server, you don't have the option to enter a different search server.

12. **Click OK.**

   The Operation in Progress page appears.

13. **Wait while the server creates the new Web application.**

   This process could take a while; the server has to create a new database on your database server and then set up a new Web application in IIS.

   The Application Created page appears if the database and Web application are created successfully. If the process fails, check the event logs in your database server and your IIS server for clues as to why the process failed.

One of the services provided by SSP is My Site personal sites, which provides each SharePoint user with a personal portal. I suggest you create a second Web application to use for your My Site personal sites. It isn't necessary to create a second Web application, but, by doing so, you isolate your My Site personal site content from your SSP content in separate applications and databases. This makes it easier to back up, restore, and move any My Site personal sites in the future. You can follow the steps you use to create a Web application for the SSP administration site to create the Web application for the My Site personal sites.

After you create Web applications to house your Shared Service Provider administrative site and My Site personal sites, you can create the SSP.

To create a Shared Services Provider, follow these steps:

1. **Browse to the Central Administration Web site.**

2. **Click the Application Management tab on the Central Administration home page.**

3. **Click the Create or Configure This Farm's Shared Services link in the Office SharePoint Server Shared Services section.**

   The Manage This Farm's Shared Services page appears.

4. **Click the New SSP button.**

   The New Shared Services Provider page appears.

5. **Accept the default name in the SSP Name section and then select the Web application you created as the SSP administration site.**

6. **Select the Web application you created for your My Site personal sites in the My Site Location section.**

7. **Type a username and password in the SSP Service Credentials section.**

   You should use the same account you used for the SSP application pool account.

8. **Accept the default values in the SSP Database and Search Database sections.**

9. **Select the front-end server you configured Search on from the Index Server drop-down list.**

10. **Accept the default value for the SSL for Web Services section.**

11. **Click OK.**

    The Operation in Progress page appears.

12. **Wait while your databases are created.**

    The Success! page appears when the SSP is created. Click OK.

Don't let this Success message give you any false hopes. You still need to follow several more steps before you can actually start using your SharePoint implementation. See the next section for a rundown of the next steps.

Performing Administrative Tasks

One feature of SharePoint is that you can use it to collaborate with members of a team to accomplish a project. I can't think of a better project that requires collaboration among many parties than installing and configuring SharePoint. Apparently Microsoft agrees; it added an Administrator Tasks list to the Central Administration Web site.

By using the Administrator Tasks list, you get a feel for how you can use SharePoint to manage tasks. In this section, you get a chance to see how to use the Administrator Tasks list to finish configuring SharePoint. (Okay, I don't actually show you how to configure the tasks, but I *do* show you how to view a *list* of tasks. The Tasks list itself does a pretty good job of explaining what's involved in each task.)

Table 2-3 lists some of the common tasks you can expect to find in the Administrator Tasks list and where (in this book) you can find more information about completing each of them.

Table 2-3	Common SharePoint Administrative Tasks
Task	*Where You Can Read About It*
Initial Deployment: Add Servers to Farm	"Creating the server farm" in this chapter
Initial Deployment: Assign Services to Servers	"Configuring SharePoint Services" in this chapter
Configure Farm's Shared Services this chapter	"Creating a Shared Services Provider" in
Incoming E-Mail Settings	Chapter 10
Outgoing E-Mail Settings	Chapter 10
Create SharePoint Sites	Chapters 3 and 4
Add Excel Services Trusted Locations	Chapter 17
Service Level Settings for SharedServices1	Chapter 18
Diagnostic Logging Settings	Chapter 18
Enable SSO in the Farm	Chapter 17

Viewing administrative tasks

When you install SharePoint, SharePoint creates a list of administrative tasks that you need to complete if you want to configure SharePoint. You may not need to complete every single task, and you may need to complete additional tasks that aren't listed. The list of administrative tasks is just a list that Microsoft believes most installations need to complete. MOSS 2007 includes additional tasks that don't apply to Windows SharePoint Services such as configured shared services.

To view the Administrator Tasks list, browse to your Central Administration site. If you aren't sure of the URL for your Central Administration site, you can access a shortcut on the front-end SharePoint server by choosing Start⇨ All Programs⇨Administrative Tools⇨SharePoint 3.0 Central Administration.

The Administrator Tasks list appears on the home page of the Central Administration site. Figure 2-11 shows a list of typical administrative tasks for MOSS 2007.

If the list includes more tasks than what can appear on the home page, click the More Items link to view the entire list of tasks.

To view a task in the Administrator Tasks list, click the hyperlinked task title. The task detail appears in the browser. Each task provides the following information:

- ✔ **Action:** A hyperlink to the page in SharePoint's Central Administration site where you perform the task described.
- ✔ **Associated Service:** The service that's involved with completing the task.
- ✔ **Description:** A high-level description of the administrative task, its purpose, and the information you need to complete it.
- ✔ **Order:** The relative order in which the tasks should be completed.
- ✔ **System Task:** A Yes/No value indicating whether the task is associated with setting up the SharePoint system.

The Administrator Tasks list is based on a standard SharePoint Tasks list. As a result, the list includes all the standard Tasks columns such as Status, Due Date, % Complete, and Assigned To. (See Chapter 4 to read more about standard Tasks lists.)

 You aren't limited to working with only the tasks created by SharePoint. You can add your own tasks to the list of Administrative Tasks. You might want to add configuration tasks that you discover on your own as part of your planning processes. Click the Add New Task link to add a new task to the list.

Assigning administrative tasks

You probably have multiple people assisting you with your SharePoint configuration. Rather than keeping track of who needs to do what, you can use the Administrative Tasks list to assign tasks to members of your team.

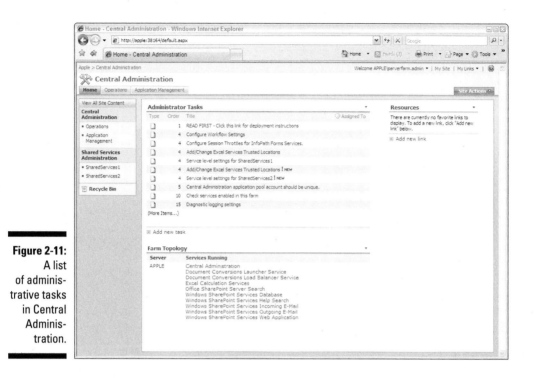

Figure 2-11:
A list
of adminis-
trative tasks
in Central
Adminis-
tration.

To assign a task to someone, follow these steps:

1. **Click the task's hyperlinked title in the Administrative Tasks list on the Central Administration site's home page.**

   The task appears in the browser.

2. **Click the Edit Item button.**

3. **In the Assigned To field, type the account name of the person you want to assign to the task, as shown in Figure 2-12.**

   If you aren't sure of the account name, click the Browse icon next to the Assigned To field to choose the account from the directory list. SharePoint gets account information from an external directory such as Active Directory. The users you assign tasks to aren't required to have access to SharePoint, unless you want them to access the tasks list and update their tasks. See Chapter 6 for more information on granting users access to SharePoint.

4. **Set the task's Start Date and Due Date.**

5. **Click OK to save the record.**

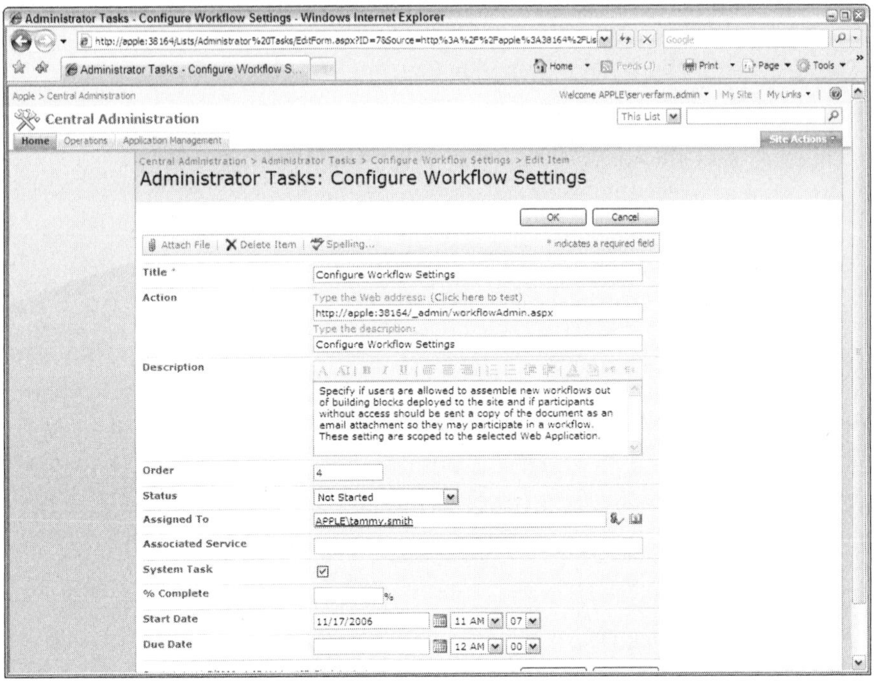

Figure 2-12:
Enter an
account
name in the
Assigned To
field.

If you configured the outgoing e-mail service, the person to whom you assign the task to receives an e-mail notifying him or her of the task assignment. You can click the Outgoing e-mail settings link on the Operations page of the Central Administration site to configure outgoing e-mail. Windows SharePoint Services includes an administrator task for this action.

Completing administrative tasks

You can use the Administrator Tasks list in several ways. In a simple configuration, you may want to step through each of the tasks and complete the task as you go. In a more complex configuration, you may need to do more research before you can complete the configuration. You should consider using the Status, Due Date, and % Complete fields to keep track of your progress. You also have the option of attaching a document to the task. This feature might be helpful if you want to create a support document that outlines your progress. I suggest you use the Administrator Tasks list, along with this book, as a roadmap for getting started with configuring your SharePoint deployment.

To complete tasks in the Administrator Tasks list, follow these steps:

1. **Click the hyperlinked title to view the task details.**
2. **Read the task's description to get a better understanding of the task.**
3. **Click the Action link to go to the page in SharePoint's Central Administration site where you perform the configuration task.**
4. **Configure the administrative task.**

   Don't be afraid to peek at SharePoint's administrative pages. If you're unsure how to complete the task, you may click Cancel and return to the page later.

Configuring an administrative task doesn't update the task's status in the Administrative Tasks list. You must manually update the status of the task. To manually update a task's status, follow these steps:

1. **Click the hyperlinked title to view the task's details.**
2. **Click the Edit Item button.**
3. **Update the Status and % Complete fields.**
4. **Click OK.**

You may choose to delete tasks after they're complete, but then you lose all your history. You may want to add a Completed Date column to the Tasks list so you know when the task was completed. See Chapter 4 for more information on adding columns to a Tasks list.

The list of Administrator Tasks that appears on the home page of the Central Administration site is displayed by using a *Web part*. (SharePoint uses Web parts to display modules of content on a page.) You may want to remove this Web part after you finish completing the administrative tasks. You may also want to change the view displayed in the Administrative Tasks Web part. See Chapter 4 for more information on modifying and removing Web parts.

Chapter 3

Creating the Site Hierarchy

SharePoint is organized into a hierarchy of containers, both physical and logical: The outermost container is the server (or server farm), which in turn contains your Web applications (all hosted on a Web server), which all in turn host one or more site collections, which in turn host the sites that end users access. (It all has a distinct Russian-nesting-doll feel to it.) The collection of Web applications within a server farm, site collections within a Web application, and sites within a site collection create a hierarchy.

Web applications and site collections are created at the server level, tasks that are usually done when SharePoint is first deployed. You might, however, add new Web applications or site collections if you decide to extend your deployment to meet additional needs in your company.

In this chapter, I show you how to create Web applications and site collections — working on the assumption that you've already planned out how many Web applications and site collections you need to create. (I discuss creating sites in Chapter 4.)

Understanding Web Applications

Web applications are the highest containers in SharePoint. In this context, a *Web application* is a Web site running on Internet Information Services (IIS), a Microsoft Web server product that runs on Windows Server 2003.

By default, an IIS Web server can serve only static content, such as HyperText Markup Language (HTML) pages. When you prepare your server for installing SharePoint, you install and enable ASP.NET for IIS, a process I explain in Chapter 2.

ASP.NET is a server extension to IIS. By enabling ASP.NET, you make it possible for IIS to serve applications created for ASP.NET — for example, SharePoint.

When you install SharePoint on the front-end Web server running IIS, an extension for Windows SharePoint Services (WSS) is added to IIS. SharePoint Web applications are IIS Web sites that are configured to use the WSS extension.

Many Web server products are available. A comparable Web server product to IIS is Apache, which runs on Linux servers. Although SharePoint consists of Web sites, it works only on servers running IIS and ASP.NET (its fellow Microsoft products). You can't install SharePoint Web sites on an Apache Web server.

Finding existing Web applications

A SharePoint implementation may have multiple Web applications — and the number of applications you create depends on how you want to use the sites hosted within the Web application. Each Web application has its own set of configuration features that you can access via the Administration page in SharePoint's Central Administration site. In fact, the Central Administration site is its own SharePoint Web application. Table 3-1 lists some separate Web applications you can expect to find in a SharePoint implementation.

Table 3-1	Common SharePoint Web Applications	
Web Application	*What It's Used For*	*Microsoft Office SharePoint Server 2007 or Windows SharePoint Services*
Central Administration	Hosts the SharePoint Central Administration site.	Both
Shared Services Provider	Hosts the SSP administrative site.	MOSS
My Site	Hosts My Site personal sites.	MOSS
Content	Hosts site collections.	Both

If you install SharePoint on a stand-alone server, the SharePoint Products and Technologies Configuration Wizard creates all the Web applications needed to run your SharePoint implementation. In a server farm, only the Central Administration Web application is created for you. You must create Web applications for your Shared Services Provider, My Site, and content.

You can have multiple Web applications for content sites. For example, you may decide to create separate Web applications for content accessed by internal users and external users.

You can determine which Web applications are already present in your deployment by looking at the list of Web sites in the Internet Information Services (IIS) Manager, as described here:

1. **Choose Start➪All Programs➪Administrative Tools➪Internet Information Services (IIS) Manager on your front-end Web server to launch the IIS Manager.**

   If you have multiple front-end Web servers, check IIS for each server.

2. **Expand the server to see a list of folders.**

3. **Click the Web Sites folder.**

   A list of Web sites appears in the pane on the right, as shown in Figure 3-1.

By default, the Web site listed at port 80 in IIS is the content site. Port 80 is the default port for *HyperText Transfer Protocol* (HTTP), which is used to communicate with Web servers. By setting the content site at port 80, you can access SharePoint in the browser without typing a port number. Other SharePoint Web applications, such as the Central Administration site, use a random port number generated when the application is created. The port number you see in the Port column for the Central Administration site is the port number that you type in the URL to access the site. For example, in Figure 3-1 the Central Administration site uses port 38164. The URL for the site is `http://apple:38164`.

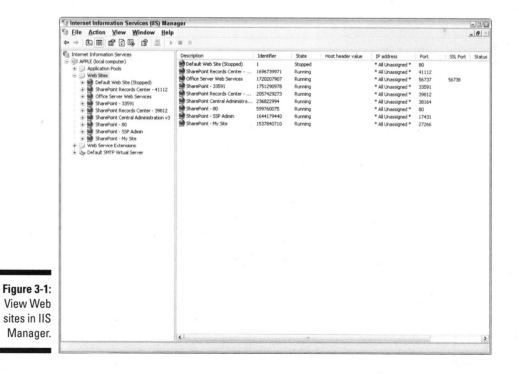

Figure 3-1: View Web sites in IIS Manager.

By default, all Web browsers use port 80 for HTTP. You don't have to use the URL, `http://servername:80`, for the content site; that would be redundant.

Setting up Web applications

You can create as many Web applications as you feel are necessary, but the big thing about creating different Web applications is that you can isolate site collections from each other. And why is isolation a good thing? Well, if each Web application has its own configuration, that means that you can then do the following:

- ✔ **Use different authentication.** Giving each Web application its own authentication scheme means you can have one Web application for internal use and another for external access.

- ✔ **Use separate application pools.** If you set it up so that each Web application uses its own application pool in Internet Information Services, you can keep the applications separate from each other on the server so they can't corrupt each other.

- ✔ **Use separate databases.** By using different databases for each Web application, you can isolate content for backup and restore operations.

The options for Web applications listed here are just that — options. You don't have to use them. For example, multiple Web applications can use the same authentication scheme, application pools, and databases. You might create a separate Web application so you have the option of using separate configurations down the road.

To create a new Web application, follow these steps:

1. **Click the Application Management tab in the SharePoint Central Administration site.**

2. **Click the Create or Extend Web Application link in the SharePoint Web Application Management section.**

   The Create or Extend Web Application page appears.

   On this page, you have two options: Create a new Web application, or extend an existing one. These steps create a new one.

   You select Extending an Existing Web Application option if you want to create a new Web application that shares an existing content database. That's a good approach if you want to make the same content available to users who are outside your corporate network.

3. **Click the Create a New Web Application link.**

   The Create New Web Application page appears, as shown in Figure 3-2.

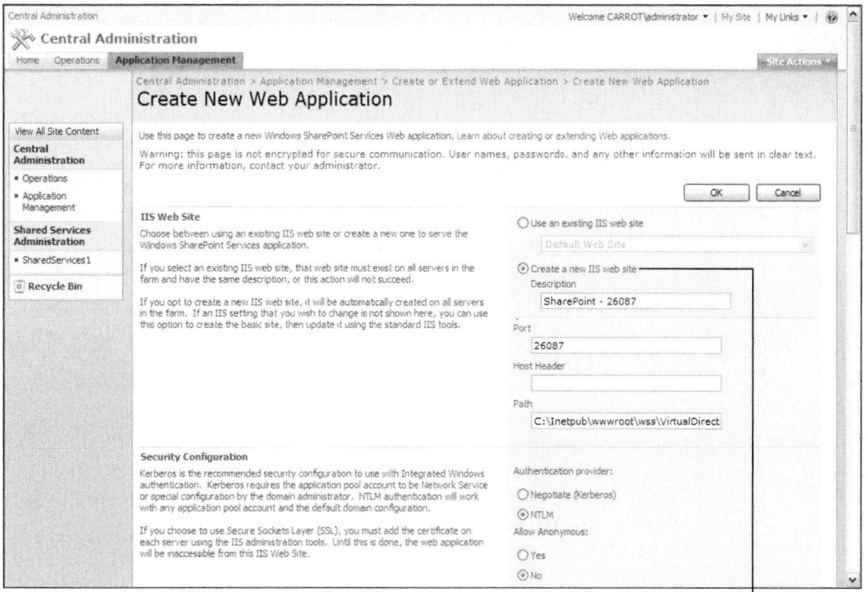

Figure 3-2:
Create a
new Web
application.

Create a new IIS Web site.

4. **In the IIS Web Site section, accept the default option to Create a New IIS Web Site.**

   Here's a list of handy things to know about this option:

   • You can select the Use an Existing IIS Web Site option if you've already created the Web site with IIS. It's best to let SharePoint handle the creation of Web sites in IIS.

   • The IIS Web Site section includes a default description and path. Accept these defaults unless you have a reason to change them.

   • You have the option to set the port that IIS uses to access the site. SharePoint randomly generates a number to use for the port. You may change it if you want. Just make sure the port number doesn't conflict with any existing port numbers.

   • Be sure to set the port to 80 if you're creating the primary content Web application. Otherwise, your users have to type the port every time they pull up the site in the browser.

   • Host headers are a new feature in this version of SharePoint; they allow you to map multiple domain names to a single Web site. Type the domain name you want to map to the Web application in the Host Header field.

You must register the domain name with your DNS server; that way client browsers can resolve ("translate") the host domain name into the IP address of the Web server. Your network administrator can assist you with this task.

5. **In the Security Configuration section of the Create New Web Application page, select the default values unless your network administrator gives you different information.**

   In this section, you have the choice to select your authentication provider. The default option is NTLM (short for Windows NT LAN Manager, an authentication protocol used for Windows NT 4.0 networks). Kerberos is more secure, however, so be sure to check with your network administrator.

   Selecting Yes in the Allow Anonymous section enables anonymous access to the Web site in IIS. You should avoid allowing anonymous access. A better approach than using anonymous access is to grant access to the domain group, Authenticated Users. (See Chapter 10 for details on how to do this.)

   If you want your Web application to use Secure Sockets Layer (SSL) for an added layer of protection, you can enable that capability by selecting the Yes radio button for SSL. SSL encrypts data sent to and from the Web application.

   If you enable SSL, you must place SSL certificates on each of your IIS servers. See your network administrator for assistance with this task.

6. **Type a URL to use as the load-balanced URL. By default, the URL is the** *servername* **and** *port.*

   The load-balanced URL is the domain that's used in all the links that point to the Web application.

7. **In the Application Pool section, accept the default option to create a new application pool.**

   By creating a new application pool, you're assured that your Web application is isolated from other Web applications on the server. If one crashes, yours won't crash as well.

   You may want to give the application pool a meaningful name. For example, I append `MySite` to the application pool name when I create a new Web application to host My Site personal sites. That way I can easily see which application pool maps to the My Site Web application in the IIS Manager.

You want to enter a username and password for the application pool to use. The username and password that you enter here is the identity used by the application pool. Microsoft recommends that you use a unique domain account for each application pool you create. The application pool account has access to all the content in the Web application. See your network or security administrator for assistance with creating domain accounts.

8. **In the Database Name and Authentication section, enter the name for the database server, database, and service account to use for database authentication.**

   The *database server* is the name of the server where your database is hosted. I suggest you give a meaningful name to the database itself. Using the same My Site example from Step 7, I append `MySite` to the database name so I can easily recognize the database.

   If you want to use an existing database with your Web application, you need to extend an existing Web application. Refer to Step 2 for more information.

   The default option for database authentication is Windows authentication. I suggest you use Windows authentication unless you have a specific need to use SQL authentication. There's no reason to create a separate set of accounts in SQL Server to manage.

9. **In the Search Server section, select a server to use as the search server for this Web application**.

   If you're using MOSS 2007, search is provided by the Office SharePoint Server Search shared service.

   See Chapter 14 for more information on setting up a search server.

10. **Click OK.**

    The Operation in Progress page appears. Wait while the Web application is created.

    The Application Created page appears after the application is created. The application has no site collections, so a link is provided to create a new site collection. (See the next section for more details on creating site collections.)

After you create your Web application, you must create a site collection before you can pull it up in the browser via the URL. You can also see the content database created for the Web application in SQL Server Management Studio and the Web site in IIS Manager.

Understanding Site Collections

First and foremost, a *site collection* is a (hierarchically arranged) logical container for grouping sites. From there, you need to know that the top-level site in a site collection is often a portal site that aggregates content from subsites — although this isn't required — and that a Web application can host multiple site collections.

The number of site collections you create depends on many factors. Every site in a collection shares navigation, security and permissions, templates, and content types. You should plan to group together sites that need to share these items and make them a site collection.

Before you create a site collection, gather several pieces of information — including these:

- ✔ **Path:** You can determine the path to your site collection before you create it. The *servername* in the URL is determined by the Web application. Your two default options are to create the site collection at the root of the URL or at the sites path. Subsites are created below this URL.

- ✔ **Administrators:** You need to choose primary and secondary administrators for the site collection.

- ✔ **Web application:** You have to decide which Web application should host the site collection.

- ✔ **Site template:** A *site template* is a boilerplate for creating SharePoint sites. When you create a site collection, you create the top-level site in the collection. You need to select the template for the top-level site. See the next section, "Configuring Web Applications and Site Collections."

- ✔ **Quota:** You may choose to select a quota that defines limits on the sizes of the sites created in the site collection.

To create a site collection, follow these steps:

1. **Click the Application Management tab in the SharePoint Central Administration site.**

2. **Click the Create Site Collection link in the SharePoint Site Management section.**

   The Create Site Collection page appears.

3. **Using the Web Application drop-down menu, select the application where you want to create the site collection, as shown in Figure 3-3.**

   This is an example of when it's important to give your Web applications meaningful names. Without meaningful names, you can have difficulty knowing which Web application to choose. If you're unsure, browse to the Web application in the browser or check your planning documentation.

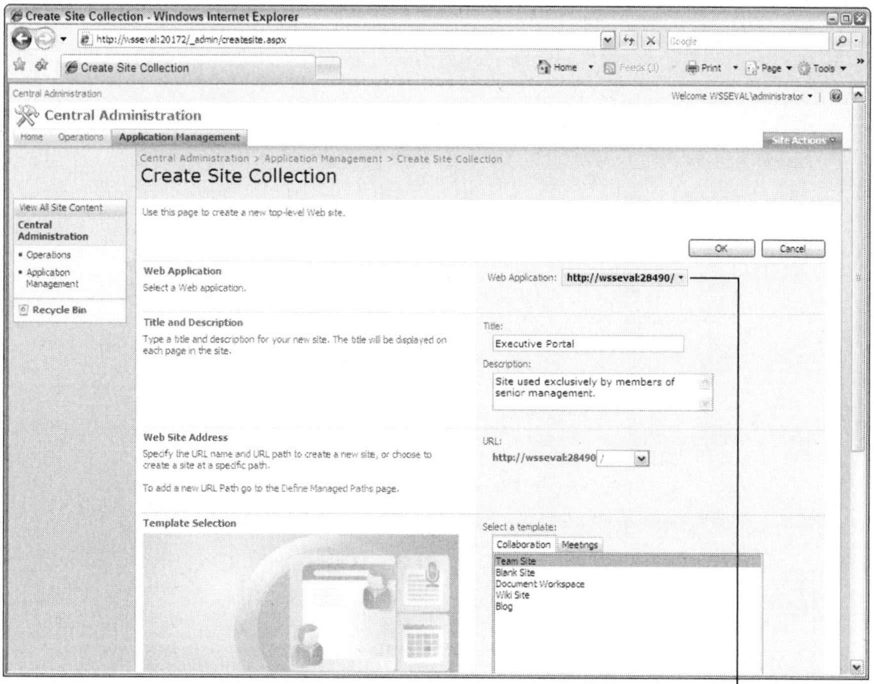

Figure 3-3:
Select a
Web appli-
cation to
host the site
collection.

Choose your Web application here.

4. **Type a title and description for the site collection.**

5. **In the Web Site Address section, type a URL for accessing the top-level site in the site collection.**

   Your default options are to use the root path, which is depicted by a forward slash (/), or to use the /sites path. You can add more paths as needed (as I describe later in this chapter in the section titled "Defining managed paths").

6. **Select a template to use for the top-level site in the site collection.**

   Your template options depend on whether you're using Windows SharePoint Services or Microsoft Office SharePoint Server 2007. WSS offers collaboration templates for small teams and project groups such as Team Site and Document Workspace. MOSS 2007 includes additional templates that are suitable for divisional portals and enterprise uses. Some MOSS 2007 site templates, such as those for collaboration and publishing portals, can only be used when you create the top-level site in a site collection. Any other site templates can be used to create sites within the site collection hierarchy. I explain site templates in more detail in Chapter 4.

7. **Type or select the primary and secondary site-collection administrators.**

   The accounts you use here are from your authentication provider (for example, Active Directory). You should generally specify two site-collection administrators. Having a backup administrator ensures that administration e-mail doesn't go unanswered in the event the primary administrator is on vacation. See Chapter 6 for more information about using authentication providers with SharePoint.

8. **Select a quota template in the Quota Template section.**

   See Chapter 18 for more information about using quota templates to monitor and control site usage.

9. **Click OK.**

   The Operation in Progress page appears.

   Wait while the site collection is created. The operation can take a few minutes while the content is added to the database.

   The Top-Level Site Successfully Created page appears. The URL for the top-level site appears in the page. You can click the link to test the site. Click OK to return to the Application Management page.

Configuring Web Applications and Site Collections

You can easily lose track of all the Web applications and site collections you have in your SharePoint deployment. The Application Management page in SharePoint's Central Administration site allows you to manage all your site collections and Web applications.

 As a rule, you shouldn't find yourself creating and configuring Web applications and site collections on a regular basis. Once you've set up your Web applications and site collections, the configuration should remain relatively stable. That doesn't mean (of course) you have any lack of further administrative tasks associated with Web applications and site collections. SharePoint provides many tools to help you monitor the health and performance of your implementation. See Chapter 18 for more information.

Configuring Web applications

For the most part, Web applications are a set-it-and-forget-it kind of feature. The only time you really need to fiddle with Web applications is when you're setting them up or if you need to move them. You can access the features you need to manage Web applications in the SharePoint Web Application Management section of the Central Administration's Application Management page, as shown in Figure 3-4.

Table 3-2 lists each of the links you find — and what they do.

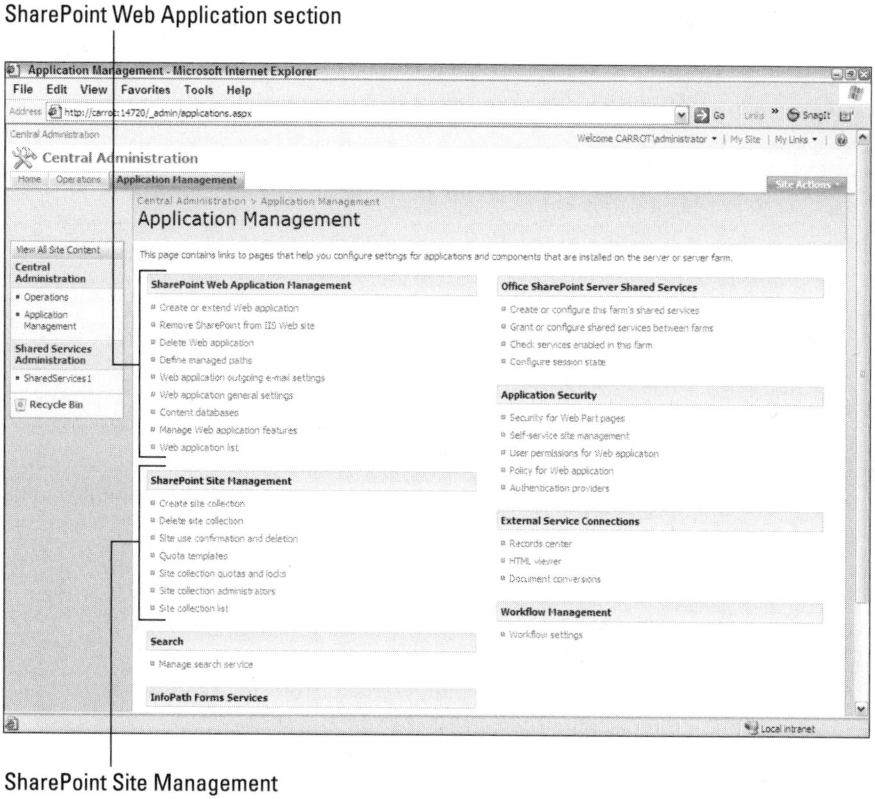

SharePoint Web Application section

Figure 3-4: Configure Web applications.

SharePoint Site Management

Table 3-2	Web Application Management Links
Link	**What You Do With It**
Create or Extend Web Application	Create a new Web application or extend an existing application.
Remove SharePoint from IIS Web Site	Choose a Web application to remove SharePoint services from or select an option to delete the IIS Web site altogether.
Delete Web Application	Choose to delete content databases and IIS Web sites for a selected Web application.
Define Managed Paths	Designate paths for the Web application's site collection to use.
Web Application Outgoing E-Mail Settings	Specify outbound mail server, From address, and Reply-To address that override SharePoint's default settings.
Web Application General Settings	Turn basic settings (such as whether the Recycle Bin is available) on or off.
Content Databases	View information about the content databases used by the Web application and add new databases.
Manage Web Application Features	Toggle features on and off for the Web application.
Web Application List	List all the Web applications.

Note that these items are configured on a per-Web-application basis. In other words, you can specify an outbound mail server for each Web application in your server farm.

Defining managed paths

Because SharePoint is a Web-based application, it's important to think about URL paths whenever you deploy. You want to try to make your paths intuitive. By default, Web applications have two paths:

- ✔ **Root:** The *root path* is the path of the server URL without anything else appended to it, such as http://*servername*. In most cases, you want to point your top-level site to this path.

- ✔ **Sites:** The *sites path* is the word sites appended to the root path, such as http://*servername*/sites. Any sites or site collections you add are appended to this URL. For example, if you create a site called Financial, the path is http://*servername*/sites/financial. You generally place all your subsites in the sites path.

You aren't limited to use just these two paths. You may create additional paths if you think it could be beneficial to your situation. For example, you may want to create a separate path for all project sites called `projects`. By adding a new path, you can select this path when you create new site collections or sites. To create a new path for a Web application, follow these steps:

1. **Click the Application Management tab in the SharePoint Central Administration site.**

2. **Click the Define Managed Paths link in the SharePoint Web Application Management section.**

   The Define Managed Paths page appears on-screen.

3. **Using the Web Application drop-down menu, select the application where you want to add the path.**

   You can work with only one application at a time.

4. **Type the name of the new path in the Path field, as shown in Figure 3-5.**

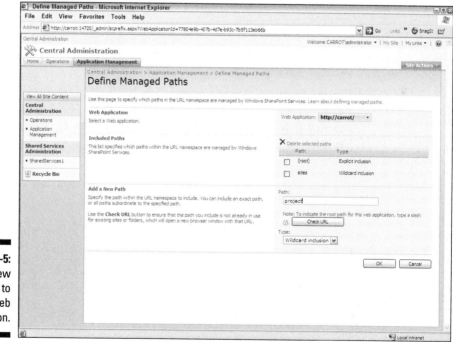

Figure 3-5:
Add a new
path to
the Web
application.

5. **Using the Type drop-down menu, indicate whether the type of inclusion is explicit or wildcard.**

   Use the Wildcard path type to indicate that the path points to a group of sites. For example, the `sites` path is used to access a group of sites in the site collection. You could also create a wildcard `projects` path that's used to provide access to a group of sites about projects. Alternatively, if you specify the `projects` path as an explicit path, then you are indicating that the path points to a portal for projects. If you want to create subsites that are accessible from the `projects` path, use a Wildcard type.

6. **Click OK.**

   The Define Managed Paths page refreshes, and the new path appears in the Included Paths section of the page.

You can use the path when you create a new site or site collection.

Configuring general settings

When you start to set general settings for your Web applications, the reasons for separating sites into Web applications becomes more apparent. You set these settings for each Web application, which means that some site collections can have features like alerts, but others can't.

To specify general settings for a Web application, follow these steps:

1. **Click the Application Management tab in the SharePoint Central Administration site.**

2. **Click the Web Application General Settings link in the SharePoint Web Application Management section.**

   The Web Application General Settings page appears.

3. **Using the Web Application drop-down menu, select a Web application that you want to specify general settings for.**

4. **Select a default time zone for the Web application.**

5. **Specify a quota for the Web application to use.**

   Define new site quotas by clicking the Quota Templates link in the SharePoint Site Management section. I cover quotas in Chapter 18.

6. **Indicate whether you want to enable the Person Name smart tag and Online Status for site members.**

   These two options provide presence information on site members.

7. **Set the maximum upload size.**

The default value is 50MB. Increasing this size can significantly impact the performance of your Web application. Note also that this is a maximum upload size, not a file size. In other words, when you upload a file, you must add together the size of the file plus the size of the overhead data to transmit the file to the server.

If you need uploads larger than 50MB, consider isolating the Web application on its own server farm away from your general purpose applications.

8. **Specify whether alerts are enabled for the Web application and set the maximum number of alerts that a single user can create.**

   Alerts require e-mail notification, which consumes server resources. You may want to accept the default value of 500.

9. **Indicate whether you want to enable RSS feeds for the Web application.**

   The clearest meaning for *RSS* is Really Simple Syndication; it's a markup language used to *syndicate* (publish and update) online news feeds. SharePoint automatically generates news feeds of site content, using the RSS file format. RSS files are displayed in a viewer that's usually browser-based. (SharePoint includes an RSS viewer that you can add to your SharePoint sites to display RSS content.) I suggest you leave RSS feeds enabled for Web applications unless you have an explicit reason to turn them off. They are a very useful way to display content from one SharePoint site in another. See Chapter 10 for more on RSS.

10. **Indicate whether to enable blogging on the Web application.**

11. **Indicate whether to enable Web page security validation. If you decide to use validation, set a period of time after which that validation expires.**

12. **Indicate whether to send a new user's name and password via e-mail.**

    If this is disabled, you must use another method to notify users of their passwords.

13. **Enable or disable backward-compatible event handlers.**

    Unless you're using event handlers from previous versions of SharePoint, you can safely disable this setting. *Event handlers* are blocks of custom code that execute when a user performs an action in SharePoint, such as uploading a file to a document library.

The event-handling model has been overhauled for SharePoint 2007, so you must explicitly enable event handlers from previous versions of SharePoint to get them to work.

14. **Specify how long to keep entries in the change log.**

    The *change log* keeps track of all the changes to site data and metadata, such as files in a document library and their properties. The change log is a table in the content database, not a file-based log. You should accept the default retention value unless you have a reason to change it.

15. Indicate whether the Recycle Bin is enabled and, if you do choose to enable, enter in how long you want to retain deleted items.

You also have the option to configure a *second-stage Recycle Bin* that stores items that have been deleted from the Recycle Bin. The second-stage Recycle Bin enables site-collection administrators to restore items deleted by end users. (See Chapter 15 for more about the Recycle Bin.)

16. Click OK.

The values are saved.

Beware that if you're changing these settings on an existing Web application that's already in production, you may get unintended consequences. For example, if you disable Recycle Bins, all documents in *existing* Recycle Bins are deleted.

Many of these settings can also be controlled at the site collection and site level. You should consider disabling a setting at the Web-application level only if you're certain that no sites or site collections need it. If you do disable a feature at the Web-application level, the site and site-collection administrators never know the setting exists.

Understanding Web application features

Each Web application has a set of SharePoint features that you can enable or disable for the entire Web application. By default, these features are enabled. You may choose to disable a feature if you know the Web application won't use them. You can enable them again later.

Features are the primary vehicle for delivering functionality in SharePoint. A basic Windows SharePoint Services installation may not have any additional Web-application features that can be enabled. However, if you install a third-party application for SharePoint, you may need to enable that program's features before you can use it.

You access Web-application features by clicking the Manage Web application features link in the Application Management page of the Central Administration site. Here are some common features you might see for a MOSS 2007 Web application:

- ✔ **Form Conversion for Archiving:** Creates archival images of an InfoPath form. If your Web application doesn't use InfoPath forms, you can disable this feature. (*Note:* This option may not show up on the Manage Web Application Features page in a default installation.)

- ✔ **Office Server Enterprise Search:** Expands the search service to include profiles, business data, and other content sources. You can disable this feature if you don't want users to search expanded sources.

- ✔ **Office Server Site Search:** Enables search service for sites and lists.

✔ **Office SharePoint Server Enterprise Web Application:** Enables features for accessing the business data catalog, forms services, and Excel services. (*Note:* This option may not show up on the Manage Web Application Features page in a Standard installation.)

✔ **Office SharePoint Server Standard Web Application:** Enables user profiles and search.

Features that apply to sites and site collections can be enabled or disabled using the Site Settings page. (See Chapter 5 for information how to access the Site Settings page.) An example of a site-collection feature in WSS is the Three-state workflow. You could disable this feature if you didn't want any sites in the site collection to use three-state workflows. (I discuss workflows in Chapter 8.)

Configuring site collections

Many administration and configuration tasks for site collections occur at the level of the site collection, using the Site Settings page. However, a few tasks must be configured by using the SharePoint Site Management section of the Central Administration site. (Refer to Figure 3-4.)

Common site-collection management tasks are listed in Table 3-3.

Table 3-3   Site-Collection Management in Central Administration

Site Management Task	What It's Used For
Create site collection	Create a new site collection.
Delete site collection	Delete an existing site collection.
Site-use confirmation and deletion	Configure server to send notices to administrators of unused site collections and configure automatic deletion.
Quota templates	Create or modify quota templates and set the storage and notification limits for the quota.
Site–collection quotas and locks	Set the lock level for a site collection to prevent access to the site collection and change the quota template.
Site-collection administrators	View or change the primary and secondary site administrators for a selected site collection.
Site-collection list	View a list of site collections for a selected Web application.

Server-farm administrators often create site collections. Then the people responsible for administering those site collections take over their day-to-day management; often these *site-collection administrators* delegate the administration of the individual sites in the collection to other people. (I discuss administration delegation in Chapter 6.)

Site-collection administrators use the Site Settings page for the top-level site in the collection to set up and configure the entire collection. Many of the configuration tasks that apply to site collections also apply to individual sites. (I discuss these configuration settings in more detail in Chapter 4 and throughout the rest of this book.)

As the server-farm administrator, you can use tasks described in Table 3-3 to view disk-storage usage and configure SharePoint to send e-mails to site-collection administrators when sites are inactive. If you don't regularly monitor the activity of your site collections, it's a pretty sure bet that SharePoint will consume more resources than you intended. (I discuss some of these monitoring and administration details in Chapter 18.)

Part II
Exploring SharePoint's Building Blocks

The 5th Wave   By Rich Tennant

In this part . . .

Get ready to get knee deep in SharePoint. You see how to use SharePoint's basic building blocks — sites, Web pages, lists, and libraries — to create an information environment. As part of the deal, I also show you the basics of site navigation and permissions management and then I take SharePoint to the next level by digging into SharePoint's data management and business process features.

Chapter 4

Introducing Sites and Site Content

In This Chapter

▶ Using site templates to create SharePoint sites

▶ Creating a Web Part page

▶ Adding and configuring Web parts

▶ Creating and configuring lists and libraries

*H*ow much effort do you think it usually takes to create a secure Web site complete with blogging, personalization, and customizable content? If you've ever built a Web site from scratch, you know it takes a great deal of effort just to get the basics, such as security, right. SharePoint makes creating secure, available, and useful Web sites as simple as using a browser.

SharePoint site templates are the key to creating powerful Web sites. A *site template* is like a boilerplate that SharePoint uses to stamp out sites. After the site is created, you can add your own content to the site or customize the site's layout. Users can use these sites for everything from collaborating on a team project to displaying financial metrics to managers.

Most of the content added to SharePoint's sites resides in lists and libraries. A *list* is a tabular view of data that consists of columns and rows. *Libraries* are a special kind of list used to store files, such as documents, spreadsheets, and slides. Users can create Web pages to display information stored in lists and libraries.

In this chapter, I show you how to create SharePoint sites and add content structures by using Web pages, lists, and libraries.

Exploring SharePoint Sites

Before your company can start using SharePoint, you must figure out how you want to create your SharePoint site structure. All content in SharePoint is organized into a hierarchy of sites. In Chapter 3, I show you how to set up a *site collection,* which is the logical container for a set of sites. The site collection creates the top-level site. After you create a site collection, you have to create the set of subsites that make up the rest of the collection.

Thankfully, you don't have to create these sites from scratch. SharePoint provides a number of site templates that you can use to create Web sites for specialized purposes. The site template you select when you create the site collection determines the top-level site's type. In Windows SharePoint Services, you'll most often select the Team Site site template. The most commonly implemented site collection in Microsoft Office SharePoint Server 2007 uses the Collaboration Portal site template. A Web site created in SharePoint is a *SharePoint site.*

Selecting a site template

Creating a SharePoint site is easy. The hard part is figuring out which kind of SharePoint site to create. SharePoint has four categories of templates. Each category is geared toward a different purpose. The four categories are as follows:

- ✔ **Collaboration:** Use these templates to create sites for sharing information with a team. These templates include features such as announcements, document libraries, and calendars.

- ✔ **Meetings:** Use these templates to create a specialized site — a *workspace.* Workspaces are usually centered around an activity, such as making a decision. Meeting workspaces are intended to organize all the artifacts associated with the meeting — agenda, objectives, and lists of attendees, for example. Despite the name, you can't use a meeting workspace to actually conduct the meeting.

- ✔ **Enterprise:** Templates in this category are intended for creating portal sites. A portal site often aggregates content from subsites and acts as a gateway to other sites or content. Portal sites are a feature of MOSS 2007. I discuss portal sites in detail in Chapter 11.

- ✔ **Publishing:** Templates in this category are intended for publishing content, such as press releases.

Some templates, such as those in the Enterprise category, create several subsites as well. The templates in the Collaboration and Meetings categories create single sites. Also, you can use any of these site templates to create the top-level site in a site collection. See Chapter 3 to read about site collections.

Just because the templates are grouped in categories doesn't mean you have to use the template for that purpose. For example, you don't have to use a Team Site template for collaboration. I often use a Team Site template for light project management, such as writing this book.

In most cases, no template is perfect, but some templates are closer to what you want than others. The best way to figure out which template to use is to start using some of the different site templates. You quickly figure out which templates work best for you. Table 4-1 lists site templates and what you might use for them.

The site templates provided by SharePoint aren't actually site templates. Rather, the sites are provisioned by using a set of XML files called a *site definition*. A site template is created in the browser and is a customized version of a site definition.

Table 4-1	Site Templates and Their Common Uses	
Category	*Site Template*	*What You Can Do With It*
Collaboration	Team Site	Use for teams who need to share calendars, tasks, and document repositories.
	Blank Site	Use when you want to build a site from scratch.
	Document Workspace	Use when individuals need to collaborate on a document and store supporting files, tasks, and calendars.
	Wiki Site	Use to create a set of pages that are linked together; can be used for brainstorming sessions or to create a knowledge base.
	Blog	Use to create an online journal called a *Web log* or *blog*.
Meetings	Meeting Workspace	Use to create a site dedicated to a meeting or a series of meetings.
Enterprise	Document Center	Use to create a central repository for managing enterprise documents.
	Records Center	Use to create a central archive for enterprise records.
	Personalize Site	Use to create a site that displays personalized content to visitors.
	Site Directory	Use to create a yellow pages directory for your site collection.
	Report Center	Use to manage reports.
	Search Center with Tabs	Use to provide customized access to search features.
	Search Center	Use to provide basic search features.
Publishing	Publishing Site	Use to create a site dedicated to authoring and publishing content.
	Publishing Site with Workflow	Use to create a site that has an approval workflow for publishing content.
	News Site	Use to publish news articles.

Only Office SharePoint Server 2007 (MOSS) has all the Enterprise and Publishing Site templates listed above. The Report Center template is only available with MOSS 2007 Enterprise Edition. The templates available in the Collaboration and Meeting categories are available in both WSS and MOSS.

Site collections include additional site templates that can only be used to create the top-level site in a site collection. These include the My Site Host template, which is used to create a site collection for hosting My Site personal sites (see Chapter 12), and the Collaboration Portal and Publishing Portal templates (see Chapter 11). These additional templates are only available with MOSS 2007. See Chapter 3 for more details on creating site collections.

Creating SharePoint sites

The two most important decisions you need to make when creating a SharePoint site are:

- ✔ Where to create the site
- ✔ Which site template to use

Although it's possible to move a site, creating sites in the right location in the first place is easier. If you choose the wrong template to create the site, you can always modify the site to look like another template, but doing so does take some time. It's a lot easier if you manage to get the right template right off the bat.

You need to have the Create Subsites permission to create a new site. This permission is granted to the Manage Hierarchy SharePoint group in MOSS 2007 and the *Site* Owners group in WSS. Only members of these groups can create new sites. The task of creating new sites is often left to a Web designer; however, if you enable Self-Service Site Creation, anyone with Read or higher permission can create new sites. See Chapter 6 for information on permissions and SharePoint groups.

Think twice about limiting site creation to only Web designers. A frequent complaint I hear from power users and other end users is that although they're excited about SharePoint, they often feel constrained by the way SharePoint is deployed. If all the decisions about creating new sites are limited to a few individuals, you can quickly erode your users' interest in using SharePoint. If you have a situation in which you must have absolute control over site creation, consider creating two separate site collections. Enable self-service site creation for one collection and keep the other collection restricted.

Sites are contained within a site collection. You must create the site collection first before you can add sites to the site collection. See Chapter 3 for information on creating site collections.

To create a new site, follow these steps:

1. **Browse to the parent site where you want to create the new site.**

   The parent site may be the top-level site of a site collection or a subsite within the site collection. It's common to create new sites using the Site Directory in MOSS 2007. You access the Site Directory by clicking the Sites tab along the top of the portal (see Chapter 11).

   The parent site you choose dictates the URL path to the site you create. For example, assume you access the home page of a WSS site collection using the URL `http://intranet`. If you create a site with the path projects, you will access the site via the URL `http://intranet/projects`. Similarly, if you create a projects site in the Site Directory of a MOSS 2007 portal located at `http://companyportal`, the URL will be `http://companyportal/sites/projects`. The sites path reflects the path to the Site Directory on the portal.

   If you're unsure of where to create a site, check with whoever sets up or administers your site collections.

   If you want the new site to be a top-level site, you must create a new site collection. See Chapter 3.

2. **Click the View All Site Content link on the Quick Launch bar.**

   The Quick Launch bar is the navigation menu on the left of the screen. See Chapter 5 for more information on using SharePoint's navigation menus.

   If the Quick Launch bar isn't visible, choose Site Actions➪View All Site Content in a MOSS portal site. In a WSS team site, you can click Site Actions➪Create and skip the next step.

   The All Site Content page appears.

3. **Click the Create button which you can find in the toolbar above the list of site content.**

   The Create page appears, as shown in Figure 4-1.

   You can use the Create page to create all kinds of content structures, not just sites.

4. **Click the Sites and Workspaces link in the Web Pages section.**

   The New SharePoint Site page appears.

5. **Enter the Title and Description for the site.**

   The Title and Description appear on the site's home page.

6. **Type a Web site address for the site in the URL Name field.**

   You're limited by the path for the current Web application and site collection. If you want to use a different path, consider using a different Web application or site collection.

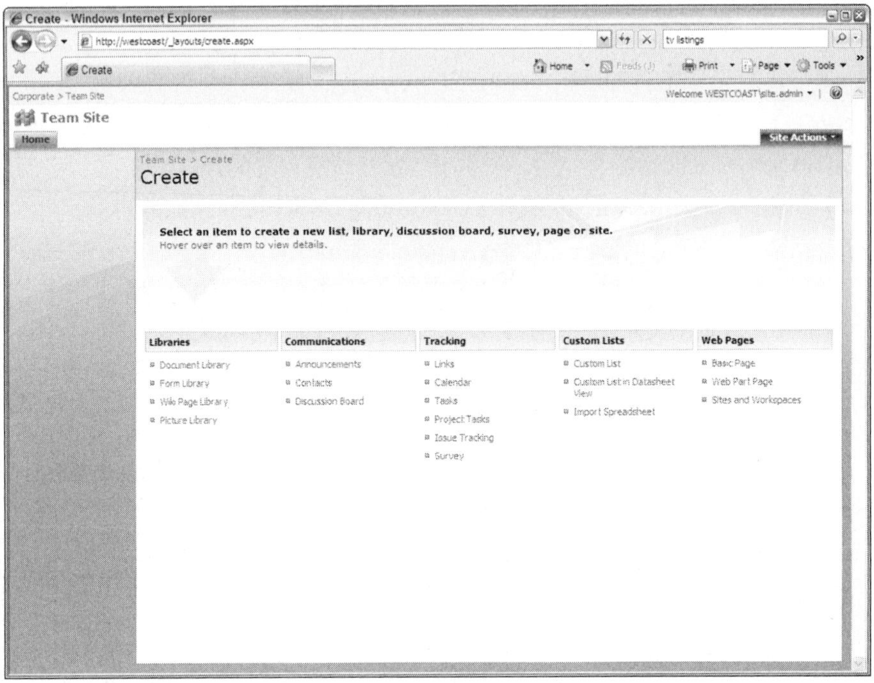

Figure 4-1:
Create new
sites with
the Create
page.

7. **Select a site template from the template gallery, as shown in Figure 4-2.**

8. **Indicate whether the site uses the same permissions as the parent site or uses unique permissions.**

   For recommendations on which approach to take, see Chapter 6.

9. **In the Navigation section, indicate whether you want the site to appear on the Quick Launch bar of the parent site.**

   You may not have the option to display the new site in the parent sites' Quick Launch and top link bars. If not, you can still add your new site to the parent site's navigation manually. See Chapter 5 for more information on managing navigation options.

10. **Indicate whether you want the site to use the parent site's top link bar.**

11. **Indicate whether you want the site to appear in the site directory. If so, select a category for the site to appear in.**

    The site directory is a feature of MOSS 2007. You won't see this option in WSS deployments. See Chapter 11 for recommendations on using the site directory.

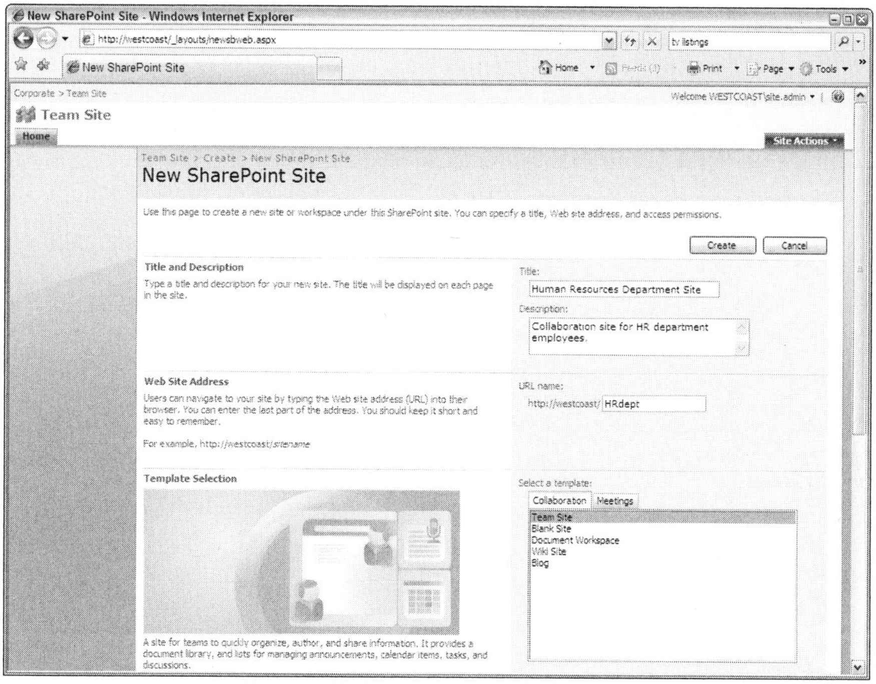

Figure 4-2:
Select a site
template.

12. **Click the Create button.**

    The Operation in Progress page appears.

    The site appears in the browser after it's created.

Browsing to SharePoint sites

SharePoint sites are Web sites, which means you have to use a browser to access the site. Just like you need to know the address of a Web site before you can pull up the site in a browser, you also must know the address of a SharePoint site.

Without any additional configuration, the address of your SharePoint site uses the server name of the SharePoint Web server. For example, if your Web server is named `JumpinJackFlash`, then you type `http://jumpinjackflash` in your browser to access SharePoint. If you're the person who installed and configured your SharePoint deployment, then chances are you know the address of your SharePoint server. If not, then you need to check with who-ever installed SharePoint.

The address of SharePoint isn't limited to the server name. You can configure a friendly name to access the server. For example, you can map the host name `http://intranet` to your server so users don't need to remember the server name.

As I describe in Chapter 3, SharePoint is capable of hosting more than one Web application and site collection. As a result, the SharePoint resource you want to access may not be available via the top-level address. Instead, you may have to use a different port or path. For example, you may have to type something like `http://intranet:23444/sites/projectsite`. Ideally, you should be able to browse to the top-level address, such as `http://intranet`, and navigate to whatever site you want to access.

If you're responsible for administering a SharePoint site collection, you should provide a friendly, easy way for users to navigate to SharePoint sites from the home page. See Chapter 5 for more information on configuring navigation.

If you don't provide adequate navigation to the sites in your site collections, users will be forced to manage a list of URLs in order to access sites. Using the Favorites feature in Internet Explorer is not the way you want users to navigate to SharePoint sites.

You aren't limited to only using a browser to access SharePoint. You can use Office clients such as Word and Windows Explorer. See Chapter 9.

Creating Structure for Site Content

All SharePoint sites are capable of hosting the same site content structures. Before end users can add content to a site, the site's structure must be created. A site template simply creates a predefined set of site content structures targeted toward a specific purpose, such as collaboration. I like to place SharePoint's common site content structures into these categories:

- **Libraries:** A repository for storing documents, forms, or other kinds of files. Examples include a Document Library, a Slide Library, and a Form Library.

- **Lists:** A custom table for storing data. SharePoint includes a number of predefined lists, including lists for Tasks, Calendar, and Issue Tracking.

- **Web pages:** A Web page hosted in a SharePoint site that displays Web parts and other HTML content. The most commonly used SharePoint Web page is called a Web Parts page. MOSS 2007 introduces a new kind of Web page called a Publishing age.

- ✔ **Web parts:** A user interface element that displays Web content on a Web page.

- ✔ **Sites and workspaces:** The logical containers that host Web pages, libraries, and lists.

By recognizing that these basic categories are the foundation of all SharePoint's content, you know you can work with any kind of content you encounter. In addition to Web applications and site collections, these are the building blocks for SharePoint. You set up Web applications and site collections as part of your initial SharePoint deployment, as I describe in Chapter 3. Afterward, all your day-to-day SharePoint activities use elements from these categories. All category elements share common navigation and features. By knowing how to create one kind of a structure in a given category, you can create many more.

SharePoint provides additional features such as content types and workflows for defining the data and behavior of the content that you want to store in these content structures. Combining content types and workflows with the content structures listed here makes it possible for you to create sophisticated business applications in SharePoint without writing custom code. See Chapter 7 for more details on content types and Chapter 8 for more about workflows.

The site structure elements you can add to a site are restricted by the features activated for that site. You can manage the features enabled for a given site or site collection by clicking the Site Features link on the site's Site Settings page. See Chapter 5 for more information on accessing and using a site's Site Settings page.

The basic steps for adding a site content structure element are the same. To add a content structure element to a SharePoint site, follow these steps:

1. **Browse to the site where you want to add the element.**

   See the earlier section "Exploring SharePoint Sites" for more information on navigating to sites.

2. **Click the View All Site Content link on the Quick Launch bar.**

   The All Site Content page appears.

   Again, if the Quick Launch bar isn't visible, choose Site Actions↪ View All Site Content in MOSS 2007 or Site Actions↪Create in WSS and skip Step 3.

3. **Click the Create button.**

   The Create page appears. (Refer to Figure 4-1.)

The page has the URL, `http://servername/sitepath/_layouts/create.aspx`.

You must be a member of at least the Designers SharePoint group in MOSS 2007 or the *Site* Owners group in WSS to access the Create page. See Chapter 6.

The Create page is divided into five categories of elements you can create: Libraries, Communications, Tracking, Custom Lists, and Web Pages.

4. **Click one of the links to create an item.**

   A page appears that allows you to create the item you select. For lists and libraries, you see a New page where you enter information such as name, description, and navigation options. Clicking any of the links in the Web Pages category brings up a customized page for creating those elements. I describe creating Web pages in the next section.

   If you hover with your mouse over an item, you'll see a description of that item.

5. **Enter the values in the page to create the item.**

MOSS 2007 includes a feature called Site Content and Structure that provides a hierarchical view of all the content structures and their content in a MOSS 2007 site collection. You can use this tool to add new structures and move existing structures. See Chapter 11 for more information on using this tool to manage site content structures.

Using Web Pages

SharePoint sites are Web sites. As such, they are made up of Web pages. The Web pages in SharePoint sites aren't just plain old HTML Web pages. They are Web pages that take advantage of the personalization and content management features of ASP.NET 2.0. Actually, SharePoint has three kinds of ASP.NET Web pages.

Windows SharePoint Services (WSS) provides the following two kinds of Web pages:

- **Basic page:** A Basic Web page is a very simple Web page with a single pane for adding content. You use the Rich Text Editor to add content to the page.

- **Web Part page:** A special Web page that enables you to select a layout and add Web parts, which are reusable content elements.

A Web Part page is very flexible; you can add content to the page from a gallery of Web parts. A Basic page, however, is limited to only a single pane for displaying content.

Microsoft Office SharePoint Server (MOSS) adds a third kind of Web page — a Publishing page. A Publishing page is similar in concept to a Web Part page in that you can add Web parts to the page. Publishing pages are special because you can use an editorial process for publishing content to SharePoint sites. Publishing pages are part of the Office SharePoint Server Publishing feature and are often used as part of a Web content management solution. I discuss Publishing pages and Web content management in Chapter 16.

Basic pages, Web Part pages, and Publishing pages are all content types. A *content type* is a set of behaviors defined for a kind of content. I discuss content types in more detail in Chapter 7.

Creating Web pages

All SharePoint sites include a home page (`default.aspx`). SharePoint automatically creates Web pages for all the lists and libraries you create in your site. That's part of what makes SharePoint so valuable — you don't have to spend your time creating Web pages. However, you can create new Web pages for your SharePoint sites any time you want to.

Similar to creating sites and lists in SharePoint, creating Web pages only requires you to fill out a form. SharePoint automatically generates the Web page using the title, description, and layout you select. You just add your content. That content could be as simple as text you type on the page. Most often you add Web parts to display content from lists and libraries on your page. Because SharePoint sites use Web pages, you can also use HTML and even JavaScript in your pages.

The most commonly used Web page in SharePoint is the Web Part page. In order to edit Web Part pages, you must have the Add and Customize Pages permission. This permission is assigned to the Manage Hierarchy and Design permission levels, which are assigned to the Designers and Hierarchy Managers SharePoint groups in MOSS 2007. In WSS, the *Site* Owners SharePoint group has the correct permissions. You must be a member of one of these groups or a custom group with the Add and Customize Pages permission to edit or create Web Part pages. See Chapter 6 for more information on permissions.

The steps for creating Basic pages and Web Part pages are very similar. You need a document library to save the new page to. By default, all the site templates usually create at least one document library. You can use that document library or create a new one. I explain how to create libraries later in this chapter. To add pages to your SharePoint site:

1. **Follow the steps to add new content structure elements to a site, as described in the "Creating Structure for Site Content" section, earlier in this chapter (see Steps 1–3).**

2. **When you come to the Create page, click either the Basic Page or Web Part Page link (refer to Figure 4-1).**

   The New Basic page or New Web Part page appears.

3. **Type the name for the new Web page in the Name field.**

   The file extension `.aspx` is appended to the file for you.

   The file extension `.aspx` is used for ASP.NET Web pages.

4. **Indicate whether to overwrite the file if it already exists.**

5. **If creating a Web Part page, select a layout template to use for it.**

   When you click the layout templates in the list, an image showing the template's layout is updated. The layout template determines where you can place content on the page.

6. **Select a Document Library to save the page.**

   If no libraries are available on the site, click the Create a New Document Library link to create a new library. (If you have to create a document library, do so and start these steps over at Step 1.)

7. **Click the Create button.**

   A Web Part page appears in Design mode. A Basic page displays a Rich Text Editor, where you enter the text that you want displayed on the page.

Because Web Part pages you create are stored in document libraries, they can be subject to versioning and check out requirements. See Chapter 15.

When a site on the MOSS server has the Office SharePoint Server Publishing feature enabled, a new menu item — Create Page — appears in the site's Site Action menu. The Create Page command creates a new Publishing page. The steps for creating Publishing pages are different than the preceding steps. See Chapter 16 for information on working with Publishing pages.

You can edit pages by browsing to the page you want to edit and choosing Site Actions⇨Edit Page.

Working with a Web Part page

Web Part pages divide the page into zones for the placement of your various Web parts. In SharePoint, a *Web part* is a user interface element that's used to display content on the Web page. The number of zones and their position on the page is determined by the layout chosen when you create the page. Although you can change the page's layout after you create the page — using tools such as SharePoint Designer 2007 or Visual Studio 2005 — it's best to get the layout right before you start editing pages. (I discuss SharePoint Designer in Chapter 16.)

SharePoint Web Parts are a kind of ASP.NET Web Part. They inherit from the `WebPart` class in the .NET Framework Class Library. In fact, you can create your own ASP.NET Web Parts to use in SharePoint. See my book, *SharePoint Designer 2007 For Dummies* (Wiley Publishing, Inc.), or the Windows SharePoint Services Software Development Kit for more information on designing Web Parts.

Publishing pages — a third kind of page that comes with MOSS — also use Web parts and Web part zones. All the rules for working with Web parts in Web Part pages also apply to Publishing pages in MOSS. (See Chapter 16 for details on using publishing pages.)

When you first create a Web Part page, all you see is a set of zones with labels, such as Header, Footer, and Left Column. (See Figure 4-3.) The zones you see are placeholders for your various Web parts. When you view the page in Published mode, you don't see those placeholders. Instead, you see the content from the Web parts you added.

SharePoint's Web Part pages support two views — Shared View and Personal View. The Shared View is the view that you modify when you first create a page or subsequently edit the page using Site Actions⊏>Edit Page. All the site's users can see the page's Shared View.

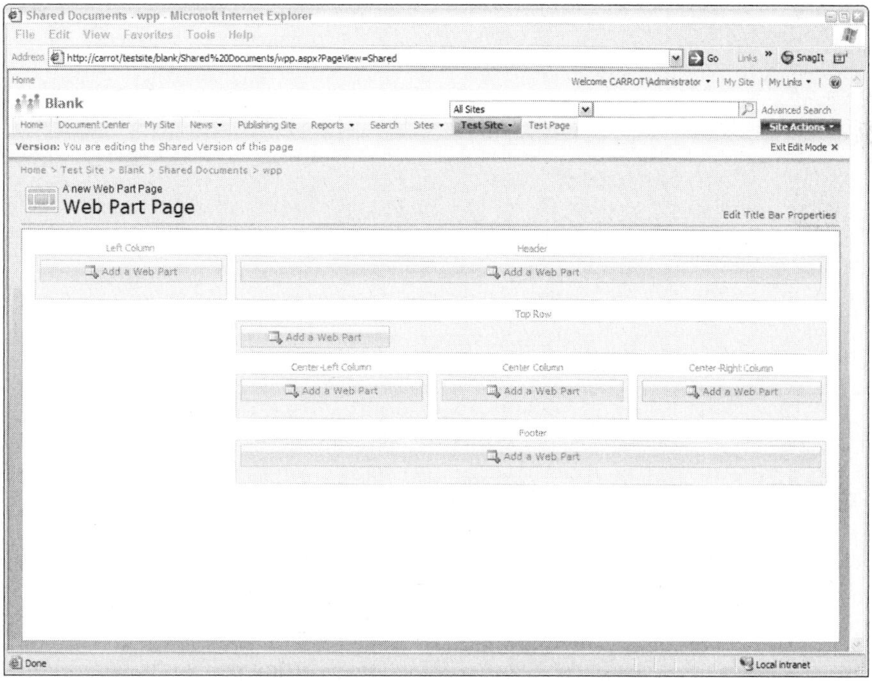

Figure 4-3:
Constructing
a Web Part
page.

Members of the site's *Site* Members group have permissions to create a Personal View of the Web Part page. Using the Personal View, a member can add or remove Web parts or change where the Web parts are positioned on the page. Personal Views are private and can only be seen by the person who creates the view. You can restrict a user's ability to customize Web parts when you add the Web part to the page, which I show you later in this chapter. Members access their Personal View by using the Welcome menu.

Users must have the Add/Remove Personal Web Parts and Update Personal Web Parts permissions in order to manage Personal Views. These permissions are granted to all members of the *Site* Members group. See Chapter 6 for more information on permissions.

Web parts are stored in the Web Part Gallery for each site collection. You can access the gallery from the site collection's top-level site's Site Settings page. (See Chapter 5 on how to access the Site Settings page.) When you edit a Web Part page, Web parts are displayed in a dialog box where they're grouped by the type of Web part. You can use the Web Part Gallery to upload new Web Parts to your site collection.

Your page has access to more Web parts than those listed in the site collection's Web Part gallery. Every list and library on the site creates a Web part that you can use to display items on your page.

To add a Web part to a Web Part page, follow these steps:

1. **Browse to the Web Part page you want to edit.**

   You can either create a new Web Part page as I describe in the preceding section or edit a SharePoint site's existing page, such as a site's Home page.

2. **Choose Site Actions⇨Edit Page.**

   The page appears in Design mode.

   You must have the proper permissions, as I describe in the earlier section, "Creating Structure for Site Content," to edit a page. If you don't see the Edit Page option, you don't have proper permissions.

   You must have the Add and Customize Pages permission to edit Web Part pages generated by SharePoint, such as a site's Home page or pages for lists and libraries. However, Web Part pages that you create are subject to the permissions of the library where the Web Part page is saved. By default, members of the *Site* Members group have access to edit the items in a library including Web Part pages. I suggest you store Web Part pages in a document library with unique permissions. Users need the Edit Items permission in order to edit Web Part pages saved in a document library. (See Chapter 6 for more details on working with permissions.)

3. **Click the Add a Web Part link in a zone where you want to add a Web part.**

The Add Web Parts Web Page dialog box appears.

4. Place a check mark next to the Web parts you want to add to the page.

You can search for Web parts by clicking the Advanced Web Part gallery and options link, which displays the gallery in a pane in the browser. Table 4-2 lists some of the common Web parts you'll find in SharePoint.

5. Click the Add button.

The Web parts appear in the page's Design view.

Web parts aren't stuck in the zones where you place them. You can drag and drop Web parts to other zones.

Table 4-2		Common SharePoint Web Parts	
Web Part Type	*WSS or MOSS?*	*What It's used for*	*Examples*
Business Data	MOSS	To display external data from business systems	Business Data List, Excel Web Web Access, IView Web Part
Content Rollup	MOSS	To display content aggregated from the portal	My SharePoint Sites, SharePoint Documents, Site Aggregator
Dashboard	MOSS	To display content on a business-intelligence dashboard	Key Performance Indicators, KPI Details
Default	MOSS	To display commonly used content	RSS Viewer, This Week in Pictures
Filters	MOSS	To filter the contents displayed in other Web parts on the same page	Current User Filter, Date Filter, Text Filter
Lists and Libraries	Both	To display content from the site's lists and libraries	Announcements, Calendar, Shared Documents
Miscellaneous	Both	To display generic content such as HTML, images, rich text, or XML	Content Editor Web Part, Page Viewer Web Part, Site Users
Outlook Web Access	MOSS	To provide users with access to e-mail on Exchange Server 2003 or later	My Calendar, My Inbox
Search	MOSS	To display search results and execute searches	People Search Box, Search Best Bets

Many Web parts require additional configuration before you can display them. The steps to access Web parts configurations are the same, and all parts have similar configuration steps in common.

To configure a Web part, follow these steps:

1. **Click the Edit drop-down arrow in the Web Part Title menu.**

   A drop-down menu appears.

   In Design mode, the Web part displays the word `Edit`. In View mode, the Web part displays an arrow.

2. **Click Modify Shared Web Part from the Edit drop-down menu**

   A tool pane appears, as shown in Figure 4-4.

3. **In the tool pane, configure properties specific to the Web part you're configuring.**

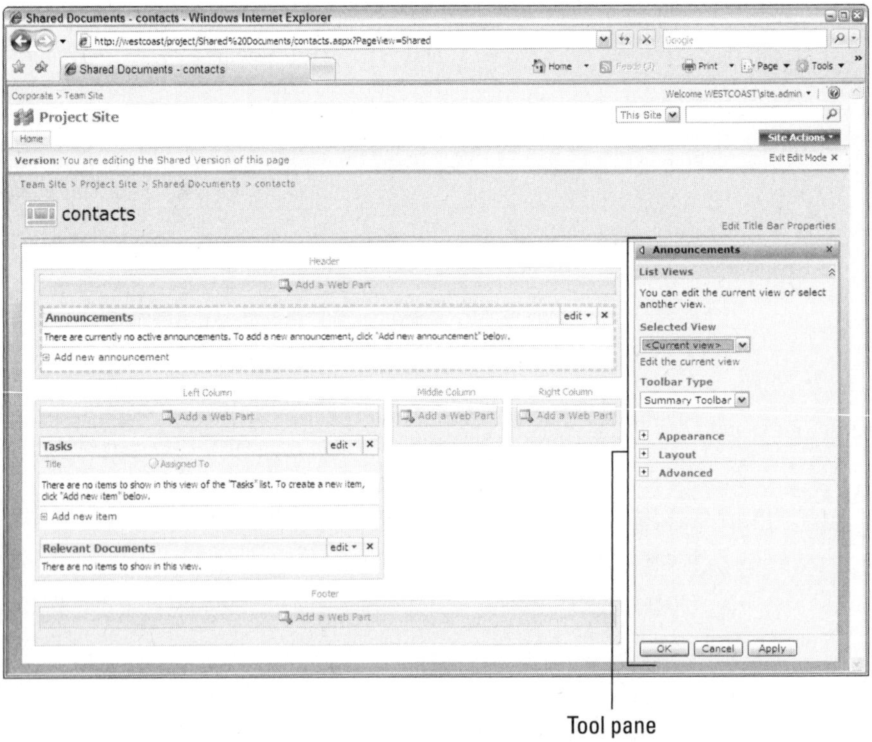

Figure 4-4:
Set the Web part properties in the tool pane.

Tool pane

For example, for an Announcements Web part, you could do the following:

- Expand the Appearance group to set properties, such as the Web part title, height, and width.

- Expand the Layout group to set properties, such as the Web part orientation, zone, and zone index.

  The zone index determines the ordering of the Web Parts in a zone.

- Expand the Advanced group to set target audiences and define additional behaviors.

4. **Click OK to close the tool pane.**

   You can click the Apply button at any time to preview your changes.

The Web Part page includes a special Web part — the Title bar. You edit the Title bar by clicking the Edit Title Bar Properties link near the upper-right corner of the Web Part page's Design view. The Title Bar Web Part enables you to set the Web Part page's title, caption, description, and header image.

Using Lists and Libraries

As I mention earlier in this chapter, two very popular site-content structures in SharePoint are lists and libraries. If you can master both structures, you are well on your way to populating your sites with well-produced content.

SharePoint has several different kinds of *libraries* — special lists you can use to store files — that can be put to a variety of uses. SharePoint also makes it easy to keep track of files by letting you add columns to the library — columns you can then use to describe the files you save. For example, you could create a column called Division, where you store the division name associated with the file.

Essentially, you can store any kind of file in a library. In fact, SharePoint comes with several specialized libraries designed to store specific kinds of content:

- **Document Library:** Store files, such as spreadsheets and documents.

- **Form Library:** Store XML files for use with Microsoft Office InfoPath.

- **Wiki Page Library:** Store customizable pages of content that are linked together.

- **Picture Library:** Store image files and include image viewers.

MOSS 2007 adds the following library types:

- **Data Connection Library:** Store files that contain external data connections.
- **Translation Management Library:** Store files for multi-language environments.
- **Report Library:** Store reports used by business intelligence features.
- **Slide Library:** Store PowerPoint slides.

Using Document Libraries is one of the ways most people start using SharePoint.

A *gallery* is another kind of library. Galleries are used to display lists of system items, such as Site Content Types and Site Templates. Galleries have a slightly different set of administrative options than a regular library. You access the galleries for a site using the site's Site Settings page.

A *list* is a tabular display of data. A list consists of columns and rows, similar to a spreadsheet. You can create your own custom lists or use any of the lists provided by SharePoint. Some of the lists you can create include:

- **Announcements:** For posting messages on a site's Web pages.
- **Contacts:** For creating a list of contacts that can be synchronized with Outlook.
- **Discussion boards:** For creating discussion threads and archiving e-mail.
- **Links:** For keeping track of a set of hyperlinks.
- **Calendar:** For tracking events, such as meetings and deadlines. Events can be exported as iCalendar files for import into e-mail applications such as Outlook.
- **Tasks:** For listing tasks that can be assigned to team members.
- **Project Tasks:** For listing tasks that include a Gantt Chart view.
- **Issue Tracking:** For tracking issues and their resolutions.
- **Survey:** For creating a survey for users to fill out online.
- **Custom:** For creating a custom list that you define your own columns for.

You can also create lists based on a spreadsheet. Instead of creating the columns from scratch, the columns are created when you import the spreadsheet.

Lists are very powerful tools that can be used to drive content on Web pages as well as support applications and business process workflows. I discuss using lists to manage your business's data in Chapter 7.

Creating lists and libraries

When you create a site using any site template other than Blank Site, SharePoint creates a number of lists and libraries, as defined by the site template. For example, most site templates create a Document Library called Shared Documents. A site based on the Team Site template also creates an Announcements list and a Calendar list.

The lists and libraries created by a site template are defined in an XML file. You can modify existing site templates so the template adds other kinds of lists and libraries. For example, you might want to modify the Team Site template so that a Slide Library is created automatically. See the Windows SharePoint Services Software Development Kit for information on modifying site templates.

In most cases, site templates don't provide all the lists and libraries that users want. It's easy to add new lists and libraries to an existing site. To add a new list or library to an existing site, you use the Create page, as I describe in the steps for adding new content to a site in the section, "Creating Structure for Site Content." The Create page groups list and library items into the following categories:

- **Libraries:** Display links to create libraries, such as Document Libraries or Form Libraries.
- **Communications:** Display links for announcements, contacts, and discussion boards.
- **Tracking:** Find links for lists that track something, such as Links or Calendar.
- **Custom Lists:** Create lists from scratch or by importing data from a spreadsheet.

Regardless of the kind of library or list you choose to create, the basic steps are the same:

1. **Follow the first three steps for adding new content to a site in the preceding section, "Creating Structure for Site Content."**

2. **When you come to the Create page, click one of the links in the Libraries, Communications, Tracking, or Custom Lists categories.**

   The New page appears.

3. **Type a name and description for the list or library.**

4. **Indicate whether you want the list or library to appear on the site's Quick Launch bar.**

   The default value is Yes.

5. **In a library, indicate whether you want the library to create new document versions each time a file is edited.**

   The default value is No. See Chapter 15 for details on using versioning.

6. **In a library, select the default Document Template for the library.**

   The default Document Template is the one used to create a new document when the user clicks the New button in the library.

7. **Click the Create button.**

   The new list or library appears in the browser.

A few lists and libraries may have additional items that you can configure. For example, the Translation Management Library asks whether you want to add a Transaction Management workflow to the library.

Navigating lists and libraries

It's important to realize that a library is just a special type of list. After you recognize that a Document Library and an Announcements list are essentially the same kind of thing, it is much easier for you to work with these structures.

The files you add to libraries and the rows you add to lists are *items*. When you add an item to a list or library, you can specify properties that describe the item — properties that are then displayed as columns in the list or library. All lists and libraries come with a common set of columns, such as Titled, Modified By, and Created By. Depending on the type of list or library you're working with, you might see additional columns. For example, a Document Library has the Checked Out To column. Just keep in mind that you can add your own columns to lists or libraries.

The columns associated with an item are the item's *metadata* or data about data. For instance, your item is the data, and the columns that describe the item are the metadata (data about the data).

Columns are an extremely important feature in lists and libraries. Columns are what make it possible for you to customize SharePoint's lists and create new lists that suit your business needs. You aren't stuck with the columns that come with an Announcements list or Task list. You can add, modify, and remove columns as you see fit. See Chapter 7 for more details on working with columns.

Lists and libraries share common navigation elements that make it possible to add new items, take actions on the list or library, and access settings. Figure 4-5 shows the standard navigation elements for a Tasks list.

Navigation bar

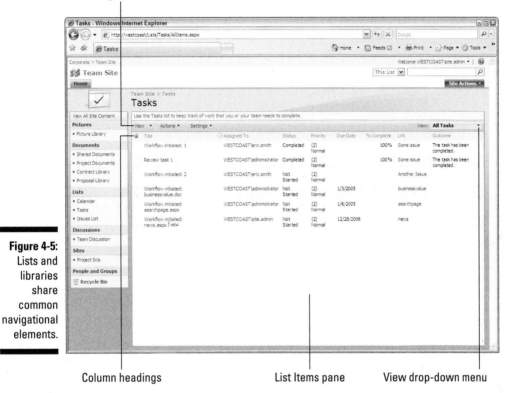

Figure 4-5:
Lists and
libraries
share
common
navigational
elements.

Column headings   List Items pane   View drop-down menu

Table 4-3 lists common tasks you can find on the main navigation bar in a list
and library.

Libraries have an additional button — Upload — as shown in Figure 4-6. Use
the Upload drop-down list to upload single or multiple files to a library.

The commands you see on each button are determined by the kind of list or
library you're accessing. For example, the Open with Windows Explorer command is available for Document Libraries.

The commands users see on the New button are determined by the Content
Types associated with the list or library. By default, each list or library is
associated with a content type. For example, a Task content type is associated
with a Tasks list and a Document content type is associated with a document
library. When a user clicks the New button in a Tasks list, SharePoint displays
a form to enter a new task. You can add or remove the content types that a
list uses in the list's Settings page. See Chapter 7 for more information on
working with content types.

Upload button

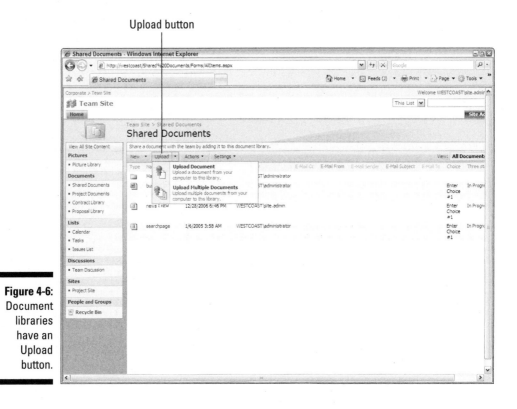

Figure 4-6:
Document
libraries
have an
Upload
button.

Table 4-3	Common Navigation Elements	
Button	**Sample Command**	**What You Use It For**
New	New Item New Folder New Document	Create a new item, folder, or document.
Actions	Edit In Datasheet	Display list items in a tabular datasheet.
	Open with Windows Explorer	Display library items in a Windows Explorer folder.
	Connect to Outlook	Synchronize list items with a SharePoint folder in Outlook.
	Export to Spreadsheet	Export the list items for the current view to a spreadsheet.
	Open with Microsoft Access	Open an Access database with a table linked to the list's items.
	View RSS* Feed	Display the RSS feed for the list's items in a browser.

Button	Sample Command	What You Use It For
	Alert Me	Receive e-mail notifications when list items are added or changed.
	Process All Tasks	Process a bulk set of workflow tasks.
Settings	Create Column	Add a new column to the list.
	Create View	Create a new view.
	List Settings	Access the list's administrative settings.

* RSS is a markup language used to syndicate site content in a newsfeed.

To change the view used to display a list or library's items, choose the View drop-down list, as shown in Figure 4-7. You can create new views by choosing Settings⇨Create View. You can set a list's or a library's default view in the Settings page.

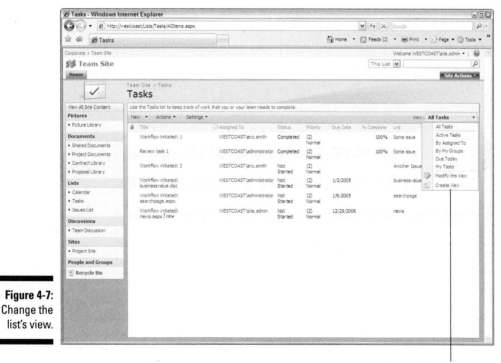

Figure 4-7:
Change the
list's view.

View drop-down menu

By default, a list's items are displayed in a Web page, called Standard View. You can switch to DataSheet view, which displays a list's items in a tabular grid, similar to a spreadsheet.

Customizing libraries and lists

In addition to adding, modifying, and deleting list items, you can take many other actions on lists and libraries including:

- **Creating custom views:** All lists and libraries are created with a standard set of views that define what items are displayed in the browser. All lists and libraries have a view that displays all items. You can create your own views that filter, sort, or group list items. Views make it possible for you to allow users to see only the list items that pertain to them. I discuss views in Chapter 7.

- **Saving versions and requiring content approval:** You can specify that items added to a list or library must be approved before they can be viewed. See Chapter 15.

- **Associating workflows:** A *workflow* is a set of steps that defines a process. You can force workflows to start each time a new item is added to the list or library or each time an item is changed. You can allow users to manually start workflows. Content approval is an example of a workflow. See Chapter 8.

- **Displaying in a Web Part:** Web parts are created for all lists and libraries. Use a list or library's Web part to display the list's contents on a Web Part page or Publishing page. You can designate the view you want the Web part to use. See the section, "Working with a Web Part page," to see how to add a Web part to a page.

- **Creating an RSS feed:** All lists and libraries have the ability to output their list items as an RSS feed. Users within your organization can subscribe to the feed using a feed reader. You can use the RSS Feed Web Part to display the feed on a page in a SharePoint site. See Chapter 9.

- **Associating with content type:** SharePoint comes with a standard set of generic content types, such as Document and Event. *Content types* define the set of columns displayed in the list or library. You can create your own content types and associate them with a list or library. See Chapter 7.

- **Setting permissions:** You can set permissions at the list or library level or at the item level. See Chapter 6.

All lists and libraries use the Customize page to configure these settings. To access the Customize page, choose Settings➪List Settings in a list or Settings➪Library Settings in a library.

The Customize *List* or Customize *Library* page is divided into the following seven sections:

- ✔ **List Information:** Display the list's or the library's name, Web address, and description.

- ✔ **Content Types:** List the enabled content types for the list or library and allows you to add new types. If you see this section, content types are enabled for the list or library in the List's Advanced Settings. If you don't see this section, it's because content types aren't enabled for this list or library. See Chapter 7 for more details on enabling content types.

- ✔ **Permissions and Management:** Manage who can access the list or library. You can also delete the list, save the list as a template, and manage workflow and information management policy settings.

- ✔ **General Settings:** Set the list's or the library's title and description, set versioning, and set advanced settings, such as whether the list's items accept attachments.

- ✔ **Communications:** Configure RSS settings and incoming e-mail settings. Your SharePoint server must be configured to accept incoming e-mail. See Chapter 10 for more information.

- ✔ **Columns:** View and modify the columns for the list or library. You can add new columns here, too.

  Before using the Create Column command to create a new column, you need to decide whether you want to create a List Column or a Site Column. A List Column is only available to the list in which it is created. Site Columns are available to all lists and libraries in an entire site collection. See Chapter 7.

- ✔ **Views:** Display and modify the list's or the library's views. You can create a new view.

You can significantly change the behavior and appearance of a list or library by using the links you find on the Customize page. The sections you use to configure a list or library depend on what you're trying to accomplish. Table 4-4 lists some common tasks you can perform on the Customize page and where you can access the settings.

Table 4-4	Common Configuration Tasks
Where You Can Find It	*What You Can Accomplish*
General Settings⇨ Title, Description, and Navigation	Remove list or library from the Quick Launch bar.
General Settings⇨ Versioning Settings	Enable content approval and versioning. Require document check out.
General Settings⇨ Advanced Settings	Enable content type management. Set item-level permissions. Enable e-mail notifications and attachments. Display New Folder command on the New menu. Enable list items to appear in search results. Set the new document template for a library. Set whether documents open in the browser or in a client application. Set a custom Send To destination for a library.
General Settings⇨ Manage Item Scheduling	Enable scheduling in a library.
Permissions and Management	Delete a list or library. Save a list or library as a template. Set access permissions for the list or library. Manage checked out files. Enable and manage workflows. Set policies for a content type.
Communications	Enable an RSS feed for a list or a library. Set the feed's title, description, and contents. Set an item limit for the feed. Enable the list to receive inbound e-mail.
Content Types	Enable new content types for the list or library. Set how content types appear on the New button.
Columns	Modify the list's or the library's existing columns. Add new list columns or site columns. Select which columns are indexed in the database for faster searching and sorting.
Views	Modify an existing view or create a new view. Set the list's or the library's default view.

Chapter 5

Navigating SharePoint

. . . .

In This Chapter

▶ Getting comfortable with navigating SharePoint

▶ Inheriting global and current navigational elements

▶ Customizing SharePoint navigation

▶ Navigating to administrative tasks

. . . .

*O*ne of the big challenges in working with SharePoint is figuring out how to find the features you need. In this chapter, I walk you through SharePoint's common navigational elements from both an end-user and an administrative perspective. I also discuss how to use administrative features to modify a site's navigation.

Exploring End User Navigational Elements

By default, SharePoint sites are set up so that they have common navigational elements. Having consistent elements across a site creates a user experience that allows you to have an expectation of what you'll find on a given page. Examples of navigational elements include the tabs across the top of a site and the links along the left of the page.

The individual links inside navigational elements are *navigational items.* By default, all the sites in a site collection share some navigational items. I discuss how to give sites their own custom navigational items in the "Modifying Navigation" section, later in this chapter.

The rest of this section deals with the various navigational elements in greater detail.

Going global with the top link bar

Each site collection has its own *top link bar* — a common navigational element used to provide access to resources available on the top-level Web site.

The top link bar is actually a series of tabs that sit in the header on a page in the SharePoint site. Figure 5-1 shows the default top link bar for a Windows SharePoint Services team site. The tabs that appear in the top link bar display the hyperlinked titles to a subsite or page in the site. Tabs with a drop-down arrow (see Figure 5-2) can expand to list a menu of content from within the site.

By default, the top link bar displays links to resources on the top-level site of the site collection. You can customize the bar so it shows only the resources for the current site and its subsites. You can even turn off the top link bar altogether on a site. See the section "Modifying Navigation" for details.

Getting personal with My Portal navigation

In a Microsoft Office SharePoint Server 2007 (MOSS) installation, a set of My Portal navigation links is in the upper-right corner of all pages. The links provide access to commonly used features of a site's members.

Top link bar

Figure 5-1:
The top
link bar.

Figure 5-2 shows the My Portal navigation links. The links are as follows:

✔ **Welcome** *Username:* Displays the logged in user. Clicking the down arrow displays a menu with the following options:

- *My Settings:* Allows the user to manage account details and regional settings, such as time zone and alerts.

- *Sign In as Different User:* Prompts for a set of different user credentials.

- *Personalize This Page:* Opens the page in Design view so you can create a personalized view of the page. This option is only visible on Web Part pages when the user has the proper permissions.

- *Request Access:* Allows the user to send the site administrator an e-mail to access a resource. This option is only visible if the site administrator has enabled access requests for the site.

- *Sign Out:* Logs out the user from the site.

✔ **My Site:** Links to the user's My Site personal site.

✔ **My Links:** Clicking the down arrow here displays a menu that the user can use to view and manage two sets of links lists:

- *My SharePoint Sites:* A list of the SharePoint sites that the user is a member of.

- *Add My Links:* Adds a link to any SharePoint resource or external URL to the My Links list.

- *Manage Links:* Displays the user's My Links list.

The My Portal links visible in Figure 5-2 are an excellent way to determine whether you're working with a MOSS 2007 site or a WSS site. The My Site and My Links options are personalization features of MOSS 2007. You only see those links in a MOSS 2007 deployment. WSS lists the Welcome *username* menu only. (See Chapter 12 for more information on personalization.)

Tracking back with breadcrumbs

SharePoint uses breadcrumb navigation to let users keep track of where they are. For those of you who remember the story of Hansel and Gretel, a bread-crumb is what you'd use to mark a trail back out of the deep, dark forest. In Web-site terms, *breadcrumbs* are site paths created to mark your progress as you navigate through the site — and they also show how to navigate back to where you started from. (Site-path breadcrumbs also have the advantage of not attracting forest animals who tend to gobble up real breadcrumb trails. Just ask Hansel and Gretel.)

MyPortal navigation links

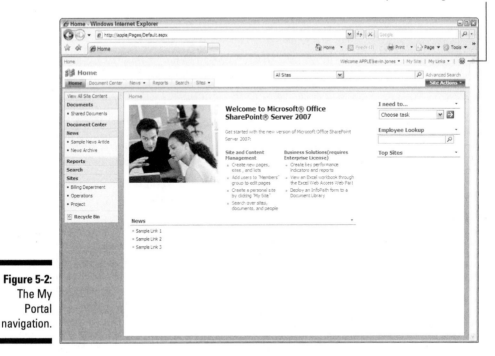

Figure 5-2:
The My
Portal
navigation.

Breadcrumbs in SharePoint look like this by default:

```
Team Site > Project Site > Shared Documents
```

In this example, you're sitting in the Shared Documents document library. You can backtrack to the Project Site or Team Site simply by clicking the link to follow the breadcrumb.

The headings displayed in the breadcrumb come from the site's title. You can change the heading by changing the site's title using the Site Settings page.

SharePoint has two kinds of breadcrumbs, as shown in Figure 5-3:

- ✔ **Global navigation:** Breadcrumb that appears at the very top of the page. This breadcrumb allows you to navigate to higher levels of site collections and portals.

- ✔ **Current navigation:** Breadcrumb that appears in the page's content that shows where you are in the present site and site collection.

You can expand a site collection's global navigation by connecting the site collection to a higher-level site collection or portal site. This is useful if you need to attach a divisional site to a company portal. You must be a site collection administrator to perform this task. To connect to a higher-level site, follow these steps:

1. **Browse to the site collection's top-level site by clicking the farthest left link (usually named Home) in the global navigation breadcrumb.**

2. **Choose Site Actions⇨Site Settings⇨Modify All Site Settings.**

   In a Web Part page, choose Site Actions⇨Site Settings.

   The Site Settings page appears.

3. **Click the Portal Site Connection link in the Site Collection Administration section.**

   The Portal Site Connection page appears.

4. **Select the Connect to Portal Site radio button.**

5. **Type or paste the URL for the portal or site collection in the Portal Web Address field.**

   For example, if the URL for the server you wish to connect to is `http://intranet`, type that value.

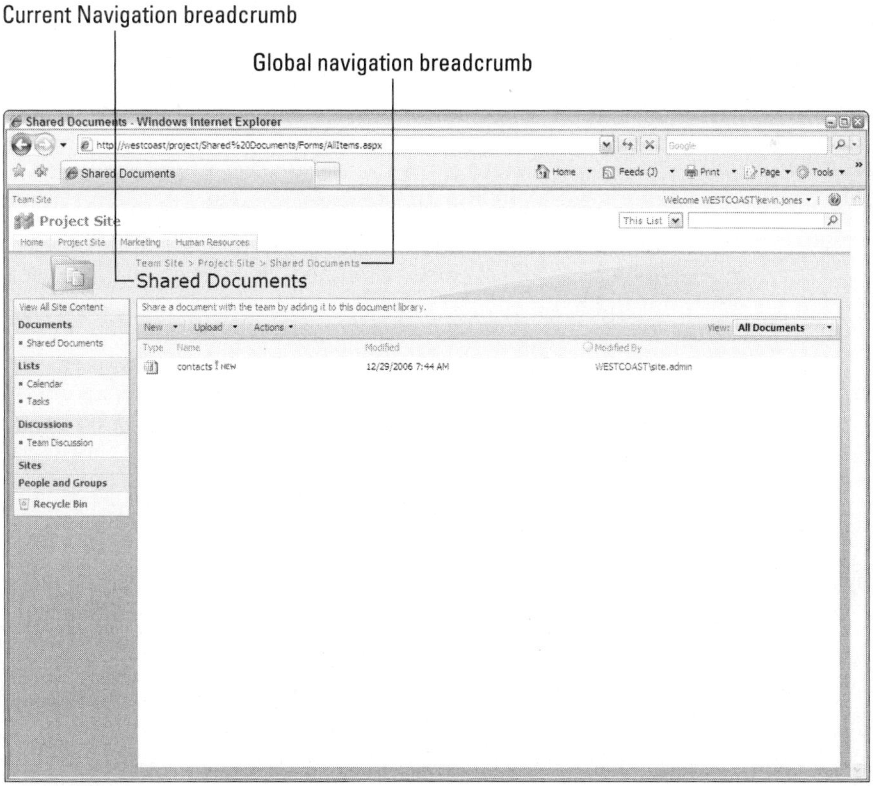

Current Navigation breadcrumb

Global navigation breadcrumb

Figure 5-3:
SharePoint's breadcrumb navigation.

6. **Type the name you want to appear in the global navigation bread-crumb in the Portal Name field.**

   The name you type doesn't have to match the name of the portal or site collection. For example, you could type **Corporate Home** instead of the actual name given to the top-level portal.

7. **Click OK.**

   The global navigation breadcrumb includes the new list, as shown in Figure 5-4.

You can use the Portal Site Connection feature to create a hierarchy of site collections and portals. This feature isn't limited to MOSS 2007, so you could connect Windows SharePoint Services site collections.

Staying local with the Quick Launch bar

Most pages in SharePoint display a list of navigation buttons on the Quick Launch bar along the left side of the page, as shown in Figure 5-5. The Quick Launch bar displays links to featured site content such as lists, libraries, sites, and publishing pages. The Quick Launch bar sandwiches the links to site content between these two important links:

- **View All Site Content link:** At the top of every Quick Launch bar, you find the View All Site Content link. This is important because it lets users quickly view all the lists, libraries, and sites that they have permissions to access. Users with the Create Subsites permissions can access the Create button on the All Site Content page.

- **Recycle Bin:** A link to the Recycle Bin appears at the bottom of the Quick Launch bar. Content deleted by users is saved to the Recycle Bin where it can be restored.

The Quick Launch bar appears on all site pages except those related to completing administrative tasks such as adding new users. You can disable the Quick Launch bar for a site or control what appears on the bar. See the section, "Modifying Navigation," later in this chapter.

Technically speaking, the Quick Launch bar is the navigation element that appears between the View All Site Content link and the Recycle Bin. You can disable the Quick Launch bar, but you can't remove the links that sandwich it. You also have the option to add a site hierarchy called Tree View below the Quick Launch bar. Because the Quick Launch bar, the Tree View, and the other links appear in the same rectangle on the page, I think it's safe to call the whole thing the Quick Launch bar. Read more about modifying the Quick Launch bar in the section "Modifying Navigation."

Global breadcrumb

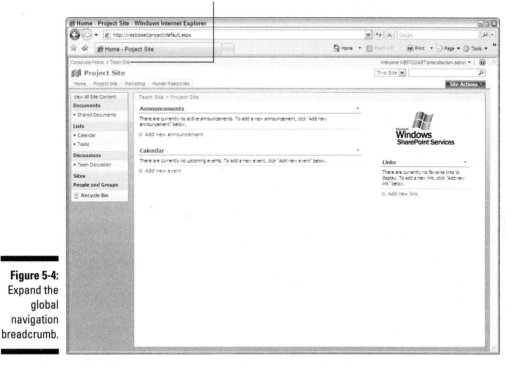

Figure 5-4:
Expand the
global
navigation
breadcrumb.

Getting specific with the search bar

A big SharePoint feature is the ability to search the SharePoint sites, lists, and libraries to find information and documents. All pages in SharePoint include a search bar by default. (See Figure 5-6.) The search bar has the following features:

- ✔ **Search Scope drop-down list:** Widen or narrow the search scope to encompass the current site or list.
- ✔ **Search term:** Type a search term in the text box.

MOSS 2007 includes a link for conducting Advanced searches and the ability to search more sources including people and business data. You can still conduct advanced searches with Windows SharePoint Services; there's no link or fancy interface (as there is with MOSS 2007). See Chapter 14 to learn more about using SharePoint search.

Figure 5-5:
The Quick
Launch bar.

Quick Launch bar

Navigating home

The *home page* is often the starting page of a Web site. A SharePoint deployment is a hierarchy of Web sites made up of nested site collections and sites — and often a rather extensive hierarchy at that. It's important for your users to know how to make their way to a particular home page, including the home pages of the following:

✔ **The current site:** While users are browsing team sites, project sites, and other kinds of sites within a site collection, they can click the site's header at any time to be taken to the home page of the current site.

✔ **The current site collection:** Users should use the global breadcrumb to backtrack to the top-level site in a site collection or higher sites.

✔ **Higher-level site collections:** Although users can use the global breadcrumb, you should also make it easier for users by featuring links to sibling site collections or higher site collections as part of the current site collection's navigational elements. See the section "Modifying Navigation" for tips on how to feature other sites.

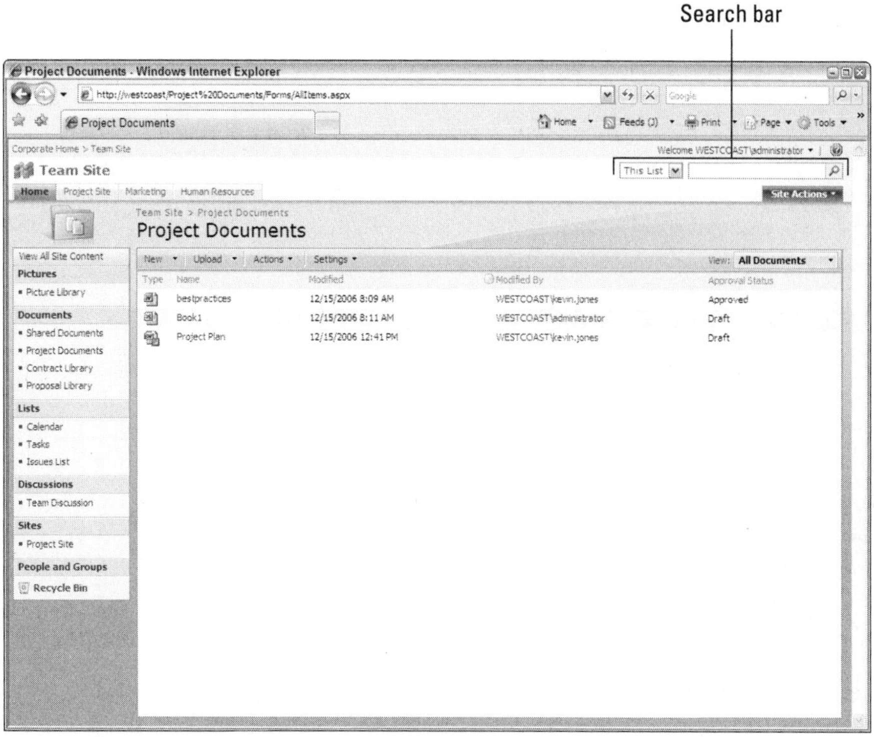

Search bar

Figure 5-6:
The search
bar.

Figure 5-7 shows an example of the Shared Documents library in a particular team site — the New Warehouse Project site, to be specific. A user can navigate to the home page of the New Warehouse Project site by clicking New Warehouse Project in the site header. The global breadcrumb at the top of the page displays the following:

- ✔ **Corporate Home:** The portal site connection.
- ✔ **West Coast Division:** The top-level site in the site collection.
- ✔ **New Warehouse Project:** The current site.

Whether the user understands that he or she is sitting in a site collection or higher isn't important. What's important is that the user knows how to make his or her way from a current site to a sibling site or higher-level site by using the navigational elements at the user's disposal.

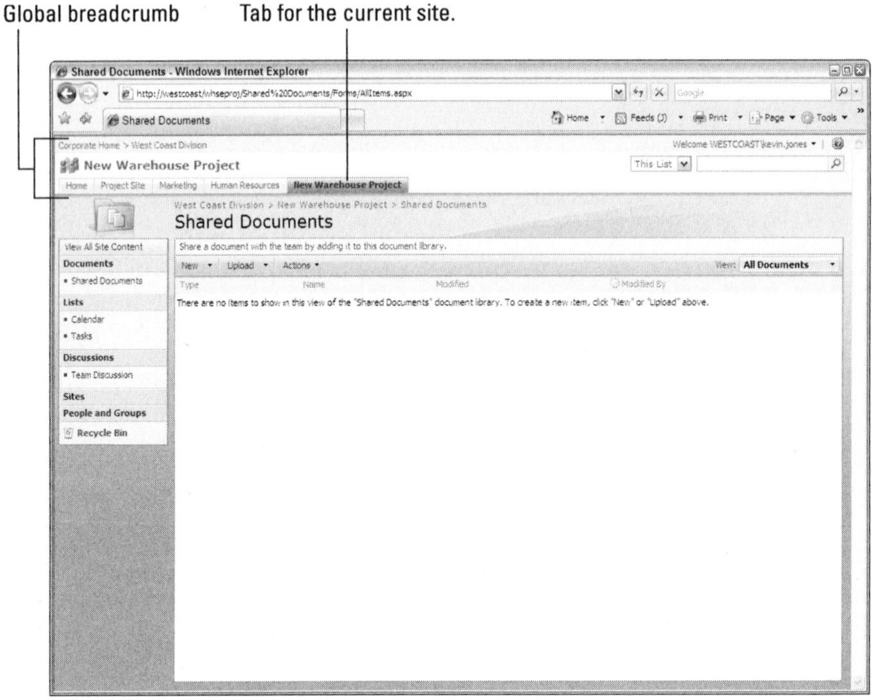

Global breadcrumb   Tab for the current site.

Figure 5-7:
Navigating
to the home
page.

Getting help

Users can access SharePoint's Help and How-to resources by clicking the Help icon in the upper-right corner of the page. The Help and How-to documentation is a combination of local and online resources displayed in a browser window.

Modifying Navigation

Rarely is site navigation a one-size-fits-all approach. Rather, navigation inherited from the parent site works best for some sites, and local navigation makes sense for others. In certain instances, creating a customized list of navigational items makes sense.

In the preceding section, I explored many navigational elements that are present in SharePoint. Of these, only two can be modified using SharePoint's administrative pages: the Quick Launch bar and the Top Link bar.

The listings that appear in the Quick Launch bar and the Top Link bar are called *navigation items*. Windows SharePoint Services allows you to manage the following navigation items:

- ✔ **Headings:** Can be used to organize links that appear in the Quick Launch bar.
- ✔ **Links:** Are used to provide shortcuts to content such as subsites, lists, and external resources. Links appear as tabs in the Top Link bar.

MOSS 2007 also supports headings and links, although MOSS provides additional support for more specific kinds of navigation items, such as these:

- ✔ **Pages;** Are links to publishing pages.
- ✔ **Sub-sites:** Are links to subsites.

Whereas WSS uses the generic Items headings and links, MOSS explicitly manages the links for pages and subsites. Headings and links can be edited and deleted in both WSS and MOSS. MOSS provides the ability to target headings and links to audiences (see Chapter 13). You can hide navigation to pages and subsites, but you can't completely delete the links. Also, you can't edit the links to pages and subsites. Users can only see the links to sites and pages that they have permission to view. I explain how to manage navigation items later in this section.

MOSS has another kind of navigation item called a *Container*, used to group together pages, subsites, headings, and links. Out-of-the-box MOSS supports two containers: Global Navigation and Current Navigation. These containers correspond (respectively) to the Top Link bar and Quick Launch bar navigation elements. There's also a Global and Current breadcrumb, and the way you configure your Top Link bar and Quick Launch bar determines what gets displayed in those breadcrumbs.

You may be wondering why MOSS goes through the trouble of using the fancy names Global Navigation and Current Navigation. Why not just refer directly to the Top Link bar and the Quick Launch bar? My guess is that Microsoft wanted to separate the organization of navigation items from the actual elements used to display those items on the screen. Creating this separation means you can (for example) replace the Quick Launch bar with a custom navigation element if need be. You could simply tell the custom navigation element to use the navigation items found in the Current Navigation container.

MOSS and WSS each have separate administrative pages for managing navigation. In the remainder of this section, I walk you through how to manage navigation. Everything I cover in the WSS section applies to MOSS, but the converse isn't true.

Navigating Sites in WSS

Site navigation in Windows SharePoint Services comprises the tabs and links you see along the top and side of a SharePoint site — and it's automatically generated at the time a site is created. You have the option to choose that the new site uses its parent's Top Link bar. When a site uses the same top link bar as its parent, it's said to *inherit* the top link bar. When the site uses its own bar, it's called *unique*. Also, you can elect to have the site listed in the Top Link bar and Quick Launch bar of the parent site. Once the site is created, you have the following options for managing site navigation:

✔ Stop inheriting the parent site's Top Link bar and manually manage navigation items.

✔ Turn the Quick Launch bar off.

✔ Enable a Tree View that displays links based on the site's hierarchy.

✔ Add or remove links for lists and libraries on the Quick Launch bar.

✔ Manage links in the Quick Launch bar and create groupings for links

The remainder of this section walks you through these activities.

Managing the top link bar

The top-level site in a site collection always uses a unique top link bar. There's no parent site to inherit from. By default, all subsites inherit the top link bar from their parent site. You can choose to use a unique top link bar at the time you create the site, or you can stop inheriting any time you change your mind.

You manage the top link bar using the Top Link Bar page. To access the page, follow these steps:

1. **Browse to the site where you wish to modify navigation.**

2. **Click Site Actions⇨Site Settings. The Site Settings Page appears.**

3. **In the Look and Feel section, click the Top Link Bar link. The Top Link Bar page appears.**

Managing the Quick Launch bar

You can manage the Quick Launch bar very similarly to the top link bar; however, the Quick Launch bar doesn't inherit from the parent site. Instead, the items that appear in the Quick Launch bar are determined by the settings in the site template you use when you create a site. Each list or library contained in a site has the option to display a link to itself on the Quick Launch bar. Site templates, such as the Team Site template in WSS, set this flag auto-matically. For example, the Team Site template displays links to all lists and libraries created in the site except the Announcements list.

You can easily add or remove a list or library from the Quick Launch bar using the list's settings:

1. **Browse to the list or library you wish to remove from the Quick Launch bar on a site.**

   For example, in a site using the Team Site template, click the link in the Quick Launch bar or click the View All Site Content link to browse to a list not included on the Quick Launch bar, such as the Announcements list.

2. **Click Settings⇨List Settings or Settings⇨Library Settings.**

   The Customize page appears.

3. **In the General Settings section, click the Title, Description, and Navigation link.**

   The General Settings page appears.

4. **In the Navigation section, indicate whether to include the list or library in the Quick Launch bar.**

5. **Click the Save button.**

   The links in the Quick Launch bar are updated to reflect your changes.

WSS also provides a Quick Launch page that behaves very similarly to the Top Link Bar page. You access the Quick Launch page by clicking the Quick Launch link in the Look and Feel section of the site's Site Settings page.

You also have the option to disable the Quick Launch bar entirely for a site. You can add a site hierarchy called a Tree View to the left navigation panel instead of the Quick Launch bar. If you leave the Quick Launch bar enabled, the Tree View appears below the Quick Launch bar. To perform either of these tasks, follow these steps:

1. **Browse to the Site Settings page for the site you wish to manage.**

2. **In the Look and Feel section, click the Tree View link.**

   The Tree View page appears.

3. **In the Enable Quick Launch section, indicate whether to enable or dis-able the Quick Launch bar.**

4. **In the Enable Tree View section, indicate whether to enable or disable a tree view in the Quick Launch bar.**

5. **Click OK.**

Navigating Sites in MOSS

The navigation features for MOSS 2007 are very similar to Windows SharePoint Services. The primary difference is that MOSS gives you a more advanced (and more complicated) tool to use for customizing navigation. Instead of manually managing the navigation items in the Quick Launch bar and Top Link bar, MOSS makes it possible to control and customize your site's navigation while allowing SharePoint to dynamically generate the links displayed.

You can modify your MOSS site's navigation options from your site's Site Settings page. Here's how:

1. **Browse to the Site Settings page for the site you wish to manage.**

   Depending on the kind of site you're accessing, you can either click Site Actions⇨Site Settings or Site Actions⇨Site Settings⇨Modify All Site Settings.

2. **Choose the Navigation link from the page's Look and Feel section.**

   The Site Navigation Settings page appears.

3. **In the Subsites and Pages section, indicate whether to show or hide subsites and pages in navigation.**

   If you choose to show subsites, then all subsites appear by default as navigation items in the Quick Launch bar and Top Link bar. The Show pages option refers only to MOSS 2007 Publishing Pages. Web Parts pages that you create aren't added as navigation items. In fact, the Show Pages option is only available on sites with the Publishing feature enabled.

   By enabling the Show Subsites and Show Pages options, SharePoint can dynamically build your Quick Launch bar and Top Link bar. See Step 8 to see how to more granularly control the visibility of individual navigation items.

4. **In the Sorting section, indicate whether to sort navigation items manually or automatically.**

   The setting you choose in the Sorting section applies to all navigation elements including the Quick Launch bar and the Top Link bar. If you choose manual sorting, you also have the option to choose automatic sorting for publishing pages listed in the navigation.

5. **In the Automatic Sorting section, select a column to sort by and whether to sort in ascending or descending order.**

   The Automatic Sorting section is only visible if you choose the option to sort automatically in Step 4.

   You can choose to sort by Title, Created Date, or Last Modified Date. Choosing to sort in descending order by Last Modified Date ensures that the most recently modified publishing pages appear at the top of the list of navigation items.

6. **In the Global Navigation section, indicate whether to display the same Top Link bar as the parent site or to display the navigation items below the current site.**

   The site's breadcrumb paths are influenced by whether the Top Link bar inherits from the parent site or is unique.

7. **In the Current Navigation section, select the navigation items you wish to display in the site's Quick Launch bar.**

   You have three options for the Quick Launch bar:

   • **Display the same navigation items as the parent site:** The site displays the same Quick Launch bar as its parent site.

   • **Display the current site, the navigation items below the current site, and the current site's siblings:** The site's Quick Launch bar displays links to the publishing pages of the current site and to any subsites and sibling sites.

   • **Display only the navigation items below the current site:** Displays links to the site's subsites in the Quick Launch bar. If the subsite's navigation is configured to show publishing pages (see Step 3), then those pages are also listed in the Quick Launch bar.

8. **In the Navigation Editing and Sorting section (you may need to scroll your browser window), reorder and modify the navigation items that appear for the site.**

   You can use this section to manually reorder links or add new headings or links to the site's navigation. The navigation items you see here are dependent upon the choices you make in the preceding sections of the Site Navigation Settings page. For example, if you opt to display the navigation items below the current site for the site's global navigation (Step 6), then the Navigation Editing and Sorting section displays navigation items for the top link bar. Otherwise, only the current navigation (Quick Launch bar) appears in the frame.

   Global navigation refers to the Top Link bar, and current navigation refers to the Quick Launch bar.

   As you click a link in the frame, a description of the link appears in the lower frame.

   Use the buttons along the top of the frame to modify the navigation items:

   • **Move Up, Move Down:** Moves the selected navigation item up or down in the list.

   • **Edit:** Opens a window so you can edit the text, URL, description, or audience of the link. You can also set the link to open in a new browser window.

- **Delete:** Deletes the link to the navigation item. This option is only available for heading and link navigation items.

- **Hide:** Hides the link to the navigation item. This option appears for all other kinds of navigation items besides headings and links. By opting to hide links to subsites and publishing pages, the link is no longer visible in the site's navigation, but it still appears in the Site Navigation Settings page.

- **Show:** Removes the hidden status for links that have been hidden. The Show button is only available for links that are hidden.

- **Add Heading:** Adds a heading that can be used to group a set of links.

- **Add Link:** Adds a link to a resource such as a site or list. You can link to external sites.

The navigation items displayed in the frame in the Navigation Editing and Sorting section depends on the option you select in the Global Navigation section (Step 6). If the site inherits its Top Link bar from its parent site, then the frame only displays navigation items for the Quick Launch bar. Otherwise, the frame displays the Global Navigation and Current Navigation containers.

9. **Click OK to finalize your changes.**

When configuring a site's navigation, I suggest you work with two browser windows open. I like to use two monitors with a browser session open in each monitor. One browser session displays the Site Navigation Settings page while the other session displays the site that I'm configuring. As I make changes in the Site Navigation Settings page, I refresh the site in the other browser to see the changes.

Exploring Administrative Navigational Elements

You'll be glad to discover that many of the administrative tasks associated with sites and site collections that were previously unavailable in SharePoint (or available only from the command line) are now available in the user interface. You can use two different menus to access all the major administrative features for site collections and sites in SharePoint:

✔ **Site Actions:** The Site Actions drop-down menu is in the upper-right corner of a SharePoint page. You must at least be a member of the *Site* Members group in MOSS or the *Site* Owners group in WSS to see the Site Actions menu. Here you find links to administrative pages and page editing features. The list of shortcuts available on the Site Actions menu depends on the features enabled in the site's template. Sites based on site templates that use the MOSS Publishing feature, such as the Collaboration Portal template, list commands related to editing publishing pages. Sites with fewer features, such as Team Sites, offer basic commands for editing Web Parts pages.

✔ **Site Settings:** You can access virtually all SharePoint's administrative pages for a site via the site's Site Settings page. The Site Settings page for a top-level site in a site collection includes a set of links related to administering the site collection. You can access a site's Site Settings page via the Site Actions menu.

You can access additional administrative features related to Web applications, site collections, and the server itself at SharePoint's Central Administration site. (See Chapter 18 for details on how to access the Central Administration site.)

Site actions

The Site Actions menu is available to users who are members of the *Site* Members group in MOSS. Members of the *Site* Visitors group and other groups that are restricted to read-only permissions can't see the Site Actions menu. WSS restricts the use of the Site Actions menu to *Site* Owners. There's no individual permission related to accessing the Site Actions menu. Rather, the ability to see the Site Actions menu is determined by whether the user belongs to a group with the permissions to access commands found on the Site Actions menu. For example, a group with the Add and Customize Pages permission is able to see the Edit Pages command on the Site Actions menu, which enables members of that group to see the Site Actions menu. See Chapter 6 for more about setting permissions.

The Site Actions menu provides shortcuts to commands commonly used by administrators, contributors, designers, and hierarchy managers when working with SharePoint sites. Which menu commands are available depends on your permissions, and on the kind of site. Table 5-1 lists the kinds of commands available on the Site Action menu, while Figure 5-8 shows you how the Site Actions menu looks for a member of the *Site* Owners group in a MOSS 2007 collaboration portal.

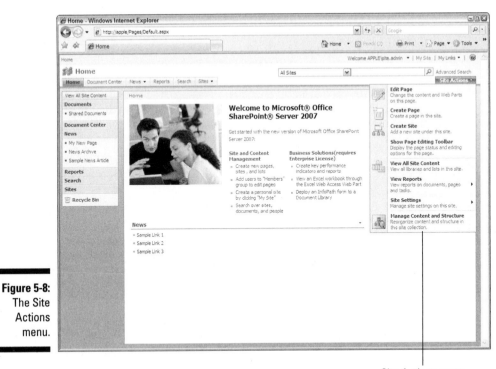

Figure 5-8:
The Site
Actions
menu.

Site Actions menu

Table 5-1		Commands on the Site Action Menu	
Command	**Who Can See It**	**Where You See It**	**What You Use It For**
Edit Page	Site Members	Publishing sites	Check out and edit a publishing page.
Edit Page	Designers (MOSS), Site Owners (WSS)	Team sites	Edit the shared version of a Web Parts page.
Add Pages	Designers (MOSS), Site Owners (WSS)	Meeting workspaces	Add a new page to the workspace.
Manage Pages	Designers (MOSS), Site Owners (WSS)	Meeting workspaces	Manage the pages in a workspace.
Create Page page.	Site Members	Publishing sites	Add a new Publishing
Create Site	Hierarchy Managers	Publishing sites	Add a new SharePoint site.

Command	Who Can See It	Where You See It	What You Use It For
Create Dashboard	Site Members	Reports site (any BI)	Display a New Dashboard page for creating a customized display of Business Intelligence data.
Create External Link	Site Members	News site	Create a page that displays an external Web page.
Create	Site Owners	Team sites	Add new lists, libraries, Web pages, and sites.
Show Page Editing Toolbar	Site Members	Publishing sites	Display toolbar for editing Publishing pages.
View All Site Content	Site Members	Publishing sites	View all the lists, libraries, and other content in a site.
View Reports	Site Members	Publishing sites	View a set of reports related to administering Web content.
Site Settings	Designers (MOSS), Site Members (WSS)	All sites	Access administrative features on the Site Settings page.
Scan for Broken Links	Site Owners	Site Directory site	Test the sites listed in the Site Directory to make sure all the URLs are good.
Manage Content and Structure	Site Members	Publishing sites	Display a Tree view of all the sites, pages, lists, and libraries in a site collection.

You always have the option to change which group has permission to access the commands on the Site Actions menu. See Chapter 6 for more information on setting permissions.

Site settings

You access a site's administrative features through the Site Settings page. To access the Site Settings page, choose Site Actions⇨Site Settings in a non-publishing site (such as Team site) or choose Site Actions⇨Site Settings⇨Modify All Site Settings in a publishing site (such as a Collaboration Portal site).

You can also access a list of all the sites created in a site collection by choosing Site Settings⇨Site Hierarchy. The Site Hierarchy link is in the Site Collection Administration column. Click the Manage link in the Site Hierarchy page to access the Site Settings page of any site listed in the site collection's site hierarchy.

The URL for the Site Settings page is:

```
http://sitepath/_layouts/settings.aspx
```

You can append the path `_layouts/settings.aspx` to any SharePoint site's path to view the site's Site Settings page.

The header of the Site Settings page displays the Site Information section, which shows the following information about the site:

- ✔ **URL:** The URL to access the site's home page.

- ✔ **Mobile Site URL:** The URL to access a mobile version of the site for use on handheld devices.

- ✔ **Version:** The version of SharePoint the site is deployed on,

The Site Settings page displays links to administrative pages in the following categories:

- ✔ **Users and Permissions:** Find links for managing people, groups, administrators, and permissions.

- ✔ **Look and Feel:** Set the site's title and configure navigation. MOSS 2007 sites also give you the option to set the site's master page, title, theme, welcome page, and other features that impact the way the site appears.

- ✔ **Galleries:** Access libraries of reusable content available to a specific site or all sites in the site collection.

- ✔ **Site Administration:** Access links for administering the site and its structure and features.

- ✔ **Site Collection Administration:** Access links relevant to administering the entire site collection. You must use the Site Settings page of the top-level site in a site collection in order to access administrative links in the Site Collection Administration column. When you view the Site Settings page of a subsite, you see the link Go to Top Level Site Settings in the Site Collection Administration column. Clicking that link takes you to the top-level site.

Chapter 6

Granting Access to SharePoint

In This Chapter

▶ Understanding authentication and authorization

▶ Viewing permissions

▶ Managing access with SharePoint groups

▶ Creating unique permissions

*W*hen considering security and permissions for SharePoint, you must understand two important elements: authentication and authorization. *Authentication* involves determining whether a user account can be reliably identified as the person they say they are. An important task, to be sure — but not one that SharePoint is in a position to take on. That is, SharePoint has no database of usernames and passwords to manage and therefore no way of determining who is really who. Rather, SharePoint assumes you already have some means to identify your users and validate that they are who they say they are.

Authorization is what allows for all the nitty-gritty stuff after a user is authenticated — granting a user access to all the objects in SharePoint, in other words — and SharePoint is definitely in a position to provide authorization services. In this chapter, I discuss authentication briefly and spend the bulk of the chapter explaining SharePoint's authorization model and how to use it.

Delegating Authentication

If you thought that working with SharePoint meant having to deal with yet another set of user credentials, you can rest a bit easier. SharePoint doesn't force you to create new user accounts and passwords. Instead, SharePoint assumes you already have some means to authenticate a user's username and password.

Rather than create a new database of usernames and passwords, SharePoint supports the use of authentication providers. These providers are external user databases that manage a user's identity. Applications that manage user accounts are *identity management systems.* SharePoint supports the following kinds of identity management systems as authentication providers:

- ✔ **Windows:** The default option in Internet Information Services (IIS) and SharePoint. Because SharePoint uses Web technologies, authentication is handled by the IIS Web server that hosts SharePoint. With Windows-based authentication, IIS uses the user's Windows credentials to access SharePoint. In most networks, Active Directory (AD) is used as the source of Windows credentials. AD isn't required for SharePoint, which is great for evaluation purposes.

- ✔ **Non-Windows:** You can enable custom authentication by using ASP.NET forms-based authentication. With forms-based authentication, you use an ASP.NET login form to access some kind of identity management system, such as a custom back-end SQL Server database or a Lightweight Directory Access Protocol (LDAP) system. Using ASP.NET requires some configuration and planning, but it's a great alternative if you don't want to use Windows-based authentication.

- ✔ **Windows Trusted:** Users can connect to SharePoint via a trusted authentication provider, such as a Single Sign-On Service (SSO). This allows the user to access SharePoint's resources without SharePoint having the user's actual credentials. You might use a trusted Windows authentication provider any time you want to authenticate users who are members of a trusted domain, such as a partner's network.

Most of the time, companies use Windows-based authentication because they already have user accounts set up — it's always easier to use what you already have in place. Just be aware that you can configure almost any kind of authentication scheme you'd like and SharePoint should be able to work with it pretty seamlessly. If you are interested in completely customizing your user identity management system, go with an authentication provider rather than sticking with Widows-based authentication.

A user's identity is made up of his or her username, password, and possibly membership in what are known as *security groups.* To give a concrete example here, the identity management system for a typical corporate Windows network is Active Directory (AD), and, in this system, there is space for setting security groups that AD refers to as domain groups. Most companies create domain groups to organize users who need similar kinds of access — groups for Marketing or Accounting or IT or HR or whatever. Then, when it comes to managing all their user accounts, administrators can treat a domain group as a single block rather than having to deal with countless individual user accounts.

Although SharePoint doesn't provide identity management, Microsoft Office SharePoint Server 2007 (MOSS) allows you to store properties about your user accounts to create user profiles. You can then use the contents of the user profiles to create social and knowledge networks. See Chapter 12 for more information about managing user profiles.

Don't confuse user profiles with user accounts. A *user account* is a user's identity in an authentication provider — such as AD — and is managed outside of SharePoint. *User profiles* are properties, such as an e-mail account or fax number, associated with a user account. User profiles are managed in MOSS. Also, don't confuse user accounts with setup accounts. When you install SharePoint, you specify a number of setup accounts that SharePoint uses to communicate between servers. Setup accounts must be Windows accounts, but they don't have to be domain accounts.

Authentication is configured at the Web application level in SharePoint. Each Web application in your server farm can use up to five different authentication providers. That means you can have five different ways for users to access the same Web application, depending on how they're authenticated.

SharePoint uses zones to manage the various authentication options for a Web application. *Zones* are simply a way to categorize the authentication options available for a Web application. When you create a new Web application, SharePoint automatically creates the Default zone and configures it to use Windows authentication. You create new zones by extending an existing Web application.

Extending a Web application is similar to creating a Web application; see Chapter 3 for more on creating Web applications.

Because authentication is managed for each Web application, you can find configuration options for authentication and security at the Central Administration site. SharePoint includes an Application Security section that provides access to these security-related administrative tasks for Web applications:

- ✔ **Security for Web Part pages:** Allows you disable access to the Online Web Part Gallery or prevent the ability to create connections between Web Parts. By default, these features are enabled. You may choose to disable them for security or performance reasons.

- ✔ **Self-service site management:** Allows you specify whether users with the Use Self-Service Site Creation permission can create new SharePoint sites. You should only enable this feature if you want to give end users the ability to create new sites. You should generally leave this option to site owners and administrators to prevent an unwieldy number of sites being created.

- ✔ **User permissions for Web application:** Allows you to specify which permissions can be assigned to users and groups at the site collection level. By default, all permissions are enabled.

> ✔ **Policy for Web application:** Allows you to specify what users or groups have either Full Control, Full Read, Deny Write, or Deny All permissions. By default, local service and network service accounts have full read permissions. You should generally allow site collection administrators Full Control permissions.
>
> ✔ **Authentication providers:** Allows you to configure authentication providers for a Web application.

In most cases, you won't need to make any configuration changes to the security settings for your Web applications. SharePoint's default settings allow you to start assigning permissions to users in your Active Directory network without any additional configuration.

There are a number of steps involved in configuring alternative authentication options for SharePoint. See the topic, "Plan for authentication," in the TechNet library at `http://technet2.microsoft.com/windowsserver/WSS/en/library/cb8409f9-cd8a-4651-b644-250ff6b86c761033.mspx` if you want more details.

SharePoint's Authorization Model

When a user tries to access a resource in SharePoint — a Web site or document library, for example — the user must be authenticated. SharePoint has no means of authenticating users, as I describe in the preceding section. Rather, SharePoint relies on your authentication provider to tell SharePoint that the user's account is valid. After SharePoint gets the thumbs up from the authentication provider, SharePoint can attempt to authorize the user's access to the resource.

You have three distinct parts to SharePoint's *authorization model* — the steps needed to authorize a user to access a resource — as seen in the following list:

> ✔ **A principal:** Principals are users granted permission to access the resource, whether they are accounts from the authentication provider or a SharePoint group, individual user accounts or domain group accounts. (Remember that SharePoint groups are groups you create for managing access for large numbers of user accounts without individually managing each user account. You can assign both individual user accounts and domain group accounts to SharePoint groups.)
>
> ✔ **A permission level:** The set of individual permissions associated with a principal. Permissions are individual rights, such as a View Page or Add Item permission. In SharePoint, permissions aren't used directly. Instead, permissions are grouped together in permission levels. Examples of permission levels are Contribute, Design, and Approve. A principal associated with the Contribute permission level has all the permissions required to add, edit, and delete list items.

✔ **A securable object:** Basically, the resources you can make *secure* (as in, limit access to) in SharePoint. SharePoint has the following kinds of securable objects:

- *Web sites*
- *Lists and libraries*
- *Folders*
- *List items*

Figure 6-1 shows the components of SharePoint's security.

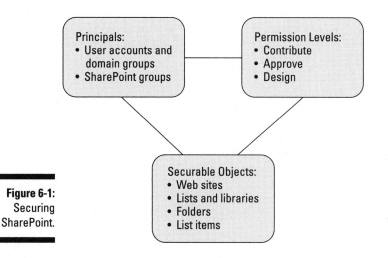

Figure 6-1:
Securing
SharePoint.

TECHNICAL STUFF

The combination of a principal (SharePoint group or authenticated user account) with a permission level assigned to a securable object is a *role assignment.*

Understanding people and groups

You access SharePoint's authorization model by using the People and Groups page. Each SharePoint site has its own People and Groups page (see Figure 6-2). You can find a link to the People and Groups page in the Users and Permissions section of the site's Site Settings page. The People and Groups page makes it possible for you to manage:

Groups

Figure 6-2:
View a site's
People and
Groups
page.

Site Permissions navigation

People

- ✔ **Groups:** Actually only one kind of group — the SharePoint group. Groups are used to conveniently provide access to multiple users without assigning the permissions to individual users.

- ✔ **People:** The user accounts and domain groups added to SharePoint from the authentication provider. Note that it isn't possible to create new user accounts using SharePoint. The user account must already exist in the authentication provider.

- ✔ **Site Permissions:** Allows you to view the permissions assigned to users and groups in the site. You can also create new permission levels.

Keep in mind through all this that a SharePoint group is a container for assigning permission levels to a user, that permission levels are a container for storing a set of individual permissions, and that permissions themselves are what confer rights to a user. In this setup, groups and people are the principals to which access is granted, whereas the site permissions are the permission assignments.

In SharePoint Portal Server 2003, SharePoint groups were referred to as *cross-site groups,* and permission levels were known as *site groups.*

Groups and people are limited in scope to the site collection level. Each site collection has its set of groups and people. All groups and people available at the top-level of a site collection are available to lower sites, lists, and libraries. The default behavior for a site or other securable object is to inherit permissions from its parent site. As a result, you may have to browse to the parent's People and Groups page to actually manage permissions for lower sites. If all sites in a site collection inherit permissions, you have to use the People and Groups page for the site collection's top-level site.

To access the SharePoint People and Groups page for a site, follow these steps:

1. **Browse to the site's Site Settings page.**

   In a Windows SharePoint Service team site, click Site Actions⇨Site Settings. In a Microsoft Office SharePoint Server 2007 publishing site, click Site Actions⇨Site Settings⇨Modify All Site Settings.

2. **Click the People and Groups link in the Users and Permissions section of the page.**

   The People and Groups page appears (refer to Figure 6-2).

   You can also access the People and Groups page by using the Site Actions menu when the site has the Office SharePoint Server Publishing feature enabled.

Each site has its own People and Groups page. The user accounts, domain groups, and SharePoint groups you see listed in the People and Groups page are shared across the entire site collection.

Understanding inheritance

If you liked the idea of using SharePoint groups to minimize the number of individual user accounts you need to manage, you're going to love the fact that you don't have to manage the individual permissions for every Web site, list, library, folder, and list item in your site collection. In the same way content structures such as sites and lists in SharePoint are organized in a hierarchy, their permissions are organized in a hierarchy as well.

By default, you grant permissions at the highest level in a site collection, and all lower level items automatically inherit their parent's permissions, users, and SharePoint groups. For example, all the permissions in the top-level site of a Web site are applied to any new sites, lists, or libraries created below the site. At the time you create a new site, you can specify that the site not inherit permissions from its parent. See Chapter 4 for details on creating new sites.

Don't think that inheritance locks you into only one way of doing things, though. You can *break* inheritance at any time — basically overriding it — if you feel the need to create a unique set of permissions for a lower-level site. You can also backtrack and discard any unique permissions you may have set and revert to inheriting the parent's permissions again. See the section, "Breaking Inheritance," later in this chapter, for details on how to use unique permissions.

Viewing Permission Assignments

A site can have all the elements of an authorization model — people, groups, and permissions, in other words — but still not be secure. The deciding factor in securing SharePoint's content lies with the permission assignments made on securable objects such as sites, lists, and libraries. A permission assignment consists of permissions, principals (users and groups), and securable objects.

Permissions are the smallest unit for managing security in SharePoint. Permissions confer rights, such as View Pages rights or Add Items rights, that a user may have. In SharePoint, you'll deal with following three permission types:

- ✔ **List Permissions:** Permissions related to accessing lists and list items.
- ✔ **Site Permissions:** Permissions related to accessing sites, pages, and permissions.
- ✔ **Personal Permissions:** Permissions related to creating personal views of Web pages.

When managed properly, you never have to work with permissions on a case-by-case basis because permissions are never assigned directly to principals. Rather, they're assigned to *permission levels,* which are assigned to default SharePoint groups. You can also assign permission levels directly to user accounts or custom SharePoint groups you create.

Follow these steps to view a list of permission levels for a site:

1. **Go the site's People and Groups page.**

2. **Click the Site Permissions heading in the Quick Launch bar.**

    A list of principals and their corresponding permission levels appear, as shown in Figure 6-3.

    Each site either inherits its site permission assignments from its parent site or has its own unique permission assignments.

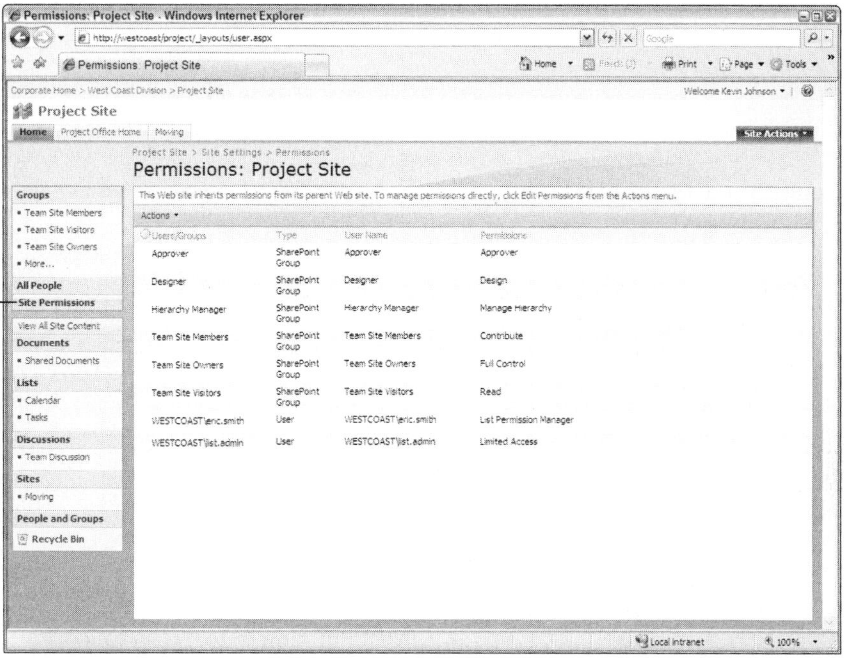

Figure 6-3:
View the
site's
permission
assignments.

Site Permissions heading

Remember that a *principal* is a SharePoint group or user account given access to a SharePoint resource. If you've assigned permission levels to user accounts or domain group accounts outside SharePoint groups, you'll see them listed here.

3. Choose Settings⇨Permission Levels from the page's main menu.

The Permission Levels page appears. You can use this page to create new permission levels or modify existing ones.

4. Click a permission level, such as Contribute, to view or modify the permissions in the permission level, as shown in Figure 6-4.

Note: The permissions you see might not be the entire set of permissions available in SharePoint. The server administrator can limit the list of permissions available to a Web application as I describe in the section "Delegating Authentication," earlier in this chapter.

Keep in mind that the Site Permissions page doesn't really show individual permissions. Instead, the page shows permission levels.

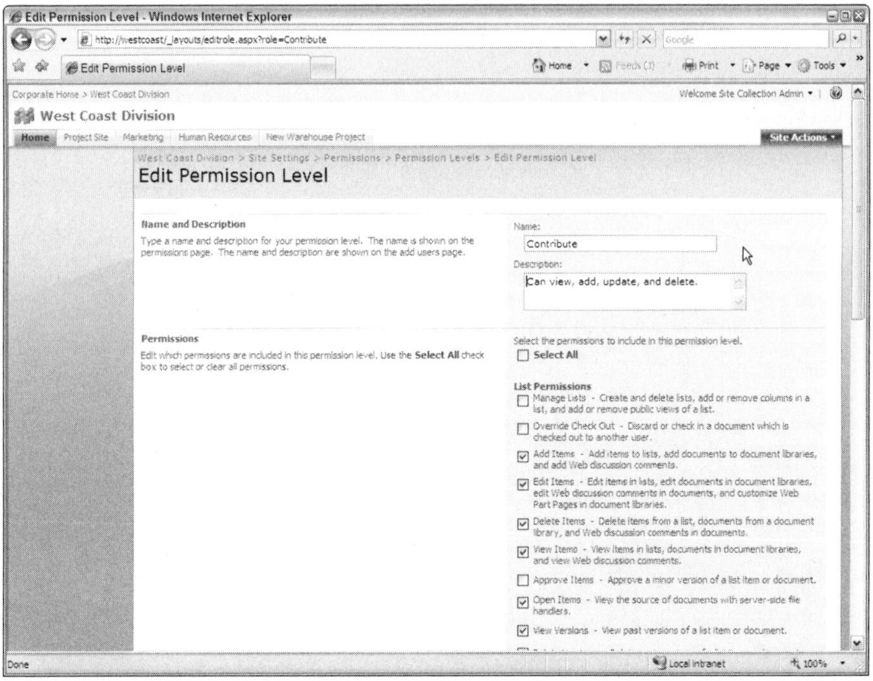

Figure 6-4:
View
permission
levels.

Table 6-1 lists the permission levels, the rights they grant, and the SharePoint group they're assigned to by default.

Table 6-1	Permission Levels	
Permission Level	*Rights Granted*	*SharePoint Group Assigned to by Default*
Full Control	Wield administrative access.	Site Owners
Design	Change the site's look and feel.	Designers
Manage Hierarchy	Manage the site's structure and permissions.	Hierarchy Managers
Approve	Approve content.	Approvers
Contribute	Add and modify content.	Site Members
Read	View all content, including history.	Site Visitors

Permission Level	Rights Granted	SharePoint Group Assigned to by Default
Restricted Read	View and open.	Restricted Readers
Limited Access	Open (same as guest access).	Quick Deploy Users
View Only	View items and pages.	Viewers

Windows SharePoint Services only includes the permission levels Full Control, Design, Contribute, Read, and Limited Access. MOSS 2007 may include additional permission levels depending on the features you have installed.

The combination of users and groups with permission levels assigned to a securable object, such as a site or a list, creates a permission assignment, as shown in Figure 6-5. I show you how to create permission assignments in the upcoming section.

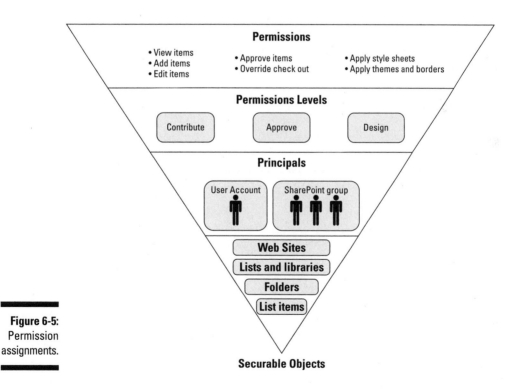

Figure 6-5:
Permission assignments.

Managing SharePoint Groups

SharePoint groups are the preferred method for granting access to SharePoint's securable objects. SharePoint creates several default SharePoint groups when you create a new site collection. SharePoint groups are only available in the site collection where they're created and can be used to grant access to any securable object within that site collection. When a SharePoint group has access to a securable object, any user account added to the SharePoint group is granted access.

Accessing a securable object via a SharePoint group is *indirect access.* In indirect access, the SharePoint group acts as the principal. Direct access occurs when the user account or domain group is the principal. Using SharePoint groups allows you to manage access for more than one user account at a time.

Instead of thinking about people who generically access your sites as users, get into the habit of thinking in terms of the roles that people play when they access SharePoint. SharePoint provides three primary SharePoint groups that effectively match users with a permission level for the purpose of fulfilling a role. The primary SharePoint groups are:

- ✔ *Site* **Members:** Confers the Contribute permission level for users, which allows them to add, edit, and modify list items and browse sites. Most end users fall into this category.

- ✔ *Site* **Owners:** Grants full control. A site owner may or may not use the site on a regular basis, but the site owner is able to delegate administrative and design tasks to others. Also, a site owner may or may not be a technical person.

- ✔ *Site* **Visitors:** Can create alerts. Users who need Read access to a site but don't need to contribute content are visitors.

A site collection has a single set of *Site* Members, *Site* Owners, and *Site* Visitors for the top-level site. The actual names of the groups are determined by the name of the site. For example, if your site is named Projects, then SharePoint calls your groups Projects Members, Projects Owners, and Projects Visitors.

By default, all sites in a site collection inherit these groups from the site collection's top-level site. For instance, anyone with Contribute access to the top-level site collection also has Contribute permissions to subsites. However, you probably don't want that. If you have a MOSS 2007 Collaboration Portal (see Chapter 11), you probably want to assign most users to the *Site* Visitors group to prevent them from making changes to portal content. Assign users to the *Site* Members group for any sites to which they contribute content, such as project and departmental sites. Each subsite can have its own set of *Site* Members, *Site* Owners, and *Site* Visitors, or you can create your own custom groups.

You must break inheritance in order to create unique permissions. See the section, "Breaking Inheritance," later in this chapter, to see how.

MOSS 2007 also provides the following set of specialized administrative groups that enable the site's owner to delegate responsibility:

- ✔ **Approvers:** Enables Approve permissions, which allow users to approve items and override document check outs.

- ✔ **Designers:** Grants permission to change the look and feel of sites with style sheets and themes.

- ✔ **Hierarchy Managers:** Enables Manage Hierarchy permissions, which makes it possible to manipulate the site's hierarchy and customize lists and libraries.

In addition to providing several kinds of administrative roles, MOSS 2007 provides the following groups for restricting access:

- ✔ **Quick Deploy Users:** Intended for scheduling Quick Deploy jobs.

- ✔ **Restricted Readers:** Can view only items and pages, but can't see any item history.

- ✔ **Viewers:** Have View Only access, but can see item history and use clients such as Office to access SharePoint.

The Quick Deploy Users group is used for moving content from one server to another, such as from a staging server to a production server. See the topic, "Planning content deployment" in the TechNet Library at `http://technet2.microsoft.com/Office/en-us/library/1d6d6040-6cbb-4685-a40e-1e9086d426831033.mspx` for details.

Figure 6-6 shows the SharePoint groups, their permission levels, and their permissions. The permissions are cumulative as you move clockwise from one o'clock on.

Creating a permission assignment

Creating a permission assignment is relatively straightforward. First, find a SharePoint group to accommodate the roles you'll need in your SharePoint deployment. (You may find that you need to create additional groups if you use consultants or contractors to perform design or administrative tasks on your SharePoint deployment.) For example, you may want to create a new SharePoint group called External Designers that doesn't grant personal permissions. You may also wish to create a group for Testers.

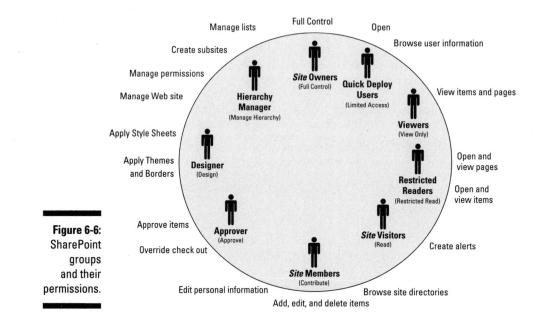

Manage lists
Full Control
Open
Create subsites
Browse user information
Manage permissions
Manage Web site
Site Owners
(Full Control)
Quick Deploy Users
(Limited Access)
View items and pages
Hierarchy Manager
(Manage Hierarchy)
Apply Style Sheets
Apply Themes and Borders
Designer
(Design)
Viewers
(View Only)
Open and view pages
Restricted Readers
(Restricted Read)
Open and view items
Approve items
Approver
(Approve)
Override check out
Site Visitors
(Read)
Create alerts
Edit personal information
Site Members
(Contribute)
Browse site directories
Add, edit, and delete items

Figure 6-6:
SharePoint groups and their permissions.

To create a new SharePoint group, do the following:

1. **Browse to the site's People and Groups page.**

2. **Click the Groups heading in the Quick Launch bar.**

   A list of SharePoint groups appears.

3. **Choose New⇨New Group.**

   The New Group page appears.

   Note: If you'd prefer to edit an existing SharePoint group, click the group's name.

4. **Type a name and a description for the new group.**

5. **Select an owner for the group.**

   The owner is the person who is going to be responsible for administering the group's membership.

6. **Indicate whether everyone or just group members can view the group's membership.**

   I suggest you allow everyone to view membership because this helps users know whom to contact if they have questions or problems about the site or group.

7. **Indicate whether the group owner or group members can edit the group's membership.**

You may want to allow the group's members to add users to groups that have fewer permissions than the group's members. For example, you could allow members to add users to the Site Visitors, Viewers, and Restricted Readers groups.

8. **Indicate whether the group should accept requests to join or leave the group and how requests should be handled.**

9. **Grant a permission level to the group from the list of permission levels provided by SharePoint.**

   Note that you are assigning permission levels to the site, not individual permissions. See the section, "Breaking Inheritance," later in this chapter to read about creating new permission levels.

10. **Click the Create button.**

    The group is created.

SharePoint groups can also be used as e-mail distribution lists. See Chapter 10 for details on setting up SharePoint groups as e-mail distribution lists.

Editing a SharePoint group's access

Permission levels group together a set of individual list, site, and personal permissions. A SharePoint group can have zero or more permission levels assigned to it. Assigning a permission level to a SharePoint group creates a permission assignment for the site, thereby granting all members of the group access.

Do the following to edit the permission level associated with a SharePoint group:

1. **Click the Site Permissions heading in the Quick Launch bar of the site's People and Groups page.**

2. **Place a check mark on the line of the SharePoint group you wish to edit. (Refer to Figure 6-3.)**

3. **Choose Actions⇨Edit User Permissions from the page's main menu.**

   The Edit Permissions page appears.

4. **Select the permission level to use for the SharePoint group, as shown in Figure 6-7.**

   For this example, I've chosen the View Only option.

   See the upcoming section for details about viewing and editing the individual permissions of a permission level.

5. **Click OK.**

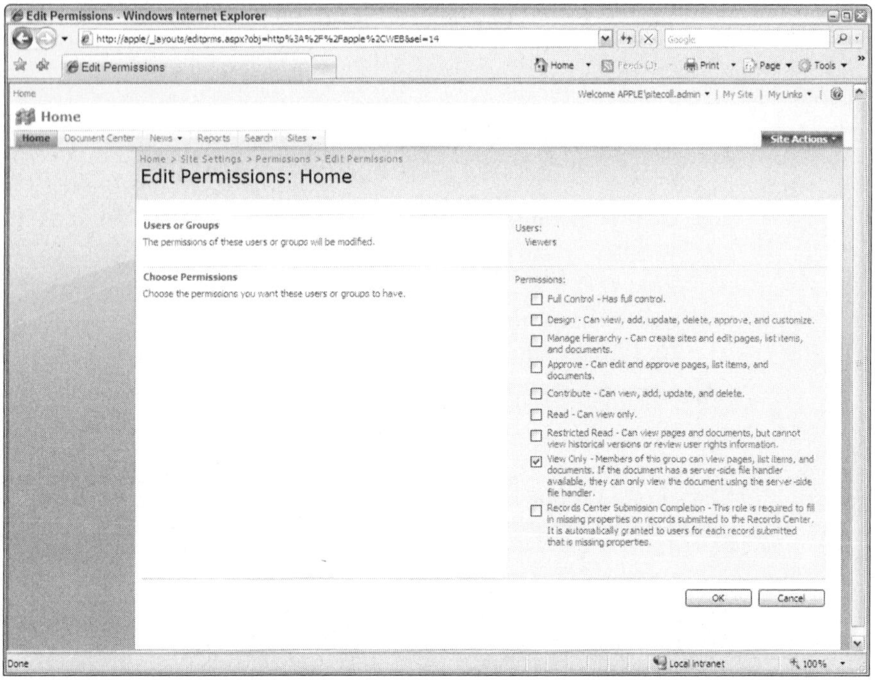

Figure 6-7:
Assigning
permission
levels to a
SharePoint
group.

Granting administrative access

You'll find a number of different administrator levels in a SharePoint deployment. Administrators usually have full access over the domain they've been charged with administering. The levels of administrators in SharePoint are:

- **Server administrators:** By virtue of having local administrator access to the physical server, a server administrator can do anything from the server console. Server administrators are usually members of the technical staff.

- **Site collection administrators:** These administrators can access everything within a site collection. SharePoint allows you to appoint a primary and secondary administrator for each site collection.

- **Site administrators:** Members of the *Site* Owners SharePoint group are the site administrators. If subsites inherit permissions, a site administrator has full access to each site.

To view all the sites for which an administrator or any SharePoint group is responsible, follow these steps:

1. **Browse to the People and Groups page for a top-level site in a site collection.**

2. **Click a group, such as *Site* Owners, for which you wish to view permissions.**

3. **Choose Settings⇨View Group Permissions.**

   The View Site Collection Permissions dialog box appears. The dialog box displays all the sites for which members of the group have access.

To set the site collection administrators for a site:

1. **Click the Site Permissions header in the People and Groups page.**

   The Permissions page appears.

2. **Click Settings⇨Site Collection Administrators.**

   The Site Collection Administrators page appears.

3. **Enter the user accounts for the people who are site collection administrators.**

4. **Click OK.**

Assigning accounts to be site collection administrators is one time when it's acceptable to use individual user accounts instead of domain groups.

Assigning users to SharePoint groups

When I discuss adding users to a SharePoint group, I actually mean individual users and domain groups. User accounts are selected from an identity management system, which may be either Active Directory (AD) in a Windows 2003 Server network domain or a custom SQL Server database. Either way, it's common to group individual user accounts together in security domain groups to make them easier to manage.

For example, many companies create domain groups to emulate their organizational structure. If the company is organized functionally with employees in Marketing, Human Resources, and Operations departments, you'll often find those same domain groups used to organize user accounts.

Always try to use domain groups whenever possible. When you add a domain group to a SharePoint group, all members of the domain groups receive the same permissions. When user accounts are added or removed from the domain group — either because of promotion or termination — you don't have to make any changes to the membership of your SharePoint groups.

You can't assign SharePoint groups to other SharePoint groups. You can assign only individual user accounts or domain groups.

Follow these steps to add users and domain groups to SharePoint groups:

1. **Browse to the People and Groups page of a site.**

2. **Click the All People heading in the Quick Launch bar.**

    A list of user accounts and domain groups appears.

3. **Choose New⇨Add Users.**

    The Add Users page appears, as Figure 6-8 shows.

4. **In the Add Users section, type the names of individual user accounts or domain groups in the Users/Groups text box.**

    You should type the names in the form of domain\account. For example, if your domain name is SP and the domain group name is Employees, you type **SP\Employees**. There's no way to browse for user accounts and domain groups from within SharePoint.

    If you don't know the names of user accounts, you can type the e-mail address. SharePoint will try to map the e-mail address for the account. For example, the e-mail address employees@sp.com resolves to SP\Employees in my domain. Chances are you can use the e-mail addresses from your address book in Outlook.

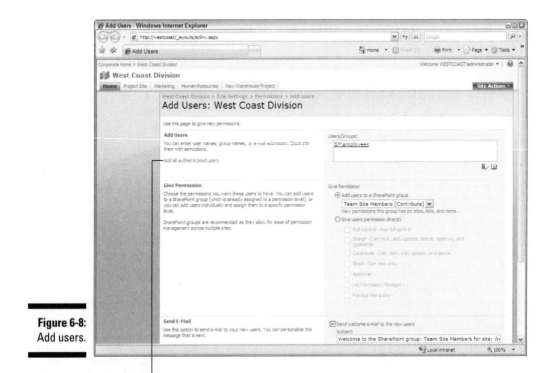

Figure 6-8:
Add users.

The Add All Authenticated Users link

To add the authenticated users domain group for a Windows authentication setup, click the Add All Authenticated Users link. (Refer to Figure 6-8.)This is a good way to ensure that all your network users have access to your SharePoint sites.

5. **Click the Check Names icon to resolve the account names with the identity management system.**

   The Check Names icon is the check mark icon below the Users/Groups text box. When you click this icon, SharePoint tries to find the user account in the identity management system, such as Active Directory (AD). If SharePoint can't find the user, then you can't add the account. If the names won't resolve, see your network administrator for assistance.

6. **Click the Browse button to select people from existing SharePoint groups.**

   The Browse button looks like a phone book and displays the Select People and Groups dialog box, as Figure 6-9 shows. You can add people that already exist in SharePoint to SharePoint groups. For example, assume you create a team site for a Marketing project. Chances are you want to add members of the Marketing team site to the Marketing Project team site. You can use the Select People and Groups dialog box to select those people.

   The controls that you use in the Add Users section are collectively known as the People Picker. You encounter the People Picker throughout SharePoint. For example, the Assigned To field in a Tasks or Issue Tracking list uses the People Picker. Any column that uses the type `Person or Group` displays the People Picker.

7. **In the Give Permission section, select a SharePoint group to add the users to from the drop-down menu.**

   You also have the option to assign permission levels directly to the users. I advise you to try to use SharePoint groups instead of granting permissions directly to user accounts. Using SharePoint groups with meaningful names such as Approver helps you to easily manage your permission assignments.

8. **Indicate whether to send a welcome e-mail to the users along with a personal message.**

   You must have e-mail configured for your SharePoint server. See Chapter 10 for details on setting up e-mail in SharePoint.

9. **Click OK.**

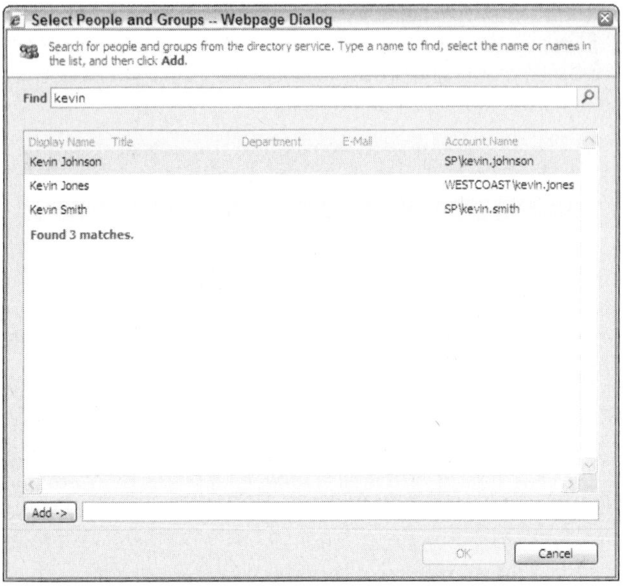

Figure 6-9:
Select
existing
people in
SharePoint.

When you assign a user account to a SharePoint group, SharePoint automatically creates a user profile in the site collection. User profiles in site collections are known as User Information to differentiate them from the User Profile feature in MOSS 2007 (see Chapter 12). User Information stores basic information about a person, such as their user account name, display name, and e-mail. You can access the User Information for a person by clicking on their name in the All People view of the People and Groups page.

If you're using domain groups instead of user accounts to assign users to SharePoint groups, then you won't see the individual user accounts in the All People page. A User Information record is generated for each user account in a domain group the first time the user logs into SharePoint.

MOSS 2007 keeps a site collection's User Information data synchronized with user profiles.

Using SharePoint groups

Members in the *Site* Owners SharePoint group create the permission structure for a site. The site owner should have a pretty good understanding of who needs to access the site and what that access should be. This means that members of the Information Technology staff usually shouldn't be site owners. Instead, you want members of the business departments to take responsibility for site ownership.

Permissions are contained within a site collection. Therefore, all the people, groups, and permission levels defined for a site collection are available to every site, list, and library within the collection. By default, all the securable objects in SharePoint inherit permissions from their parents.

Web sites, lists, libraries, folders, and list items are all securable in SharePoint.

When a site collection is created, all the content structures within the site collection inherit permissions from the site collection. For example, when you create a new site collection using the Collaboration Portal (see Chapter 11), all the sites, lists, and libraries in the portal inherit permissions from the top-level site. The default permissions configuration for a site collection is as follows:

✔ The *Site* Owners, *Site* Visitors, and *Site* Members groups are created.

✔ The primary and secondary site collection administrators are added to the site's Site Owners group. These administrators are specified at the time the site collection is created.

✔ Default SharePoint groups, such as Approvers and Hierarchy Managers, are created and given appropriate permissions.

The site collection's site owner should take responsibility for planning the permissions. If desired, the site owner can delegate the responsibility of implementing the permissions to members of the Hierarchy Managers group.

Now that you know how to add new users and domain groups to a SharePoint group (see the previous section) finish setting up security for a site collection by doing the following:

1. **Add user accounts or domain groups to the *Site* Visitors group.**

   The Site Visitors group has Read permissions, which enables this group to view the site collection's content.

   I suggest you add the Authenticated Users domain group to the Site Visitors group. This enables all your network users to access your site collection.

2. **Add user accounts or domain groups to the *Site* Members group.**

   Members of the Site Members group have Contribute permissions, which allow them to add content to the site collection.

3. **Add users to the Hierarchy Manager and Designers groups.**

   You may want to create a separate permission level for consultants. WSS doesn't have these groups by default, but you can create similar groups if you need that kind of role.

4. **Configure unique permissions for content structures in and below the top-level site.**

You have to stop inheriting permissions from the top-level site before you can create unique permissions for sites, lists, and libraries. See the next section, "Breaking Inheritance," for details.

5. **Add sites to the site collection.**

You have the option to inherit permissions or use unique permissions at the time you create the site.

Remember that everything *in* the site collection inherits *from* the site collection by default. Make sure your site collection permissions don't grant too many people access.

To make contacting site owners and designers easy, consider adding the Contact Details and Site Users Web parts to your sites, as shown in Figure 6-10.

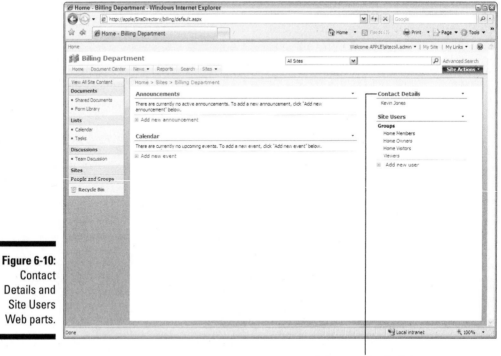

Figure 6-10:
Contact Details and Site Users Web parts.

A Contact Details link

Breaking Inheritance

In theory, you could set up security once for a site collection and allow everything to inherit. In reality, you may not want everyone to have the same access. You have the option to create unique permissions at the time you create a site. If you change your mind later, you have to break inheritance.

To stop inheriting permissions from a parent site, follow these steps:

1. **Browse to the People and Groups page for a site.**

2. **Click the Site Permissions header in the Quick Launch bar.**

   The Site Permissions page description displays `This Web site inherits permissions from its parent Web site.`

3. **Choose Actions⇨Edit Permissions.**

   A dialog box appears confirming that you wish to stop inheriting permissions.

4. **Click OK.**

   The site's permissions levels and SharePoint groups are no longer Read-Only.

To re-inherit permissions from the parent site, choose Actions⇨Inherit Permissions. Any changes you've made are discarded, and the site inherits the parent's permissions.

After you stop inheriting permissions, the parent's permissions are copied to the site. I suggest you delete the parent's permissions and start fresh with your custom permissions. Otherwise, it's easy to get confused about which permissions you want to use.

Follow these steps to remove existing permission assignments:

1. **Browse to the Site Permissions page.**

2. **Place check marks next to the permission assignments you wish to remove.**

3. **Click Actions⇨Remove User Permissions.**

4. **Click OK to confirm the deletions.**

   All the permissions are deleted.

Chances are you'll need to create new *Site* Owners, *Site* Members, and *Site* Visitors groups for the site. Instead of creating each group individually, SharePoint has a way to create the groups all at once.

To create a unique set of SharePoint groups for a site, do the following:

1. **Browse to the site's People and Groups page.**

   You must be a member of the site's Site Owners SharePoint group to create a new group. The site must have unique permissions.

2. **Click the Groups heading in the Quick Launch bar.**

3. **Choose Settings⇨Set Up Groups.**

   The Set Up Groups for this Site page appears, as shown in Figure 6-11.

4. **Select the Use an Existing Group or Create a New Group option to use for the *Site* Visitors, *Site* Members, and *Site* Owners groups.**

   If you choose a new group, use the text fields to add new users to the various new groups.

5. **Click OK.**

It's usually sufficient to allow a site's content structures to inherit permissions from the site. You shouldn't try to secure everything individually. But there may be times when you need to secure a folder in a library or limit access to a list. You may want to delegate ownership to a list or to library administrators.

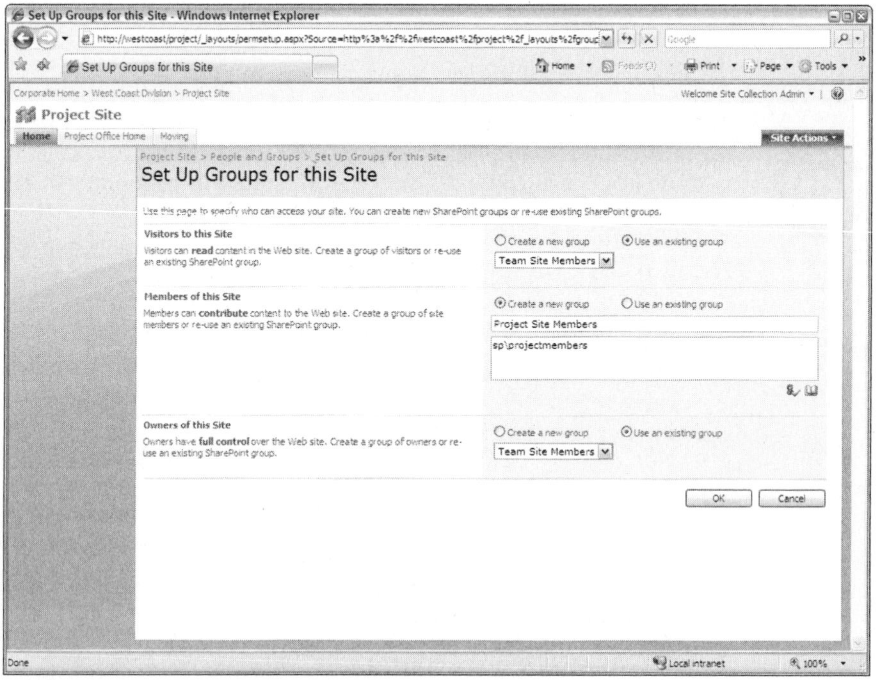

Figure 6-11:
Set up groups for a site.

In order to manage permissions, the user must have the Manage Permissions permission.

To create unique permissions for a list or library, follow these steps:

1. **Browse to the list or library.**

2. **Choose Settings⇨Document Library Settings or Settings⇨List Settings.**

   The Customize page appears.

3. **Click the Permissions for This Document Library link or the Permissions for This List link.**

   The Permissions page appears.

4. **Choose Actions⇨Edit Permissions.**

   A confirmation dialog box appears.

   You must be a member of the Hierarchy Managers group to edit permissions.

5. **Click OK.**

6. **Manage the permissions.**

   Managing permissions on lists and libraries is the same as managing permissions for sites. See the section, "Managing SharePoint Groups," earlier in this chapter, for details.

Follow these steps to create unique permissions for a list item, document, or folder:

1. **Browse to the list or library where the item is stored.**

2. **Click the item's drop-down list.**

   A contextual menu appears.

3. **Click Manage Permissions.**

   The Permissions page appears.

4. **Follow Steps 4–6 in the preceding list.**

You can't create new SharePoint groups in lists and libraries. You can, however, add existing groups to the list or library. To add an existing SharePoint group to a list or library, do the following:

1. **Browse to the Permissions page for the list, library, or list item as described in the two preceding sets of steps.**

2. **Choose New⇨Add Users.**

   The Add Users page appears.

3. **Use the People Picker in the Add Users section to add the SharePoint group.**

   See the section, "Assigning users to SharePoint groups," earlier in this chapter, for details on using the People Picker.

4. **Assign permissions to the group.**

5. **Click OK.**

   The SharePoint group has access to the list, library, or list item.

Be careful about adding users to groups at the list or library level. You're actually adding users to the entire site collection group. Individual lists and libraries don't have their own SharePoint groups.

Chapter 7

Managing Data with SharePoint

. . . .

. . . .

*A*ll businesses need a means to store and process data. That most often means using a database or a spreadsheet, sometimes both. Using multiple tools that aren't easily connected together creates islands of information. Sure, you can use Excel to query a database. But how easy is it to upload data from an Excel spreadsheet to a database?

SharePoint gives you the best of both worlds when it comes to managing data. Users can use familiar tools, like Excel and an Internet browser, to interact with data and files in SharePoint lists and libraries. The data entered into lists and libraries is stored in databases where it can be backed up, monitored, and queried. In other words, *managed.*

SharePoint provides a number of predefined lists and libraries that most companies find very useful right out of the box. A Tasks list is very useful in tracking project tasks, and the Shared Documents document library is very useful for managing documents on a team site.

Keep in mind that SharePoint is more than just a repository for dumping files and filling out task forms. SharePoint's strength lies in its toolset of powerful features that make it possible for you to use lists and libraries to manage data that's pertinent to your organization. The building blocks for customizing SharePoint's lists and libraries include:

✔ **Columns:** Define the name/value pairs users fill out when they add a document or list item to a library or list.

✔ **Views:** Organize data and provide ad-hoc reporting tools.

✔ **Content types:** Associate a set of columns with workflows and other properties to create reusable entities.

Underlying these building blocks is a Web site creation framework for lists and libraries that generates Web pages and fill-in Web forms with columns, views, and content types you define. This framework makes it possible to use SharePoint's lists and libraries as full-fledged data entry applications.

For example, instead of creating a custom ASP.NET Web page with a set of labels, textboxes, drop-down lists, and a Submit button, you can customize a SharePoint list by defining the columns for which you wish to capture data. SharePoint automatically generates forms for creating new entries and editing existing ones. What's more, you don't have to manage a database and worry about administrative tasks like backup jobs. SharePoint takes care of that for you.

You can use columns, views, and content types with any of the predefined lists and libraries provided by SharePoint. Alternatively, you can start from scratch and create your own custom lists. In this chapter, I explain how to customize lists and libraries in SharePoint so they match the specific data needs of your organization.

Defining Columns

Columns are a defining characteristic of lists and libraries in SharePoint. When you browse to a list or library in SharePoint, you see column headings across the top of the view. The columns you see are determined by the kind of list or library you create, the content types associated with the list or library, and the current view being displayed. For example, a document library includes columns such as Type, Name, and Modified. I discuss views and content types later in this chapter.

Columns are the name/value pairs used by a list or library to describe content. Columns defined for use with a single list or library are *list columns.* You can also create *site columns,* which aren't associated with a list or library. Rather, they separate the column's definition from being tied to a single list or library so that they can be reused across the entire site.

Columns are also called fields or properties, depending on the context of how the list item or document is viewed. When a user is interacting with a document in Word or Excel, columns are referred to as *properties*. When a developer is defining columns for a list, columns are referred to as *fields.* Also, the fields in an InfoPath form template map to columns in a library. InfoPath form templates are used to create electronic forms. See Chapter 8 for more information on InfoPath.

The data captured in columns, fields, and properties is often called *metadata,* or data about data. When used with a document in a document library, columns describe additional properties about the document, such as whether the document is confidential or when the document can be destroyed. When used with a list item in a list, columns are the list item itself. For example, a Tasks list has columns such as Title, Assigned To, and Due Date. The values entered into these columns are the list item.

You aren't stuck only with the columns defined for existing types of list and libraries. You can create your own custom columns in order to capture data unique to your business. The four properties that define a SharePoint column are:

- ✔ **Column name:** This is the name displayed for the column. Think of the name as a caption rather than as an identifier. SharePoint creates unique identifiers for all the columns you create, so the column name is really just a descriptive name.

- ✔ **Column data type:** The column data type defines the kind of information that's stored in the column and how that information is stored and displayed. For example, use a `number` data type if you want to use the column's value in a calculation. SharePoint includes its own set of data types. Some of these types correspond to familiar types (such as `number` and `string`), but others are created just for SharePoint, such as `Person` or `Group`. I list the SharePoint data types and their corresponding data types in the .NET Framework in Table 7-1.

  Choosing the right column data types is important because the data type stored in the column determines how the data is stored in the database and how the data is formatted on the screen. For example, you can't add together two text values, but you can add currency and number columns.

- ✔ **Column group:** You can define groups for categorizing your columns. SharePoint includes a set of groups that's used for defining the default SharePoint columns.

- ✔ **Optional data type settings:** Each data type has its set of properties that further defines the column. Examples include the ability to enter a formula for a calculated column or the ability to specify the maximum number of characters for a text column. You also have the option to specify a default value for the column and mark the column as required.

Table 7-1	SharePoint Column Data Types	
Column Data Types	*.NET Data Type*	*What It's Used For*
Single line of text	System.String	Collects and displays a single of text, including numbers used as text (such as telephone numbers).
Multiple lines of text	System.String	Collects and displays multiple lines of text.
Choice	System.String	Displays a menu list of options.
Number	System.Double	Stores numerical values that may be used for calculations.
Currency	System.Double	Stores and formats numerical values of money.
Date and Time	System.DateTime	Stores and formats dates and times.
Lookup	System.String	Allows user to select a value from another list on the site.
Yes/No	System.Boolean	Stores true/false information with a check box.
Person or Group	System.String	Displays the names of users or SharePoint groups.
Hyperlink or Picture	System.String	Displays a hyperlink to a Web page or an image,
Calculated	N/A	Displays results of a formula.
Business Data	N/A	Looks up data from the Business Data Catalog.
Publishing HTML	System.String	Edits and displays HTML.
Publishing Image	System.String	Stores links to images for publishing on a Web page.
Publishing Hyperlink	System.String	Stores links for publishing on a Web page.
Summary Links	System.String	Displays a Publishing page's set of links.
Audience Targeting	System.String	Displays information on audience targeting.

Site columns also define the default control used to display the column's information. For example, the Choice column type allows you to select whether to use a drop-down list, radio buttons, or check boxes for collecting and displaying data.

Defining list columns

When you create a new list or library, it comes with a default set of columns. For example, the document library has columns for Title, Type, and Modified By. The columns are the fields you use to enter data about the list item or document. In the case of a list item, the columns *are* the list item. For example, when you enter a list item into an Announcements list, the list item is the announcement, which in turn is made up of columns such as Title, Body, and Expires.

In the case of a document, you can think of the columns as the document's properties. More often than not, you want to store more information about a document than just its title, its type, or whether it has been modified. For example, you may also want to categorize the document and specify whether the document is confidential.

No problem. In SharePoint, it's easy to add new columns to your lists and libraries. Just keep in mind that you'll more than likely want to add the columns right to your list and library and that, when you add the column to the list or library, the column is available only to that particular list or library. Columns added directly to the list or library are *list columns*.

To add a new column to an existing list or library, follow these steps:

1. **Browse to the list or library where you wish to add the column.**

   You can click the View All Site Content link on the left side of your SharePoint site to view a list of all the lists and libraries on your site.

2. **Choose Settings⇨List Settings (for a list) or Settings⇨Document Library Settings (for a document library.)**

   The Customize page appears.

   You must have the Manage Lists permission to access the list or library's Customize page. Members of the Designers and Manage Hierarchy SharePoint groups have this permission by default.

3. **Click the Create Column link in the Columns section.**

   The Create Column page appears.

4. **Type a name for the column in the Column Name field.**

   The name you enter here is the name that appears in the list.

5. **Select the type of information you plan to store in the column.**

   This is where you select the column's data type, such as currency or date and time.

6. **Enter additional column settings.**

   Depending on the type of column you create, different settings are available for configuring the column. At a minimum, you can enter a description and indicate whether the column is required. You may be able to enter formulas and formatting information or select other lists to use to display data depending on the column's type.

7. **Click OK.**

   The column appears in the list of columns on the Customize page.

You can edit an existing column by clicking the column in the Customize page. You can edit some of the columns settings (such as Name and Description), but you can't always change the column type.

Changing a column type could result in loss of data. Make a backup of the data before changing the type.

You can also use the Customize page to set the order in which the columns appear when the user edits the list item. Click the Column Ordering link in the Columns section to specify the position from the top for each column. If you want to control whether a column appears in the list, you can customize the list's view as I describe in the section, "Get a New View," later in this chapter.

Any time you have large quantities of data in a SharePoint list, you may want to mark a column for indexing. An *indexed column* is stored in the database with a pointer to the actual record, similar to a card catalog in a library. The index improves performance because SharePoint doesn't have to sort, filter, or query all entries in a list. When you choose a column for SharePoint to create an index on, SharePoint stores the lookup ID for all the records and the value of the indexed column. You can mark a column to be indexed by clicking the Indexed Columns link in the list or on the library's Customize page.

I recommend indexing a column only in situations where you anticipate performance issues with a list. I also suggest indexing a column when you have views that take advantage of the column for sorting or filtering.

Indexing a column in SharePoint doesn't create an index in SQL Server.

Defining site columns

Sometimes, you may want to reuse column definitions across multiple lists or even across multiple libraries. SharePoint makes this possible by allowing you to set up *site columns* — columns that you define at the site level and then make available to all the lists and libraries in the site collection. For example, if you want to capture the customer associated with a list item or document, you may choose to define the customer column only once at the site level and then reuse it throughout the site.

Site columns are also called *column templates* or *column definitions.*

When you use a site column in a list, the column is copied to the list and becomes a list column. You can modify the column just like any other list column.

Even though site columns are copied to lists, you can make global changes to the site column and propagate those changes to lists where the column is used. Click an existing column in the Site Column gallery and select the option to update all list columns based on the site column.

Before you can add a site column to a list, you first have to create the site column itself. Site columns are created at the site or site collection level. The site column can be used only in the site where it's created and any subsites below it. I recommend creating site columns at the top-level of the site collection unless you know that you need the site column only for a limited group of sites.

Each site has its own Site Column gallery where you can create and manage site columns. By default, the columns in the gallery are grouped according to the kinds of column they are, but you're free to create your own custom groups if the default groupings don't fit your purposes.

SharePoint has a site column category — Hidden — which is reserved for built-in columns that you can't modify.

Creating a new site column is very similar to creating a list column. To create a site column, do the following:

1. **Browse to the Site Settings page of the site where you wish to create the site column.**

   In a MOSS 2007 site, choose Site Actions⇨Site Settings⇨Modify All Settings. In a WSS site, choose Site Actions⇨Site Settings.

   In most cases, create the site column in the top-level site of the site collection.

2. **Click the Site Columns link in the Galleries section.**

The Site Column Gallery appears.

3. **Click the Create button**.

The New Site Column page appears.

4. **In the Name and Type section, enter the site column's name and column type.**

Refer to Table 7-1 for a list of column types.

5. **Select a site column group, such as Custom Columns, to categorize the column.**

You can place your column into any existing site column group or create a custom group by selecting the New Group radio button. The column group determines where the site column appears in the Site Column Gallery.

6. **Enter additional column settings.**

Similar to list columns, each column type includes a set of additional options that you can specify, such as the maximum number of characters and the default value.

7. **Click OK**.

The site column appears in the Site Column gallery below the group that you select in Step 5.

You can also modify existing site columns with the Site Column gallery. Click any of the site columns you see in the gallery. You can modify the column's name, group, and some additional column settings, but you can't change the column's type.

You use site columns with content types or as list columns in a list or library. I discuss using site columns with a content type later in this chapter. Follow these steps to use a site column as a list column:

1. **Browse to the list or library where you wish to use the site column.**

You can click the View All Site Content link on the left side of your SharePoint site to view a list of all the lists and libraries on your site.

2. **Choose Settings➪List Settings (for a list) or Settings➪Document Library Settings (for a document library).**

The Customize page appears.

3. **Click the Add from Existing Site Columns link in the Columns section.**

The Add Columns from Site Columns page appears.

4. **Click a column from the list of available site columns in the left list box.**

When you click any of the available site columns, you see the column's description and group below the list box.

5. **Click the Add button to move the column to the Columns to Add list box on the right, as shown in Figure 7-1.**

6. **In the Options section of the Add Columns from Site Columns page, use the check box to indicate whether to add the site column to all content types used in the list or library.**

   Each item in the list or library is associated with a content type. You can use content types as a way to specify which columns are associated with a certain kind of document or list item. See the section, "Enabling Content Types," later in this chapter.

7. **Still in the Options section, use the appropriate check box to indicate whether to add the column to the list's (or library's) default view.**

8. **Click OK.**

   The column appears in the list of columns on the Customize page.

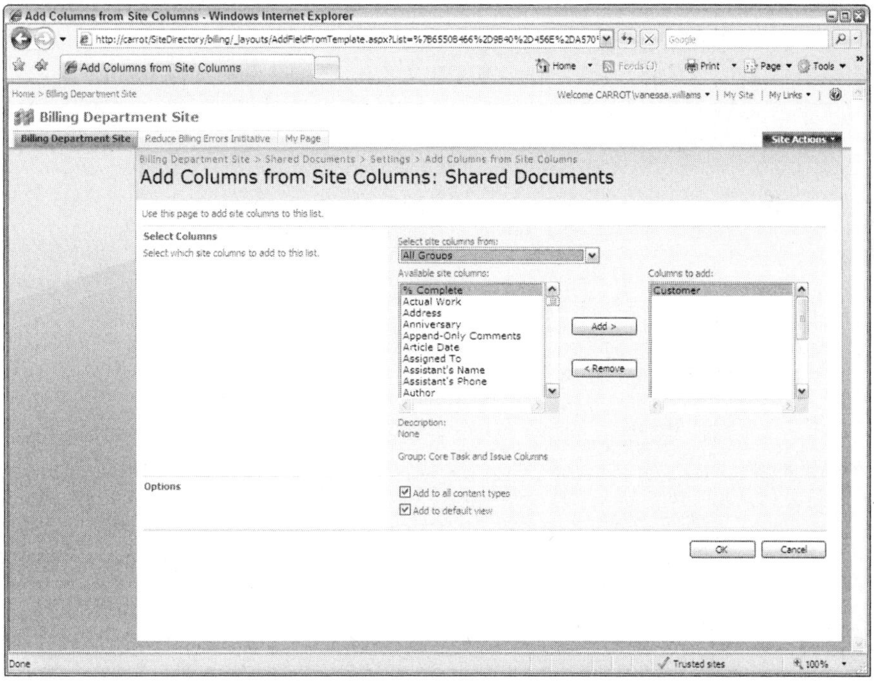

Figure 7-1:
Add the site column to the list or library.

After you add a site column to a list or library, the column is copied to the list and becomes a list column. You can modify the column's name, types, and additional settings just like you would any list column. You can also update the list column by editing the site column in the Site Column gallery and choosing to update list columns based on the site column.

Get a New View

When you browse to a list or library in SharePoint, you see the default view. *Views* define the list columns that are displayed on the Web page. You can modify existing views or create entirely new views. You assign a name to the view, and, from then on, it can be selected via the View menu, as shown in Figure 7-2. The View menu also provides options to modify the current view or create a new view.

You can also manage views with the list or library's Customize page.

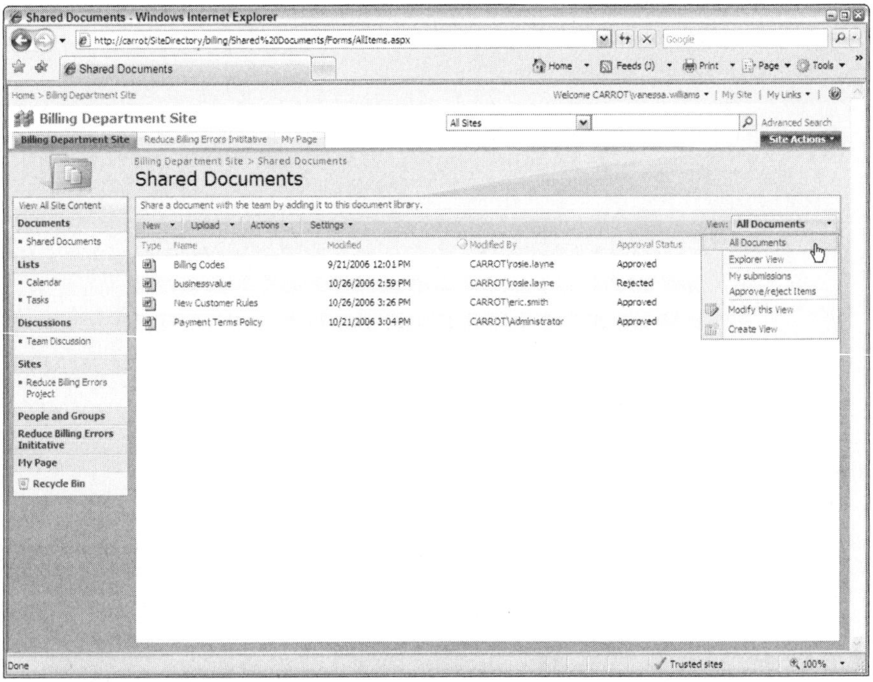

Figure 7-2:
Use the View menu to change or modify the view.

Modifying views

Views are an excellent way to customize information display. Unlike a traditional Windows file folder, you aren't limited to using folders only as a means to organize data. You can use views to display list items or documents with any built-in or custom list column.

In addition to defining the list columns that are displayed, you use views to define column positioning, sorting, filtering, grouping, and totals. You can also define some styling and layout properties for the view.

Before you create a new view, I suggest you make sure that an existing view doesn't already meet your needs. Also consider whether you have all the columns you need to create your view. If not, create those columns first and then create the view.

You can use *calculated columns* in your views — columns that use formulas. You can also use calculations to create filtered views. Using formulas in columns and filters allows you to create unique ways to display data.

To create a new view, follow these steps:

1. **Browse to the list or library where you wish to create the view.**

2. **Choose View⇨Create View.**

   The Create View page appears.

3. **On the Create View page, choose either a view format (for example, Standard View) or an existing view on which you wish to base the new view.**

   The Create View page appears..

   I explain view formats in the upcoming section, "Using special views."

   Keep in mind that not all the same view settings are available for all view formats. Just to keep things (relatively) straightforward, the steps I outline here walk you through all the options for views with the Standard View view format.

4. **In the Name section, type a name for the view and use the check box to indicate whether the view is the list or library's default view.**

5. **In the Audience section, select whether the view is personal or public.**

   By default, all views are public. You can create your own personal views, but only you can use this view. Personal views might be useful for list administrators or content approvers who need to look at the list or library's content differently than general users.

6. **In the Columns section, place a check mark next to the columns you want to display in the view and indicate their position from the left of the screen.**

7. **In the Sort section, select up to two columns by which you wish the list sorted.**

8. **In the Filter section, create a filter by selecting a column as well as an operator and then entering a value, as shown in Figure 7-3.**

   You can use multiple columns to filter.

9. **In the Group By section, select any columns by which you wish to group the list items.**

   You can also choose whether to show groups collapsed or expanded. The default option is Collapsed. I like to use the Collapsed option because it allows the user to see all the groups on a single page.

10. **In the Total section, select totalizing formulas for columns you wish to total.**

    The totalizing choices available depend on the type of information stored in the column. For example, you can add a count total for text columns, but you can use Minimize, Maximize, Average, and Sum for number columns.

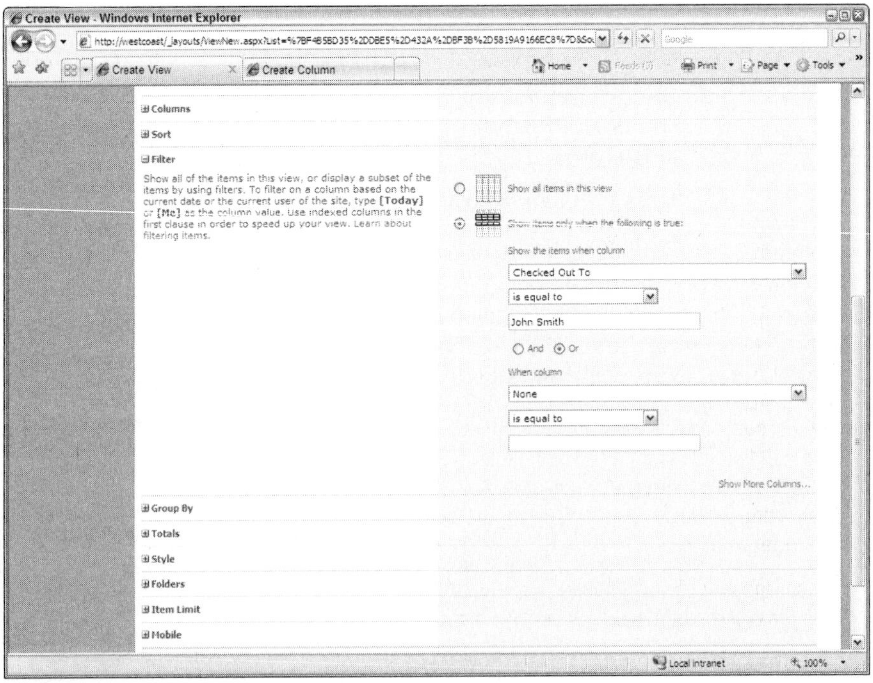

Figure 7-3:
Create a
filter.

11. **In the Style section, select the style to use for displaying the view.**

    SharePoint includes several styles that you can use to control the layout of information in the view. The Default view presents a tabular view of the data.

12. **In the Folders section, select whether to display items in folders or without folders.**

    I discourage users from using folders in lists or libraries because files can be hard to find in a mess of nested folders, but sometimes it's necessary to meet permissions requirements. You can use the Folders option of a view to ignore the folder structure and display all items in a flat list.

13. **In the Item Limit section, select whether to display all items or limit the number of items returned on a single page.**

    Users can page forward to see additional items.

14. **In the Mobile section, indicate whether SharePoint should create a mobile version of the view.**

    I suggest creating unique views for mobile use rather than trying to create a dual purpose view.

15. **Click OK.**

Creating a parent/child view with folders

Folders often get a bad rap in SharePoint because they're so easily misused. If you've ever had to double-click through a half dozen folders to get to a file, you know how frustrating it can be to have a folder structure forced on you. I often advise people to resist the temptation to use folders solely as an organizing tool. Using columns and views allows you to create multiple ways of organizing the same list of data without limiting yourself to a single folder structure. If ten people are sharing a document library, those ten people can each create their own view of the library. If the files are placed inside folders, users tend to assume that they're stuck with a single organizing structure — however, the folders are organized.

One purpose for folders, however, can't be easily created with columns and views. A folder in a list or library is nothing more than a list item. As such, it has all the same characteristics of list items, including the ability to store metadata. Using one content type to define a folder and another to define the list's items makes it possible to display a parent/child relationship between the folder and the list item contained within.

A classic example of parent/child relationships is the Master/Detail view. For example, you could use a folder to display order header data with list items as the order items. SharePoint discussions boards are another good example. The discussion board consists of discussion folders that represent discussion threads. Each discussion container has its own set of metadata and contains all the messages for the thread.

Creating a new view often involves a lot of modifying after the fact to get the view the way you want it. Choose View➪Modify This View while you're in the list or library to modify the view.

You can sort and filter a list's contents with the list or library's column headers without creating a view. In fact, this is a great way to use SharePoint as an ad hoc reporting tool. Each column header expands to display a menu of sorting and filtering options, as shown in Figure 7-4.

Each view of a list or library has a unique URL. You can use the URL of a view on the site's Quick Launch navigation or any time you want to take users to a specific view of the list or library. See Chapter 5 for more details on modifying site navigation.

Using special views

SharePoint provides several view formats that you can use to display the contents of your lists and libraries. You combine these formats with other view settings, such as column order and filters, to create unique views of your lists and libraries.

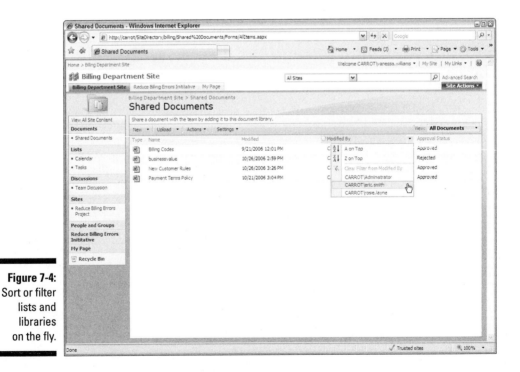

Figure 7-4:
Sort or filter lists and libraries on the fly.

The view formats available depend on the kind of list you're working with. The four view formats you'll see most often are:

- ✔ **Standard:** This is the default Web page view that you see when you first access a list or library.

- ✔ **Datasheet:** This is a grid view of the list or library similar to a spreadsheet. Any Standard view can be converted to Datasheet view by choosing Actions➪Edit in Datasheet. Datasheet view includes a pane that allows you to export the list's contents to Access or Excel. See Chapter 9 for more information about working with lists and libraries in Access and Excel.

- ✔ **Calendar:** As its name implies, this is a Calendar view of data, which displays a day, week, or month view of a calendar. A default Calendar view is created for all events lists. You can create custom views with the Calendar view format.

- ✔ **Gantt:** This creates a view that displays a Gantt chart along with a list of tasks. Gantt views make it possible for you to use SharePoint for light project management, such as managing tasks.

SharePoint includes other view formats for specialized kinds of lists. For example, the Discussion list includes view formats for displaying discussions as thread or in a Chronological Flat view.

Document libraries have an Explorer view that allows you to drag and drop files into the library by using a Web page. You can also open the library in a Windows Explorer folder by choosing Actions➪Open with Windows Explorer in the Library.

In addition to these view formats, you can use a few other built-in views to view a list's contents. These include:

- ✔ **Mobile:** By default, SharePoint creates pared-down, text-only views of sites, lists, and libraries suitable for viewing on a mobile device, such as a Smartphone. You can find the URL for mobile versions of a list by looking in the Mobile section of the Edit View page. If you don't see a Mobile section, SharePoint doesn't generate a mobile version for that view format.

- ✔ **Detail:** Any time you want to view an individual list item, you can click the item to display a menu with the View Properties and Edit Properties menu items. Both of these options display a form view of the column values for the selected item.

- ✔ **RSS:** SharePoint generates RSS feeds for all lists and libraries. See Chapter 10 for more information on enabling RSS for a list or library and view the RSS feed.

All views associated with a list or library are ASP.NET pages stored in the Forms folder of the list or library. When you create a custom view, SharePoint generates an ASP.NET page of the same name and places the file in the Forms folder. I discuss using Visual Studio 2005 or SharePoint Designer 2007 to edit ASP.NET pages in Chapter 16. Table 7-2 lists some of the default views and ASP.NET page filenames.

Table 7-2	Views and ASP.NET Page Filenames Used in SharePoint
View	*ASP.NET Page Filename*
Standard	`AllItems.aspx`
Datasheet	Not applicable — uses parameter `ShowInGrid=True` in the form's URL
Calendar	`Calendar.aspx`
Explorer	`WebFldr.aspx`
View Properties	`DispForm.aspx`
Edit Properties	`EditForm.aspx`

Enabling Content Types

Imagine being able to configure a document library so it could store only contracts. Imagine further that, when a new contract is added, it must be routed to a member of the legal department for review. The set of properties that define a document's data as well as how to handle that data is a *content type*.

Content types go beyond simple name/value pairs. In fact, they go beyond documents. Not only can you create complex properties with fields (such as multi-valued drop-down lists and Yes/No check boxes), but you can also associate document templates and workflows with content types. Content types can be used to define electronic forms, items in lists and libraries, and every kind of content you could think to store in SharePoint. A task is a content type. A Web Part page is a content type. A picture is a content type. Without content types, SharePoint would consist of lonely generic containers — lists and libraries with no sense of purpose.

A Web Part page as a content type? Surely, I've lost my mind. To the contrary, everything you work with in lists and libraries is a content type — contacts, issues, and even Web Part pages. Web Part pages are stored in libraries (see Chapter 4). They're files. Where else would you save them to? One of the properties that gets defined for content types is the document template. The template for a Word file or Excel spreadsheet automatically launches a blank file in those applications. The Web Part Page content type specifies a template that creates Web Part pages — the New Web Part Page. After you complete the New Web Part Page, SharePoint creates a new Web Part page in your document library.

MOSS 2007 adds a content type for Publishing Pages, which is another kind of SharePoint Web page. The document template for the Page content type launches the Create Page page. By default, Publishing Pages are saved to a site's Pages library. See Chapter 16 for more details on working with Publishing Pages.

SharePoint provides a predefined set of content types. The content types you create inherit from these content types to create a parent-child relationship. Some content types included with Windows SharePoint Services (WSS) are Item, Document, and Folder. (Document and Folder inherit from Item.) A whole slew of list-specific content types — types like Contact, Issue, and Task — inherit from Item. The columns and behaviors you see in the lists and libraries you create are determined by these content types.

Previous versions of SharePoint didn't include the concept of a content type. Instead of using generic lists and libraries that are given purpose by content types, previous versions of SharePoint defined each list individually — a Tasks list, an Announcements list, and so on. There was no way to define content in one place (a content type) and reuse it.

Microsoft Office SharePoint Server (MOSS) 2007 adds additional content types to support the extra features it provides. You'll find content types for Business Intelligence, InfoPath, Page Layout, and Publishing. All these content types inherit from the Item content type in WSS.

Content types make it easy to separate a content's properties from its storage. In previous versions of SharePoint, you define properties in a single document library or list. Content types associate properties with the content. As a result, you can reuse content types across multiple lists and libraries within a site collection.

Content types created in WSS allow you to define the following set of properties and behaviors:

 ✔ *Site columns* define the set of properties that appear in the list or library.

 ✔ *Workflows* define the workflows associated with the content type.

You can create list- or library-specific columns instead of creating site columns and site content types. You can also create site columns in a list or library without using a site content type. I suggest you use site columns or site content types any time you need to reuse a column or other properties more than two times.

MOSS 2007 adds the following additional properties:

- **Document Information Panel:** Here you can define an InfoPath form as way of collecting property data in an Office 2007 client. By default, SharePoint uses a default template to generate the form, but you can create a custom InfoPath form.

- **Information Management Policies:** A great way to define the policies that apply to this content type. See Chapter 15 for more on policies.

- **Document Converters:** Use this feature to determine the options available for converting documents from one format to another. Choices available include Word Document to Web Page and InfoPath Form to Web Page.

Defining content types

Content types are created at the site collection level. All the document libraries and lists within the site collection have access to the content type, including libraries created within the Document Center and Records Center in MOSS 2007. Follow these steps to create a new content type:

1. **Browse to the Site Settings page for the site where you wish to create the content type.**

   In a MOSS 2007 site, choose Site Actions⇨Site Settings⇨Modify All Settings. In a WSS site, choose Site Actions⇨Site Settings.

   Content types created in the top-level site of the site collection are available to all sites in the site collection. If a content type pertains only to a particular subsite, you may wish to create it at the subsite level.

2. **Click the Site Content Types link in the Galleries section.**

   The Site Content Type Gallery page appears.

3. **Click the Create button.**

   The New Site Content Type page appears.

Content types as global objects

If you've done any computer programming, you might equate the data and behaviors captured in a content type with objects in object-oriented programming. Although that's not technically accurate, I think it's a useful analogy for figuring out how you want to use content types in your organization.

The obvious use for content types is to define the types of documents that your company uses. Using content types for documents makes it easy to ensure that libraries that store those documents capture the right information every time.

A not-so-obvious use for content types is as global objects for use with lists. The columns defined for a list become the list item. You can use a content type to essentially create a template of columns, workflows, and other settings that can be used in lists. For example, you could create a content type called Customer or Invoice. The content type would display a set of site columns that define what it means to be a Customer or an Invoice. You could associate workflows with the content types to ensure that an action always occurs when a user creates a new Customer list item or an Invoice list item.

4. **Type a name and description for the content type.**

   The name and description that you enter appears in the New menu when you associate the content type with a list or library. Include a description that informs users of when they should use the content type. For example, if you create a Short Term Lease Contract content type that's intended for use with leases of less than six months, provide that description.

5. **Choose a Parent Content Type from the Select parent content type from drop-down list.**

   A list of related content types appears in the Parent Content Type drop-down list.

   Content types related to documents inherit from the Document Content Types parent type.

6. **Choose a content type from the Parent Content Type drop-down list.**

   Choose the content type closest to the type of content you're creating. For example, choose Document for Word documents and Excel spreadsheets or Task to create a new content type, such as Project Task.

   You can create a new content type to use as a parent if you want to create a hierarchy of content types. For example, you could create a new content type called Spreadsheet that you could use to associate properties with spreadsheets. The trick when it comes to deciding whether you should create a content type or use an existing type is whether you need a separate set of properties that you can't find in an existing type.

7. **In the Group section, select an existing group to put the new content type into or create a new group.**

   For example, if you want to create a group of content types for contracts, you could create that group here.

8. **Click OK.**

   The Site Content Type page for the new content type appears. You can use this page to associate workflows, site columns, and other properties with the content type.

You use the Site Content Type page to define the properties for the site content type. Every time you associate the site content type with a document library or list, you take that bag of properties with you. Table 7-3 lists the properties you can manage for a site content type. Note that the links listed in Table 7-3 include links for WSS and MOSS 2007. Document information panels, information management policies, and document conversion are available in MOSS 2007.

Table 7-3	Site Content Type Properties	
Property	*Link Used to Set Property*	*What It's Used For*
Parent content type	Parent	View the parent content type's properties.
Document template	Advanced Settings	Set the template used after the user clicks New in the Library.
Workflows	Workflow Settings	Set the workflows associated with the type.
Property template	Document Information Panel Settings	Set whether the library displays a default template for capturing properties or a custom InfoPath form.
Information management policies	Information Management Policy Settings	Set policies for the content type.
Document conversion	Manage Document Conversion for This Content Type	Set properties to convert the document to other languages.
Metadata	Add from Existing Site Columns	Select site column to associate with the content type.

Using content types

The default content types provided by SharePoint are somewhat generic. Consider creating your own content types that are specific to your business. For example, you may define several custom content types that inherit from the Document content type. These custom document types might include contracts, proposals, and request forms. You define the columns and behaviors that you want to see for all documents of the type Contract or Proposal by using the steps defined in the preceding section.

Whether you use built-in content types or create your own custom types, you need to associate the content types with lists and libraries before they can be used. By default, lists and libraries don't use content types. By enabling content types in a list or library, the list or library uses the columns, document templates, workflows, and other properties defined in the content type. You can even indicate what content types appear on the New menu in the list or library.

To enable content types in a list or library, do the following:

1. **Browse to the list or library where you wish to use the content types.**

   You can click the View All Site Content link on the left side of a site to view a list of all the lists and libraries on the site.

2. **Choose either Settings⇨List Settings (for a list) or Settings⇨Document Library Settings (for a document library).**

   The Customize page appears.

3. **Click the Advanced Settings link in the General Settings section.**

   The Advanced Settings page appears.

4. **Select the Yes radio button in the Content Types section.**

5. **Click OK.**

   The Content Types section appears in the Customize page.

You must associate a content type, such as content types for managing contracts, with the list or library.

Use the Content Types section (see Figure 7-5) to associate specific content types with the list or library or manage existing types:

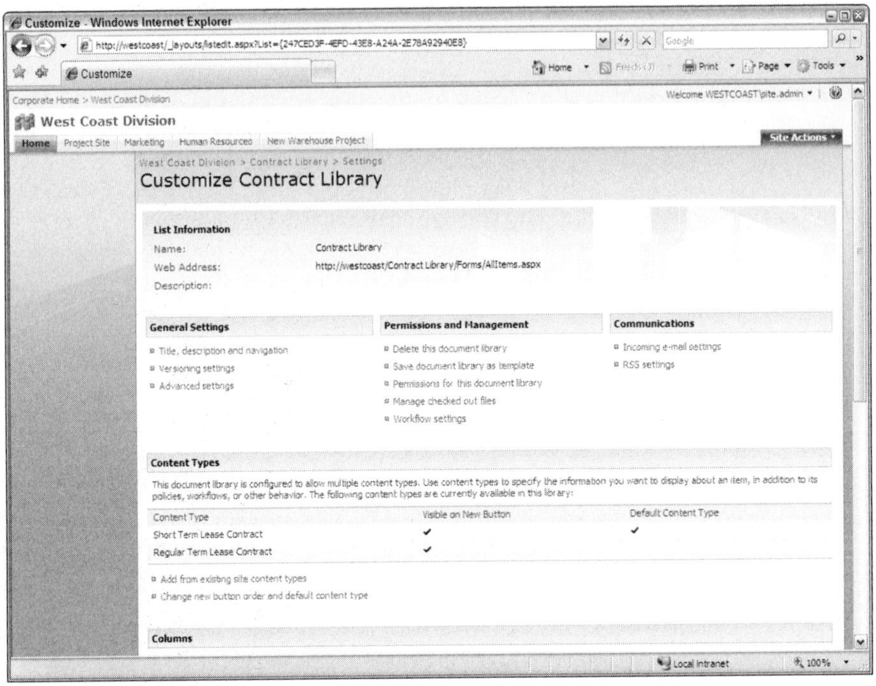

Figure 7-5:
Manage list content types.

Click the hyperlinked name of a content type listed to make changes to the content types. Any changes you make are limited in scope to the current list or library and don't affect the site content type.

After you associate a content type with a list or library, the content type is copied to the list or library and becomes a list content type.

Click the Add from Existing Site Content Types link to add new site content types to the list or library. See the section, "Defining content types," earlier in this chapter for information on creating site content types.

When a user saves a file to a library that uses a content type, the user is prompted for the document type. After the user selects a type, he or she is prompted to complete the properties defined for the content type selected.

Click the Change New Button Order and Default Content Type link to set the order in which content types appear on the New menu. The first content type is the default content type. When a user uses the New menu to create a new document, SharePoint uses the document template associated with the content type. Figure 7-6 shows the New menu with two content types.

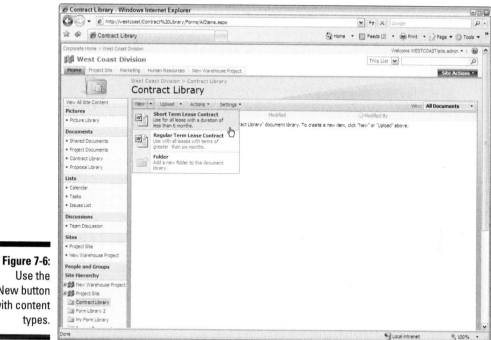

Figure 7-6:
Use the
New button
with content
types.

Chapter 8

Managing Business Processes with SharePoint

In This Chapter

▶ Associating workflow templates with lists, libraries, and content types

▶ Initiating and participating in workflows

▶ Keeping track of workflow instances

▶ Deploying and managing InfoPath form templates

▶ Using forms libraries

---

*A*ll businesses have loads of business processes and the forms that support them. There's a process for requesting to use the conference room. There's a process for getting an expense report approved. In many organizations, there are many kinds of processes that fall outside the scope of traditional information systems. As a result, these processes remain mostly manual.

Having a manual process for requesting a conference room may be annoying, but automating it probably doesn't create a competitive advantage. This explains why so many trivial processes are still manual. However, important processes, such as approving expense reports and escalating customer complaints, often aren't automated. And I don't count filling out a Word document and e-mailing it to the boss as automated.

SharePoint provides extensive support for managing business processes by using *workflows*. I like to think of workflows as executable flowcharts. After a series of steps is identified, SharePoint generates tasks and other kinds of list items to facilitate movement through the workflow.

Another important feature that SharePoint uses to support business processes involves the use of electronic forms. Unlike the Word documents that you e-mail to your boss, these forms use InfoPath 2007 to create an intelligent form complete with data validation and the ability to save the form's data separate from the form itself. Better yet, Microsoft Office SharePoint Server (MOSS) 2007 can display InfoPath forms in the browser so users don't need any special software installed on their computers.

Using Workflows

If you look at many of the documents stored in document libraries, they're used to support or initiate some kind of business process. For example, it's common to use spreadsheets to support calculations used for tax and regulatory filings. Oftentimes, only the person who completes the filing truly understands all the support documents required to create the filing. Heck, he may be the only one who even knows when the filing is due! Another common business process is document review and approval where a document must be routed to several people for feedback.

Rather than keeping all the information about business processes locked away with the people who do the work, SharePoint has a workflows feature that triggers and tracks the business processes associated with documents.

Workflow features in SharePoint are made possible by Windows Workflow Foundation (WF), which is part of version 3.0 of the .NET Framework.

Workflows can be used for more than just routing documents. Windows SharePoint Services (WSS) 3.0 includes a three-state workflow that makes it possible to track the status of list items and documents. The *three-state work-flow* allows you to assign three statuses, or *states,* that are used to trigger an action. The most obvious use for a three-state workflow is a SharePoint Issues list. Issue items in an Issues list have three possible states — Active, Resolved, and Closed. When an issue's status is updated, the three-state workflow creates tasks that notify assigned users of actions they need to take.

MOSS 2007 includes several document management workflows, including these:

- ✔ **Approval:** A serial workflow that sends a document to a series of approvers.

- ✔ **Collect Feedback:** A parallel workflow that requests feedback on a document from several reviewers.

- ✔ **Collect Signatures:** A workflow that's initiated in Office 2007 clients to gather electronic sign-off on the document.

- ✔ **Disposition Approval:** A workflow that allows approvers to determine whether expired documents are retained or deleted.

MOSS 2007 also includes a Translation workflow that's enabled for use with translation libraries.

The basic process for enabling and using workflows in SharePoint goes like this:

1. **An administrator associates a workflow with a list, library, or content type.**

In order for an administrator to associate a workflow, the workflow must be deployed to the server. Workflows are enabled as site features in a site collection.

2. **A user initiates an instance of the workflow with a document or list item.**

   The user may explicitly start the workflow, or the workflow may start automatically when an item is added to a list or library. The initiation experience is determined by the workflow.

3. **Workflow participants interact with the workflow through the various tasks that the workflow generates.**

   As actions are taken on the workflow's tasks, a workflow history is updated. When all the workflow tasks are complete, the workflow instance is complete.

At any time after a workflow instance is started, users or administrators may modify or terminate the workflow instance.

Associating workflows

Before users can use a workflow in a list or library, you must associate the workflow with the list or library. You can have multiple workflows of the same type in a single library. For example, you might have two approval workflows. One approval workflow routes to the immediate supervisor, and the other workflow routes to the supervisor's boss.

You can associate workflows with site content types. Instead of creating workflows in individual lists and libraries, associate the workflow with the content type to be assured that the workflow is always available. For example, you could create a content type for all Human Resources (HR) documents that includes a workflow that routes all documents to a member of the HR staff for review.

You can create custom workflows by using SharePoint Designer 2007 or Visual Studio 2005. To see a list of all the workflows available for a site collection, view the Workflows gallery in the site collection's Site Settings page. See Chapter 5 for details on accessing a site's Site Settings page.

WSS provides access to the workflows features of Windows Workflow Foundation (WF). The workflows described in this section are installed by MOSS 2007.

Okay, by now you know that you have to associate a workflow with a list or library before you can actually use that workflow with a list or library. Here's the part where you actually find out how to do that. It should come as no surprise that you associate workflows to a list or library with the Add a Workflow page. To access the Add a Workflow page for a list or library, do the following:

1. **Browse to the Customize page for the list or library.**

   The easiest way to do this is to choose Settings⇨List Settings or Settings⇨Library Settings from the list or library. The Customize Page appears.

2. **Click the Workflow Settings link in the Permissions and Management section.**

   The Add a Workflow page appears. If the list or library already has workflows associated with it, the Change Workflow Settings page appears. You can click the Add a Workflow link to associate another workflow with the list or library.

You can also associate workflows with a list or library by using a content type in the list or library that's associated with a workflow. See Chapter 7 for more information on creating content types.

To access the Add a Workflow page for a content type, follow these steps:

1. **Browse to the Site Content Type page for the content type in the Site Content gallery.**

   See Chapter 7 for more information on accessing the Site Content gallery.

2. **Click the Workflow Settings link.**

   The Change Workflow Settings page appears.

   On this page, you can add and remove workflows associated with the content type.

3. **Click the Add a Workflow link to access the Add a Workflow page.**

By default, the Approval, Collect Feedback, and Collect Signatures workflows are associated with the Document site content type in MOSS 2007.

To associate a new workflow with a list, library, or content type using the Add a Workflow page, follow these steps:

1. **Browse to the Add a Workflow page for the list, library, or content type as described in the preceding steps.**

   Figure 8-1 shows the Add a Workflow page.

2. **Select the workflow template you wish to associate with the list, library, or content type, such as Approval or Collect Feedback.**

3. **Type a name for the workflow.**

   The name you type identifies the workflow to users. For example, instead of using the generic name Approval workflow, use the name that's relevant to your business, such as Qualified Prospect Approval.

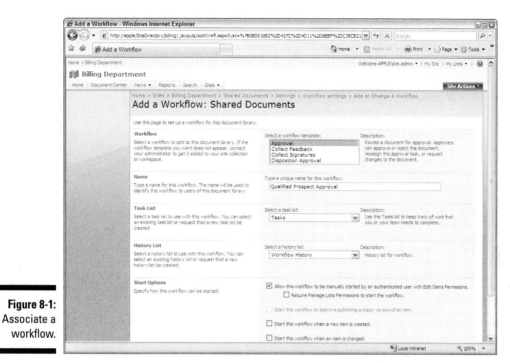

Figure 8-1:
Associate a
workflow.

4. **Select a task list and history list to store tasks and history associated with the workflow.**

   You can choose to use existing lists or create new lists. In the case of a content type workflow, enter the names you wish to use for the tasks list and history list. These lists will be created on the list or library that uses the content type.

   Make sure you assign someone to review tasks and history lists. Otherwise, tasks created by new workflows may not be processed. See the later sections, "Managing individual workflows" and "Getting the workflow big picture," for more information on using tasks and history lists with the workflows.

5. **Specify the start options for the workflow.**

   The start options you see are defined by the workflow template you select in Step 2. Usually, you must choose whether to allow the workflow to start manually or automatically. If you choose to start the workflow automatically, you can specify whether the workflow starts at the time the new item or document is created or when the item is changed.

6. **Select the Yes or the No radio button to indicate whether to add the workflow to the content type's children content types.**

   This step applies only to content types, not lists and libraries.

7. Click Next to access additional configuration steps for the workflow or click OK if the workflow doesn't have any additional configuration steps.

If the workflow template has additional configuration steps, that information appears in an InfoPath form after you click Next. Additional configuration includes things such as defining how many levels of routing are required for the workflow.

After the workflow is associated with a list or library, it can be initiated. See the section, "Managing individual workflows," later in this chapter, for details on what happens when a workflow starts.

In order to associate a workflow template, the template itself must be activated for the site collection. Use the site collection's Workflows gallery to see a list of the available workflow templates. Use the Site Collection Features page to activate and deactivate workflow templates. Both links are accessible via the Site Settings page of the site collection's top-level site.

SharePoint uses forms to collect information for configuring the workflow. Each workflow has its set of forms associated with the workflow. You can expect to see three kinds of workflow forms when configuring a workflow:

- ✔ **Association and initialization:** Forms associate the workflow with the list or library and allow you to configure parameters. Association forms are displayed to the list administrator when the workflow is associated with the list. Initialization forms are displayed to the user when the workflow is actually started for an individual list item. Often, the association and initializations forms display the same data. This allows the administrator to define the association while allowing the end user to set parameter values specific to their list item.

- ✔ **Modification:** Forms make it possible for users to modify a workflow instance once it has been started.

- ✔ **Task:** Forms make it possible to define custom tasks for workflows.

WSS uses ASP.NET forms, and MOSS 2007 supports InfoPath forms. By using InfoPath forms, Office 2007 clients can interact with workflows initiated with MOSS 2007.

All workflows have association forms that the administrator uses to create the initial association between the workflow and the list or library. Beyond association forms, all forms are optional.

Managing individual workflows

Workflows can start automatically or manually depending on how the workflow is configured. When a new workflow is created for a document or list item, the workflow is a workflow *instance*. For workflows configured to start automatically, SharePoint fires off a new workflow instance every time an item or document is created or edited, depending on how the workflow is configured.

Creating a workflow instance is also called *instantiating* the workflow. The concept of instantiation comes from object-oriented programming, where a programmer uses a class to instantiate an object. The *class* is a template that defines data and behavior, and the *object* represents the data and the actions taken upon it. For example, a program may have a Customer class that's used to instantiate a unique customer object with the name Smith, John. In the case of SharePoint, the workflow template is like the Customer class, and the workflow instance associated with the document or list item is like an individual customer's record.

SharePoint adds a column to the list or library when the workflow is associated. This column has the same name as the workflow and displays the status of a workflow instance. You can use this column to create views to filter on a certain workflow status or group by workflow status. See Chapter 7 for more information on creating views.

When a workflow starts, it may or may not display an initiation form. If not, the user may be totally unaware that a workflow instance has started. For example, SharePoint's three-state workflow doesn't display an initiation form.

After a workflow's initiation, users participate with the workflow through the various tasks that the workflow creates. The workflow fires off whatever the first activity is in the workflow. This activity could be creating a task and assigning it to someone or sending an e-mail reminder. Until that person follows up on the task, the workflow stays in its present state. For that reason, managing workflows is just as important as starting them.

Each item or document in a workflow-enabled list or library has its own Workflows page where you can manually start workflows and manage existing workflows. Follow these steps to access the Workflows page:

1. **Browse to the list or library where you wish to start the workflow instance.**

2. **Hover your mouse over the list item or document you wish to work with.**

   A drop-down arrow appears.

3. **Click the drop-down arrow to display the Edit menu.**

4. **Click the Workflows link on the Edit menu.**

   The Workflows page appears, as shown in Figure 8-2.

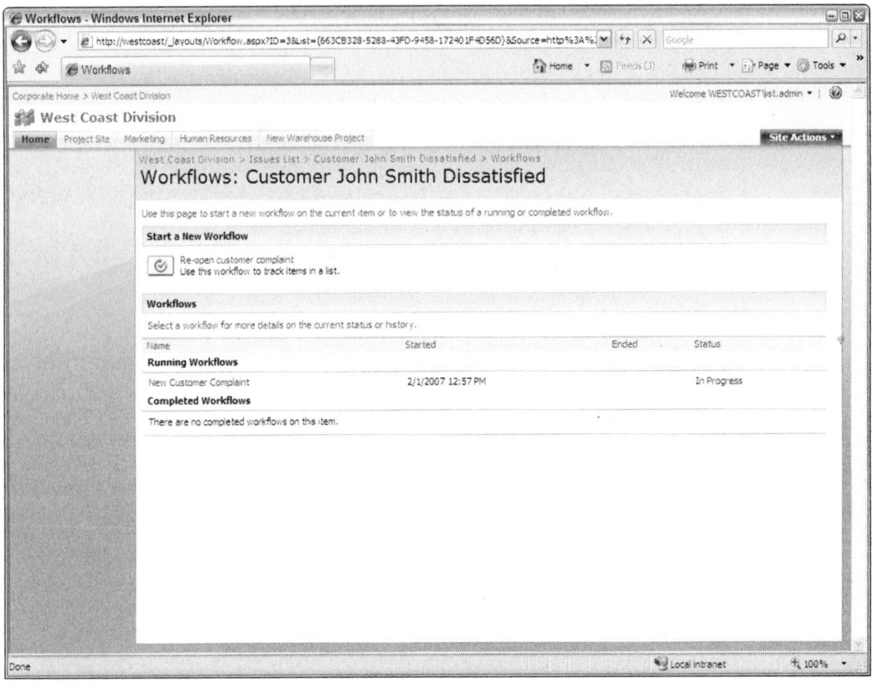

Figure 8-2:
View an item's workflows.

Alternatively, you can click the View Properties link on the item's Edit menu and then click the Workflow button to access the Workflows page.

You use the Workflows page to manually start and manage workflow instances associated with a list item or document. The Workflows page lists all the workflows associated with the list or library. To manually start one of these workflows, click the Workflow link in the Start a New Workflow section.

You can have only one running workflow instance for a list item or document. After you start a new workflow instance, you can't start another workflow instance with the same workflow type until the first instance completes.

When a workflow starts, the events of the workflow fire. This usually involves creating tasks and assigning them to users. Users and administrators can view the tasks list and workflow history list associated with the workflow to check the status of the workflow. Alternatively, you can access the Workflows page for a document or list item to access the tasks and history of the workflow instance.

The Workflows page is the place to view all the workflow instances running for a list item or document. You can also see a list of all the completed workflows. To view the details of a running or completed workflow, click the workflow instance you wish to view. The Workflow Status page appears.

The Workflow Status page, as shown in Figure 8-3, lists the following information:

- ✔ **Initiator** of the workflow. If the workflow instance started automatically, the initiator is listed as System.
- ✔ **Date** and **time** the workflow was started and when it last ran.
- ✔ **Status** of the workflow instance.
- ✔ **Tasks** associated with the workflow.
- ✔ **Event history** associated with the workflow.

You can click any of the tasks listed in the Tasks table to open the task. In MOSS 2007, you can click the Terminate This Workflow Now link in the Workflow Information section to force the workflow instance to stop when an error occurs. MOSS 2007 also provides workflow reports. Click the View Workflow Reports link in the Workflow History section to access reports about the workflow.

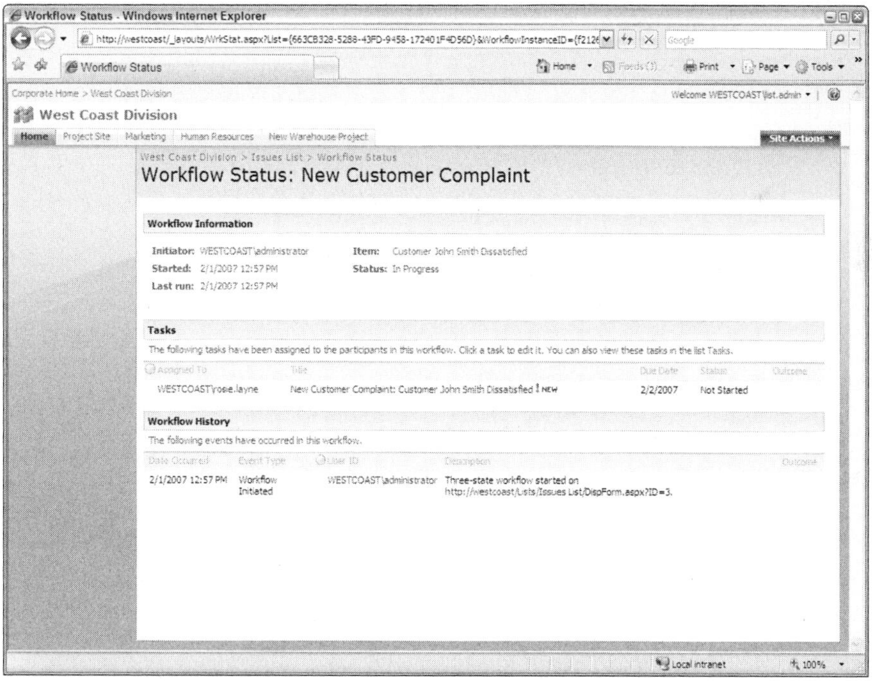

Figure 8-3: Manage a workflow with the Workflow Status page.

Creating and customizing workflows

You can create your own custom workflows with SharePoint Designer 2007 and Visual Studio 2005. SharePoint Designer 2007 includes a workflow designer that allows you to add actions, such as sending e-mail messages and assigning tasks to a workflow. You can use Visual Studio 2005 to create custom workflow actions that you can use in SharePoint Designer 2007.

Visual Studio 2005 makes it possible to create reusable workflow templates that can be used against any list, library, or content type. SharePoint Designer 2007 can only create workflows to act against a specific list or library.

You can download sample workflow project templates for Visual Studio 2005 by using the Workflow Developer Starter Kit. You can download the kit for free from the Microsoft Download Center at www.microsoft.com/downloads.

Getting the workflow big picture

The activities from workflows manifest themselves as items in lists, such as tasks lists. Thinking about how you want to manage the big picture view of workflows is important. If people in your company are prone to ignore manual requests, they'll ignore electronic ones, too.

Thankfully, MOSS 2007 provides a set of reports you can use to view the status of workflows in a list or library. MOSS 2007 provides these two reports:

- ✔ **Activity Duration Reports** provide details about how long it takes users to complete each action in the workflow, such as closing a task. The report also shows how long it takes the workflow to complete.

- ✔ **Cancellation & Error Reports** show which workflows have been cancelled or have encountered errors.

You can access these reports using the Workflow Status page, as I describe in the preceding section. You can also access the reports from a list or library's Customize page. To access the reports, choose Settings⇨Document Library Settings⇨Workflow Settings ⇨View Workflow Reports or Settings⇨List Library Settings⇨Workflow Settings ⇨View Workflow Reports. (The first command path works for libraries, while the second works for lists.)

You can view a summary of all the workflows in progress for an entire site collection in the Site Collection Workflows gallery. To access the gallery, click the Workflows link in the Galleries section of the site collection's Site Settings page.

You can keep track of workflows in a number of additional ways so items don't get lost in the shuffle. Here are some suggestions:

✔ **Use views** to make it easier for list and workflow administrators to quickly see the status of all items.

✔ **Create dashboard pages** that display views from several lists so administrators can easily jump around from list to list.

✔ **Use Outlook tasks** to ensure that workflow tasks appear in a user's task list.

✔ **Create an RSS feed** for the list that includes the status of workflows. See Chapter 10 for more information on working with RSS feeds.

Filling Out InfoPath Forms

Filling out forms is part of life. We fill out paper forms, forms in Word documents, forms in e-mail, and forms in Excel spreadsheets. The IRS even uses fill-in tax forms in PDF files. SharePoint provides a special content type — a *Form* — that makes it possible to create electronic versions of forms. And unlike those electronic versions of forms that people create with Excel and Word, these forms make it possible to extract the data entered by users.

The Form content type in SharePoint is made possible by InfoPath 2007, which is a client application in the Office 2007 suite. *InfoPath* is a tool for designing and filling out electronic forms. InfoPath provides a toolbox with textboxes, labels, check boxes, and all the other widgets necessary for laying out and designing forms. The file that stores all the design information is the *form template*. The file that stores the values that a user types is a *form*.

Form templates use the file extension .xsn, and forms use the extension .xml. Understanding the difference between form templates and forms is important. The form is what the user fills out; the form template defines the form's design.

SharePoint provides a special kind of document library — a *form library* — for managing InfoPath forms. You associate an InfoPath form template with the form library in the same way that you might associate a Word document or an Excel spreadsheet as the template for a document library. When the user clicks the New button in the library, SharePoint opens a blank form based on the form template. When the user saves the form, the data the user enters is saved in the form file in the form library. The completed form file is a document in the library, just as a Word document or an Excel spreadsheet are documents in a document library.

You aren't restricted to using InfoPath forms with forms libraries. You can use InfoPath forms with any kind of library, but they usually work best with forms libraries.

InfoPath 2007 includes a number of sample form templates that you can modify, which means you don't need to start your forms from scratch. Microsoft is supposed to release a set of InfoPath forms that you can use with SharePoint.

You can use InfoPath forms in workflows. See the Software Developer Kit (SDK) for more information.

Before you start making extensive use of InfoPath forms services, make sure that you have server capacity to handle it. See the Plan for Forms section of the MOSS 2007 TechNet documentation at:

```
http://technet2.microsoft.com/Office/en-us/library/
        2aefdd4d-e520-4ecf-a56e-b984ece63a711033.mspx
```

Configuring InfoPath forms services

In previous versions of SharePoint, an end user had to have the InfoPath client installed on his or her computer to open the blank form. As a result of this requirement, not many companies deployed InfoPath forms. InfoPath 2007 has a new feature that makes it possible for form template designers to make forms browser-enabled. When used with a compatible server program (such as the InfoPath Forms Services feature of Microsoft Office SharePoint Server 2007), InfoPath forms can be displayed and filled out using a Web browser.

InfoPath Forms Services is a component of MOSS 2007 and is activated by default. InfoPath Forms Services adds a section to the Application Management page of the Central Administration site for administering the service.

The basic issue with managing InfoPath Forms Services comes down to managing form templates. Here are two kinds of InfoPath form templates that must be managed:

- **Administrator-approved:** Templates that use managed code and other sophisticated features of InfoPath for manipulating data and data sources. These forms must be uploaded to the server by a farm administrator, as I describe in the section, "Managing form templates," later in this chapter.

- **User:** Templates that don't have any advanced features, which therefore can be uploaded to the site collection by users. I describe these in the section, "Managing form templates." Even though the form templates don't require administrative approval, administrators can set a number of settings to influence the range of behaviors available for use in user form templates.

The following links are available for managing form templates with InfoPath Forms Services:

- ✔ **Manage Form Templates:** Use this link to upload, activate, and deactivate administrator-approved form templates to the server farm. See the section, "Managing form templates," later in this chapter for more information.

- ✔ **Configure InfoPath Forms Services:** Configure settings related to security.

- ✔ **Upload Form Template:** Use this link to verify and upload administrator-approved templates.

- ✔ **Manage Data Connection Files:** Use this link to manage data connection files that store data connection information shared among InfoPath forms.

- ✔ **Manage the Web Service Proxy:** Use this link to configure proxy connections used by data connection files.

The settings you make with the Configure InfoPath Forms Services page (see Figure 8-4) affect all InfoPath forms. Table 8-1 lists some of the settings you can configure.

Figure 8-4:
Configure
InfoPath
Forms
Services.

Table 8-1 **Configuration Options for InfoPath Forms Services**

Setting	What It Does
User Browser-Enabled Form Templates	Allows user form templates to be viewed in the browser.
Data Connection Timeouts	Specifies the default and maximum timeout for connection to data sources in a browser-enabled form.
Data Connection Response Size	Sets the maximum size of responses processed by data connections.
HTTP Data Connections	Requires use of the Secure Sockets Layer protocol (SSL) before transmitting passwords over the network.
Embedded SQL Authentication	Prevents the use of SQL usernames and passwords in forms.
Authentication to Data Sources	Prevents user form templates from using authentication information in data connection files.
Cross-Domain Access for User Form Templates	Prevents user forms from accessing data from another domain
Thresholds	Sets the maximum number of postbacks and actions per postback for each user session.
Form Session State	Sets the location for storing form session state.

All the configuration options listed in Table 8-1 have default values set. If you're unsure of the purpose of an option, leave the default setting. Most of the settings relate to preventing users from inadvertently accessing or revealing usernames and passwords. Other settings, such as the Thresholds settings, serve to prevent the form from consuming too many server resources.

Consider deviating from the Session State Service default value for the Form Session State Configuration setting if you have a smaller group of users using InfoPath Forms Services. Essentially, Session State Service uses more memory on the database server because each session is stored in the server's memory. Form View Session State Management stores session data on the client, thus increasing network bandwidth because session data is transmitted between the server and the client.

Deploying form templates

InfoPath form templates can be deployed by users so long as the forms don't have any managed code. InfoPath form templates can be as sophisticated as custom Web parts created in Visual Studio. Users can upload the forms template just like they would any other document template. Users can also use the InfoPath 2007 Publishing wizard to publish their templates to SharePoint.

Form templates are stored in the Forms folder of a document library.

To publish a form template to a document library via InfoPath 2007, follow these steps:

1. **Open the template in design view in InfoPath 2007.**

2. **Choose File⇨Publish.**

   The Publishing Wizard starts.

   You may be prompted to save the form template first. If so, save the template.

3. **In response to the question, "Where do you want to publish the form template?" select the To a SharePoint Server with or without InfoPath Forms Services radio button and then click Next.**

4. **Type the URL of the SharePoint site where you wish to publish the form template and click Next.**

   You might be prompted to enter your credentials to access the site. If so, enter your username and password.

5. **If the SharePoint server has InfoPath Services enabled, the Publishing Wizard prompts to enable the form to be filled out in a browser.**

   Enable the form to be filled out by a browser unless the form has special features that won't work in a browser. By displaying the form in a browser, users aren't required to have InfoPath 2007 installed on their local computers.

6. **Select the Document Library radio button to indicate that you want to publish the form template to a library, as shown in Figure 8-5.**

   By selecting Document Library, you can deploy the form to any kind of document library including a forms library. Your other choices are to save the form template as a content type or as an administrator-approved form template.

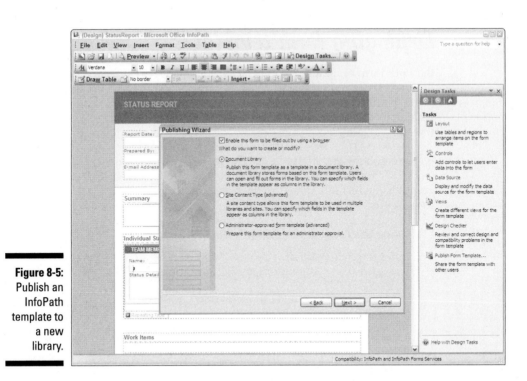

Figure 8-5:
Publish an
InfoPath
template to
a new
library.

7. **Click Next.**

   A list of existing libraries appears in the wizard.

8. **Select the Create a New Document Library radio button and click Next.**

   You can also select an existing library from the list.

9. **Type a name and description for the new document library and then click Next.**

10. **Click the Add button to add fields from the form template to use as columns in the library and then click Next.**

    The fields in the form become the columns in the form library. You can also add new columns in the library to describe the form. These columns don't become fields in the InfoPath form.

11. **Review the summary information and click the Publish button.**

    InfoPath creates the library with the columns you specify in the preceding step and uploads the form template as the library's default template.

12. **The wizard displays a summary of the actions. Click the Close button to close the wizard.**

Browse to the library and test the form template.

Managing form templates

InfoPath form templates are very powerful and can include custom code that accesses databases. Form templates that use code and other advanced features must be deployed to the server by an administrator. An administrator-deployed form template is a *managed form template*.

You need to have a business process in place for deploying managed form templates. If you plan to have a lot of form templates to deploy, consider using a workflow to manage the process. Here are the high-level steps for deploying managed form templates:

1. **A developer or power user creates the form template and notifies a farm administrator that the template needs to be deployed.**

2. **A farm administrator uploads the template to the Managed Form Templates library in Central Administration.**

    The upload process verifies that the form template doesn't contain any errors before uploading the template. If errors are found, the administrator must notify the developer or power user and tell them to correct the errors.

3. **A farm administrator activates the form template to a selected site collection.**

    The form template can't be used by a site collection until it's activated in that site collection. The farm administrator must have administrator rights to the site collection in order to activate the form template. Otherwise, a site collection administrator can activate the form template from the site collection.

4. **Site collection administrators or their delegates consume the form template as a site content type or in lists, libraries, or workflows.**

For all this to work, the farm administrator must upload the form template to the server, as I describe in Step 2. To upload the form template, do the following:

1. **Browse to the Application Management page in Central Administration.**

2. **Click the Upload Form Template link in the InfoPath Forms Services section.**

    The Upload Form Template page appears, as shown in Figure 8-6.

3. **Click the Browse button to browse to a form template or type the path to the template in the File Name textbox.**

You can browse to a file share or type the Universal Naming Convention (UNC) path to a SharePoint library if you're using a library to manage templates before they're deployed.

4. **Click the Verify button.**

InfoPath Services validates the form template and displays warning and error messages.

If error messages appear, you must correct the problem before you can upload the form template. Share warning messages with the developer to see whether they need to be corrected.

5. **Deselect the Upgrade the Form Template If It Already Exists check box.**

You can use this option to upgrade an existing form template to a new version and indicate what should happen to existing forms using previous versions of the template.

6. **Click the Upload button.**

SharePoint uploads the form template to the server farm.

7. **Click OK to close the Upload Form Template page and go to the Manage Form Templates page.**

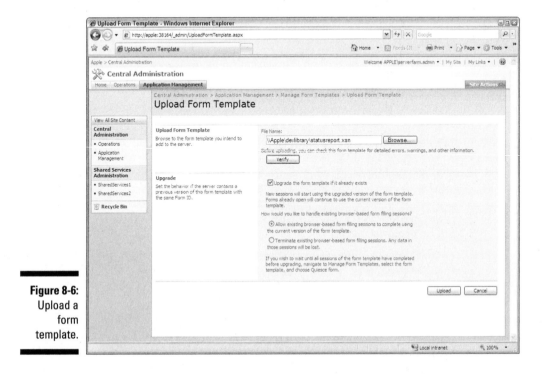

Figure 8-6:
Upload a form template.

Before the form template can be used, the template must be activated to a site collection. The farm administrator can activate the template or a site collection administrator can. After form templates are uploaded to a server farm, they appear as site collection features. Thus, any site collection administrator can activate the form template by using the Site Collection Features link in the site collection's top-level Site Settings page.

Follow these steps to activate the form template as a farm administrator:

1. **Click the Manage Form Templates link on the Application Management page of Central Administration.**

   The Manage Form Templates page appears.

2. **Click the template you wish to activate.**

   A menu appears.

3. **Choose Activate to a Site Collection.**

   The Activate Form Template page appears.

4. **In the Activation Location section of the page, choose the site collection you wish to activate the form template to.**

   You must have administrative permissions on the site collection to activate the form template. You may need to change Web applications in order to find the site collection you wish to activate to.

5. **Click OK.**

   The form is activated to the site collection.

Forms activated to a site collection appear in the Form Templates library of the top-level site of the site collection. You can use the form template like you would any other form template. For example, you could set the form template as the template for a library or create a new content type that uses the form template as its template.

Working with forms libraries

A form library is a kind of document library specifically intended for storing forms. You don't have to use a form library. You can store forms in any kind of document library. A form library includes all the features of a regular document library, such as check-in and versioning.

A few features that you might be interested in using are the item menu options in form libraries. The form item menu is the menu that appears when you click the arrow for a form in the library. The menu includes options to edit the form in InfoPath or the browser. The menu also provides the option to convert the XML forms and InfoPath forms to a Web page. See Chapter 16 for more information on converting documents and forms to Web pages.

All the setting and configuration options for forms libraries are similar to document libraries. One feature that you might consider enabling is the browser-enabled documents option. By default, all libraries are configured to open files in the default client application. For example, Word files are opened in Microsoft Word. In most cases, clients don't have InfoPath installed on their machines, so you'll want the blank form to open in the browser. To open browser-enabled documents in the browser, follow these steps:

1. **Browse to the form or document library.**

2. **Choose Settings⇨Form Library Settings.**

   The Customize page appears.

3. **Click the Advanced Settings link.**

4. **In the Browser-enabled Documents section, select the Display as a Web Page radio button.**

5. **Click OK.**

In order for the blank form to appear properly in the browser, it must be a browser-enabled form and the server must be running InfoPath Forms Services. When a user clicks the form in the library, the form appears in the browser, as shown in Figure 8-7.

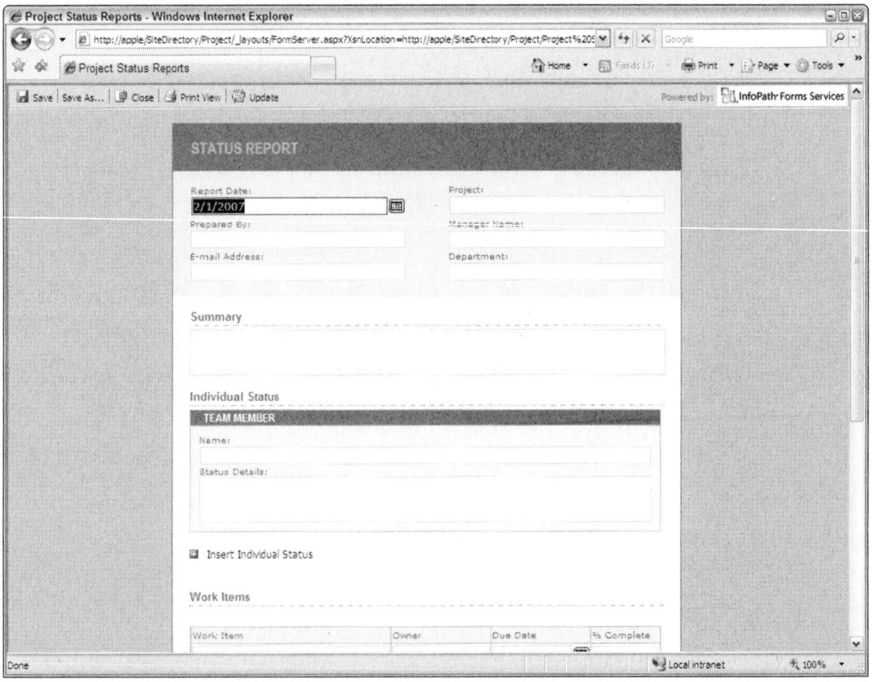

Figure 8-7: Browser-enabled blank forms appear in the browser.

By default, InfoPath forms are saved to the forms library. However, you aren't restricted to saving forms in a forms library. Forms can be saved in any kind of library. More importantly, you can redirect the data from a form to another store such as a database. To do so, simply configure the form's Submit button to send the data elsewhere for storage. For example, you could create a form template for submitting expense reports. The expense report could be accessed and entered in SharePoint, but the data submitted by the user would actually be transmitted to a line-of-business application for processing.

To quickly change the destination for data entered when a user clicks the submit button, choose Tools⇨Submit Options in the InfoPath 2007 client. The Submit Options dialog box appears, which allows you to select a destination for the form (such as e-mail, SharePoint document library, or Web service).

You also have the option to use data connections in InfoPath to submit data to another kind of back-end data storage, such as a database. Choose the Tools⇨Data Connections option in InfoPath 2007 to create and access data connections. You can store these data connections on the SharePoint server farm. Follow these steps to manage data connection files on the SharePoint server farm:

1. **Browse to the Application Management page in Central Administration.**

2. **Click the Manage Data Connection Files link in the InfoPath Forms Services section.**

   The Manage Data Connection Files section appears.

3. **Click the Upload button.**

   The Upload Data Connection File page appears.

4. **Browse to the filename of the data connection file.**

5. **Type a category name for the file.**

6. **Indicate whether clients can access the data file over HyperText Transfer Protocol (HTTP).**

   Enable this option if you want InfoPath and other clients to use the data connection file.

7. **Click the Upload button.**

   The file appears in the library.

You can use the InfoPath 2007 client to access the file as a data connection for InfoPath form templates.

Part III
Improving Information Worker Collaboration and Productivity

The 5th Wave   By Rich Tennant

"...and that's pretty much all there is to converting a document to an HTML file."

In this part . . .

Start using SharePoint with familiar desktop clients, like Word, Excel, and Outlook, and then see how users can make SharePoint personal through portals, personalization, and My Site. Because no portal is complete without search, I close by getting you up to speed on using and configuring SharePoint search.

Chapter 9

Using SharePoint for Collaboration

In This Chapter

▶ Accessing SharePoint from Office 2007 clients

▶ Using the Office Ribbon to publish to SharePoint

▶ Using Windows Explorer and Web Folders to access SharePoint

▶ Extending SharePoint with other Microsoft server products

*P*art of what makes SharePoint a good choice to use for document management, collaboration, or business process management is that users don't have to know a new user interface along with a new series of menu commands. In fact, users can use the existing tools that they're already using — Office applications, Web browsers, and Windows Explorer, for example.

In this chapter, I explore some of the different ways that users can interact with SharePoint sites and resources.

Using SharePoint with Office 2007

All the Office 2007 client applications are capable of accessing SharePoint resources. Some clients, such as Outlook, are especially useful for interacting with SharePoint sites. Here are some of the ways that your users can use Office 20007 clients to access resources on SharePoint:

- ✔ Publish documents to a document library with Word 2007.
- ✔ Create new entries on a SharePoint blog with Word 2007.
- ✔ Publish individual slides or entire slideshows to a slide library with PowerPoint 2007.
- ✔ Link to and update SharePoint lists with Excel 2007.
- ✔ Display charts and Excel spreadsheets with Excel Services.

✔ Post announcements with Outlook 2007.

✔ Archive e-mail threads to discussion boards with Outlook 2007.

✔ Synchronize tasks, contacts, and calendars in Outlook 2007.

✔ Create electronic forms with InfoPath 2007.

✔ Customize SharePoint sites with SharePoint Designer 2007.

Managing documents

A common problem that users and administrators have with Office clients is figuring out how to manage all the various files created by using the various Office applications. When users interact with centralized information systems, the data they enter is stored automatically in a database. The user doesn't give any thought about where a customer's order goes after it's entered into the screen. The user clicks OK and knows that he can pull up that customer's record at any time. The same thing can't be said about documents and files created with Office applications.

When a user needs to save a file created with an Office application, the user has to decide on the location to save the file. The user may choose a private or shared network location, a local hard drive, or removable media. Obviously, some of these locations are better than others.

Office 2007 offers two features that take some of the guesswork out of saving and managing files created with certain Office applications:

✔ **Document Management Server:** Office 2007 applications that sport the new Ribbon interface provide support for publishing documents to a document management server such as SharePoint. The applications that offer this feature are Word 2007, Excel 2007, and PowerPoint 2007.

PowerPoint 2007 includes the ability to publish individual slides to a slide library in Microsoft Office SharePoint Server (MOSS) 2007. A *slide library* is a centralized location for storing reusable slides. Users can then pull these reusable slides into their own slide presentations.

Other Office 2007 applications can save documents to SharePoint, but they don't provide the convenient Ribbon interface. See the following section for more information.

✔ **Document workspaces:** Certain Office 2007 applications, such as Excel and Word, can create a SharePoint Document workspace and publish a file to the workspace. *Workspaces* are used to create a document-centric SharePoint site used for collaboration on a document.

Outlook 2007 supports the creation of Meeting Workspaces, which is a similar concept. Users can create a meeting-centric SharePoint site at the time they create a meeting request in Outlook. The Meeting workspace can be used to store agendas, objectives, attendees lists, and other information pertinent to conducting the meeting and tracking progress on the meeting's action items.

The ability to publish files to a Document Management Server works with any kind of document management system, not just SharePoint. When used in conjunction with SharePoint document libraries, users can manage versions, check out documents for editing, and save additional properties about the document. See Chapter 15 for more information on using these document management features of SharePoint.

MOSS 2007 provides several specialized document management features, including a centralized Documents Center for storing enterprise-wide documents on a SharePoint collaboration portal and the Records Center for long-term document archival. See Chapter 15.

To publish a document to a SharePoint library via Word, Excel, or PowerPoint 2007, follow these steps:

1. **Create a new document, chart, spreadsheet, or presentation.**

2. **Click the Office Button.**

   The Office menu appears.

3. **Choose Publish⇨Document Management Server.**

   The Save As dialog box appears.

4. **Type the URL of the SharePoint document library where you wish to save whatever you created in Step 1.**

   To get the URL, browse to the library in SharePoint and copy the URL into the File Name text box. Alternatively, you can type the URL of the SharePoint server name and browse to the library. For example, for a server named abcinsurance, you would type **http://abcinsurance**. After you browse once to the server, the server appears in the My Network Places folder.

5. **Type a filename for the file and click Save.**

6. **Fill in any prompts related to the file's properties.**

   You can require that a user completes properties before saving a file to a document library. These properties can be marked as required in the document library or by using a content type with the document library.

   The file is saved to the library.

After a file is published to SharePoint, users can access features, such as Check Out and Version History, by choosing Office Button➪Server in the Office 2007 application.

When users need to collaborate on a document, saving the document to a Document Workspace site might be better than using a document library in a team site. A *Document Workspace site* stores the document and all the supporting documents and tasks required for collaboration on the document. Saving files to an existing Document Workspace site is the same as saving to any other SharePoint site.

What's unique about Document Workspace sites is that users with permissions to create sites in SharePoint can create their Document Workspace site inside some Office 2007 applications. Follow these steps to create a Document Workspace site in Word 2007, Excel 2007, or PowerPoint 2007:

1. **Create the document you wish to save to the site.**

2. **Choose Office Button➪Publish➪Create Document Workspace.**

   The Document Management pane appears.

3. **Type a name for the Document Workspace site.**

4. **Select the location for the workspace from the drop-down list or type a URL where you want the workspace created.**

5. **Click the Create button.**

   The Office 2007 application creates the Document Workspace site in SharePoint.

You can use the Document Management pane to check the status of the document; view and add new members to the site; and review tasks, links, and other documents founds on the Document Workspace site.

You can create a Document Workspace site by sending an attached Office 2007 document in an e-mail via Outlook to invitees as members of the workspace site. After the document is attached to the e-mail, simply click the Attachment Options button in the Include section of the Message tab. On the Attachment Options pane, select the Shared Attachments radio button and enter the URL for the SharePoint site where you want to create the workspace site.

Document Workspace sites are a great way to keep track of the work required to create a particular document. After the document is completed, consider moving the document to a document library on a team site. Also consider changing Document Workspace sites to Read Only after the work on the document is complete. This prevents users from adding more information to the workspace site after the fact. You may also want to have a policy about how long you retain these sites. It might be sufficient to archive them to backup after you've determined no one needs to access them.

Protecting documents

Protecting corporate assets requires more than managing permissions and having a good backup strategy in place. Authorized users can still sometimes misuse corporate assets by sharing documents with unauthorized parties or inappropriately discarding a hard copy of a sensitive document. SharePoint's lists and libraries support the use of Information Rights Management (IRM) to limit the actions that authorized users can take when it comes to providing access to documents. Common uses for IRM include preventing users from copying, forwarding, or printing a document.

For IRM protection to work, the server must have a protector program for the type of file being accessed. MOSS 2007 includes protectors for the following file types:

- ✓ InfoPath forms
- ✓ Word, Excel, and PowerPoint files in 97–2003 file formats
- ✓ Word 2007, Excel 2007, and PowerPoint 2007 files in the Open XML Format
- ✓ XML Paper Specification (XPS) format

Deploying rights management requires significant configuration before you can start using IRM in SharePoint. Enabling IRM in SharePoint requires the following:

- ✓ Rights Management Server deployed on the network
- ✓ Rights Management Server client deployed on SharePoint Web servers and client computers
- ✓ Information Rights Management enabled in Central Administration
- ✓ Information Rights Management enabled in each list or library where you wish to use rights management

Find more information about deploying rights management along with the server and client software on the Windows Server 2003 Rights Management Server page on TechNet at:

```
http://technet2.microsoft.com/windowsserver/en/technologies/
               featured/rms/default.mspx
```

Using lists with Excel and Access

Commonly, individual departments use Excel spreadsheets and Access databases for analyzing and keeping track of data. Just as commonly, the

Information Technology (IT) department is completely unaware of these informal applications. As a result, IT may have a problem on its hands when a spreadsheet blows up or a department outgrows its database.

The answer that many in IT resort to involves forcing departments into the company's formal information systems or creating custom applications to replace these niche applications. The unfortunate side effect of these approaches is that the departmental solutions usually reflect a lot of work and worker knowledge about the department. Rather than discard these solutions, SharePoint provides extensive features for integrating Excel 2007 spreadsheets and Access 2007 databases.

In both Excel 2007 and Access 2007, you have the option to create a one-to-one relationship between a table in a spreadsheet or database and lists in SharePoint. Whether a relationship is maintained between the list and the table depends on the kind of action performed:

- ✔ **Importing** data from a table to a list or a list to a table doesn't maintain a connection between the table and the list. A copy of the data is moved from one to the other.

- ✔ **Exporting** data from a table to a list or a list to a table doesn't maintain a connection between the table and the list. Whether an operation is considered an import or export depends on the perspective of the application. For example, if you're moving data from a list to a table, you're exporting from SharePoint to Excel or Access.

- ✔ **Linking** data creates a connection between the list and the table such that changes made in the table are made in the list and vice versa.

Data is imported into a custom list in SharePoint. The columns of the table become the columns in the custom list. Importing a spreadsheet or Access table is an easy way to get data into a list without manually entering the data.

SharePoint lists are a natural repository for working with Excel and Access tables. Lists are columns and rows of data just like a table. As a result, SharePoint provides a number of features that facilitate importing and exporting data, including the following:

- ✔ **The Datasheet view Task pane:** All SharePoint lists have a special view — a Datasheet view — where data is displayed in cells similar to a spreadsheet. The Datasheet view includes a Task pane, which provides several menu options for working with Excel and Access.

- ✔ **The Export to Spreadsheet command:** This command can be found on the Actions menu of lists and libraries. The Export to Spreadsheet command creates an Excel query that Excel executes. The query displays the list's contents in an Excel spreadsheet. Even though the command exports the list's data, SharePoint still creates a link between the spreadsheet and the list.

✔ **The Import Spreadsheet command:** In the Custom Lists section, the Create page offers the Import Spreadsheet command, which you can use to import a spreadsheet to a custom list. The spreadsheet's columns become the list's columns, and the spreadsheet's data becomes list items.

You can save spreadsheets and databases that are linked to SharePoint lists in SharePoint libraries.

The Task pane in a list's Datasheet view is the easiest way to use data from existing SharePoint lists in Excel spreadsheets or Access databases. To access the Task pane, do the following:

1. **Browse to the list or library you wish to work with.**

2. **Choose Actions⇨Edit in Datasheet.**

   The Datasheet view appears.

3. **Choose Actions⇨Task Pane.**

   The Task pane appears, as shown in Figure 9-1.

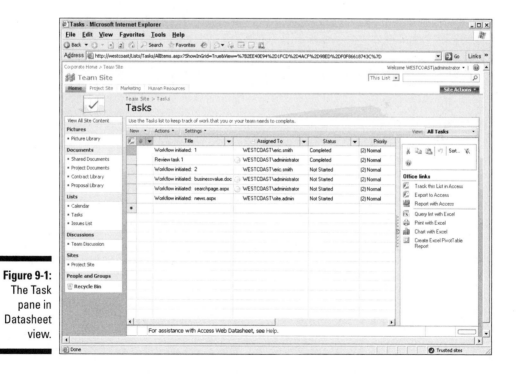

Figure 9-1: The Task pane in Datasheet view.

The Task pane includes links to most of the features you could want. Your options in MOSS 2007 include:

- **Track This List in Access:** Creates a linked table in Access.
- **Export to Access:** Creates a static table in Access that isn't linked to the SharePoint list.
- **Report with Access:** Creates a linked table in Access and generates a report in Access based on the linked table.
- **Query list with Excel:** Creates an Excel query that can be refreshed in Excel to see the latest data from the SharePoint list.
- **Print with Excel:** Creates an Excel query and displays the Print dialog box in Excel.
- **Chart with Excel:** Creates an Excel query and starts the Chart Wizard in Excel.
- **Create Excel Pivot Table Report:** Creates an Excel query and starts the Pivot Table Wizard in Excel.

WSS includes a similar set of options as MOSS 2007.

Many of these commands also work with Office 2003.

The top of the Task pane includes a set of icons for cutting, copying, pasting, undoing, sorting, and filtering the data you see in the Datasheet view.

You can use the `Paste` command to paste data you copy from a spreadsheet or other table into the datasheet. This is an excellent way to populate a SharePoint list without being forced to import data into a custom list.

Excel 2007 and Access 2007 also provide their own set of commands for importing, exporting, and linking data in SharePoint lists. Access 2007 provides additional features that make it possible to publish a database to a document library. Access 2007 also includes a Move to SharePoint Site Wizard that migrates an Access 2007 database to SharePoint lists. See my book, *Office 2007 and SharePoint Productivity For Dummies* (Wiley), to get more information on using Excel 2007 and Access 2007 with SharePoint.

The Many Faces of SharePoint

Users can access SharePoint content in many ways. In the preceding section, I describe several ways in which users can use Office 2007 clients to interact with SharePoint. Of course, the Web browser is another important way that users access SharePoint content. Other access choices include these:

- ✓ **Office 2003 clients,** which do have some built-in support for accessing SharePoint resources, similar to Office 2007. See my book, *Microsoft SharePoint 2003 For Dummies* (Wiley), for ideas on how you can use Office 2003 with SharePoint.

- ✓ **Mobile devices,** which often can access special mobile views of lists and libraries. SharePoint provides a mobile framework that automatically creates these views. You can determine the mobile view of a site by looking for the mobile site URL in the site's Site Settings page. The URLs for mobile list and library views can be found in the Mobile section of the Edit Views page.

- ✓ **Web Folders,** which make it possible for users to access SharePoint resources from any application, not just Office applications. Web Folders use a URL to access resources. After a user accesses a resource from within an application, the URL is saved as a Web Folder in My Network Places.

- ✓ **Windows Explorer,** which can access SharePoint resources by using Universal Naming Convention (UNC) paths. The easiest way to access a list or library in Windows Explorer is to use the special Windows Explorer view that's automatically created by SharePoint.

Users aren't restricted to just using Internet Explorer to access SharePoint. SharePoint sites work fine in Firefox and Safari browsers.

SharePoint also provides extensive access to administrative features using Web services. See the Windows SharePoint Services Software Development Kit (SDK) for more information on the Web services available.

Integrating with Other Servers

Microsoft offers a vast array of client and server products. Most of these products build upon the features of another product to provide a sophisticated information technology infrastructure.

SharePoint is just one of many server products offered by Microsoft. Some server products enhance or provide services to SharePoint, whereas others are actually built as applications on top of SharePoint. Take a look at these servers:

- ✓ **Exchange Server 2007** is an e-mail server that can be used to ensure that only authenticated e-mail is received by SharePoint. See Chapter 10 for more information on configuring inbound e-mail.

✔ **ForeFront Security for SharePoint** protects SharePoint deployments from virus threats, prohibits uploading of certain file types, and scans for inappropriate content.

✔ **Forms Server** is a server application built on Windows SharePoint Services (WSS) 3.0 for serving browser-based InfoPath forms. InfoPath Forms Services is an equivalent product that's built into MOSS 2007.

✔ **Groove Server** is a platform for collaborating on documents with other users. Groove provides support for working with documents offline. Content created in Groove can be stored in SharePoint document libraries.

✔ **Live Communications Server 2005** provides presence and real-time communications including voice, video, and instant messaging. Live Communications Server provides presence information to SharePoint and Office clients that enable users to know when someone is online so that they can easily start a real-time conversation with that person.

✔ **Microsoft Operations Management Server:** A systems management server that is available as a free download from TechNet. Microsoft provides management packs for all their popular servers including SharePoint.

✔ **Project Server:** A server application built on MOSS 2007 for managing project resources and analyzing project performance.

✔ **Visual Studio 2005 Team Foundation Server:** Supports the special collaboration needs of software development teams. Team Foundation Server is built on WSS 2.0.

Forms Server, Groove Server, Live Communications Server, Project Server and SharePoint Server are considered Office servers because they're part of Microsoft Office.

To find out more about these servers, see Office Online at http://office.microsoft.com and TechNet at http://technet.microsoft.com.

Chapter 10

Communicating with SharePoint

*M*ost business users live and die by e-mail. Because users already spend so much time with e-mail, it only makes sense that SharePoint has features for integrating e-mail.

Instead of just generating a bunch of new e-mail for users to sort through, SharePoint provides smart integration with Outlook 2007 that enables users to easily manage the areas of overlap between SharePoint and Outlook. Users can use the browser to access SharePoint, or they can use Outlook 2007 to access contacts, calendars, and tasks from SharePoint. Users can even use the categorization and search features of Outlook 2007 on items they download from SharePoint.

In addition to being able to use Outlook to manage their resources on SharePoint, users can send e-mail directly to lists and libraries. The e-mail attachments become documents, and the body of the e-mail becomes a list item. You can even configure a distribution list based on SharePoint groups. When users send e-mail to the distribution list, all their e-mail communications are archived in a discussion board on SharePoint.

In this chapter, I show you how to configure SharePoint so users can use Outlook 2007 and e-mail to communicate with lists and libraries that are relevant to them.

Integrating with Outlook

A great deal of overlap occurs between Outlook and SharePoint. For example, both Outlook and SharePoint have tasks, calendars, and contacts. It only makes sense that users can use Outlook to interact with SharePoint. Outlook 2007 and Windows SharePoint Services (WSS) version 3 offer many points of integration.

Integrating SharePoint lists and libraries with Outlook 2007 is as simple as clicking a single menu command in SharePoint. After you connect, you can view the contents of the list or library in Outlook. If the list or library is enabled to receive incoming e-mail, users can even use Outlook to send replies to discussion threads and add meetings to team calendars.

To connect a list or library to Outlook 2007, do the following:

1. **Using a browser such as Internet Explorer, browse to the list or library you wish to access in Outlook 2007.**

   For example, if you want to access the Shared Documents library on a team site called Projects, browse to the Projects team site and go to the Shared Documents library.

2. **Choose Actions➪Connect to Outlook.**

   Outlook prompts you to connect the list, as shown in Figure 10-1.

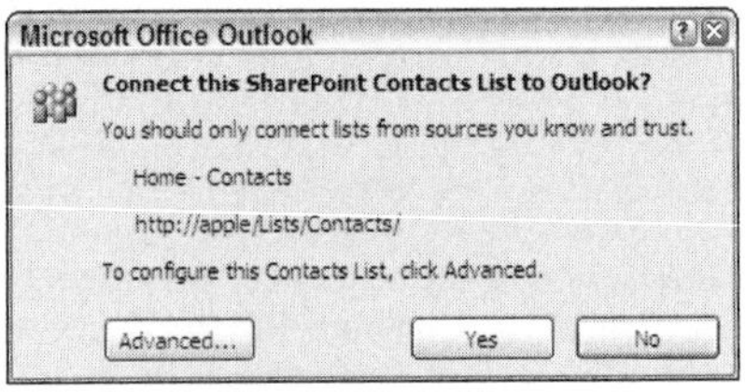

Figure 10-1: Create a connection between Outlook and SharePoint.

Microsoft Office Outlook

Connect this SharePoint Contacts List to Outlook?
You should only connect lists from sources you know and trust.

Home - Contacts

http://apple/Lists/Contacts/

To configure this Contacts List, click Advanced.

[Advanced...] [Yes] [No]

3. **Click the Yes button.**

   The list appears in Outlook 2007.

Where the list appears in Outlook 2007 depends on the kind of list you're connecting to. You can find all your SharePoint connections with the Outlook 2007 Navigation pane. SharePoint calendars appear in the Other Calendars section of the Calendars pane. SharePoint contacts appear in the Other Contacts section of the Contacts pane. Document libraries and other kinds of lists (such as discussion boards) appear in the SharePoint Lists folder. The content downloaded to the SharePoint Lists folder from SharePoint is stored in an Outlook data file on the user's local hard drive.

After connecting to a SharePoint list in Outlook 2007, users can send an e-mail link to other users inviting them to connect to the same list in Outlook. This feature is especially helpful if a team site owner wants to make it easy for teammates to view site content in SharePoint. To send a link, follow these steps:

1. **Make a connection to a list or library in SharePoint, as outlined in the preceding set of steps.**

2. **Right-click the connected list in the Outlook 2007 Navigation pane.**

3. **Choose Share List Name from the shortcut menu.**

   A new e-mail appears.

4. **Enter recipient information and then click the Send button to send the e-mail.**

The recipients of the e-mail receive an e-mail form with a Connect to This Document Library button in the form's toolbar — a button that allows them to connect the list or library to Outlook, as shown in Figure 10-2.

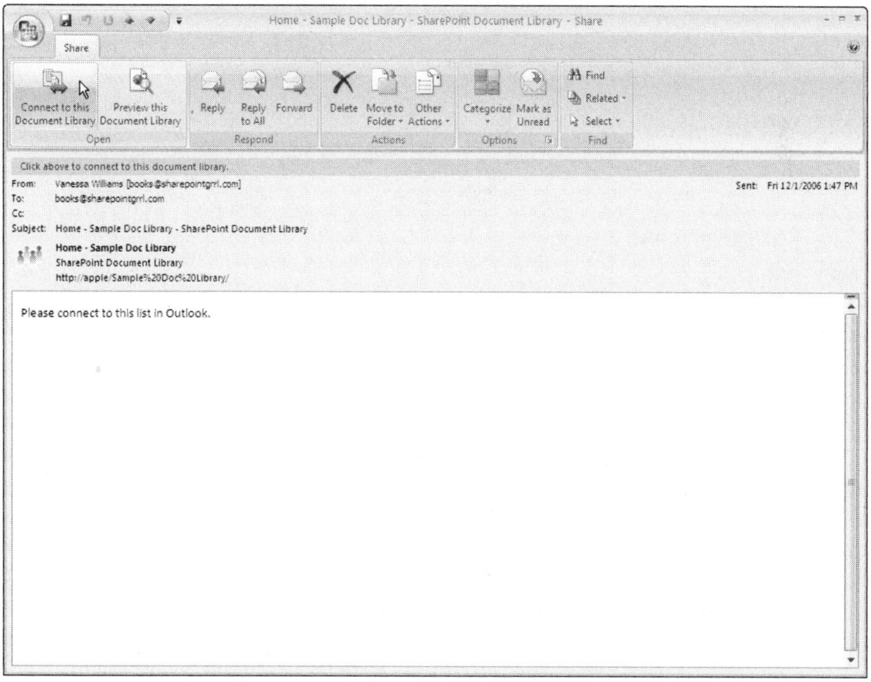

Figure 10-2:
Share Outlook connections with other users.

Users can interact with the content from SharePoint lists in Outlook the same way that they can interact with other Outlook content. For example, users can create new contacts, meeting requests, and tasks in Outlook. Users can also use Outlook to download offline copies of document libraries for use while on the road. Users can synchronize changes made in Outlook to SharePoint by using Outlook's Send/Receive function.

Unlike previous versions of SharePoint and Outlook, users can see tasks assigned to them in SharePoint in their local tasks list.

Users can also use roll-up Web parts in My Site to see all their tasks and documents. (See Chapter 12 for more about My Site.)

In Outlook, the connections to SharePoint are maintained as accounts similar to e-mail accounts. Users can *view* their connections to SharePoint lists in Outlook by using the Account Settings dialog box. The dialog box can be accessed in Outlook 2007 by choosing Tools➪Account Settings. This dialog box lists all the connections, as shown in Figure 10-3. (Keep in mind that users can use the Account Settings dialog box to change or remove a connection, but they can't *add* SharePoint lists from this dialog box.)

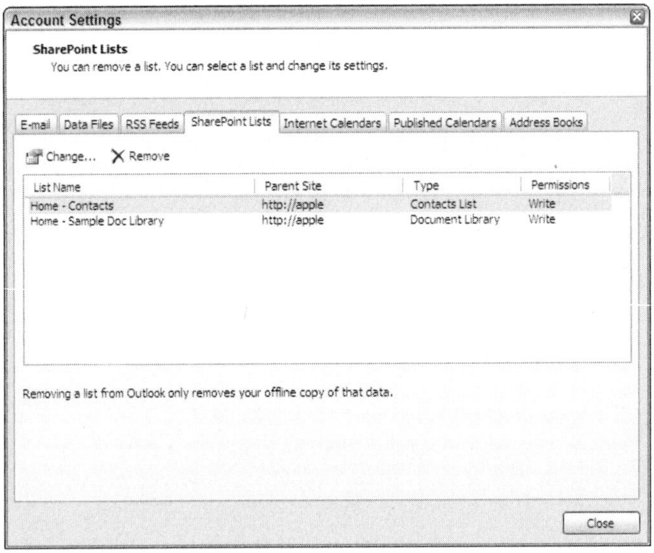

Account Settings

SharePoint Lists
You can remove a list. You can select a list and change its settings.

| E-mail | Data Files | RSS Feeds | SharePoint Lists | Internet Calendars | Published Calendars | Address Books |

📝 Change... ✕ Remove

List Name	Parent Site	Type	Permissions
Home - Contacts	http://apple	Contacts List	Write
Home - Sample Doc Library	http://apple	Document Library	Write

Removing a list from Outlook only removes your offline copy of that data.

Close

Figure 10-3:
View SharePoint lists in Outlook 2007.

Working offline with Outlook

Users can create new contacts and events, and can even reply to discussion threads in Outlook without being connected to SharePoint. When the user is connected to the network again, he can use the Send/Receive command to send new posts to SharePoint and download any content from the lists. Users can also use Outlook to work with documents in document libraries in an offline status.

Users connect to document libraries in Outlook like any SharePoint list. The contents of the list are grouped by *Downloaded Documents,* documents that have been downloaded from the server, and *Available for Download,* documents that are on the server but haven't been downloaded to Outlook yet.

Users can preview the contents of downloaded documents in the Outlook 2007 Preview pane, as shown in Figure 10-4.

Users can also edit the file offline and upload their changes to the document library at a later time. When a file — such as a Word document or Excel spreadsheet from a connected SharePoint library — is opened from Outlook 2007, the Office 2007 application displays an Offline Server Document toolbar. By clicking the Edit Offline button, the downloaded file is copied to the local SharePoint Drafts folder in the user's My Documents folder. The user has the option to upload the file during that editing session, or the file can remain in the SharePoint Drafts folder until the user reconnects to the network.

Figure 10-4:
Preview
documents
in Outlook
2007.

Users can also open documents from Outlook 2007 with previous versions of Office; however, the Offline Server Document toolbar won't appear. The same is true of non-Office documents also. In those instances, browse to the SharePoint library using the browser and then use the Check Out feature to download a local copy of the file to the SharePoint Drafts folder.

Keeping track with notification

SharePoint provides three ways for users to keep up-to-date with the updates on lists and libraries in SharePoint sites. Instead of manually pulling up SharePoint sites in the browser to check for new announcements or see whether any tasks were assigned to you, use one of the following SharePoint features:

- ✔ **E-mail notifications:** Tasks and issues lists can send e-mail notifications to a user at the time the task or issue is assigned to the user. E-mail notifications show up in the user's e-mail Inbox.

- ✔ **Syndicated feeds:** View syndicated feeds of content from SharePoint sites in your favorite feed reader, Outlook 2007, or Internet Explorer (IE) 7. All lists and libraries in SharePoint can deliver an updated list of items added to the list or library by using a special file — an RSS feed. *RSS* is an eXtensible Markup Language (XML) file that requires a reader or style sheet to render the file contents to HyperText Markup Language (HTML) in a Web page.

- ✔ **Alerts:** Subscribe to receive an e-mail notification in the form of an alert any time items are added, deleted, or changed in a list or library.

Three levels of configuration are required for these features to work:

- ✔ **Server farm:** The server farm must be configured to send outbound e-mail. Otherwise, none of these features can work. Type the name of your Simple Mail Transfer Protocol (SMTP) server in the Outgoing E-Mail Settings page, which you can access by clicking the Outgoing E-Mail Settings link on the Operations page of the Central Administration site.

  Additionally, alerts and RSS feeds can be disabled for each Web application. By default, these features are turned on. You can access these settings by clicking the Web Application General Settings link on the Application Management page of Central Administration. You can also configure these settings when you create a new Web application.

- ✔ **Site collection and sites:** RSS feeds can be disabled for all sites in a site collection by turning off the feature on the top-level site. If RSS is enabled for the site collection, each site can be configured to disable RSS. Access the RSS configuration options by clicking the RSS link in the Site Administration section of the site's Site Settings page. You can access the Site Settings page in WSS by clicking Site Actions➪Site

Settings. In the MOSS 2007 publishing site, click Site Actions⇨Modify All Site Settings⇨Site Settings.

RSS must be enabled at the server farm in order to see the RSS link on the Site Settings page.

You can manage all alerts found on a site by clicking the User Alerts link in the Site Administration section of the site's Site Settings page.

✔ **List or library:** At the individual list or library level, list administrators can enable RSS for the list or library and configure what content appears in the feed. List administrators can also enable e-mail notification for tasks and issues lists. List users can create alerts on items in a list or library if they have the Create Alerts permission.

Enable e-mail notifications on tasks and issues lists by using the Advanced Settings link on the list or library's Customize page. Click Settings⇨List Settings to access the Customize page. After the task or issue is assigned ownership, the user receives an e-mail notification.

Users can subscribe to alerts for an entire list or an individual item in a list. Users can choose Action⇨Alert Me in a list or library to subscribe to the entire list or library. By clicking an individual item and choosing Alert Me from the menu, they can receive an alert based on the individual item. The alert contains a notification of the kind of change that occurred along with a link to the item or list.

SharePoint automatically generates RSS feeds for all lists and libraries. Follow these steps to determine how much information to display in a feed:

1. **Browse to the Customize page for the list or library where you want to configure the feed.**

   Access the Customize page by using the list or library's Settings menu as in Settings⇨List Settings.

2. **Click the RSS Settings link in the Communications section.**

3. **In the List RSS section, indicate whether to enable an RSS feed for the list or library.**

4. **Specify the feed's channel information, such as Title, Description, and Image URL.**

5. **In the Document Options section, indicate whether to include file enclosures or links to files.**

   This section only appears for document libraries. The default values are No.

6. **In the Columns section, select the columns to include in the feed.**

7. **In the Items section, Indicate the maximum number of items and days to include in the feed.**

8. **Click OK.**

Users can view the feed for a list or library by choosing Actions⇨View RSS Feed in the list or library. The feed appears in the browser. In most cases, users want to use a feed reader to subscribe to the feed. By creating a subscription, users can automatically view feed updates without browsing to the feed.

Outlook 2007 and Internet Explorer (IE) 7 provide integrated feed reader support. Many other feed readers are available. The nice thing about using IE 7 and Outlook 2007 is that RSS subscriptions are synchronized between the two applications. If your organization hasn't chosen a preferred feed reader, it should probably do so before implementing SharePoint.

To subscribe to a feed by using IE 7, follow these steps:

1. **View the RSS feed for the list or library by using IE 7.**

   If IE 7 is your default browser, you can click Actions⇨View RSS Feed in the list or library. Otherwise, you can allow the feed to open in your default feed reader or browser and paste the feed's URL in IE 7.

2. **Click the Subscribe to This Feed link, as shown in Figure 10-5.**

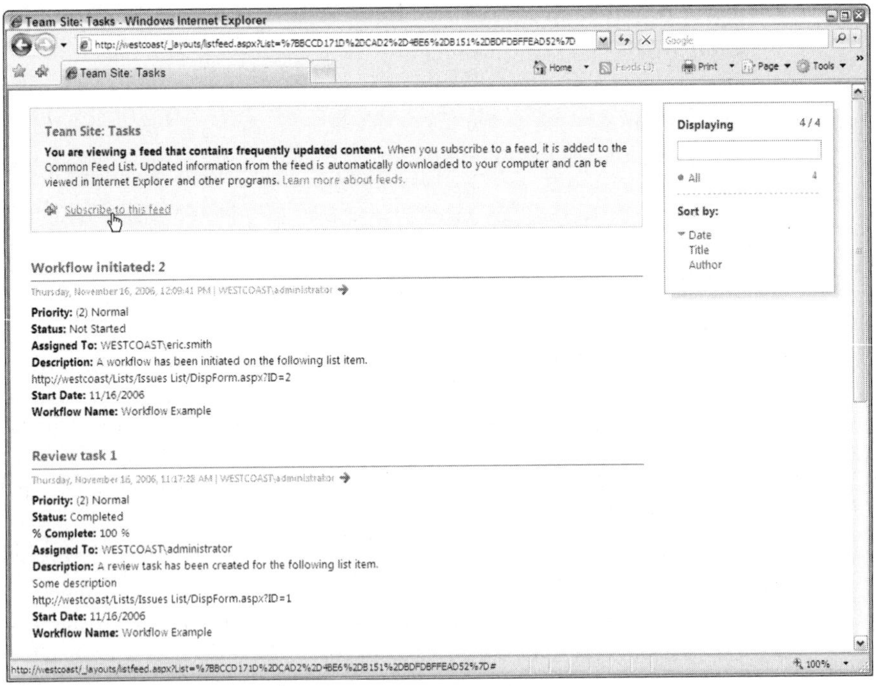

Figure 10-5:
Subscribe to
an RSS feed
in IE 7.

IE 7 prompts you for a location to store the feed.

By default, IE 7 stores feeds in the Favorites Center, which has one tab for Web pages and another for RSS feeds.

3. **Click the Subscribe button.**

IE 7 saves the feed.

Both IE 7 and Firefox include menu commands that make subscribing to RSS feeds a snap.

Sending E-Mail to SharePoint

One challenge facing organizations is managing e-mail. Everyone's e-mail Inbox seems to be overflowing. E-mail administrators have no way of knowing how much e-mail should be saved and how much is wasted space, so they set arbitrary limits to keep e-mail Inboxes from getting too large.

E-mail can be a useful way to add content to your SharePoint sites. Rather than uploading documents via the browser or Office applications, you can send attachments and e-mail contents to your SharePoint site.

You have two basic options for sending e-mail to a SharePoint site:

✔ **Configure an e-mail address for a list or library:** You can configure an e-mail address for an individual list or library. Users send content to the list or library by including the e-mail address in the To or Cc lines of their e-mail. This configuration in considered the *basic e-mail integration configuration* in SharePoint.

✔ **Use SharePoint Groups as distribution lists:** You can use a SharePoint group as a distribution list for sending content to a SharePoint site. Users can use the e-mail address of the SharePoint group to send e-mail to the group's members as well as lists within the site. This option requires the configuration of the SharePoint Directory Management Service and is considered an *advanced configuration*.

Before you can configure SharePoint to accept e-mail, you must configure the e-mail service on your SharePoint Web server. E-mail is handled through SMTP, which means that it is responsible for sending e-mail. In this case, the e-mail is being sent to SharePoint, not to a third party via the Internet as SMTP usually does.

Use the Manage Your Server dialog box to add the Mail Server role to your Web server. See the section, "Preparing your server," in Chapter 2, for more information on adding roles to your server. After you step through the wizard, the Manage Your Server window displays the Mail Server (POP3, SMTP) role. You don't need to make any other configuration settings on the server for SharePoint to use the service.

You can use the Internet Information Services (IIS) Manager to manage the SMTP server, including changing the domain name used in the e-mail addresses of your lists and libraries.

SMTP runs on port 25. You can test to ensure the SMTP service is working by opening a telnet session on port 25. To open a telnet session, type **telnet servername 25** at a command prompt. If the telnet service can't connect, your SMTP service isn't working properly. To test the service after you establish a telnet session, you can type the command **EHLO**. Of course, using Outlook to send a test e-mail is easier.

Sending e-mail to lists and libraries

Before users can start sending e-mail to SharePoint, the server farm must be configured to accept incoming e-mail. You use the Configure Incoming E-Mail settings for both basic and advanced configurations.

Here's how you configure basic e-mail settings for SharePoint:

1. **Browse to the Operations page in Central Administration.**

2. **Click the Incoming E-Mail Settings link in the Topology and Services section.**

   The Configure Incoming E-mail Settings page appears.

   You can also access this page from the Administrative Tasks list on the Central Administration site's home page, as I describe in Chapter 2.

3. **Click the Yes radio button under Enable Sites on This Server to Receive E-Mail?**

4. **Accept the Automatic default settings.**

   The other option is Advanced, which allows you to enter the folder where SharePoint should look for e-mail messages. By default, the SMTP service drops mail in the folder `C:\Inetpub\mailroot\Drop`. You may choose a different location, for example, if you want to move the drop folder to a disk drive different than the operating system. You can also use a Universal Naming Convention (UNC) path to configure SharePoint to pick up mail from a different server altogether. The downside of this approach is that SharePoint has no way of knowing if the SMTP service on the other server isn't working.

5. **Accept the No default value in the Directory Management Service section.**

   Configuring the Directory Management Service is discussed in the following section.

6. **Type the domain name used to display e-mail server addresses in the E-Mail Server Display Address textbox.**

   The value you type here is used to create e-mail addresses for lists and libraries. If you want to use a user-friendly domain name, you can change it in the SMTP server.

   The e-mail server address value must match the default domain in the SMTP server. Use Internet Information Services (IIS) Manager to configure the domain.

7. **In the Safe E-Mail Servers section, indicate whether to accept e-mail from all servers or to accept mail from only specified servers.**

   Use this option if you want to accept e-mail from only an e-mail server, such as Microsoft Exchange Server.

8. **Click OK.**

   SharePoint is enabled to accept incoming e-mail into lists and libraries. You must manually configure the lists or libraries you wish to receive e-mail.

You can submit many different kinds of content through e-mail. Simply by including the e-mail address of a list or library in the To or Cc lines of an e-mail, team members can do the following:

- ✔ **Archive e-mail threads to a discussion board** instead of each member saving the e-mail in their Inbox. Members can add new comments to the thread via e-mail or browser, or they can use Outlook 2007 to view new comments posted to the discussion board.

- ✔ **Post announcements to the team site** at the same time you e-mail them to team members. If the site has a Web part displaying announcements on the site's home page, e-mailed announcements appear automatically on the page.

- ✔ **Send meeting requests to a team calendar.** The meeting request must be in the iCalendar format, which is the default for Outlook.

- ✔ **Upload documents to a document library** by attaching them as attachments to an e-mail. You can also send pictures as attachments and upload those to a picture library.

- ✔ **Submit a completed InfoPath form** by e-mailing it to a form library.

- ✔ **Add a new entry to a SharePoint blog** by e-mailing the post to the blog.

For these features to work, the various team calendars, announcements lists, blogs, and other lists and libraries that users want to target must be configured to accept e-mail. The steps for enabling e-mail are similar for all lists and libraries:

1. **Browse to the list or library where you want to enable incoming e-mail.**

2. **Choose the Settings menu and then choose a menu option to access the list or library's settings page.**

   The Customize page appears.

   For example, choose Settings⇨Document Library Settings for a library or choose Settings⇨List Settings for a list.

   You must have the Manage Lists permission to access the Settings menu.

3. **In the Communications section, select the Incoming E-Mail Settings link.**

   The Incoming E-Mail Settings page appears.

   If you don't see the link in the Communications section, there are two possible causes. Either incoming e-mail isn't enabled for the server farm, or the list or library type can't be configured to use incoming e-mail. To determine whether e-mail is enabled on the server farm, check another list or library, such as a document library, to see whether you see the link.

4. **In the Incoming E-Mail section, click the Yes radio button to allow the list or library to accept incoming e-mail.**

5. **Type an e-mail address for the list or library in the E-Mail Address textbox.**

   The domain name of the e-mail address is determined by the settings in the server farm's Configure Incoming E-Mail Settings page in Central Administration.

   If your server farm is configured to use SharePoint's Directory Management Service, the e-mail address appears automatically in the address book of your e-mail server, such as Microsoft Exchange Server. Otherwise, your e-mail administrator must manually add the e-mail address.

   Place the e-mail address in the list or library's description so users readily know they can e-mail their content to the list or library.

6. **Configure the remaining e-mail settings for the specific list or library you're configuring.**

   See Table 10-1 for a list of configuration settings you'll encounter.

7. **Click OK.**

   The list or library is configured to receive inbound e-mail.

You can also enable a list or library to accept incoming e-mail when you create the site.

Table 10-1	Inbound E-Mail Settings	
Setting	*What It Does*	*Where You'll Find It*
E-Mail Attachments	Determines how attachments are handled.	Libraries, calendars, announcements, and discussions
E-Mail Message	Determines whether to save the original e-mail.	Libraries and discussions
E-Mail Meeting Invitations	Determines whether to save e-mailed meeting invitations.	Libraries and discussions
E-Mail Security	Determines whether to accept e-mails based on list or library permissions or from anyone.	Libraries, calendars, announcements, discussions, and blogs
Post Publishing	Determines whether to save e-mailed posts as drafts or published versions.	Blogs

To configure incoming e-mail settings for a blog, you must enable incoming e-mail for the Posts list on the blog site.

Sending inbound e-mail to a list or library is as simple as addressing the list or library's e-mail address in the To or Cc lines of the e-mail. How the e-mail's contents are saved in the list or library depends on the type of list and how the content is sent, as I describe here:

✔ **Message body** is saved intact as posts to discussions and blogs.

✔ **Meeting requests and appointments** become events in a SharePoint calendar.

✔ **Attachments,** such as pictures, forms, and documents, are saved as files in a library.

Using distribution lists

SharePoint also makes it possible to send e-mail messages to an entire group of users in SharePoint. SharePoint provides the Directory Management Service as a means to manage e-mail distribution lists with SharePoint. By configuring the service, you can synchronize a SharePoint group with a distribution list in Active Directory (AD). When you add members to the SharePoint group, the members are added as contacts to the distribution list in AD. This allows users to send an e-mail to a distribution list that is actually maintained in SharePoint. By adding list and library e-mail addresses to the distribution list, users can send content to all the members of the list and have the e-mail and any attachments archived in SharePoint.

Before you configure the Directory Management Service in SharePoint, you must create a container in AD to store the distribution lists. The container is a new organizational unit. I suggest giving the container a name, such as SharePoint Groups, so it's easily identifiable in AD.

After you create the organizational unit container, you can enable the service in SharePoint. Follow these steps to enable the Directory Management Service in SharePoint:

1. **Browse to the Operations page in the Central Administration site.**

   See Chapter 18 for more details on the Central Administration site.

2. **Click the Incoming e-mail settings link.**

   The Configure Incoming E-mail Settings page appears.

3. **Click Yes in the Directory Management Service configuration section.**

   A list of options appears.

4. **Type the path to the AD container where new distribution lists should be created.**

   AD uses *distinguished names* (DN) to uniquely identify objects, such as users and containers. The *DN notation* is a series of attributes separated by commas. For example, assume you have an AD container called SPGroups in the AD domain of mycompany.com. In this example, SPGroups is the *organizational unit,* mycompany is the *domain-name domain component,* and com is the *top-level domain-name domain component.* The distinguished name is OU=SPGroups, DC=mycompany, DC=com.

   If you don't type the correct distinguished name, SharePoint gives you a warning message.

5. **Type the domain name of the SMTP Mail server for incoming mail.**

6. **Indicate whether to accept e-mail from authenticated users only.**

7. **Indicate whether distribution lists can be created from SharePoint sites.**

   If you choose Yes, you must select the request approval settings.

8. **Click the OK button.**

   See the preceding section if you need more details on completing the configuration of the incoming e-mail settings.

In order to use a SharePoint group as a distribution list, you must enable the group to use e-mail. You can enable e-mail for an existing SharePoint group or you can enable it whenever you set up groups for a site. Either way, the steps are straightforward.

To enable e-mail for an existing SharePoint group, follow these steps:

1. **Browse to the People and Groups page for the site you wish to manage.**

   You can find a link to the People and Groups page in the Users and Permissions section of a site's Site Settings page. (See Chapter 6 for more about using the People and Groups page.)

2. **Click the group you wish to enable from the Quick Launch bar.**

   For example, click the *Site* Members group if you wish to enable e-mail for the group.

3. **Choose Settings⇨Group Settings.**

   The Change Group Settings page appears.

4. **Scroll to the E-Mail Distribution List section and then click the Yes radio button to create an e-mail distribution list for the group.**

5. **Type an e-mail address for the group.**

6. **In the Archive E-Mail section, indicate whether you want e-mail sent to the group archived on the site. If so, select a list or enter the name of a new list.**

7. **Click OK.**

   SharePoint creates the new distribution list in the organizational unit in AD that you specified when you configured the Directory Management Service. If you're using Microsoft Exchange Server, the e-mail address for the distribution list appears in the address book.

Users can use the e-mail address of the SharePoint group to e-mail all members of the group. When the group's membership changes in SharePoint, the distribution list is updated in AD.

If you enable inbound e-mail for SharePoint groups at the time the site is set up, SharePoint automatically associates an e-mail-enabled discussions list and calendar with the SharePoint group. The default e-mail addresses for these lists are *groupname.discussions* and *groupname.calendar*, respectively. The e-mails that users send to the SharePoint group's e-mail address are archived in these lists.

You can manually add e-mail–enabled lists and libraries to a SharePoint group with the Add Users page. Just type the e-mail address of the list or library instead of using a user account name.

Chapter 11

Using Portal Sites

In This Chapter

▶ Creating portals with SharePoint templates

▶ Customizing collaboration portals

▶ Listing sites in the Site Directory

▶ Configuring a Publishing Portal site

*I*n other chapters, I show you how to use various site templates included with SharePoint — templates associated with team sites, wikis, and blogs, for example. Site templates are used to create a single SharePoint site, and, within each SharePoint site, you can choose a site template to create another SharePoint site.

Microsoft Office SharePoint Server (MOSS) 2007 adds a new kind of site template — a portal site template. The *portal site template* lets you define a hierarchy of sites that can be created all at once. So, instead of creating sites one at a time with site templates, portal site templates create a set of multiple sites that are intended for use together.

MOSS 2007 provides extensive support for creating portals. MOSS has two portal site templates that you can use to create commonly used portals:

✔ **Collaboration Portal:** This site template includes a set of sites that are frequently used in internal division portals, such as sites for records and document management.

✔ **Publishing Portal:** This site template lets you build a site suitable for creating an Internet-facing portal for providing content, such as press releases or investor communications.

These two templates are available only when you create a new site collection. I explain how to create site collections in Chapter 3.

In addition to the two portal site templates, SharePoint also provides the following templates for creating specialized portals:

- **My Site** is essentially a personal portal that each portal member uses to manage access to resources in SharePoint. I discuss My Site in Chapter 12.

- **Personalization Sites** make it possible to create portals that display content personalized to each user, such as My HR portal. See Chapter 13 for more information on personalization sites.

Exploring Collaboration Portals

The Collaboration Portal site template provides several subsites that enable collaborating, sharing information, and connecting among employees of a division or small- to medium-sized enterprise.

Many of the subsites in the Collaboration Portal are called *Centers* instead of sites. The Centers and sites created by the Collaboration Portal include the following:

- **A top-level publishing site:** Provides the portal's home page and access to all the portal's resources.

- **A Document Center:** Provides a centralized repository for storing enterprise documents. The Document Center is essentially a document library for the company. I discuss the Document Center in Chapter 15.

- **A News site:** Provides a centralize site for publishing news articles. I discuss publishing sites like news sites in Chapter 16.

- **A Report Center:** Provides a site for creating a business intelligence portal. See Chapter 17 for more information on business intelligence.

- **A Search Center:** Provides a site for searching the portal's content. See Chapter 14 for more information on search.

- **A Site Directory:** Lists all the sites found within the portal.

You can access these sites by using the top link bar across the top of the portal, as shown in Figure 11-1.

You can delete any of the sites that you don't want to use. I explain how to delete sites in the section, "Getting the big picture," later in this chapter. Also, the Collaboration Portal includes plenty of sample content that may not be useful to your business. For example, the portal home page (seen in Figure 11-1) shows an image of two people intently working on a project. You probably want to delete that image. In fact, I insist that you do. The Collaboration Portal consists mostly of publishing sites, which I explain how to edit in Chapter 16.

Top Link bar

Figure 11-1:
Access
portal sites
with the top
link bar.

Managing portal content

Each of the sites contained in a Collaboration portal is its own SharePoint
site. As such, it has all the features you expect SharePoint sites to have,
including navigation, lists, and libraries. Each site has its own Site Settings
page where you can manage the settings relevant to that particular site.

By default, all the sites inherit their permissions from the top-level sites.
However, you can break inheritance any time. (See Chapter 6 for more information on permission inheritance.)

Changing default settings

Part of the setup process when creating a portal site involves you choosing
your initial site owners and naming the portal site. Don't feel that you're
stuck with your choices here, though. You can easily change these settings
down the road using the Site Settings page of the top-level site in the portal.
See Chapter 5 for more using the Site Settings page.

To change the owner of the portal site, follow these steps:

1. **Click the Site Collection Administrators link in the Users and Permissions section. The Site Collection Administrators page appears.**

2. **Type the names of the new site owners or use the Select People dialog box to select the users.**

3. **Click OK.**

You can also manage site collection administrators from the Application Management page in the Central Administration site.

Follow these steps to change the portal site's title and other default settings:

1. **Click the Title, Description, and Icon link in the Look and Feel section of the Site Settings page.**

    The Title, Description, and Icon page appears.

2. **Type a new title and description for the site.**

3. **Enter a URL to the image you want to use for the site's icon.**

4. **Click OK.**

    The site's header and global breadcrumb update to reflect the changes.

Linking to another portal

All the sites in a portal use the same top link bar by default; however, each site uses its own settings for the Quick Launch bar. You can change these settings at the Site Settings page, as I describe in Chapter 5.

You can create a hierarchy of portal sites that enables a lower-level divisional site to link to a higher-level enterprise site. The link to the higher-level portal appears in the portal's global breadcrumb. To connect the portal site to another portal, follow these steps:

1. **Browse to the top-level site in the portal site.**

2. **Choose Site Actions⇨Site Settings⇨Modify All Site Settings.**

    The Site Settings page appears.

3. **Click the Portal Site Connection link in the Site Collection Administration section.**

   The Portal Site Connection page appears.

4. **Select the Connect to Portal Site radio button.**

5. **Type the portal URL in the Portal Web Address textbox.**

6. **Type the name you want to appear in the global breadcrumb in the Portal Name textbox.**

   For example, you can connect to a portal called `Corporate Home`.

7. **Click OK.**

   The higher-level portal appears in the global breadcrumb, as shown in Figure 11-2.

You can use these same steps to connect any site collection to another site. You aren't restricted to using portal sites only.

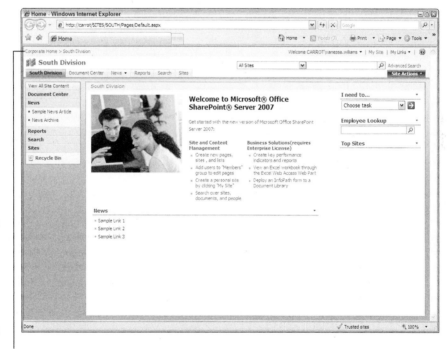

Figure 11-2:
Create a
breadcrumb
path to
another
portal.

Global breadcrumb

Getting the big picture

MOSS 2007, with its Site Content and Structure page provides you with a tree view of your portal's site collection that allows you to easily see the portal's hierarchy. You can use the page to do the following:

- ✔ Access common site management links — links such as Site Settings and Permissions — for any site in your portal's site collection.
- ✔ Access publishing features, such as Check In and Discard Check Out, for list and library items.
- ✔ Add new list items, lists, and subsites.
- ✔ Copy subsites or lists to another subsite in the hierarchy.
- ✔ Move list items or subsites.
- ✔ Delete list items or subsites.
- ✔ View reports and properties for the items in the hierarchy.

SharePoint automatically updates all links and navigation anytime you copy, move, or delete content.

You can access the Site Content and Structure page by choosing Site Actions➪Manage Content and Structure. You can also click the Content and Structure link in the Site Settings page.

The Site Content and Structure page uses a Windows Explorer-like interface, as shown in Figure 11-3. The Navigation pane on the left displays the site hierarchy. By clicking the plus (+) sign next to the items in the Navigation pane, you can see subsites and lists contained within. The List pane displays the contents of the container selected in the Navigation pane. When you click a site in the Navigation pane, you see the subsites and lists contained within the site. When you click a list, you see the individual list items.

You take action on the items in the site hierarchy through context menus. The commands that are available depend on the kind of object you're accessing and the permission level of the user. You must have at least Contributor permissions to access the Site Content and Structure page.

To take action on an item, follow these steps:

1. **Position your cursor over the item until the drop-down arrow appears.**

2. **Click the drop-down arrow to display a context menu.**

3. **Choose the action from the menu.**

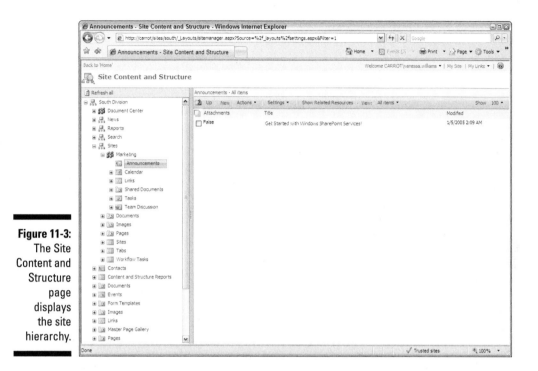

Figure 11-3:
The Site
Content and
Structure
page
displays
the site
hierarchy.

For example, assume you want to remove the Search Center that uses tabs and instead add the generic Search Center to a newly created portal. Here's how you'd do that using the Site Content and Structure page:

1. **Click the drop-down arrow for the Search site.**

2. **Choose Delete from the context menu.**

   A confirmation dialog box appears.

3. **Click the OK button to confirm the deletion.**

   The site is deleted.

4. **Click the top-level site in the hierarchy.**

5. **In the List pane, choose the New menu, as shown in Figure 11-4.**

6. **Choose Site.**

   The New SharePoint Site page appears.

7. **Add a new site based on the Search Center template.**

   You can find the template in the Enterprise tab.

   The site appears in the Site Content and Structure page.

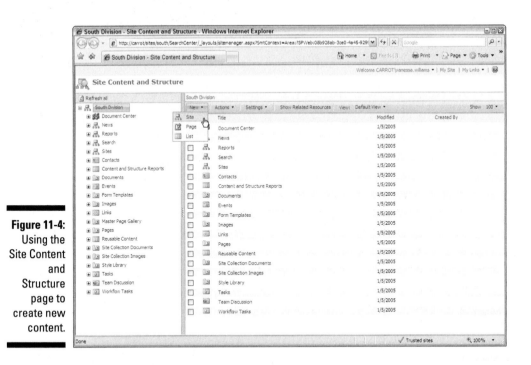

Figure 11-4:
Using the
Site Content
and
Structure
page to
create new
content.

Using the Site Directory

The Collaboration Portal includes the Site Directory site, which is essentially the Yellow Pages for your portal. You can add sites to the Site Directory during or after site creation.

By default, all portal sites have a Site Directory. You access the Site Directory by clicking the Sites link on the top link bar of the portal site. Figure 11-5 shows the Site Directory. You can add a Site Directory to any top-level site by following the steps to create a site and selecting the Site Directory template.

You can add a Site Directory to a subsite, but the directory still lists the sites in the entire site collection. This means that even when you add a Site Directory to a subsite, the directory lists all the sites found in the site collection, not just the sites that are below the subsite.

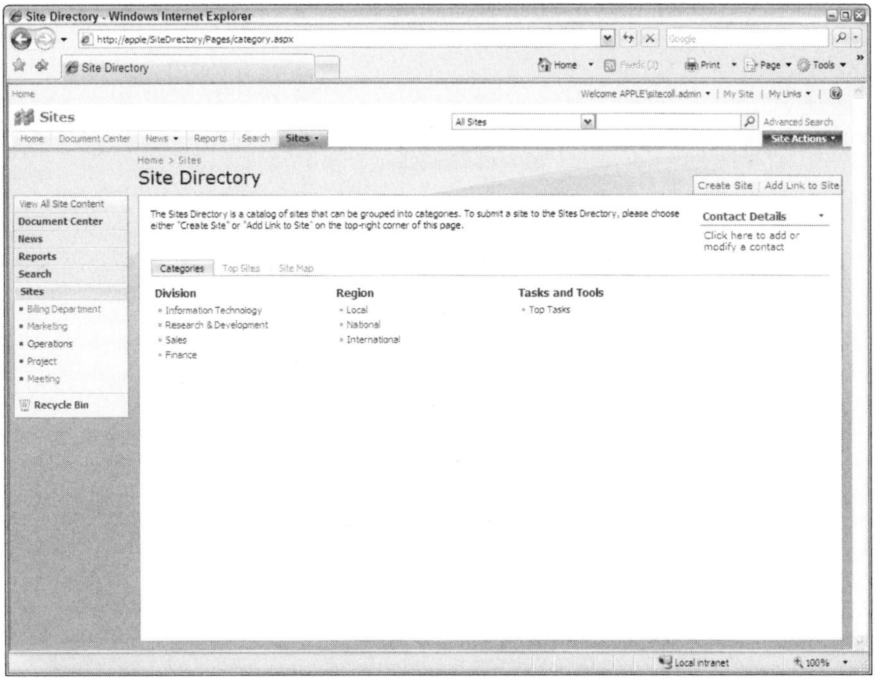

Figure 11-5:
The Site
Directory.

The Site Directory displays the following three tabs, which provide different ways of viewing the sites in the site collection:

✔ **Categories:** Displays a set of categories that are used to organize sites. SharePoint provides a default set, but you can create your own.

✔ **Top Sites:** Displays a list of sites marked as Top Sites.

✔ **Site Map:** Displays an automatically generated hierarchical list of the site collection.

Before you start adding sites to the Site Directory, you should use the following general steps as a guide when setting up the Site Directory:

1. **Customize the Sites list.**

   The content you see in the Categories and Top Sites tabs is driven by the Sites list in the Site Directory. I explain how to modify the Sites list in the "Managing categories" section.

2. **Modify the Site Directory home page.**

   You can add new tabs or change the order of the tabs that appear in the Site Directory home page. Choose Site Actions⇨Edit Page to put the page in Edit mode.

3. **Add your Contact Details.**

   The Site Directory home page includes a Contact Details Web part where you can enter the name and contact information of the person responsible for managing the Site Directory. If you don't want to use the Contact Details Web part, you can remove it when you modify the Site Directory home page.

Managing categories

The Site Directory makes it easy to organize your sites any way you want by using categories. SharePoint provides categories — for example, Division and Region with choices, such as Sales and Finance or Local and National. SharePoint provides two additional organization options — Top Sites as well as Tasks and Tools. Sites marked with the Top Sites designation appear in the Top Sites tab in the Site Directory. The Task and Tools category is an example of using the Site Directory to create a list of site links directed toward completing an activity.

Because all the site content is managed in a Sites list, everything you know already about working with lists (see Chapter 4) applies to managing categories in the Site Directory. Follow these steps to manage categories for the Site Directory:

1. **Click the View All Site Content link in the Quick Launch bar.**

   The All Site Content page appears.

2. **Click the Sites link in the Lists section.**

   The Sites list appears.

3. **Choose Settings⇨List Settings.**

   The Customize page appears.

4. **In the Columns section, click the Division, Region, or Tasks and Tools columns (see Figure 11-6) that you want to change and then make those changes.**

   For example, you might decide to add new choices or remove all the existing choices. You can also choose to delete a column entirely.

5. Click the Create column link to add a new category.

For example, if you want to display a list of sites based on projects or product lines, you could create columns to represent those choices. Using categories in this way makes it possible for you to draw attention to sites in ways that go beyond organizational hierarchy. See Chapter 7 for more information on working with columns.

You can create a new Tab on the Site Directory home page if you want to display a single category of sites. The Top Sites tab is an example of this. You can create new tabs when you place the Site Directory home page in Edit mode.

6. In the Views section, click the Categories link to change the order that categories appear on the Site Directory home page.

See Chapter 7 for more details on working with views.

7. Click the Site Creation Categories view to set the categories that appear when a new site is created.

The Site Directory site uses the publishing features of MOSS 2007. You can use the publishing features to make extensive changes to the look and feel of the site. See Chapter 16 for more information.

Managing sites

Sites don't just magically appear in the Site Directory when you create them. To the contrary, a site only shows up in the Site Directory if a list item for the site is created in the Site Directory's Sites list. Here are a few ways to get a site into the Sites list:

- ✔ Indicate whether you want the site included in the Site Directory when you create the site.
- ✔ Click the Add Link to Site button on the Site Directory.
- ✔ Add the site directly to the Sites list.

By default, content approval is enabled for the Sites list. Thus, new sites added to the Sites list must be approved before they appear in the Site Directory. Use the Submitted Sites view in the Sites list to see a list of sites awaiting approval.

You can turn off content approval for the Sites list by clicking the Versioning Settings link in the Customize page. Conversely, you can enable workflows, such as the Approval workflow, if you want to use an advanced approval process. See Chapter 8 for more information on workflows.

Adding sites via the Sites list or the Add Link to Site link is exactly the same process. That's because the Add Link to Site link takes you to the New Entry form for the Sites list. You use this form to add a new link to the site, as shown in Figure 11-7.

You aren't limited to adding sites from SharePoint. You can add a link to any Web site or resource. Also, you don't have to list every SharePoint site in the Site Directory. You only want to add those sites that you want people to find. For example, the Sales department and the Marketing department each have their own SharePoint site that they use within their departments. They may not want these sites listed in the Site Directory. However, if they create a collective SharePoint site called Sales and Marketing Initiatives that's intended to educate employees, then they probably do want that site listed in the Site Directory.

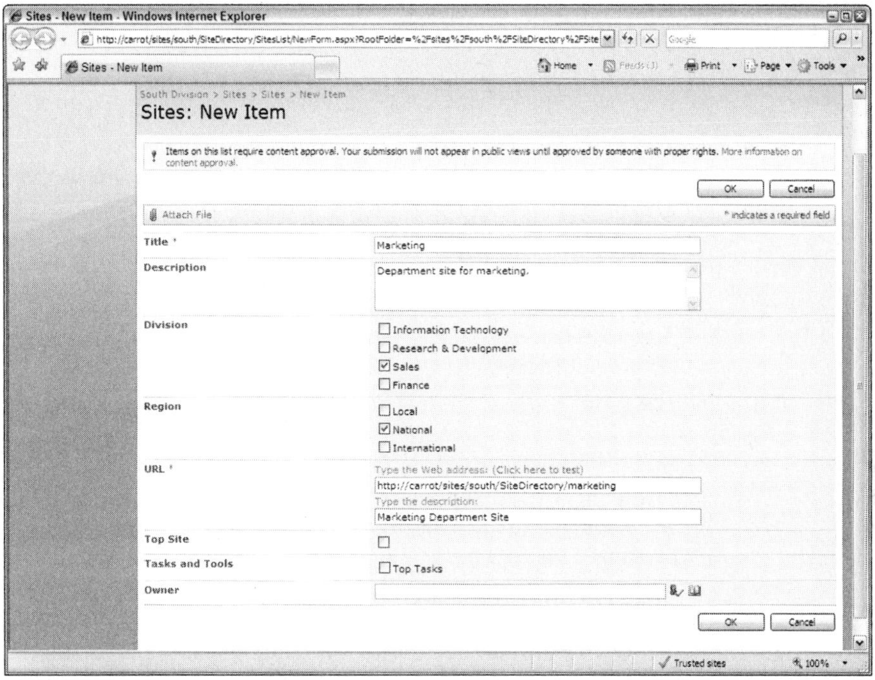

Figure 11-7:
Add links
to sites
in the Site
Directory.

If you don't see the categories or the choices you want in the New Entry form, you can always modify them to suit your needs, as I describe in the preceding section.

Keep in mind that you're only adding links to sites here, not actually creating new sites. Users with permissions to create sites can use the Create Site link on the Site Directory home page to create new SharePoint sites.

You aren't required to create sites with the Site Directory. The Site Directory is simply a listing service. Note that sites created using the Create Site link are subsites of the Site Directory. Make sure this is your intention before using this feature. See Chapter 4 for more information on creating SharePoint sites.

Scanning for broken links

One feature unique to the Site Directory is the ability to check for broken links. Just like sites aren't magically added to the directory, neither are they deleted when a site is removed. By checking for broken links, you can ensure that your directory is validated.

Follow these steps to check for broken links in your Site Directory:

1. **Choose Site Actions⇨Scan for Broken Links.**

   The Broken Site Directory Links page appears.

2. **Select a view to scan.**

   The views you see listed are the same views that exist in the Sites list.

   The scan can scan only 1,000 sites. If you have more sites than that, create additional views in the Sites list to filter the scans.

3. **Click OK.**

   The Broken Links Scan page appears.

   The scan goes through each site in the view and tests for broken sites. If any broken sites are found, the entries in the Sites list are marked as broken.

4. **Click OK after the scan completes.**

   You go to the Broken Sites view of the Sites list.

5. **Remove or fix any broken entries.**

You can also scan for broken links with the Site Directory Links Scan in the Central Administration site. Click the Site Directory Links Scan link on the Operations page.

Setting the default Site Directory

You have the option of setting the path for the site to be used as the Site Directory for your portal. By default, the Sites site that is created with the Collaboration portal is used as the Site Directory path. To change the path to the Site Directory for the portal, follow these steps:

1. **Browse to the home page of the portal.**

2. **Choose Site Actions⇨Site Settings⇨Modify All Site Settings.**

   The Site Settings page appears.

3. **Click the Site Directory Settings link in the Site Collection Administration section.**

   The Site Directory Settings page appears.

4. **In the Site Directory Location section, set the path for the Site Directory.**

   The Site Directory must already exist at the URL before you can set the path. You can create a new Site Directory with the Site Directory template.

5. **In the Site Creation Metadata section, indicate whether categories are required when a new site is listed in the Site Directory.**

6. **In the Site Collection Creation section, indicate whether new site collections can be created from the Site Directory.**

   Self-Service Site Creation must be enabled before this option is available. You can enable Self-Service Site Creation by clicking the Self-Service Site Management link in the Application Security section of the Application Management page in the Central Administration site. By default, the Site Directory displays the Create Sites link to users with the correct permissions. By enabling site collection creation in the Site Directory, users also see a link for creating new site collections. With this feature disabled, the only way to create new site collections is through the Central Administration site.

7. **Click OK.**

   The settings are saved.

You can set the path to a master Site Directory where you want to list all site collections. This might be useful if you have a farm with several Web applications and site collections. A master Site Directory lists all the site collections created across several portals. Click the Manage Site Directory Settings link in the Operations page of the Central Administration site

Reaching Out with Publishing Portals

The Publishing Portal site template is a good example of how the look and feel of a SharePoint portal site can be customized. The Publishing Portal is intended for use as an Internet-facing site; The Collaboration Portal and Publishing Portal site templates are available only when you create a new site collection. See Chapter 3 for more details on creating site collections. The Publishing Portal has these features:

- ✔ A top-level site with custom home page.
- ✔ A subsite called Press Releases for managing the publication of press releases.
- ✔ A Search site that provides search services to the site.

The portal is a Publishing Portal because it's intended for publishing content to a site. The expectation is that the site has more readers than contributors. Also, the portal uses the publishing features of MOSS 2007 for managing content. See Chapter 16.

The portal's home page includes a list of actions that you should consider taking to customize your portal for Internet use. The following action links take you to the administrative pages where you can implement the features:

- ✔ **Enable Anonymous Access:** Before the general public can access your site, you must enable anonymous access to the site. I discuss enabling anonymous access in Chapter 6.

  Enabling anonymous access isn't something to take lightly. You must take steps to ensure that anonymous users can't gain access to other resources on your server. I discuss accessing SharePoint sites from the Internet in Chapter 3.

- ✔ **Manage Navigation:** You can customize the site's navigation with this link. By default, the Search site is hidden from the site's navigation. See Chapter 5 for more information on managing site navigation.

- ✔ **Go to Master Page Gallery:** This link takes you to the Master Page gallery for the portal. *Master pages* define the site's look and feel. See Chapter 16 for more information on working with master pages.

- ✔ **Manage Site Content and Structure:** This link takes you to the Site Content and Structure, which I describe earlier in this chapter.

- ✔ **Set Up Multilingual Support:** You can configure your site so that it can display content in multiple languages.

- ✔ **Add Users to the Approvers and Members Groups:** You must grant access to anyone who needs to add content to your site. Anonymous users have Read Only access. By default, the Press Releases subsite inherits permission from the top-level site. See Chapter 6 for information on managing permissions.

Of course, you can access all these administrative settings from the portal's Site Settings page. Choose the Site Actions menu to access the site's administrative pages.

Before allowing users to access the site, remove or change the default content provided with the portal site template. The portal uses publishing pages. You can use the Site Actions menu to place the page in Edit mode. (See Chapter 16 for step-by-step instructions on checking, editing, and actually publishing your publishing pages.)

Figure 11-8 shows an example of the home page for a Publishing Portal. In this figure, the user is logged in as `lisa.west` who is a member of the *Site Visitor* SharePoint group. If the user was logged in as a member of the *Site Members* group, the Site Actions button would appear next to the user's login information. If the site was accessed anonymously, no login information would be visible.

Press Releases subsite link   Search box

Figure 11-8:
The home
page of a
Publishing
Portal.

Actions list

Chapter 12

Configuring Profiles and My Sites

· ·

In This Chapter

▶ Administering and customizing My Site personal portals

▶ Viewing My Site from an end user's perspective

▶ Setting up user profile properties

· ·

*W*indows SharePoint Services (WSS) provides you with the basic collaboration features you'd expect — the ones that allow site members to work on documents, coordinate meetings, and manage project tasks. Microsoft Office SharePoint Server (MOSS) 2007 extends the collaboration features of WSS by allowing site members to take advantage of user profile and personalization features that help site members better manage their personal view of the portal, make connections with other members, and view content targeted directly to them.

In MOSS 2007, all these features are accessible via a personal portal that MOSS 2007 has dubbed My Site. The My Site personal portal gives the member the following:

✔ **My Profile:** A page that displays public properties of the member's user profile along with documents and links the member wishes to share. The layout for the My Profile page is the same for all site members.

✔ **My Home:** The site member's private home page of his or her personal site. The personal site is a full-fledged WSS site where the user is the site owner. As site owner, the user can grant other users access to subsites, Web Part pages, and other content the member adds to the personal site.

✔ **Personalization sites:** Special kinds of sites created with content targeted to the user. For example, your Human Resources (HR) department may create a personalized site — My HR — that displays personalized HR content.

In this chapter, I explain My Profile and My Home as well as their supporting technologies, user profiles, and My Site personal sites. I cover personalization features in Chapter 13.

Planning for My Site

The My Site feature is activated by default when you create a Shared Services Provider (SSP). You must specify a Web application to host My Site at the time you create the SSP. I show you how to do this in Chapter 2. Creating the My Site host requires very little planning because the feature is enabled by default.

You need to decide whether to host My Site in a separate Web application or in an existing Web application, such as the primary Web application. The benefit of using the primary portal is that users can access their My Site personal portals with port 80, which makes the URL very simple. If you use a separate Web application, you have to use a different port.

In Chapter 3, I explain the advantages of separating applications in their own Web applications. All these advantages apply here. Because most users access their My Site personal site via the My Site link in SharePoint pages, using a different Web application won't hurt anything.

Whether you host My Site in its own application or in a separate Web application, My Site is created in its own site collection. Each SSP has only one My Site site collection, but you can share a My Site Web application across multiple SSPs. The SSP administrator shares My Site hosts across SSPs by using the Trusted My Site Host Locations list in the Shared Services Administration site. I describe how to access the Shared Services Administration site in Chapter 18.

MOSS 2007 provides a My Site Host site template that's used to set up a My Site site collection. As I explain in Chapter 2, the My Site feature is created automatically when you create the Shared Services Provider. The template is available only when creating a new site collection from within the Central Administration site, as I describe in Chapter 4.

A SharePoint user accesses his or her My Site personal portal by clicking the My Site link in the upper-right corner of a SharePoint site, as shown in Figure 12-1. The address associated with the My Site link is

```
http://mysite_site_url/_layouts/MySite.aspx
```

as shown in the status bar in Figure 12-1. The My Site link attempts to open the user's My Site personal portal. If the user doesn't have a My Site personal portal, one is created automatically for the user. Otherwise, SharePoint redirects to the My Home page of the My Site personal portal using a URL that's similar to the following:

```
http://mysite_site_url/personal/username/default.aspx
```

My Site link

Figure 12-1:
Access the
My Site
personal
portal.

URL in Status bar

Each user's My Site personal portal is its own site collection within the My Site host. The user's personal site is the top-level site in his or her My Site site collection. The user's private home page, My Home, is the `default.aspx` page for the personal site. The URL for the private home page is:

```
http://web_app/my site path/user_name/default.aspx
```

For example, the following URL

```
http://carrot:25444/personal/shaun_combs/default.aspx
```

breaks down like this:

✔ The Web application is `carrot:25444`. The server name is `carrot`, and the HTTP port number is `25444`. This My Site host is hosted in its own Web application. (If the My Site site collection is hosted in the same Web application as the primary Web application — the one that uses port 80 — you don't need to type the port number.)

 ✔ The **My Site path** is `/personal`. This is the default path, but you can change it.

 ✔ The **username** is Shaun Combs and is accessed by using the naming convention `shaun_combs`.

 ✔ The **home page** is `default.aspx`.

I explain how to set the My Site path and naming conventions for user names in the section, "Configuring My Site," later in this chapter.

The default public access for a user's My Site personal portal is the public view of the My Profile page. The public view of the My Profile page is accessed via a URL like this one:

```
http://my_site_url/Person.aspx?accountname=user_name
```

Restricting access to My Site

My Site personal portals are created for all users who access the My Site link. In other words, if the user can see the My Site link in the upper-right corner of the SharePoint page, the user can create his or her very own My Site personal portal. Of course, you may not want every Tom, Dick, and new temp to have a My Site personal portal. You — in the role of SharePoint administrator — manage access to My Site and other personalization features with the Personalization Services Permissions link in the Shared Services Administration site. By default, all authenticated users are granted authority to access personal features and personal sites.

If you don't want everyone who has access to the portal to have their own personal sites, remove permissions for all authenticated users and then grant permissions to the users or groups you want to have personal sites. For example, in my domain, I have a security group called Employees and another called Consultants. I want employees to have rights to create personal sites but not consultants. Follow these steps to remove all rights for all authenticated users and then grant rights to a security group, such as an Employees group:

1. **Browse to the Shared Services Administration site.**

   You can find a link to your Shared Services Administration site on the SharePoint Central Administration site, which is accessible from a SharePoint server by choosing Start➪Administration Tools➪SharePoint 3.0 Central Administration. See Chapter 18 for more details.

2. **Click the Personalization Services Permissions link.**

   The Manage Permissions page appears.

3. **Select the NT Authority\Authenticated Users check box.**

4. **Click the Remove Selected Users button.**

   A confirmation prompt appears.

5. **Click OK to accept the confirmation dialog box.**

   The group is deleted.

6. **Click the Add Users/Groups button.**

   The Add/Users Groups page appears.

7. **In the Choose Users section, type the names of the security groups (such as Employees) or accounts you wish to grant permissions to.**

8. **In the Choose Permission section, select the Create Personal Site and Use Personal Features check boxes, as shown in Figure 12-2.**

9. **Click the Save button.**

   Only users who belong to the accounts or groups you entered in Step 7 have access to the My Site personal portal feature. Users who already have My Site personal portals can still access their portals. Because My Site portals are site collections, you must delete the user's My Site site collection through the Central Administration site. See Chapter 3 for details on working with site collections.

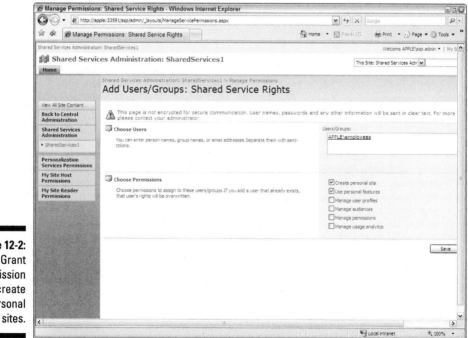

Figure 12-2:
Grant
permission
to create
personal
sites.

You can also use the Shared Service Rights page, as shown in Figure 12-2, to grant administrators permission to manage user profiles and audiences.

Access to the My Site host is enabled by default with the Office SharePoint Server Standard Web application features. The features are enabled by default on every Web application created in MOSS. If you want to prevent a portal from using My Site, you can create the portal in a separate Web application and disable the feature for the Web application. Do this, for example, if you're creating an Internet-facing public SharePoint site, such as a Publishing portal. See Chapter 3 for more information about disabling Web application features.

You could also edit the Master page so that the My Site and My Links links don't appear in the upper-right corner of the page. That prevents users from accessing the My Site host.

The My Site personal site is a kind of WSS site collection. Each user who has his or her own My Site personal portal is the site owner and administrator for their My Site site collection. As a result, the member can change permissions so that users can access content in the personal site. The My Site personal site and the public view of the My Profile page share a common Quick Launch navigation bar, which makes it possible for users to share documents and other content with everyone in the organization.

Because each user is the site owner and administrator of his or her own My Site personal portal, he or she has access to administrative features, such as Site Actions menu and the Site Settings page.

By default, all authenticated users have Read permissions on the content in a user's My Site personal site. Users with Read permissions are the *Default Reader Site Group*. You can change the default settings for who has Read permission on the Manage Permissions page (see the preceding set of steps) or the My Site Settings page (see the following section).

Configuring My Site

You can configure a number of properties for the My Site host. My Site is managed with the Shared Services Administration site (see the upcoming steps). Many of these settings, such as the path used to access My Site personal portals, apply only to new My Site personal sites, so configure these settings before users start creating their My Site personal sites. Sites created before changes are made retain their previous settings.

You can access the My Site configuration features by writing a program that uses the `Microsoft.Office.Server.UserProfiles` namespace in the `Microsoft.Office.Server.dll` assembly. The `My Site` object model is documented in the MOSS 2007 Software Development Kit (SDK) if you wish to programmatically make changes to existing My Sites.

To configure the My Site host, follow these steps:

1. **Browse to the Shared Services Administration site for the Shared Services Provider (SSP) that you wish to administer.**

   You can find a link to Shared Services Administration sites on your SharePoint farm's Central Administration site. Most server farms have only one Shared Services Administration site. See Chapter 18 for more information about accessing the Central Administration and Shared Services Administration sites.

   A quick way to see all the Web applications and SSPs in a SharePoint farm is to click the Create link or configure this farm's Shared Services link in the Office SharePoint Server Shared Services section on the Application Management page of the Central Administration site.

2. **Click the My Site Settings link in the User Profiles and My Sites section of the Shared Services Administration site.**

   The My Site Settings page appears, as shown in Figure 12-3.

3. **In the Preferred Search Center section, specify a preferred Search Center.**

   By default, the preferred Search Center is the URL for the Search Center in SharePoint. When a user executes a search by using the search box in the upper-right corner of My Site, the preferred Search Center is used to conduct the search. See Chapter 14 for more details on search.

4. **In the Personal Site Services section, type the URL for the Web application that hosts the My Site sites.**

   The *personal site provider* is the Web application that hosts all your My Site sites. You can point to a new Web application if you wish to move your My Site host.

5. **In the Personal Site Location section, type the path used for My Site personal portals.**

   The value you enter here determines the path where personal sites are created in the My Site Web application. The default location is personal.

6. **In the Site Naming Format section, select the format you wish to use for naming My Site personal sites.**

   The site-naming format determines how sites are named via the user account. The format you choose determines how easy it is to resolve conflicts when naming new sites.

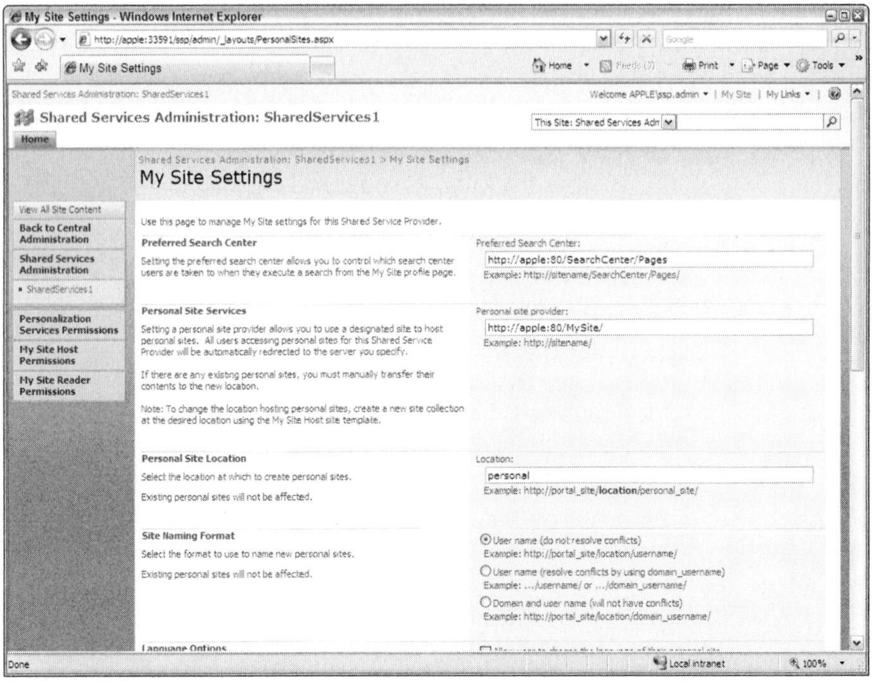

Figure 12-3:
The My Site
Settings
page.

7. **In the Language Options section, select whether users can choose the language of their personal site.**

   The default value is No.

8. **In the Multiple Deployments section, select whether to support multiple deployments of My Site.**

   Enabling this feature makes it possible to share a My Site host across multiple SSPs. If you enable this feature, use the Trusted My Site host locations link in Shared Services Administration to associate users with a different My Site provider.

9. **In the Default Reader Site Group section, select a default reader site group.**

   The default value is the Active Domain Security Group Authenticated Users, which grants all authenticated users Read permissions to the public views of My Site sites. You may wish to change this group if you want to further restrict who has the ability to read My Site profiles, especially if you have consultants and non-employees using SharePoint.

10. **Click OK.**

The My Site Settings page includes three links in the Quick Launch navigation bar that allow you to manage permissions. (Refer to Figure 12-3.) With these links, you can manage the following permissions for My Site:

- ✓ **Personalization Services Permissions:** Allows you to manage who has permission to view, use, and manage personalization features, as I describe in the preceding section, "Restricting access to My Site."

- ✓ **My Site Host Permissions:** Takes you to the People and Groups page of the My Site site collection. From here, you can see and manage all the people and groups set up to use My Site. See Chapter 6 for more information on managing permissions.

- ✓ **My Site Reader Permissions:** Takes you to the My Site Settings page. Look back at Step 9 of the preceding Steps list to see how to set the default reader site group.

Modifying the templates

Each of the three primary features of My Sites — personal sites, profiles, and personalization — has its own site templates. The easiest of these to modify is the My Profile template. The My Profile page has a single view for all users. I explain how to modify the template for public profiles later in this chapter. Personalization sites are usually customized by the site owner responsible for creating the personalization site (see Chapter 13). Each user has the authority to modify his or her personal site.

If you want to make changes across all personal sites, public profiles, and personalization sites (such as changing color schemes or navigation), you have to modify the underlying site templates for each of these sites. See the WSS or MOSS 2007 Software Development Kits (SDKs) for details on modifying site templates.

Exploring My Site

I like to sell the My Site personal site as each person's jumping-off place into SharePoint. It's a great starting point for getting people used to the idea of using SharePoint. I always suggest training sessions where users are encouraged to move content from other sources — such as network file shares, local hard drives, and e-mail Inboxes — to their My Site personal site. The more your users use My Site, the more they'll use the rest of your SharePoint implementation.

Using My Home and personal site

Every My Site personal portal includes a personal site with a private home page — My Home. The My Home page is the portal user's personal SharePoint site for the following:

- ✔ Managing personal information by displaying e-mail, calendar entries, and contact lists from Exchange Server.

- ✔ Providing publicly viewable information via his or her user profile.

- ✔ Connecting by using blogs and discussion threads.

- ✔ Staying up to date with colleagues' birthdays, profile updates, and new blog posts.

- ✔ Sharing documents with his or her personal Shared Documents document library.

- ✔ Aggregating all his or her SharePoint site memberships, documents, and tasks from across the entire SharePoint portal.

- ✔ Consolidating all his or her private files from various repositories — such as file shares, local hard drives, and removable media — to a private document library.

- ✔ Collaborating with colleagues and other co-workers with team sites and workspaces created in his or her My Site personal site.

My Site users need to understand that by default the members of the default My Site Readers group have permissions to read most of the content found on their personal site, such as the Shared Documents folder. Also keep in mind that My Site is a WSS site, and the users are the owners of their own My Site personal site. Each user can use the My Site personal site to create their own collaboration sites if they wish.

As the site owner, the user has access to the Site Actions menu, which allows them to edit the page and access the site's Site Settings page. Because each user is their own site owner, it's a good opportunity for them to get accustomed to the tasks required to administer a SharePoint site — tasks like managing permissions and adding lists and libraries.

The user can personalize the view of their My Home page by choosing Site Actions➪Edit Page. Of special interest to users of the My Home page are the Content Rollup and Outlook Web Access Web parts. Table 12-1 lists some Web parts that users should know how to use.

Table 12-1	Helpful My Home Page Web Parts	
Type	*Name*	*What It Does*
Content Rollup	Colleague Tracker	Lists colleagues and their SharePoint activity.
	My Pictures	Displays pictures from Picture library.
	My SharePoint Sites	Lists documents from all document libraries.
	My Workspaces	Lists sites created in the My Site personal site.
	Recent Blog Posts	Lists most recent blog posts.
	SharePoint Documents	Lists documents from sites where the user is a member.
	Site Aggregator	Lists sites of the user's choice.
Outlook Web	My Calendar	Displays Exchange Server 2003 or later calendar.
Access	My Contacts	Displays Exchange Server 2007 contacts.
	My Inbox	Displays Exchange Server 2003 or later Inbox.
	My Mail Folder	Displays Exchange Server 2000 or later calendar.
	My Tasks	Displays Exchange Server 2003 or later tasks.

Another popular Web part is the RSS Viewer. Because virtually all SharePoint content (including search results, document libraries, and lists) is available as syndicated RSS feeds, the RSS Viewer Web part is an easy way for users to subscribe to content from any SharePoint site. The RSS Viewer Web part can display feeds from external sites, too.

Users may also benefit from adding the Table of Contents Web part to their My Home page. This Web part displays a customizable site map of all the content in their personal site. This might be helpful if users have difficulty remembering where they put content in their My Site personal site.

Showing off the My Profile page

The My Profile page in a user's My Site personal portal is the public view of a user's user profile. A *user profile* is a set of name/value pairs that describe the user. See the section, "Managing User Profiles," later in this chapter, to read more about profiles from an administrator's perspective. The My Profile page is a user's opportunity to interact and manage his or her user profile.

The My Profile page has three views:

- **Personal:** This is the view seen by the user (see Figure 12-4). The user sees this private view by default when he or she is logged into SharePoint and accesses his or her My Profile page.

- **Shared:** This is the view seen by readers of a user's My Profile page. Each user determines what content is visible to people who view their profile.

- **Designer:** This is the view seen by an administrator who wants to modify the shared view of the My Profile page.

Adding and filtering content

By default, the My Profile page is a template that allows users to add content in Personal view. Users can't add or remove Web parts to the My Profile page, but they can add content to the existing Web parts. Figure 12-4 shows the Personal view of the My Profile page for a user named Rosie Layne. The page has the following Web parts:

- **Details and organization hierarchy:** Displays the user's profile properties and position in organization chart.

- **Documents:** Shows a list of all the user's public documents on his or her My Site personal portal. Users should understand that documents published to the Shared Documents document library in their My Site personal site appear in the Documents Web part on their public profile page.

- **Colleagues:** Displays a list of co-workers the user identifies as colleagues.

- **In Common with You:** Displays a list of things the visitor to the page has in common with the profiled owner, such as managers, colleagues, and memberships.

- **Memberships:** Lists the sites that the user belongs to.

- **Links:** Displays a set of hyperlinks the user wishes to share with other users. Note this is the same list of links accessible via the My Links link in the upper-right corner of the navigation bar. Users can add links any time by choosing My Links⇨Add to My Links.

Table 12-2 lists the default My Profile features and the URLs used to access them. The URLs are relative to the path for the My Site Web application, not the individual user's My Site personal site.

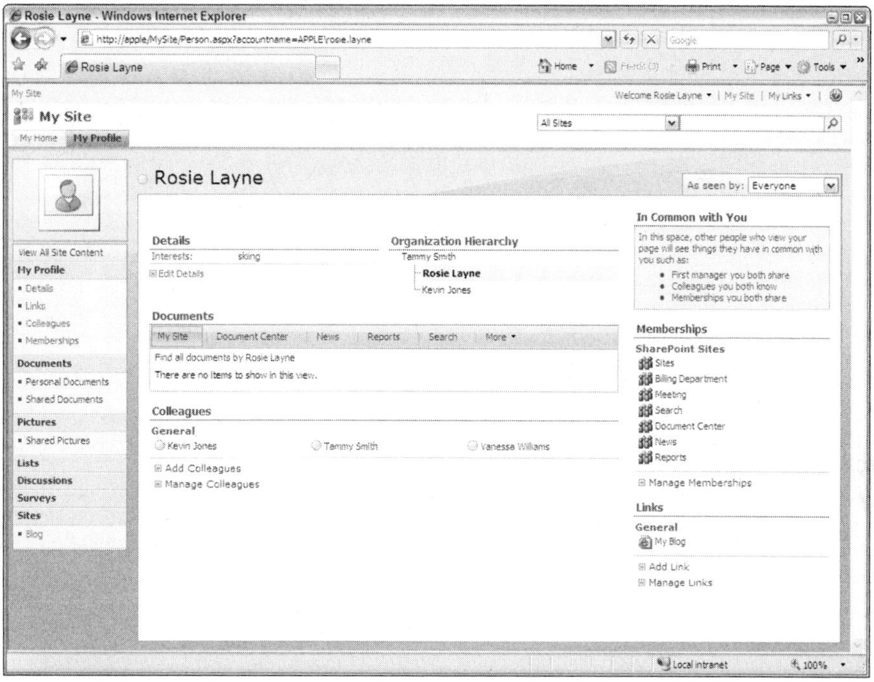

Figure 12-4:
Personal
view of the
My Profile
page.

Table 12-2		My Profile Features and URLs
My Profile Feature	*What It Does*	*URL Used to Access*
My Colleagues	Displays a list of colleagues.	`/_layouts/MyContactLinks.aspx`
My Links	Displays a list of hyperlinks.	`/_layouts/MyQuickLinks.aspx`
My Memberships	Lists sites and distribution lists that the user belongs to.	`/_layouts/MyMemberships.aspx`

Figure 12-5 shows the shared view of the user profile page for Rosie Layne. This view is shown from the perspective of her colleague, Kevin Jones. You can see both Rosie and Kevin report to Tammy Smith in the Organization Hierarchy.

The user adds content to his or her profile — such as identifying his or her colleagues — by using either the My Profile page or links on the Quick Launch bar of the My Home page. The Web parts in the My Profile page list include links for adding content. For example, the Colleagues Web part displays links to Add Colleagues or Manage Colleagues. The My Home page displays links to the My Profile features in the Quick Launch bar, as shown in Figure 12-6.

The user can specify privacy groups for profile properties, colleagues, memberships, and links. Users use the privacy groups to filter the content displayed in Web parts in the shared view of their My Profile page. This determines who can see what on the My Profile page. Table 12-3 lists the privacy groups and what they do.

Table 12-3	Privacy Groups in My Profile
Privacy Group	**Limits View To**
Everyone	Everyone with default My Site Reader permissions, as I describe in the section, "Configuring My Site"
My Colleagues	Manager, peers, direct reports, and anyone else manually added
My Workgroup	Same as My Colleagues and anyone else manually added
My Manager	Manager only
Only Me	User only

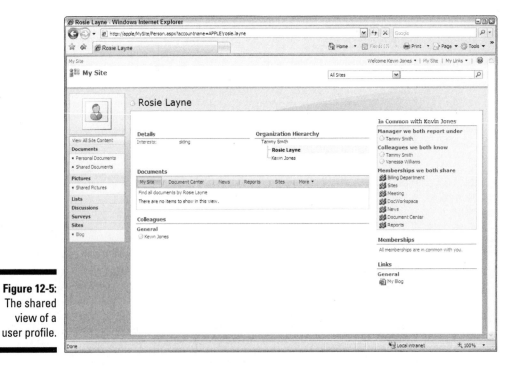

Figure 12-5:
The shared view of a user profile.

Figure 12-6:
Access My
Profile
features
from the My
Home page.

My Profile links

The user determines what content can be seen by a privacy group at the time
the content is added. For example, to set a privacy group for a colleague
added to the My Colleagues list, do the following:

1. **On the My Profile page, click the Add Colleagues link in the Colleagues
   Web Part in the lower section of the page. You may need to scroll
   down to see the Web Part.**

   The Add Colleagues page appears.

   You can only add content to your own My Profile page. You can't pull up
   another user's page and add content to it. An administrator can manage
   some user profile properties, as I describe in the section, "Managing
   User Profiles," later in this chapter.

2. **In the Identify Colleagues section, type the names of the people you
   wish to add as colleagues. You can also browse the directory to see a
   list of names.**

   The people you add here become members of the My Colleagues
   privacy group.

3. **In the Privacy and Grouping section, choose a privacy group from the
   Show These Colleagues To drop-down list, as shown in Figure 12-7.**

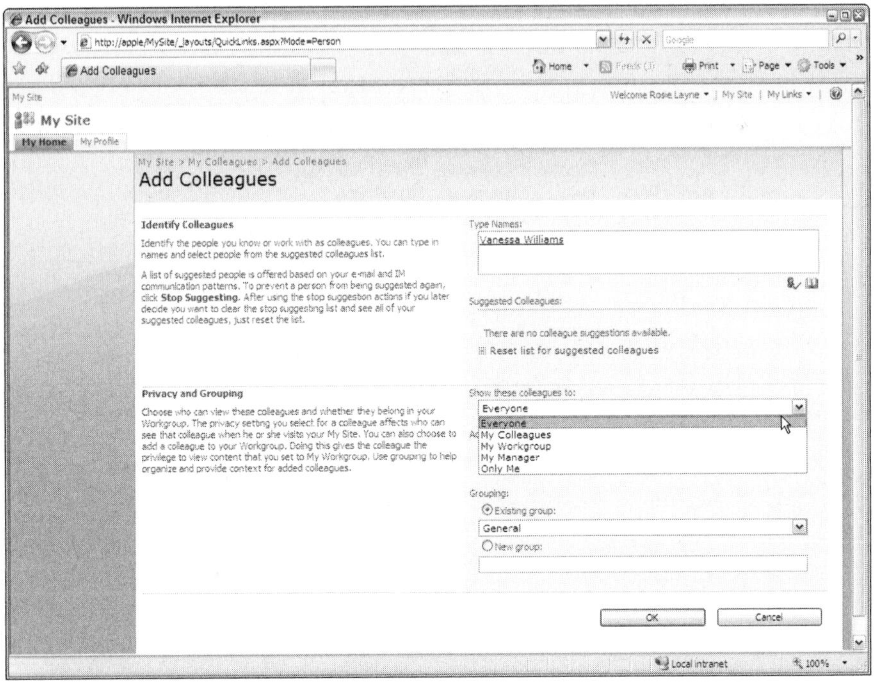

Figure 12-7:
Select a
privacy
group
for the
colleagues.

The privacy group you select here determines who can see this colleague's name in your list of colleagues on the profile's shared view.

4. **Select the Yes or No radio button next to Add Colleagues to My Workgroup to add the colleagues you enter in Step 2 to the My Workgroup privacy group.**

   The My Workgroup privacy group is intended to list only those colleagues who are closest to you. By selecting the Yes option, you add these people to the My Workgroup privacy group.

5. **Select a group to add the colleague to in the Grouping drop-down list.**

   Groups are used to organize colleagues.

6. **Click OK.**

The My Memberships list also makes use of privacy groups. The documents listed in the Documents Web part on the shared view of the My Profile page are filtered based on the privacy group selected in My Memberships. By restricting the view of a site membership with a privacy group, only those users who can see the membership can also see documents from the membership in the Documents Web part. For example, if you set a site membership entry in the My Memberships list to the My Workgroup privacy group, only colleagues added to the My Workgroup privacy group can see the documents from that site in the shared view of the My Profile page.

The MOSS 2007 People search feature also uses the privacy groups to determine whether a user's profile is returned in the search results. Setting the privacy group for a membership to anything besides Everyone restricts the People search results. If you're having trouble accessing users via People search, it might be because of the user's memberships privacy settings.

At any time, users can test the views of a privacy group by selecting a group from the As Seen By drop-down list in their My Profile page, as shown in Figure 12-8. The content is filtered to match the view of the privacy group selected.

Modifying the Shared view of the My Profile page

The My Site administrator has the ability to modify the My Profile page by adding or removing Web parts. The My Profile page has only one Shared view, so all users see the same content for each user.

To modify the My Profile page, the root My Site site collection administrator navigates to any My Profile page for any user, including his or her own. From there, he or she can then choose Site Actions⇨Edit Page to edit the shared version of the page.

Figure 12-8: Filter the view by privacy group.

You can manage the administrators for the My Site site collection from within the Central Administration site. (Keep in mind that the Central Administration site is hosted on the first machine on which you installed SharePoint. On that machine, choose Start⇨All Programs⇨Administrative Tools⇨SharePoint 3.0 Central Administration.) On the Application Management page, click the Site Collection Administrators link. The Site Collection Administrators page appears, as shown in Figure 12-9.

The site collection administrator is somewhat limited in terms of the kinds of Web parts he or she can add to the My Profile page because you can't add Web parts for lists and libraries from an individual user's My Site personal site. Instead, if you have information you want to share across all profile pages, you must store that information at the root site collection level.

For example, assume you want to add an Announcements Web part to the My Profile page. The underlying announcements list must be created at the root site collection of My Site. The relative URL for the View All Site Content page is `_layouts/viewlsts.aspx`. To access the View All Site Content page for the root site collection of My Site, append that URL to the URL of

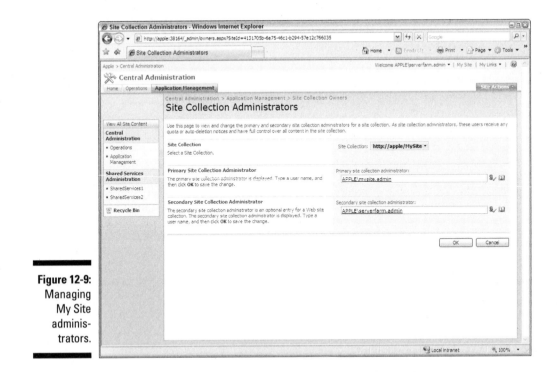

Figure 12-9: Managing My Site administrators.

the My Site root. If the root is `http://apple/MySite`, use the URL

```
http://apple/MySite/_layouts/viewlsts.aspx
```

to access the View All Site Content page. From there, you can add lists or libraries that you can display on the My Profile page.

Be careful of crowding too much information on the My Profile page. I suggest concentrating on content related to actually using My Site and My Profile as well as adding tips on how to get the most out of People search. The star of the My Profile page should be the person being profiled, not the company picnic.

Managing User Profiles

User profiles are a set of name/value pairs used to describe a user. The name/value pairs in a profile are *properties*. User profiles are a feature of MOSS 2007 and are used to provide content to My Site personal sites. User profile properties are also used to conduct a People search. Some of the properties defined by default in SharePoint are `First Name`, `Last Name`, `Department`, `Manager`, `Account Name`, and `E-Mail`.

As I mention in Chapter 6, user profiles are distinct from user accounts. A *user account* is a security account that defines someone's username and password. User accounts are managed in identity management systems, such as Active Directory (AD). In Chapter 6, I explain the kinds of identity management systems you can use with SharePoint.

AD is the most common identity management system used with SharePoint.

Some identity management systems also store a user's profile. Rather than manually enter profile data into SharePoint, you can import this information from your identity management system. SharePoint supports importing profile data from AD or any Lightweight Directory Access Protocol (LDAP) directory.

You can also import profile data from virtually any data source, including databases and flat files with the Business Data Catalog. AD and LDAP sources are considered primary user profile sources, whereas other data sources are secondary sources used to provide supplemental properties. Any property that you don't provide via a primary source is a *supplemental property.* For example, you may wish to import the `sales territory` for users from a line-of-business application. I show you how to set up and use the Business Data Catalog in Chapter 17.

Before you import or create any user profiles, make sure you have properties set up in SharePoint. User profiles are a feature of the Shared Services Provider (SSP) and are managed via the Shared Services Administration site, which you access via the Central Administration site. Click the User Profiles and Properties link in the User Profiles and My Sites section to access the User Profiles and Properties page, as shown in Figure 12-10.

The User Profiles and Properties page is divided into two sections. You use the top section, the Profile and Import Settings section, to manage user profiles and configure SharePoint to import user profiles from an identity management system. The bottom section, User Profile Properties, is where you create and manage user profile properties. Table 12-4 lists the links on this page and what you can do with them.

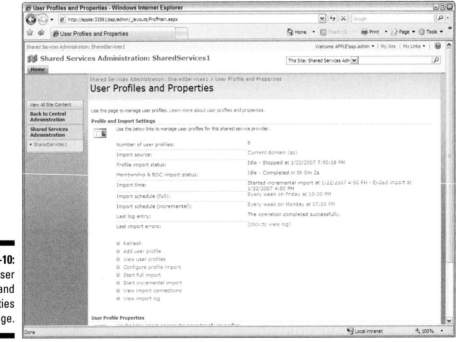

Figure 12-10: The User Profiles and Properties page.

Table 12-4		Links for Managing User Profiles and Properties		
Section	*Link*	*Relative URL*	*Page Title*	*What It's Used For*
Profile and Import Settings	Add User Profile	_layouts/ProfNew.aspx	Add a user profile.	Add a new user profile.
	View User Profiles		View user profiles.	Manage existing user profiles or add new profiles.
	Configure Profile Import	_layouts/SetImport.aspx	Configure a profile import.	Select a data source and create full and incremental import schedules.
	Start Full Import	N/A	N/A	Immediately start a full import of the user profile properties.
	Start Incremental Import	N/A	N/A	Immediately start an import of any user profiles that changed since the last import.
	View Import Connections	_layouts/MgrDSServer.aspx	View import connections.	Create a new connection to an import data source.
	View Import Log	_layouts/logviewer.aspx	Crawl Log.	Check import status.
User Profile Properties	Add Profile Property	_layouts/EditProperty.aspx	Add a user profile property.	Add a new property to user profiles.
	View Profile Properties	_layouts/MgrProperty.aspx	View profile properties.	Display a list of existing properties.

Setting up user profiles is something you do only once unless you discover that you need to modify properties. You don't have to worry about getting updated profile information from your identity management system to SharePoint. After you configure an import schedule, SharePoint automatically imports user profiles. You should, however, periodically check the status of your imports to make sure profiles are importing properly.

Although you *can* use the User Profiles and Properties page to manually add and edit user profiles, I suggest you import this data from your identity management system. Otherwise, you'll be managing data in two different sources. The exception, of course, is if you create a property that you want users to complete. For example, you might want users to enter information about their hobbies. There's no need to manage that kind of information in an identity management system.

Here are the high-level steps for setting up user profiles in SharePoint:

1. **Identify external data sources from which you can import profile data.**

   If you plan to use data sources other than AD or an LDAP-compliant directory service, you need to configure the Business Data Catalog connection. See Chapter 17.

2. **Identify user profile properties that you want to use in SharePoint.**

   Use the View Profile Properties link in the User Profiles Properties section, as I describe in Table 12-4, to see what properties already exist. Be sure to look at your existing identity management system to see what profiles you want to import. You may find that you need to bring in data from HR and payroll software to populate properties like birthday and service anniversary dates.

3. **Configure the Business Data Catalog to access any non-LDAP sources you intend to use in gathering property data.**

   See Chapter 17 for more details on working with the Business Data Catalog.

4. **Click the Add Profile Property link in the User Profile Properties section to create new properties,**

   I walk you through adding a new property in the next section.

5. **Modify any existing properties to fit your requirements with the View Profile Properties link.**

   Click any property to view the Edit User Profile Property page. The Edit User Profile Property page allows you to map the SharePoint property to the data connection.

6. **Click the View Import Connections link to set up new data connections to your identity management systems and Business Data Catalog resources.**

   You'll need to know how to access and search your identity management system. You may need to check with your network administrator for the details on these specific tasks.

7. **Click the Configure Profile Import link to set up the import schedule.**

   You have the option to set up full and incremental schedules. Schedule the full import during non-busy times, such as weekends or after hours. I suggest you schedule a daily incremental import.

   Make sure someone in your IT (Information Technology) staff knows how to start an incremental import on demand. Should the need arise to have the profiles of several users available before the next scheduled update, you want someone who knows how to make it happen.

8. **Click the Start Full Import link when you're ready to immediately start the import.**

   For the first import, I like to manually start the full import after work hours. Alternatively, you can schedule the import and then check it when you return to work. The only problem with this approach is that it doesn't leave you any recovery time if the import fails. Just make sure you have plenty of time to test the import before you actually plan to start demonstrating or using the user profile features.

9. **Check the status of the import on the User Profile and Properties page (refer to Figure 12-10).**

   The following entries tell you everything you need to know about the status of your import:

   - *Number of user profiles:* Make sure this number matches with the number of user accounts you have in your identity management system.

   - *Last log entry:* This tells you whether the job completed or had problems.

   - *Last import errors:* This displays the number of errors on the last import.

10. **Click the View Import Log link to deal with any errors.**

    If you do encounter errors, try to determine the source of the error and correct it.

User profiles are stored in the user profile store. You can configure and access the user profile store with the user profile object model. You can find user profile objects in the `Microsoft.Office.Server.UserProfiles` namespace. You can also use the user profile Web service at:

```
http://site url/_vti_bin/userprofileservice.asmx
```

See the MOSS 2007 Software Development Kit (SDK) for more information on using the object model and Web services to access and configure SharePoint.

Managing profile properties

It's convenient to think of a user profile property as a name/value pair, such as `name=Vanessa`. If you ever had to add a new property or edit an existing one, you quickly find out how complex properties really are. To create a new profile property, follow these steps:

1. **Click the Add Profile Property link in the User Profile Properties section of the User Profiles and Properties page (refer to Figure 12-10).**

   The Add User Profile Property page appears, as shown in Figure 12-11.

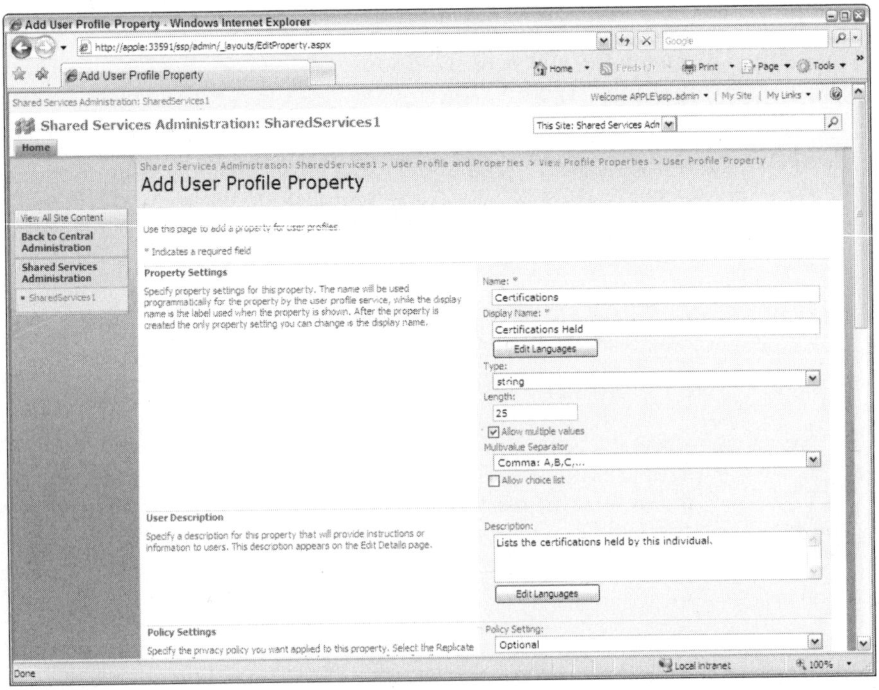

Figure 12-11:
Create a new profile property.

2. **In the Property Settings section, enter the name and select the data type for the user profile property.**

   Each user profile property is associated with a data type, such as `string` or `URL`. The data type may have additional settings, such as `length`, for you to provide. The `string` data type allows you to specify whether to allow multiple values and also lets you display a choice list.

3. **In the User Description section, enter text that explains the properties purpose to end users.**

4. **In the Policy Settings section, select whether the property is required, optional, or disabled in the Policy Setting drop-down list.**

5. **Still in the Policy Settings section, select the default privacy setting for the property from the Default Privacy Setting drop-down list and indicate whether the user can override the setting.**

   The privacy group that you select here determines who can see the profile's value in the user's My Profile page (see the section, "Showing off the My Profile page," earlier in this chapter). The `First name` and `Last name` properties are examples of properties where the user can't override the default privacy group of Everyone. This prevents users from preventing site visitors from seeing their name.

6. **Still in the Policy Settings section, select the Replicable check box if you want the property replicated to all site collections.**

   User profiles in MOSS 2007 and the user information found in WSS is synchronized. If you want a user profile property to synchronize to WSS, you must mark it as replicable. A property must be visible to everyone (see Step 5) before it can replicated.

   You can see a list of all user profile and personalization policies by accessing the Shared Services Administration site from the Central Administration site (see Chapter 18). In the User Profiles and My Sites section, click the Profile Services Policies link.

7. **In the Edit Settings section, indicate whether users can edit the property's value in their own user profiles.**

   Any values that are imported from other sources should be disabled for editing.

   Users with the Manage Profile permission have the authority to edit any property value. User accounts and groups with the Manage Hierarchy permission level have the Manage Profile permission by default, as I describe in Chapter 6.

8. **In the Display Settings section, indicate the properties visibility settings.**

This profile property lets you indicate whether the property is visible in the user's My Profile page or the Edit Details page. You can also specify whether the changes to the property's value appear in the Colleague Tracker Web part.

9. **In the Search Settings section, indicate whether the property is aliased or indexed.**

   If a property is an `alias` property, it can be used to search for users. E-mail is often an `alias` property that's used to work with user accounts. Indexed properties can be searched.

10. **In the Property Import Mapping section, select the data connection to use as the source for the user profile property.**

    Your identity management system is the Master Connection. You can configure additional data connections if you want to import from other sources such as the Business Data Catalog. See the section, "Managing User Profiles," earlier in this chapter for more details on configuring your import.

Getting the most out of user profiles

You may be wondering what the point is in displaying lists of colleagues, site memberships, and interests. How is it of value to the business to know that there are six people who like to ski or play *Dungeons and Dragons?* Can't you find out that stuff at the water cooler?

User profiles are more than just trivia. The information collected in user profiles is used to show relationships among the people in your organization. The colleagues list is a no-brainer. The list shows the formal relationships in your organization — an employee's boss, peers, and direct reports.

The memberships list takes the relationship one step further because it shows the sites and e-mail lists that people have in common. If your sites and e-mail lists mirror your organizational chart, the memberships list may resemble the colleagues list. However, say you have a task force that cuts across functional departments. If you create a team site for the task force, the membership list shows relationships that extend beyond the organizational chart.

Taking memberships a step further, the values (such as `interests`, `skills`, and `hobbies`) found in the user profile make it possible to show relationships among people based on different kinds of information. The user profile makes it possible to create a social network where people connect with each other based on common interests, similar to public social networks like MySpace.

MOSS 2007 has a new People search feature that makes it possible for end users to search based on the properties in user profiles. By connecting with people of similar interests, employees can meet new people in the organization. And similar to MySpace, after employees find each other's My Site pages, they can read each others blogs, find colleagues and memberships in common, and get to know each other better.

Because features, such as People search, rely on user profiles, it's important that your users complete their user profile data. Otherwise, users might not be able to connect. For example, assume you create a user profile property that indicates whether the employee is interested in participating in a car pool. If nobody bothers to complete their profile, there's no way to know who has an interest in car pooling.

Chapter 13

Personalizing Sites

*P*ersonalization isn't exactly the hottest topic on the Web right now. That's because personalization is old news. *Personalization* is the ability to give a site's user the choice to change the color scheme, add and remove widgets, and see customized and targeted content, including advertisements.

What is news is the ability to provide personalization features to users inside the corporate firewall via the company portal. Microsoft Office SharePoint Server (MOSS) 2007 provides personalization services along with a delegated administration model.

Human Resources (HR) wants a special site that targets employees based on their position, skills, and benefits grouping? No problem. The executive team wants key financial performance indicators shared with people based on their position and involvement with certain projects? Easy as pie. Marketing wants to share the latest promotions with people based on their relationship with certain products and territories? Consider it done.

Of course, I mean consider it done by Marketing. One of the key features of SharePoint is delegated administration. Therefore, instead of creating a long list of requests for the Information Technology department to fulfill, departments can implement these features themselves. Marketing doesn't have to wait for their turn in the never-ending, always reprioritizing line of IT projects. With a little training, Marketing can use MOSS 2007 to reach the people who are closest to the customers.

Personalization is about targeting content. In order to target content, you need two pieces of information: whom to target and what to target. In this chapter, I show you how to use audiences to build groups of users for targeting content — the Whom to Target part — and I discuss how you can use those audiences to target everything from individual items in a list to an entire SharePoint site — the What to Target part.

Knowing Your Audience

A key component in providing personalized content is having a way to filter content. SharePoint uses audiences to target content to groups of users. SharePoint has three kinds of audiences:

- **SharePoint groups:** Groups of users created for managing membership and permissions in a SharePoint site collection.

- **Distribution lists and security groups:** Groups that are external to SharePoint and can be found in sources such as Exchange Server and Active Directory, respectively.

- **Global audiences:** Groups of users created based on rules that query the user profile store.

SharePoint groups, distribution lists, and security groups are all groups that you should already have defined. (If this isn't ringing a bell, check out Chapter 6, where I discuss defining SharePoint groups as part of your security and user access planning). But not to worry. You can always create new SharePoint groups for use as audiences any time you want. You don't even have to worry about assigning permissions to any new SharePoint groups you create to use as audiences, so long as audience members already have permissions to access the resource. Generally speaking, SharePoint groups, distribution lists, and security groups often reflect a user's membership in a department, team, or project. You can assign groups directly to the content you wish to target, as I describe in the section, "Targeting Content," later in this chapter.

When you want to target content based on something other than formal membership in a group, your best bet is to build a global audience. Audiences that are global can be used across multiple site collections, whereas you can only use a SharePoint group in the site collection where the group is created.

A global audience is like a query that you build based on the values in the user profile store. In Chapter 12, I discuss the process for discovering user profile properties and how to add new properties. Oftentimes you discover user profile properties that you need to create in order to build audiences. For example, if Sales wants to target content to its sales representatives based on sales territory, you need to add a new user property — `Sales Territory`.

The queries you create for building global audiences are *rules*. You can build two kinds of rules for global audiences:

✔ **User-based rules** allow you to select users based on their membership in a security group, distribution list, or their reporting relationship in the organizational hierarchy. (Keep in mind that you can't add a SharePoint group to a user-based rule because SharePoint groups are specific to the site collection where they're created.)

✔ **Property-based rules** allow you to include people based on whether the selected property is equal to, not equal to, contains, or doesn't contain a value.

Global audiences are managed via the Audiences link in the Audiences section of the Shared Services Administration site. (You can access the Shared Services Administration site via the Central Administration site. See Chapter 18.) The Audiences link opens the Manage Audiences page, which displays the status of the audience services and a set of links for managing audiences. Use the Manage Audiences page to create new audiences and view existing audiences.

You can create up to 10,000 audiences per Shared Services Provider (SSP). Global audiences can be shared across all the site collections in an SSP.

To create a new global audience, follow these steps:

1. **Click the Create Audience link on the Manage Audiences page**.

   The Create Audience page appears.

2. **Type a meaningful name for the audience in the Name field.**

   The value you type here appears in the Select Audiences dialog box when you target content. Make sure you use a name that reflects the audience's membership.

3. **In the Owner field, type or select an owner who's responsible for managing the audience.**

4. **Choose a radio button to indicate whether to include users who Satisfy All Rules or Satisfy Any of the Rules.**

   Requiring that users satisfy all the rules is a stricter requirement. If the user doesn't meet every single rule, the user is excluded. Use this option any time you have a very specific audience in mind that you want to target. Use the (more lenient) option of including users who satisfy any of the rules if you want to include a larger pool of users in your audience.

   Satisfy All Rules is equivalent to using an AND operator, while Satisfy Any of the Rules is equivalent to using an OR operator.

5. **Click OK.**

   The Add Audience Rule page appears.

6. **Add a new rule, as I describe in the upcoming set of steps.**

You add audience rules when you create a new audience. You can add new rules or modify or delete existing rules for an existing audience. Click the View Audiences link on the Manage Audiences page to access the rules for an existing audience.

To add a new rule, follow these steps:

1. **Go to the Add Audience Rule page either by adding a new audience — as outlined in the preceding steps — or by editing an existing audience.**

2. **In the Operand section, select the operand for the rule.**

   Your choices are either User or Property.

3. **If you select a property-based rule, select the property you want to base the rule on.**

   If you don't see the property you want, you need to add the property to the user profile store. See Chapter 12.

4. **Select an operator from the Operator drop-down list.**

   For user-based rules, your choices are Reports Under and Member Of. Property-based rules allow you to choose an Equality or Contains operator.

5. **For a user-based rule, select a user, security group, or distribution list that satisfies the operator you choose in Step 4.**

6. **For a property-based rule, type a value in the Value text box.**

   You don't need to use quotations or worry about case sensitivity; however, you do need to make sure you spell the value correctly.

7. Click OK.

The View Audience Properties page appears. Your rule appears in the Audience Rules section of the page. Click the Add Rule link to add additional rules.

You can add up to six rules to an audience via the View Audience Properties page. If you need to add more than six rules or want to create more complex rules, you can use the `Audience` object model. You access the `Audience` object model via the `Microsoft.Office.Server.Audience` namespace in the `Microsoft.Office.Server.dll` assembly. You can't modify complex rules in the browser, but you can view the audience's membership.

Because audiences are based on rules that are basically queries, the audience's membership must be recalculated periodically. You use the Manage Audiences page to schedule audience compilation. Click the Specify Compilation Schedule link to create a new compilation schedule. I suggest compiling audiences every night.

Targeting Content

Personalizing content is an important aspect of any portal application. MOSS 2007 offers several options for targeting content to users. In all cases, the steps needed to select a particular audience as a recipient of targeted content stay the same.

It's important to realize that the content and the display of that content are usually separate. In other words, you may end up using a Web part to display content originally stored in a list. You can target your audience at the content itself or via the content's display. MOSS 2007 gives you the best of both worlds with the Content Query Web part, which can be used to display content targeted at the list level.

For example, assume the Human Resources department has a list of job openings on a SharePoint site. They could use multiple Web parts to target the job openings to different audiences. One Web part might display job openings to members of the Sales team, while another Web part might display openings to members of the IT department. Another approach might be to target the job openings at the list level and use a single Content Query Web part to display the openings. The Content Query Web part respects the audiences selected for the list items (job openings, in this case).

Don't make the mistake of assuming you can just use audiences and content targeting as a way to manage access permissions. You need to use groups and permissions for all the permissions stuff, as I describe in Chapter 6. The purpose of audiences is to display relevant content, *not* to restrict access. The hard and fast rule when it comes to deciding between audiences and permissions is to ask yourself whether you want to restrict access or if what you really want to do is filter out irrelevant content. If the answer is to filter, use audiences.

With that out of the way, check out the following (general) steps for targeting audiences:

1. **Identify the content and audience you want to target.**

   Make a list of the content you want to target and who the various audiences are. For example, you may have information about benefits that only applies to people based on their years of service.

2. **Determine the connection between the content and the audience.**

   You need to configure your content to match the audience. For example, if you want to display content based on the value of a property in that content, such as `Division` or `Sales Territory`, make sure that the property is associated with the content. Otherwise, you can't make a connection between the content and the audience.

3. **Determine the appropriate level of targeting.**

   It's important that you target at the right level. For example, it's possible to target content at the list item level and use the Content Query Web part to automatically filter the display based on audiences. There may be other times, however, when you want to target a Web part to a specific group.

   For example, assume you have an announcements list called Manager Announcements. These announcements only apply to managers. You also want executives to see these announcements, but you don't want staff or line employees to see the announcements. Rather than individually targeting each announcement, you could display the Manager Announcements List Web part (recall that each list has its own corresponding Web part that displays its contents; see Chapter 4) and target the Web part to the audiences Managers and Executives. Only members of those audiences would be able to see the Web part.

4. **Select the audiences you want to target.**

   Selecting audiences is the action of entering an audience in the Target Audiences field. The Target Audiences field is usually a text box with two buttons next to it, as shown in Figure 13-1. The left button is the Check Names button. You click it after you type the name of the audience, and if you wish to validate that you've entered a legitimate audience. The right button is the Browse button, which opens the Select Audiences dialog box. Figure 13-1 shows the Target Audiences text box for a list item.

In most cases, you're going to want to click the Browse button so that you can use the Select Audiences dialog box to find the particular audience(s) you want. The Select Audiences dialog box has a Find control, which allows you to search for audiences among the three kinds of audiences available: global audiences, distribution lists and security groups, and SharePoint groups. You can target multiple audiences by using the Add button to add each audience you wish to target. Figure 13-2 shows an example of the Select Audiences dialog box.

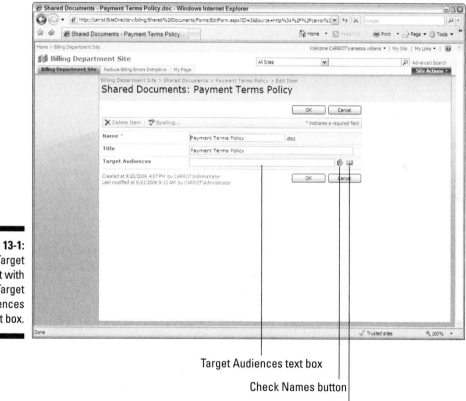

Figure 13-1:
Target content with the Target Audiences text box.

Target Audiences text box

Check Names button

Browse button

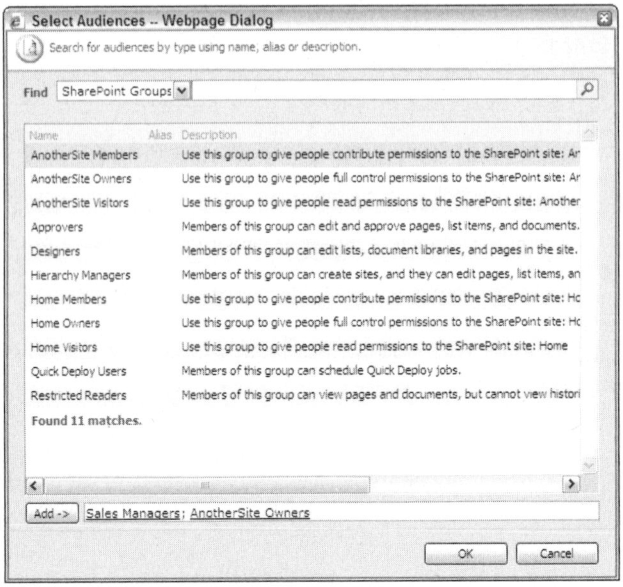

Figure 13-2:
Search and
select
audiences
to target.

Targeting list items

A list item is the most granular item you can target in SharePoint. In order to target list items to a particular audience, you must enable audience targeting in the list or document library. After audience targeting is enabled, you can edit a list item to select an audience to target.

To enable audience targeting in a list or library, follow these steps:

1. **Browse to the list or library with the targeted content.**

2. **Choose Settings⇨Document Library Settings or Settings⇨List Settings.**

   The Customize page appears.

   You must have the Manage Lists permissions, which is assigned by default to the Design and Manage Hierarchy permission levels, to access the Settings menu.

3. **Click the Audience Targeting Settings link in the General Settings section**.

   The Modify List Audience Targeting Settings page appears.

4. **Select the Enable Audience Targeting check box.**

5. Click OK.

The Target Audiences column appears in the Columns section of the Customize page.

You can modify the Target Audiences column to indicate which types of audiences can be selected. By default, all three types of audiences are available for the column. (See Chapter 7 for information on editing columns in lists and libraries.) Figure 13-3 shows the Change Column page, which you can use to edit the Target Audience column.

Target Audiences is a site column, which means that it's a global column that's defined for all lists and libraries. See Chapter 7 for more information on site columns.

Targeting an audience for a list item is simply a matter of editing the list item. Anyone with Edit Items permissions can target a list item to an audience. Therefore, anyone who is a Contributor to the list can use audience targeting if audience targeting is enabled for the site.

Audience targeting of list items is honored in Web parts and RSS feeds.

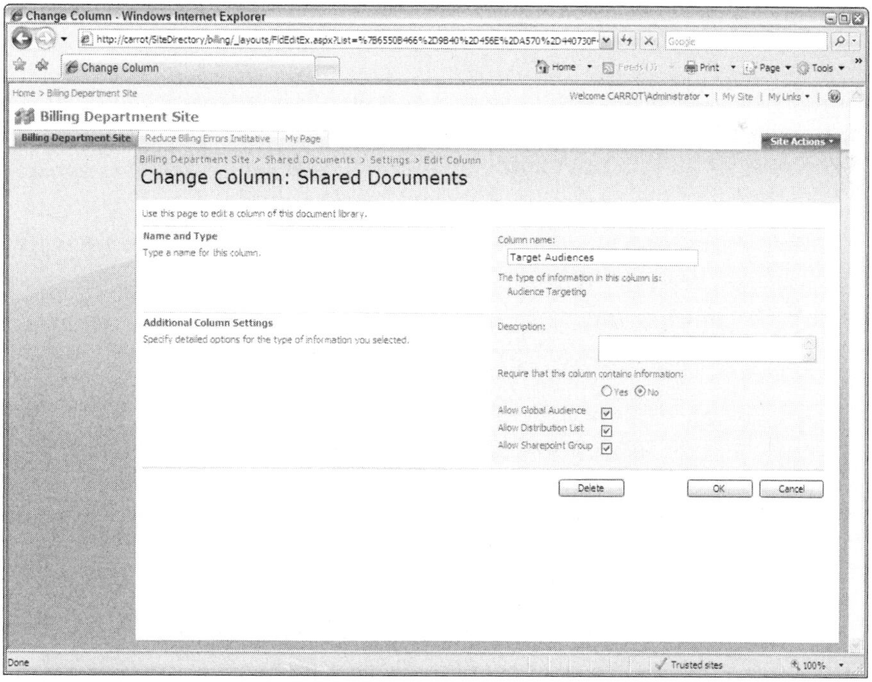

Figure 13-3:
Modify
settings for
the Target
Audiences
column.

One example where audience targeting of a list item makes sense is in the Published Links to Office Client Applications list. The Published Links list is a list in the Shared Services Administration site that defines sites to appear in a user's My SharePoints folder in an Office 2007 client. By default, audience targeting is enabled in the Published Links list. For example, you could define a published link that points to a document library on the team site for Marketing. If you target that published link to an audience that consists of members of the Marketing staff, then only those users can see the published link in an application like Word 2007. You access the Published Links list via the Published Links to Office Client Applications link in the Shared Services Administration site.

Targeting Web parts

Instead of targeting individual items in a list or library, you can target content in a Web part. The Target Audiences text box is available on all list and library Web parts and most other kinds of Web parts, too. To target content in a Web part, follow these steps:

1. **Add the Web part to a Web parts page or modify a Web part on an existing page.**

   You must have the Add and Customize pages permission to add Web parts and modify their settings. This permission is usually restricted to Designers and Hierarchy Managers. (See Chapter 4 for more information about modifying Web parts pages.)

2. **In the Web parts tool pane, click the plus sign (+) to expand the Advanced properties for the Web part.**

3. **Scroll down to the Target Audiences text box and add audiences, as shown in Figure 13-4.**

4. **Click OK.**

   The Web part's content is now visible only to members of the audiences you select in Step 3.

You can also use the Content Query Web part to display content that's targeted at the list item level. The Content Query Web part is a very powerful Web part that makes it possible for you to display content by creating queries based on your SharePoint content. To use the Content Query Web part, follow these steps:

1. **Add the Content Query Web part to an existing Web Parts page.**

   The Content Query Web part is in the Default group of Web parts in the Web Parts gallery.

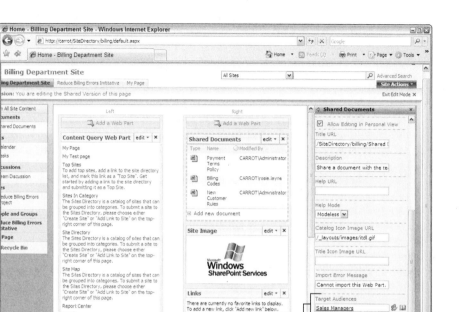

Figure 13-4:
Target
audiences
in a Web
part.

Target Audiences text box

2. **Click Edit➪Modify Shared Web Part.**

   The tool pane appears.

3. **Click the plus (+) sign to expand the Queries section.**

4. **Select the Show items from the following list radio button.**

5. **Click the Browse button and select the list you wish to display.**

   You can choose a list from anywhere in the site collection, not just the site you're working in.

6. **In the List Type section of the tool pane, select the kinds of items you wish to query.**

   For example, if you're querying a Tasks list, choose Tasks.

7. **In the Audience Targeting section, click the Apply Audience Filtering check mark.**

8. **Click the Include Items that are Not Targeted check mark if you want those items to be visible to everyone.**

   Any list item without an audience target appears in the Web part if you select this option.

9. **Click the OK button.**

The Content Query Web part uses the audience settings of the list's items to filter the contents displayed.

Targeting navigation

It is possible to target audiences by customizing SharePoint's navigation features, but, if you go down that road, I suggest you do so sparingly unless you plan on spending quite a bit of time actively managing your navigation features. In Chapter 5, I describe the navigation options SharePoint makes available to you. In most cases, you want to configure your navigation so that SharePoint can dynamically generate the navigation bars and breadcrumbs appropriate for your (general) needs. With audience targeting, the idea is for you to create unique navigation bars for different groups of people. Given that SharePoint already only shows navigation links that the user has permissions to, it may not make much sense to use audience targeting with your navigation.

One exception where you may wish to use audience targeting as a navigation aid is if you have an area of your portal you'd like to profile a bit more. For example, assume that Human Resources identifies that they receive a disproportionate number of phone calls from the Customer Service department for information that's readily available via the HR knowledge base. You could add a navigation link to the HR knowledge base that's targeted just to the members of customer service. An alternative approach is to add the site to the My Site navigation, as I describe in the section, "Creating personalization sites," later in this chapter.

To set up targeted navigation links for a specific audience, do the following:

1. **Choose the Site Settings➪Modify Navigation link on the Site Actions menu of the site you wish to modify.**

The Site Navigation Settings page opens.

You must have at least the Design permission level to modify navigation. See Chapter 5 for specifics on modifying navigation.

2. **In the Navigation Editing and Sorting page, add a new link or edit an existing link.**

The Navigation Link dialog box appears.

3. **Enter an audience for the Navigation link, as shown in Figure 13-5.**

You can type the audience name or use the Browse button to select the audience.

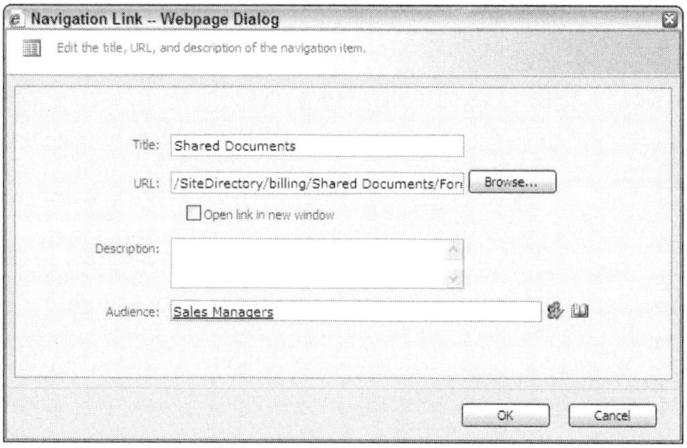

Figure 13-5:
Target
navigation
links.

4. **Click OK.**

   The navigation link can only be seen in the site's navigation by members
   of the audience.

Getting Personal

When it comes to an intranet portal, less is more. When you first create your
portal, chances are many departments will rush to add new information.
Department managers will dream of hours of uninterrupted productivity
because everyone will turn to the portal for information instead of ringing
their phones incessantly. Tell your managers to get real. Pushing loads of
policy documents and forms to the portal doesn't mean they don't have to
answer the phone.

Instead, they'll probably get the same number of phone calls from people
asking where they can find such and such form on the portal. Rather than
dump everything in the portal, encourage your users to figure out whether
they can provide users with a view of the portal that's personalized to meet
their needs.

A personalized view of the portal creates a user experience where the portal
anticipates the user's information requirements. Think I'm dreaming? Think
again. You might already have the information you need to create a personalized experience.

For example, each new hire very likely needs to receive the exact same set of paperwork and policy documents. People who aren't (yet) participating in child-care services or the 401k program need to be sent reminder notices when the time comes to elect for those services. And people with specialization training or certifications need to know when training classes are coming up or certifications are expiring.

If you know who these groups of people are — and in most cases you do — you can anticipate the forms and questions these folks have before they ever ask for them. Instead of sending out blast e-mails or posting blanket announcements on the home page of the SharePoint portal, encourage content providers to create a personalized experience just for those people who need it.

Personalizing Web parts

SharePoint provides a number of personalized Web parts that allow you to display information based on a user's identity or profile property. Personalized Web parts are used extensively in My Site. For example, the Outlook Web Access Web parts, such as My Inbox and My Calendar, are personalized Web parts. The content rollup Web parts, such as the Colleague Tracker and My Links, are also examples of personalized Web parts.

Personalized Web parts are different than targeted Web parts. A *targeted* Web part uses an audience to create a group of people who can see the content. A *personalized* Web part displays content that pertains only to the current user. This makes it possible to create personalized sites, such as My Site, where all the content pertains to the current user.

Personalized Web parts are used most frequently with the My Site templates for personal sites, the public profile page, and personalized sites. Personalized Web parts aren't restricted to those sites, however. You can use personalized Web parts on any kind of site to display information you want to target to an individual. For example, you could place a Web part on the portal's home page that displays the current user's progress toward a predefined set of goals.

SharePoint provides a number of filter Web parts that make it easy to personalize the content in a Web part. The most obvious filter Web part is the Current User Filter Web part. This Web part appears by default in the personalize site template.

The Current User Filter Web part allows you to identify the value of the current user by either selecting the current user name or by using a value from the user's profile. You then use that value to filter values in another Web part. For example, you could filter on an account number identifier that's stored in the user profile. The account number could then be used to filter a business data Web part that displays data from another source such as a payroll or human resources database.

You can use the Advanced Filter Options to determine how the filtered value is used in connection with other Web parts on the page. Your options include the ability to insert text before or after the filtered value. For example, you could add leading zeros to an account number. Figure 13-6 shows the filtering options for the Current User Filter Web part.

The filter Web parts, such as the Current User Filter, can be used with almost any kind of Web part. They're frequently used with list and library Web parts and business data Web parts. You filter the values displayed by creating a connection between the filter Web part and another Web part. The filtering Web part is the *provider,* and the filtered Web part is the *consumer.*

To create a connection between a providing Web part such as a Current User Filter Web part and a consuming Web part such as a Tasks List Web part, follow these steps:

1. **Browse to the page where you wish to use the filter Web part.**

   Filter Web parts are often used with personalization sites (see the next section) but they don't have to be. You could use them on the home page of a team site or on a Web parts page that you add to a site. I've often seen them used on sites to provide data filtered to the current user. For example, a company might use a SharePoint team site to manage their help desk requests. They could filter a list of requests so that the current user only sees the requests that pertain to him or her. Of course, the manager needs a view that shows all requests, which might be accomplished with an entirely separate Web parts page.

2. **Choose Site Actions⇨Edit Page.**

3. **Add the provider Web part and consumer Web part to the Web Parts page.**

   For example, you can use the Current Filter Web part to provide the user name to a Tasks List Web part.

4. **Click the Edit button on the provider Web part, such as the Current User Filter Web part, to display the Edit menu.**

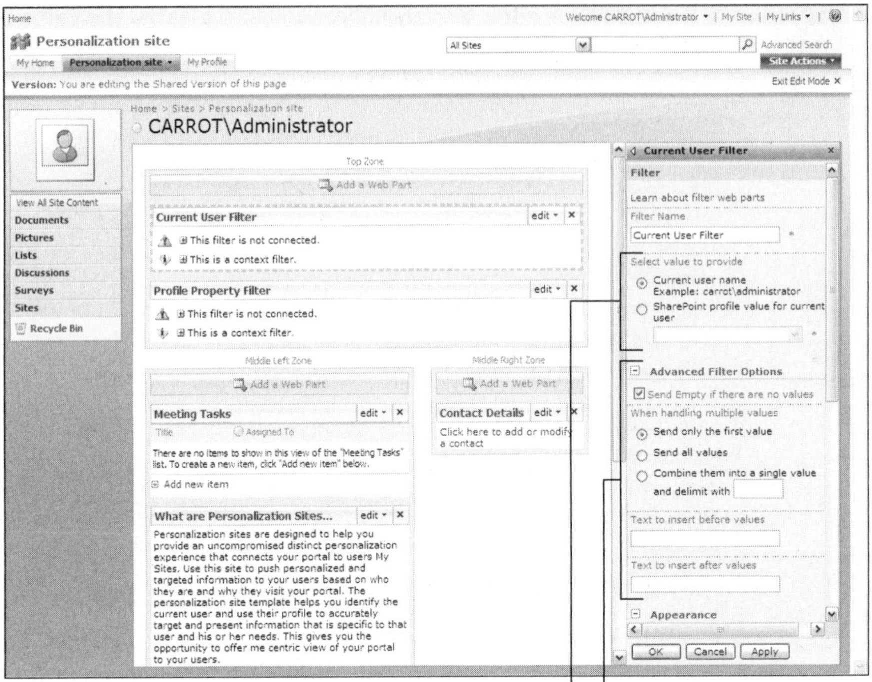

Figure 13-6:
Filter values
based on
a user's
identity.

Filter by user name or profile value.

Advanced Filter options

5. **In the Edit menu, choose Connections➪Send Filtered Values To.**

   A submenu of consuming Web parts appear.

   Note: Only Web parts that are capable of being filtered appear.

6. **Select the Web part that you wish to filter.**

   If you add a Tasks List Web part to the page, then you see the Tasks List Web part listed.

   The Configure Connection dialog box appears.

7. **Select the field from the consuming Web part that you want the provider Web part to filter.**

   For example, the Current User Web part can be configured to supply the username of the current user. You can select the Assigned To field from a tasks or issues Web part to filter the list to the current user, as shown in Figure 13-7.

If you don't see the fields you need, click the Cancel button and add the fields to the consuming Web part or reconfigure your filter provider to match a field in the consumer.

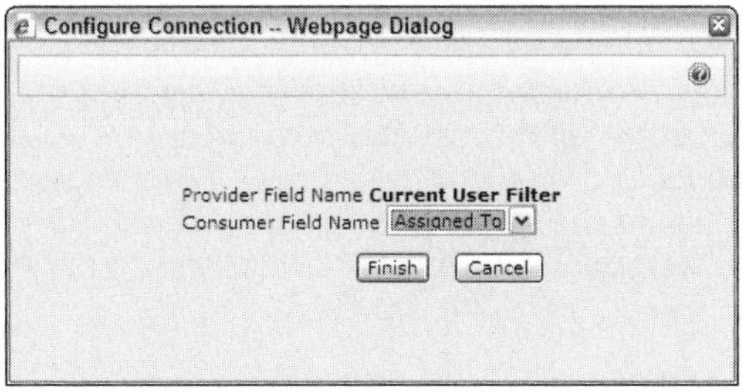

Figure 13-7:
Select
the field
to filter by.

Configure Connection -- Webpage Dialog

Provider Field Name **Current User Filter**
Consumer Field Name Assigned To ▾

[Finish] [Cancel]

8. Click the Finish button.

The consuming Web part is filtered by the values provided by the provider Web part. In this example, the current user sees his or her tasks by default.

A provider Web part can filter multiple consuming Web parts on a page.

Creating personalization sites

You use personalized Web parts to create entire sites whose content is filtered by the current user. The entire site may not be personalized, but the home page of the site is personalized. The rest of the site may contain content, such as lists and libraries, that support the personalization process.

Microsoft identifies three kinds of personalization sites that companies often create:

- ✔ **Content:** In this personalization site, content is created by one group, such as HR, and published to a personalized site, such as My HR. Note that no My HR site template exists in SharePoint. Rather, you create a site with the Personalize Site site template and then add Web parts that display content created by the HR department.

- ✔ **Data:** Here, the site displays business data that is filtered to the current user. For example, you might create a data personalization site for your help desk or call center employees to provide a customized view into their open tickets or call queue. Again, SharePoint doesn't provide specific templates for call centers or help desks. You create the site by using Web parts that query data from business applications.

✔ **Personalized views of group content:** This kind of personalization site displays the content of a team site filtered by user. This is a good way to ensure that team members see documents, tasks, and issues that pertain to them.

Audience targeting can be combined with personalization sites to further customize the user experience. For example, you can add Web parts targeted to all the developers on a project to call their attention to important deadlines — the team side of things — while displaying the overdue and upcoming tasks that pertains to the individual user in a separate personalized Web part. Combining audience targeting with personalization sites is a great way to make sure to communicate important announcements and deadlines.

The actual steps involved in creating personalization sites are quite simple. The challenge is planning the sites. The planning steps are similar to what you would go through if you were creating a custom solution. You have to identify your users, what content you wish to display, where the content is coming from, and how you're going to connect the user with the content.

You aren't restricted to just using content that's stored in SharePoint. You can use the business intelligence and business data Web parts to query business databases. You may need to involve a developer or database administrator to help with this task.

After you have all the pieces of your personalization site, follow these high-level steps to actually create it:

1. **Create the personalization site with the Personalization Site template.**

   You may not need an entire site just to display your personalized data. You can use personalized Web parts on any kind of SharePoint Web site. See the preceding section, "Personalizing Web parts," in this chapter on using personalized Web parts. See Chapter 4 for information on creating SharePoint sites.

   You can display personalized content in multiple sites. For example, you could display a personalized view of goals and objectives on a public page and also on a personalization site.

2. **Add personalized content and Web parts.**

   You need to add the data for your Web parts (most often to lists and libraries), configure filtering Web parts (such as the Current User Filter Web part), and create connections between those Web parts (as I describe in the preceding section, "Personalizing Web parts").

3. **Register your personalization site with the My Site host.**

   By registering your personalization site with the My Site host (see the next set of steps), the personalization site appears in the user's My Site navigation. This is a great way to provide access to personalization sites such as My HR.

Registering personalization sites is done by the administrator for the Shared Services Provider. Registering all personalization sites isn't necessary, but it makes it easy for users to find the site. If you don't register the site, be sure to provide some alternative way for people to access the site.

To register a personalization site with the My Site host, follow these steps:

1. **Browse to the Shared Services Administration site.**

   You must have administrative rights to access this site. If administrators wish to delegate management of registering personalization sites, they can modify the permissions on the Personalization Site Links list.

2. **Click the Personalization Site Links link in the User Profiles and My Sites section.**

   The Personalization Site Links for My Site Navigation page appears.

   The Personalization Site Links page is a SharePoint list. You navigate it like you do any other SharePoint list.

3. **Click the New button.**

   The New Item page appears.

4. **Type or paste the URL of the personalization site in the Web Address field and then type a description for the URL.**

   The description you type appears in the My Site navigation.

5. **Type or select an owner for the link in the Owner field.**

6. **Type or select an audience for the link in the Target Audiences field.**

7. **Click OK.**

   The site appears in the My Site navigation, as shown in Figure 13-8.

 You aren't restricted to only adding personalization sites to the Personalization Links list. You can add any kind of SharePoint site and use the Target Audience field to determine who can see the navigation. This is a great way to customize My Site navigation and provide easy access to project sites, team sites, and department sites.

Figure 13-8:
Add sites to the My Site navigation bar.

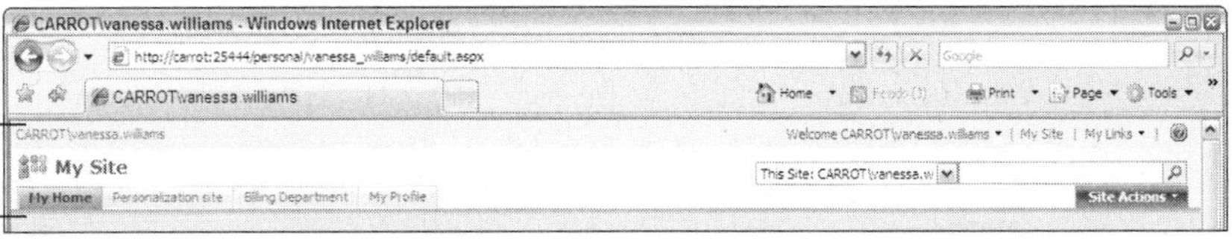

Sites registered with My Site navigation.

Personalizing the view

Many of the sites you create in SharePoint include a personal view and a shared view. Administrators and designers can edit the shared view, while each user modifies the personal view to suit their tastes. As a site owner or designer, you may wish to restrict the extent to which users can modify their personalized view.

Administrators modify the shared view of a page by choosing the Site Actions➪Edit Page command. Users modify the personal view by choosing the Welcome Username➪Personalize This Page command. The information about which version is being edited appears in the page header, as shown in Figure 13-9.

Many Web parts include a set of Advanced properties that allow an administrator to determine whether a Web part can be edited in personal view. The properties must be enabled by the Web part's developer, so not all Web parts have the properties.

Shared Version

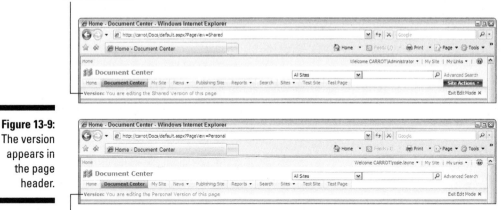

Figure 13-9: The version appears in the page header.

Personal Version

The properties are only accessible in shared view and can be found in the Advanced properties, as shown in Figure 13-10. The Allow Editing in Personal View property determines whether users can modify the Web part in the page's personal version. The Allow Zone Change property allows users to move the Web part into a different zone. The other properties, such as Allow Hide and Allow Minimize, make it possible for a user to disable the Web part in the page.

Even if you disable editing for all Web parts, users still have the ability to add Web parts to their personal views. Creating personal views is a feature of the page's site template. You have to modify the page if you want to remove the personal view completely from the page.

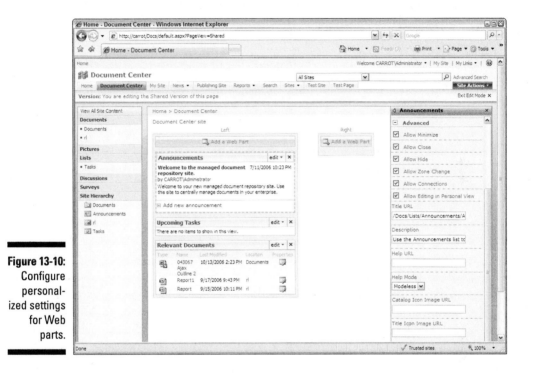

Figure 13-10:
Configure personalized settings for Web parts.

Chapter 14

Searching the Enterprise

*B*eing able to find the documents, events, and contacts that you store in SharePoint is an important requirement. You might not always remember exactly where a certain list or library is stored in the site hierarchy, so it's a real plus that SharePoint provides search services that make it easy to find these items.

At a minimum, you expect to be able to search for a file based on properties, such as the filename and who created it. SharePoint can also search *inside* documents so you can find the spreadsheet that lists all your software product keys even if you gave the file some ridiculous name, like Ice Cream Flavors. SharePoint search does more than just extend navigation to content; search makes it possible for users to find unstructured information very quickly.

SharePoint search has two flavors:

- ✔ **Windows SharePoint Services (WSS)** provides non-configurable search of the content found within a single SharePoint site collection.

- ✔ **Office SharePoint Server Search,** which is built on top of WSS search, provides a highly configurable search service that makes it possible to search content sources inside and outside SharePoint.

The features found in Office SharePoint Server Search turn search into a full-blown application. Deploying and maintaining Microsoft Office SharePoint Server (MOSS) Search requires a significant investment in time and people, but it makes it possible to use SharePoint to search content throughout your entire enterprise.

In this chapter, I explain the search features available in WSS and MOSS 2007, and I explain the steps required to configure, deploy, and maintain SharePoint search.

SharePoint's Search Offering

Search is a big deal. Just ask Google. Or, better yet, ask Microsoft. Microsoft identifies search as a huge opportunity for its business. It's no surprise to see SharePoint positioned as one of the key tools for delivering Enterprise search.

WSS does provide a very robust search engine, but it's limited to just searching within SharePoint site collections. There are no administrative pages for administering WSS search.

MOSS 2007 search features are built on top of WSS and provide administrators with the ability to search many kinds of content sources outside SharePoint. As such, it lets you completely customize the search experience in SharePoint.

The official name of the MOSS 2007 search feature is Office SharePoint Server Search. This feature can be found in more products than just MOSS 2007, such as:

- **Office SharePoint Server 2007 for Search:** This product is available in Standard and Enterprise Editions. This product is a good option for companies that want to create custom search applications. Both editions can index content from file shares, Web sites, SharePoint sites, and Exchange public folders. The Standard Edition is limited to 500,000 items in the content index. Enterprise Edition has no limit.

- **Office SharePoint Server 2007 Standard Edition:** This product adds the Search Center interface and the ability to search for people.

- **Office SharePoint Server 2007 Enterprise Edition:** This product adds the ability to index content from the Business Data Catalog.

Office SharePoint Server Search is a shared service that's delivered via the Shared Services Provider (SSP). See Chapter 2 for more information on the SSP.

SharePoint Search consists of two logical servers: a *search query* server (sometimes called the *search server* or *query server*), and an *index* server (sometimes called an *indexer*). The search server accepts user's search queries and passes them off to the index server for fulfillment. A single physical server can host both logical servers; however, Microsoft recommends deploying at least two servers. You can have multiple physical query servers, but you need only one physical index server.

Implementing search

Office SharePoint Server Search is a multifaceted product that requires configuration at the farm, Shared Services Provider (SSP), site collection, and site levels. A great deal of planning, coordinating, and monitoring is required to implement a good search solution. Depending on the size of your organization, you may need to create a search team to help match the organization's needs with the SharePoint capabilities.

Your team should include someone with a high-level understanding of your company's information needs as well as individuals who represent smaller organizational units' information needs. You may need Web designers and developers to help you customize the end user experience. Plan on identifying a search application administrator who is responsible for managing and monitoring search results. Involve Information Technology (IT) staff to plan for capacity and availability requirements.

Windows SharePoint Services Search and Office SharePoint Server Search are both very powerful search tools. If you want to maximize your return on these investments, you must plan on training your users to get the most out of them. Both these services are powerful enough to provide users with relevant and effective searches without training. However, showing users a few tips, such as how to conduct keyword searches in WSS and advanced searches in MOSS, can go a long way toward improving the user's search experience.

See the TechNet library on Microsoft's Web site for more information on planning for Office SharePoint Server Search at www.microsoft.com/technet/prodtechnol/office/spsearch.

Searching SharePoint

Most Web sites nowadays let you search the site. It should come as no surprise to end users to see the familiar search box in the upper-right corner of all SharePoint sites. Users can use this search box to search the site or list they're viewing.

Figure 14-1 shows the search box. The drop-down list on the left displays the search scope. The *scope* defines the context for the search. WSS defines two scopes: This Site and This List. The user types the search term in the textbox and clicks the Submit button.

MOSS 2007 includes two additional scopes: All Sites and People. You can create additional search scopes for MOSS, but WSS search is limited to the two default scopes.

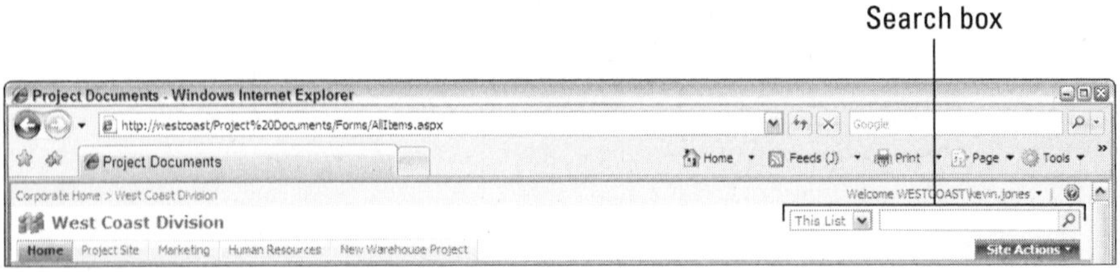

Search box

Figure 14-1:
Use the
search box
to search in
SharePoint.

SharePoint supports two kinds of search queries:

✔ **Full text searches** query the database with free-form text typed in the search box. All searches are full text searches by default.

✔ **Keyword searches** query the values of a set of properties based on the text you enter in the search box. Advanced searches in MOSS 2007 create keyword searches.

You can manually create keyword searches in either MOSS 2007 or WSS. Creating manual keyword searches is your only option for conducting an advanced search in WSS. The syntax for creating a keyword search consists of the following:

✔ **Keyword value:** This is the value you want to search for.

✔ **Property filter:** This is the property you want to filter on.

✔ **Inclusion and exclusion characters:** You use a plus (+) character to include the property or a minus (–) character to exclude the property. By default, properties are included so it isn't necessary to use the inclusion character.

For example, to create a keyword search based on the `author` property, type the following in the search box:

```
author:"John Smith"
```

You can use multiple properties to create OR and AND statements. Using two of the same property filters is equivalent to an OR statement, whereas using two different property filters effectively creates an AND statement. For example, the following statement searches use the `site` and `author` properties:

```
site:http://company/sitedirectory author:"John Smith"
```

You can mix full text queries with keyword queries, as shown here:

```
sharepoint -author:administrator
```

The preceding statement searches for all instances of the word sharepoint when the author isn't administrator.

You can use manual keyword queries to execute advanced searches in WSS. Although you can use keyword syntax in MOSS 2007, it isn't usually necessary because MOSS 2007 provides an advanced search interface.

See the WSS and MOSS 2007 Software Development Kits (SDKs) for more details on executing keyword searches. See the section, "Managing properties," later in this chapter, for more information on properties.

Search results are returned to the results page. The results page in WSS is pretty simple. By default, the search results are listed by relevance, but users have the option to search by modified date. Additionally, no advanced search options are displayed on the WSS results page.

Using the Search Center

Searches conducted in MOSS 2007 use a special results page that's part of the Search Center. The Search Center is an example of a search application built using the features of MOSS 2007. The Search Center is deployed automatically in the Collaboration Portal template, as I describe in Chapter 11.

By default, a link to the Search Center appears in the portal's top link bar. Also by default, search results appear in the Search Center. Administrators can change the search results page, as I describe in the section, "Other administrative tasks," later in this chapter.

There's no equivalent feature to the Search Center in WSS. However, you can create a link to the search results page if you want to display a dedicated search page. The search results page uses the relative URL _layouts/searchresults.aspx. You also have the ability to use the WSS Search Web service to provide a custom search experience.

The Search Center is a vital component of the search functionality provided by MOSS 2007. You can use the Search Center to conduct simple searches similar to WSS searches in the search box. A key feature of the Search Center is the ability to conduct advanced searches using different operators, languages, and properties.

The Search Center with Tabs is the default template used in the Collaboration portal. The two tabs that appear in the Search Center with Tabs — All Sites and People — are examples of search scopes. A *scope* filters the content that's searched. In a search using People scope, the search is limited to data found in the User Profile Store. See the section, "Scoping out," later in this chapter for more about scopes.

You can customize the Search Center by adding tabs and creating custom search results pages. The Search Center includes Web parts — the Search Box Web Part and the Advanced Search Web Part. You can configure these Web parts to change the search options that are available to the user. See the topic, "Customizing the Search Center," in the MOSS 2007 SDK for more details.

The Search Center uses Publishing pages like the other sites in the Collaboration portal. See Chapter 16 for more about working with Publishing pages.

Figure 14-2 shows an example of the Search Center conducting a keyword search with the People search scope.

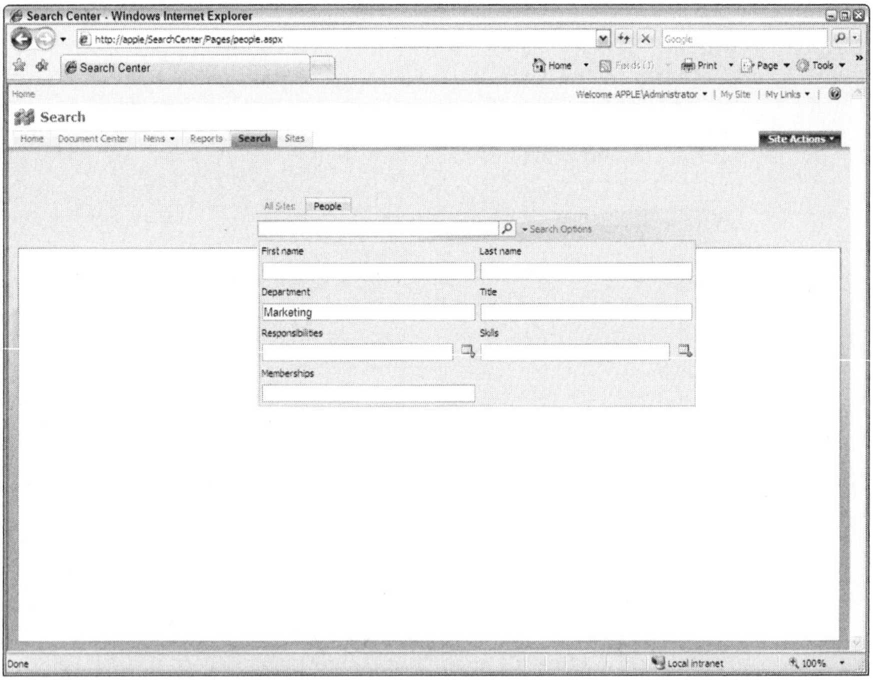

Figure 14-2:
Conduct
searches
with the
Search
Center.

Searching people

People search is an important feature of MOSS 2007's user profiles service. MOSS 2007 provides three user-interface options for searching for people: the People scope, the People tab in the Search Center, and the Employee Lookup Web part, which is featured on the home page of Collaboration portals.

The MOSS 2007 People search features are more than just a directory service. Using user profile information about colleagues, interests,

and custom user profile properties, People search makes it possible for users to connect with other users who have shared interests and experience.

Adding the Knowledge Network feature to SharePoint increases the power of People search to connect the employees in your organization with relevant people inside and outside the organization. I discuss user profiles and knowledge networks in Chapter 12.

Taking action on search results

The search results returned by MOSS Search allow the user to do more than just click results links. Results are returned based on several relevance factors, such as modified date and proximity of the result to the site's home page.

In addition to improved relevance, MOSS Search provides features, such as Did You Mean? prompts, that give the user alternative spellings of terms. Users also have the option to subscribe to search alerts and subscribe to an RSS feed of the search results.

Ensuring that search results appear on the first page of results is an important goal. Users generally don't take the time to scroll through numerous pages of results. They expect the results to be right on top. Improving search relevancy requires a combination of approaches that includes identifying the relative value of pages and sites. Pages of higher relevance, such as the portal home page, are *authoritative pages,* whereas sites of lesser importance are *demoted sites.* You can also establish an editorial process for highlighting search content by using Keywords and Best Bets, as I explain in the section, "Managing properties," later in this chapter.

MOSS 2007 includes a number of additional ways to tweak search results that require you to break out your crack programming skills. If you find that your search relevancies leave something to be desired, see the topic, "Search Relevance Architecture Overview," in the MOSS 2007 SDK.

Configuring Search

From an end-user perspective, search is pretty straightforward. You type your search term in a search box and then scroll through the results. After all, it's just search, how hard can it be? Well, getting the right results in the right order requires significant configuration.

Before you can start to understand how to configure Office SharePoint Server Search, you must first understand the major components of search:

- **Content sources:** These are the SharePoint sites, network shares, external Web sites, and other sources you want to be able to search within SharePoint.

- **Crawl process:** Searching a content source each time someone executed a query would be very resource-intensive. Instead, SharePoint prepares for searches by creating a list of words from the content source. A *crawl* is when the search service searches a content source. Administrators create rules that define what and when content sources get crawled.

- **Index:** SharePoint creates a reference list — an *index* — of the words it collects from a crawled content source. Actually, SharePoint creates two kinds of indexes. One index uses properties, such as `author` and `modified date`, to create an index of properties and their values. These are *crawled properties*. The second index is the content index, which stores all the words associated with the content source.

- **Query:** A query is when a user executes a search in SharePoint. SharePoint passes the user's query through a *wordbreaker* that breaks the query down into individual words. Afterward, the words are passed through a program, or a *stemmer,* that generates language-specific inflected forms of the words. Wordbreakers and stemmers allow SharePoint to generate additional search terms that make the query more effective.

- **Scope:** Scopes allow an administrator to define groups of content that are used to filter the context index. WSS automatically creates This Site and This List scopes, and MOSS adds All Sites and People scopes.

This terminology points out an important distinction: End users search, the server indexes. When you configure a content source, you're configuring SharePoint to index the content. Only after the content is indexed is it available to be searched by an end user. Indexing is made possible when SharePoint crawls the content.

All the components identified here are present in WSS and MOSS 2007. The primary difference between these two search services is that MOSS 2007 search is configurable. WSS search defines defaults for these components, which makes it simple to manage but provides fewer features.

Even though there's no user interface for configuring search in WSS, you can use the `stsadm` command line application to interact with some search features.

Office SharePoint Search is a component of the Shared Services Provider (SSP). When you configure your SSP, you specify the search database along with the Index server. After you create your SSP, you're ready to start configuring Office SharePoint Search. See Chapter 2 for a walkthrough of creating an SSP.

You manage search using the Search section of the Shared Services Administration home page, which you can access via the Central Administration site. The Search section has the following two links:

- ✔ **Search Settings** provides access to administrative pages for all the major components of search.

- ✔ **Search Usage Reports** provides a set of reports you can use to determine the effectiveness of your search application in providing results to user's queries. Your designated search application administrator should use the reports to tweak the search configuration over time.

I refer to SharePoint search as a search application to remind you that search must be administered in order to stay healthy and relevant. Like any application, search atrophies without the proper monitoring and auditing. Use the reports in the Search Usage Reports page along with the crawl logs (keep reading) to get feedback on your search application. Also, conduct periodic searches to test the search application.

Defining content sources

Content sources define the content that administrators can configure for users to search. Office SharePoint Server Search allows you to create the following kinds of content sources:

- ✔ **SharePoint sites:** By default, SharePoint automatically creates a default content source called Local Office SharePoint Server Sites and adds the top-level URL for each site collection to it.

- ✔ **Web sites:** You can create content sources based on internal or external Web sites.

- ✔ **File shares:** Content stored in networked file shares can be added as a content source.

- ✔ **Exchange public folders:** You can configure search to access content in public folders.

- ✔ **Business data:** With the Business Data Catalog, you can add an application database as a content source. You must first configure the Business Data Catalog to access the data. See Chapter 17.

MOSS 2007 provides support for creating content sources for Lotus Notes, but it isn't configured by default. See the MOSS 2007 SDK for more information.

Keep the number of content sources minimized. Each content source can contain only a single type of content, so you need at least one content source for each content type you plan to index. For example, you need separate content sources for SharePoint sites and file shares.

You can only create content sources in MOSS 2007. WSS doesn't make any content source management features available.

To create a new content source, do the following:

1. **Browse to the Shared Services Administration site for your SSP.**

   You can navigate to the Shared Services Administration site from the Central Administration site.

2. **Click the Search Settings link in the Search section.**

   The Configure Search Settings page appears.

3. **Click the Content Sources and Crawl Schedules link.**

   The Manage Content Sources page appears.

   You should see the default content source for SharePoint sites.

4. **Click the New Content Sources button.**

   The Add Content Source page appears.

5. **Type a name for the content source.**

6. **Select the type of content to be crawled from the list of content source types.**

7. **Type the start addresses where you want to begin crawling.**

   You should specify the top-level address. You can always add crawl rules if you want to exclude specific content from the address.

   If the content source type is Business Data, you select an application to crawl from the Business Data Catalog in this step.

8. **In the Crawl Settings section, select the options for how you want the content source crawled.**

   Generally speaking, the crawl options allow you to determine whether the crawl searches subfolders or just the top-level address. Each content type has slightly different settings.

9. **Select a crawl schedule or create a new schedule in the Crawl Schedules section.**

   You should generally schedule both full crawls and incremental crawls. A *full crawl* crawls the entire content source, whereas *incremental crawls* cover only content that has changed since the last full crawl.

10. **Select the Start Full Crawl of This Content Source check box.**

    Crawling content is very resource-intensive. Try to schedule crawls during after hours. Full crawls can take a really long time, so wait to start them at the end of the day.

11. **Click OK.**

Even though you can create multiple content sources, SharePoint maintains a single content index. Users' search queries are executed through search scopes, which are used to create meaningful search groups based on the content index. See the section, "Scoping out," later in this chapter, for more information on search scopes.

Adding content sources is one thing, but managing them is another. To manage an individual content source — including viewing the crawl status of a content source — go back to the Manage Content Sources page and click the link for the content source you're interested in. Doing so opens the menu shown in Figure 14-3, which lets you edit or delete the content source; start, pause, or stop a crawl; and view the crawl log.

Make it a point to check the crawl log to see the status of your content crawls. Click the Crawl Logs link in the Configure Search Settings page — the page from Step 2 in the preceding steps list.

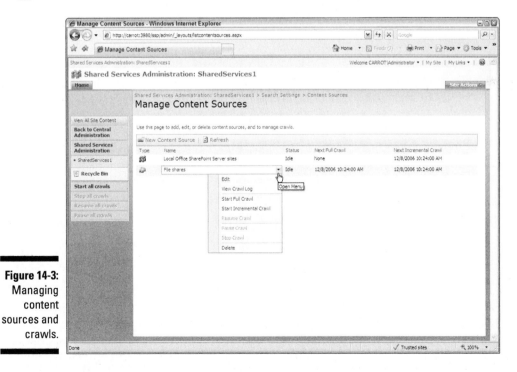

Figure 14-3:
Managing
content
sources and
crawls.

Crawling content

The act of opening content in content sources in order to build a context index is known as *crawling*. When you create a content source, specify a starting address and schedule that determine what gets crawled and how frequently the crawl occurs. SharePoint allows you to create *crawl rules* to provide more granular management of what gets crawled in a content source.

You use crawl rules to define whether specific paths should be excluded or included when the content is crawled. You can also specify a different authentication account to use besides the default content account. Follow these steps to create a crawl rule:

1. **Click the Crawl Rules link in the Configure Search Settings page.**

   See Steps 1–2 in the preceding section to see how to get to the Configure Search Settings page.

   The Manage Crawl Rules page appears.

2. **Click the New Crawl Rule button.**

   The Add Crawl Rule page appears.

3. **Type the path you wish to include or exclude in the Path textbox.**

   You can use the wildcard character asterisk (*) in pathnames. For example, to include all the folders under the file share `\\file-server\departments`, you enter the following path:

   ```
   \\file-server\departments\*
   ```

4. **In the Crawl Configuration section, indicate whether to include or exclude the path in the crawl.**

5. **If you choose to include the path, you can enter alternative authentication information in the Specify Authentication section.**

   Oftentimes, the default content access account, which is set to `NT Authority\Local Service` by default, might not have the permissions required to access the content source. You can specify a different account to be used for this crawl rule.

   You can change the default content access account on the Configure Search Settings page. Be sure not to use an administrator account; otherwise, SharePoint may crawl unpublished documents.

6. **Click OK.**

   The rule appears in the list of crawl rules.

You can test your crawl rules to see if a path matches any of the rules you define. To test your rules, paste a path in the textbox on the Manage Crawl Rules page and click the Test button. SharePoint indicates whether the path is included or excluded, as shown in Figure 14-4.

Don't use the crawl rules as a means to define content sources. Instead, define the content source first and then use crawl rules to further define the crawl's behavior.

Starting with a more specific start address in your content source is better than using crawl rules to create inclusions and exclusions. Narrow your content source first and then create any crawl rules as necessary. It's easy to overwhelm your server resources by creating very wide content sources.

SharePoint has another kind of crawl rule that pertains to external content sources. You use *crawler impact rules* to define rules to limit how many times SharePoint requests content from an external source, such as a Web site on the Internet.

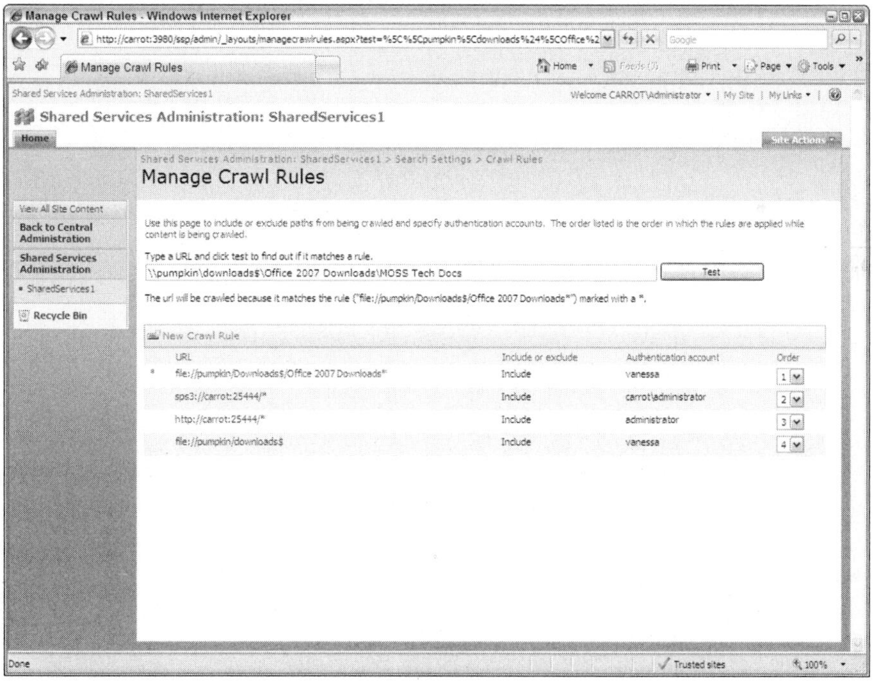

Figure 14-4:
Test your
crawl rules.

Crawling content sources uses resources on the server being crawled. For that reason, minimize the amount you crawl external servers by using crawler impact rules. You can define crawler impact rules by using wildcards so that the rule applies to a set of external sources. For example, defining a rule using the site name *.com includes all sites that end with .com in their URLs.

You define crawler impact rules with the Manage Search Service page in the Central Administration site. See the section, "Other administrative tasks," later in this chapter, for more on crawler impact rules.

An alternative approach for allowing users to search external Web sites is to incorporate Google search into your SharePoint portal. Google already crawls public Web sites, so you can take advantage of Google's results instead of creating your own index. Google provides the Google Free Web search service that you can use to display a Google search box that's limited to a single Web domain. All you have to do is download the Google Free code, create an HTML file with the code, and use the Page Viewer Web part to display the HTML file on a SharePoint site. Using Google Free is a great way to provide users with a limited search scope. You can download Google Free at www.google.com/searchcode.html. Figure 14-5 shows an example of the Google search box using Google Free to conduct a search of Microsoft's TechNet Web site.

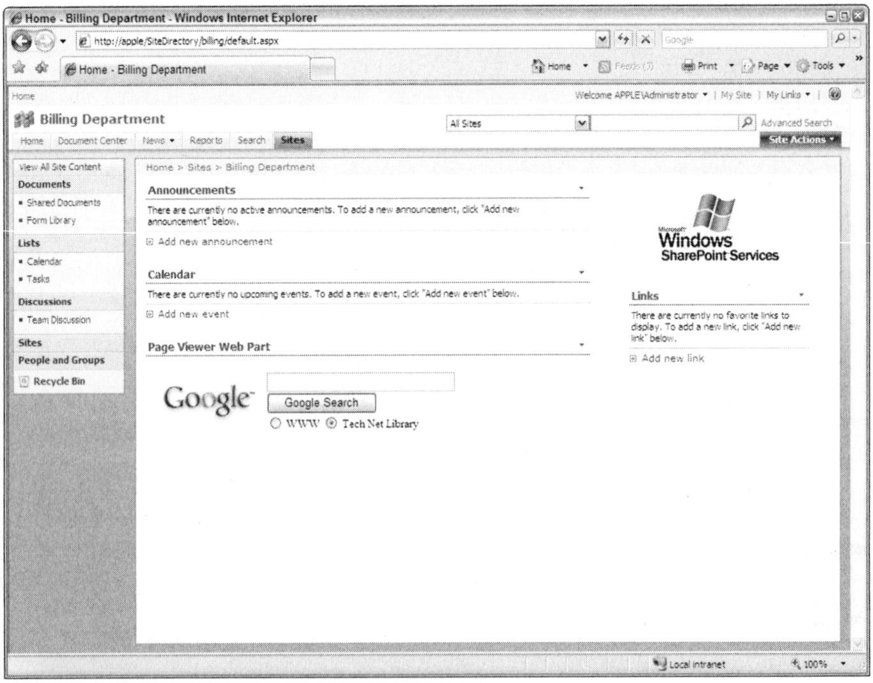

Figure 14-5:
Use Google Free to search external Web sites.

Scoping out

Office SharePoint Server Search has a single content index that stores text from all the crawled content sources. SharePoint uses *search scopes* as a way to filter the content index. By limiting the user's query to filter subsets of the content index, SharePoint increases the probability of returning a relevant results set.

SharePoint has two kinds of search scopes. *Shared* scopes are managed by the SSP and are shared across site collections. (SharePoint provides two default shared scopes: All Sites and People.) In addition, though, each site collection can have its *own* set of scopes that are available for only that site collection.

Search scopes are built by creating a set of rules that determines what content is included from the content index. Here are four kinds of search scope rules you can create:

- ✔ **Web address:** Allows you to build rules based on locations, such as a site, list, or folder in a document library.

- ✔ **Property query:** Allows you to build rules based on managed properties, such as `author`. I explain managed properties in the next section.

    Rules based on managed properties use the `IsExactly` operator, which means that results aren't returned unless the search term exactly matches the value in the content source.

    You may be inclined to think using properties is of limited value. However, you can create properties for content sources based on data from the Business Data Catalog. Therefore, you have the opportunity to create properties based on business data, such as `Sales Territory` or `Product Category`.

- ✔ **Content source:** Allows you to limit the scope to a specific content source for shared search scopes.

- ✔ **All content:** Includes all content in the content index in the scope.

You create one rule at a time based on these rule types. You can include, require, and exclude items matching the rules to create the search scope's filter criteria.

Users need to understand how to use scopes. If you have too many scopes, their use might not be obvious. For example, the All Sites shared scope includes everything in the content index except People. If a user conducts a People search using the All Sites search scope, he won't get the same results he would if he were to use the People scope, which is limited to content from user profiles.

You can add scope rules to existing scopes. Before you create a new scope, decide whether the scope should reside at the SSP or the site collection. Scopes created at the SSP are available to all site collections, whereas those created in a site collection are available only in that site collection. The steps for creating scopes are similar.

To create scopes on a site collection, follow these steps:

1. **Browse to the Site Settings page of the top-level site of the site collection where you wish to create the scope.**

   To create shared scopes, click the View Scopes link in the Configure Search Settings page. See the earlier section, "Defining content sources," for details on getting to the Configure Search Settings page.

2. **Click the Search Scopes link.**

   The View Scopes page appears.

3. **Click the New Scope button.**

   The Create Scope page appears.

4. **Type a title and description for the scope.**

5. **In the Display Groups section, place a check mark next to each display group where you wish to display the search scope.**

   By default, MOSS 2007 includes two display groups — Search Dropdown and Advanced Search. These display groups correspond to the MOSS 2007 default search options — search and advanced search, respectively. The scopes included in the Search Dropdown display group appear in the Scope drop-down list in the search box that appears on SharePoint sites (refer to Figure 14-1). Choosing to add your scope to the Search Dropdown display group displays the scope in the Scope drop-down list.

   You can create new display groups with the View Scopes page. This option doesn't apply when you create a new scope in the SSP. However, you can add SSP scopes to a site collection's display groups. For example, the All Sites and People scopes are created at the SSP, but they're added to the Search Dropdown display group.

6. **Indicate whether to use the default search results page.**

   The results page for People searches is an example of using a different results page.

7. **Click OK.**

   The scope appears in the display group you selected on the View Scopes page.

Because no rules are defined for the new scope, no search results are returned when it's used. To add new scope rules, follow these steps:

1. **Click the scope from the list of scopes on the View Scopes page.**

   A contextual menu appears.

2. **Click the Edit Properties and Rules command.**

   The Scope Properties and Rules page appears.

3. **In the Rules section, click the New Rule link.**

   The Add Scope Rule page appears.

4. **Select the rule type from the Scope Rule Type section.**

5. **Specify the path for Web Address rules or the property for Property Query rules.**

6. **In the Behavior section, indicate whether to include, require, or exclude the content.**

7. **Click OK.**

   The rule appears.

You can click the New Rule link to add as many rules as necessary to properly limit the scope.

Managing properties

All content sources have properties that are native to that source. For example, Word documents have properties such as `author`, `title`, and `subject`. SharePoint discovers these properties as part of the crawl process and adds these properties — as well as their values — to the property store. Properties discovered by the crawler are known as *crawled properties.*

There's no question about the usefulness of searching properties. The problem arises, however, when you have so many content types that the properties overlap. For example, a Word document has a subject and so does an e-mail. Also, not all crawled properties are meaningful for search. To manage the glut of crawled properties, SharePoint allows you to map crawled properties to managed properties.

Managed properties are the crawled properties identified by an administrator as being search-worthy. SharePoint creates a predefined set of managed properties, such as `author`, `description`, and `type`. You can see managed properties in action in the Advanced Search interface in the MOSS 2007 Search Center and when users execute keyword searches.

Managed properties are administered on the Configure Search Settings page in the Shared Services Administration site. Click the Metadata Property Mappings link on that page to get to the Metadata Property Mappings page, where you can view existing managed properties, create new properties, and manage the mappings between managed properties and crawled properties.

From a planning perspective, you may find it both useful and overwhelming to use the Metadata Property Mappings page to view managed properties and crawled properties. This can give you some clues about the kinds of searches that people need to conduct. However, it might be more productive to identify a list of properties before viewing managed properties.

Two crawled properties that SharePoint maps for you are `Best Bets` and `Keywords`. These are two features of Office SharePoint Server Search that you can use to create a dictionary of search terms (`Keywords`) and a set of sites that are highly relevant to those terms (`Best Bets`).

Don't confuse Keywords with conducting a keyword search. A *keyword search* simply refers to performing a search using managed properties, such as `author:smith`. A *Keyword* is a glossary term. You can conduct a keyword search using the `Keyword` managed property. For example, assume you create a Keyword called `Widget`. A keyword search for this term looks like `Keyword:widget` with `Keyword` as the managed property.

Keywords and Best Bets are managed at the site collection level. Follow these steps to create a new Keyword:

1. **Browse to the Site Settings page of the top-level site of the site collection where you wish to create the Keyword.**

2. **Click the Search Keywords link.**

   The Manage Keywords page appears.

3. **Click the Add Keyword button.**

   The Add Keyword page appears.

4. **Type the search term you wish to define in the Keyword Phrase textbox.**

5. **Type any words that are synonymous with the keyword phrase in the Synonyms textbox.**

6. **Click the Add Best Bet link.**

   The Add Best Bet dialog box appears.

7. **Select an existing Best Bet to associate with the Keyword or create a new Best Bet.**

Best Bets and Keywords have a many-to-many relationship. *Best Bets* are hyperlinks to resources that float to the top of the search relevancy. Each Best Bet must have a unique URL.

8. **Click OK to close the Add Best Bet dialog box.**

9. **Type the definition of the keyword in the Keyword Definition textbox.**

10. **Specify a contact that is responsible for the keyword.**

11. **Enter dates in the Publishing section for publication start date, end date, and review date for the Keyword.**

12. **Click OK.**

When a user executes a search using the keyword, the information you define for the keyword appears to the right of the search results, as shown in Figure 14-6.

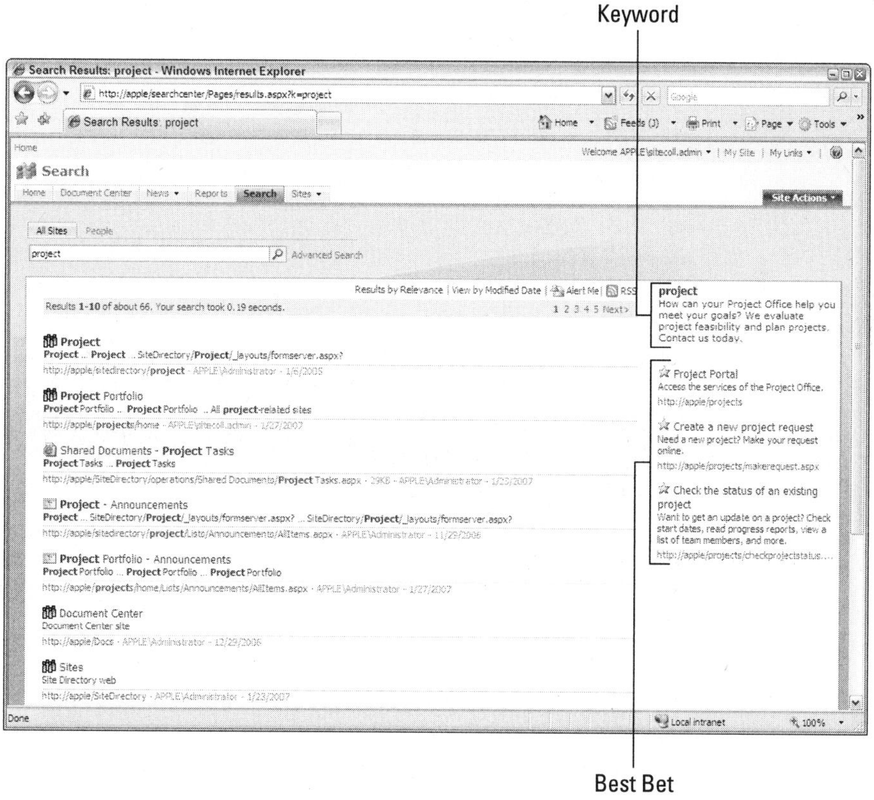

Keyword

Figure 14-6:
Searching for defined Keywords.

Best Bet

Other administrative tasks

Despite all the configuration settings I cover in this chapter, you may need to set a few more settings:

- ✔ **Search visibility in sites** determines whether the site appears in search results. You can also specify whether ASP.NET pages found in the site are indexed. Click the Search Visibility Link on the Site Settings page for the site you wish to manage.

- ✔ **Search settings for the site collection** determines whether the site collection uses the Search Center and shared scopes. Click the Search Settings link on the Site Settings page of the site collection's top-level site.

- ✔ **Set database authentication** for the search database and the path for the index file locations at the Edit Shared Services Provider page. Click the Create or Configure This Farm's Shared Services link on the Application Management page of the Central Administration site to get to the Edit Shared Services Provider page.

- ✔ **Set crawler impact rules and farm-wide settings** by clicking the Manage Search Service link on the Application Management page of the Central Administration site.

- ✔ **Stop or start search services** using the Services on Server page. Access the page through the Operations page in the Central Administration site. MOSS 2007 uses the Office SharePoint Server Search service to deliver all the search features that I describe in this chapter. MOSS uses the Windows SharePoint Services Help Search, which is the same as the WSS Search service used by WSS server, to index help files.

- ✔ **Map indexed addresses to new address in search results, disable search-based alerts, remove items from search results, and use authoritative pages to influence search relevancy** with the Configure Search Settings page in the Shared Services Administration site.

Part IV
Enterprise Applications for SharePoint

The 5th Wave   By Rich Tennant

In this part . . .

1 introduce you to the heavy hitting features of SharePoint Server 2007 — the stuff you can use to create enterprise-quality applications, even if you aren't a large enterprise. You'll see how to use SharePoint for document and records management, how to publish content to SharePoint sites, and how to integrate data and create business intelligence applications.

Chapter 15

Exploring Document and Records Management

Microsoft has made much of the fact that Microsoft Office SharePoint Server (MOSS) 2007 is capable of providing Enterprise Content Management services. SharePoint has always offered document management features via document libraries, but they waited until MOSS 2007 before adding ECM to their features set. To qualify SharePoint for use as an ECM solution, Microsoft had to make the following changes:

✔ **They improved document management features,** such as content approval and routing. Document management involves storing and sharing documents among a group of people, such as a team, department, or an entire enterprise.

✔ **They added the Records Center special site template,** which is essentially a records management application. *Records management* involves managing anything that needs to be retained for a certain length of time, including documents and e-mails.

✔ **They added publishing features** that make it possible to manage Web content, whether that content is used for the internal portal or a public-facing Internet site.

SharePoint brings in features of Microsoft Content Management Server 2002 to address the special needs of managing Web content.

In this chapter, I describe the document and records management features of SharePoint. The records management features of MOSS 2007 expand on the document management features of Windows SharePoint Services and a few new features that are distinctive to managing a records repository. I discuss publishing and Web content features in Chapter 16.

Managing Documents

Document management has always been the cornerstone feature of SharePoint. In many organizations, the document library is the first SharePoint feature they find out how to use. *Document libraries* are repositories for storing documents of all types, including Word documents, Excel spreadsheets, images, and audio files.

Virtually all document management features are delivered via document libraries. The collective technologies of Windows SharePoint Services (WSS) and MOSS 2007 provide many features that make document libraries more than just passive containers for storing documents.

WSS provides the following document management features:

- ✓ **Versioning** saves previous versions of the document. You have the option to save only published versions or all draft versions as well.

- ✓ **Check in and check out** requires that users explicitly check out a document before editing. Only versions that are checked in are visible by other users.

- ✓ **Content approval** requires that a separate user, who acts as the Approver, has to change the status on new versions of a document before they're visible.

- ✓ **Content types** identify the kinds of documents that are stored in the document library. A *content type* is a collection of properties used to describe the document. Keep in mind that content types *can* include an optional document template that's associated with the document.

- ✓ **Information Rights Management (IRM)** protects documents from unauthorized copying, forwarding, and printing.

Most of the features for managing documents in WSS are delivered through document libraries. Generally speaking, the document libraries created in Windows SharePoint sites are intended more for collaboration than document management. The features are important, but they're primarily there to enable collaboration among team members.

MOSS 2007 adds some additional content management features that graduate from managing documents in teams to managing documents for an entire organization. These features include:

- ✓ **Information management policies** that define rules for auditing and retaining content. Policies can be applied to content types, libraries, or lists.

- ✓ **Document Information Panels** that collect document metadata from users in Office 2007 clients. MOSS 2007 allows you to associate custom Document Information Panels with content types.

✔ **Document workflows** that route documents to users who need to complete a document management task, such as approving the document for publishing or collecting signatures. You can optionally associate workflows with a content type.

Workflows are enabled by WSS. MOSS 2007 includes several document management workflows out-of-the-box. You can create custom workflows to use with WSS.

✔ **Item scheduling** that allows you to schedule when a document is visible.

✔ **A Document Center** is a centralized repository for managing an enterprise's documents. The Document Center is the document library for the entire enterprise, but it doesn't replace all the document libraries found in individual team sites.

✔ **A Records Center** is a records management application intended for managing the archiving of a company's records for compliance purposes.

The Records Center site template is an implementation of the Records Center Web service of WSS. Users of both WSS and MOSS aren't limited to using the Records Center site template. They can use the Records Center Web service to send documents to a different records repository.

MOSS 2007 adds additional publishing features for managing Web content published to SharePoint sites and portals. See Chapter 16 for details on these features.

Because so much of the document management functionality is delivered via document libraries, I cover document management features in the context of the document library. Understand that document libraries can be found in team sites, portal sites, Document Center sites, and Records Center sites. Create document libraries and enable the document management features that are relevant to the site where it's created.

Managing drafts and published versions

Many of the fundamental document management and collaboration features of SharePoint are made possible through document libraries. Document libraries are a feature of WSS and are, therefore, available to both WSS sites and MOSS 2007 sites.

You can think of document libraries as being like network shares except they have many more features. Document libraries are more transparent when it comes to security. That is, it's much easier to see who has access to what simply by having the user click the Edit menu on a document. Clicking the Edit menu on a document shows the list of commands that the user can take on that document. For example, members of the SharePoint Group *Site* Members have permissions to delete documents in a document library. You may be surprised to realize that users can delete documents other than their own. However, you can easily customize permissions for document libraries.

When you create a new document library, you have to make several decisions that relate to enabling document management features. One of those decisions is whether SharePoint should create a new version of a file each time the file is edited. By default, the answer is no. However, you can enable versioning when you create the library or after the fact.

Many kinds of document libraries are in SharePoint, such as picture libraries and form libraries. Each of these libraries has the same features as a document library. Also, because a document library is a kind of list, lists share some of the features of document libraries, including versioning. I explain the different kinds of lists and libraries that you encounter in WSS and MOSS 2007 and walk you through creating lists and libraries in Chapter 4.

When creating a document library, decide whether the library should store previous versions of documents. You can opt to store each major version, or you can opt to store each draft version as well. *Draft versions* are minor versions and are represented by the decimal number in a version, such as 0.2 or 1.3. When a document is published, the document's version number is rounded to the next whole number and is considered a *major version.* You can opt to store only major versions and not interim draft versions.

Deciding whether to use versions is usually driven by the business's need to retain draft copies, not concern for disk storage. Storage is relatively cheap. You can, however, restrict the number of major and minor versions retained in the library. Take into consideration the number of versions you plan to retain when calculating storage requirements. Because you're storing more than one version of the same file, expect your disk requirements to increase.

If you decide to enable draft versions, you must determine who can see draft items in the library. By default, any user with read permissions can see draft items. Your other options are to restrict draft items to users with editing permissions or users with approval permissions.

You use the Versioning Settings page to enable versions, content approval, draft item security, and Check Out for document libraries. To enable these features, follow these steps:

1. **Browse to the document library.**

   If you click the View All Site Content link in the left side of a SharePoint site, you'll see a list of all the libraries on the site.

2. **Choose Settings⇨Document Library Settings.**

   The Settings page appears.

3. **Click the Versioning Settings link in the General Settings section.**

   The Versioning Settings page appears, as shown in Figure 15-1.

4. **In the Content Approval section, select the Yes radio button to enable content approval.**

   Enabling content approval requires that submitted documents be explicitly approved by an Approver before they're visible.

5. **In the Document Version History section, indicate whether to use no versions, major versions, or major and minor versions.**

   If you opt for major or minor versions, you can optionally limit the number of major and minor versions to retain.

6. **In the Draft Item Security section, select who can see draft items in a document library.**

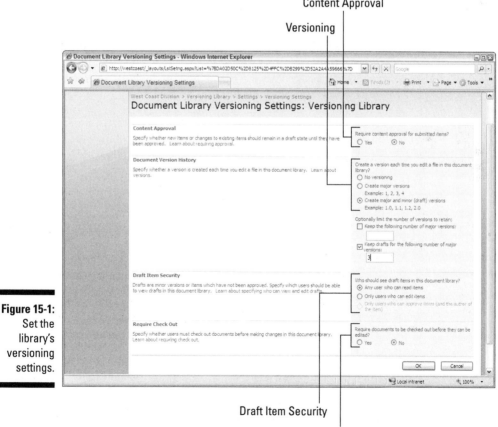

Figure 15-1:
Set the library's versioning settings.

By limiting draft items to Editors or Approvers, you prevent others from seeing the documents in the library.

7. In the Require Check Out section, indicate whether users must check out documents before they edit them.

I usually suggest requiring check out for documents because doing so allows every one to see who's working on a document.

8. Click OK.

The versioning settings are saved.

A user's experience with document libraries depends on how the user accesses the library. Accessing the library through a browser is the most predictable user experience, but it's the least practical. Users have two ways to access library features through a browser. They can use the document's Edit menu or view the document's properties. The features enabled in the library dictate the commands available via the Edit menu or Properties view. Figure 15-2 shows two Edit menus. The Edit menu on the left shows default settings for a document library. The Edit menu on the right shows a library where all versioning settings are enabled. The state of the file and the user's permissions determine exactly which menu commands are available. For example, the Discard Check Out menu item appears only when the file is checked out. Table 15-1 lists common menu commands, the default SharePoint groups that can access the command, and when you can expect to see them on the Edit menu.

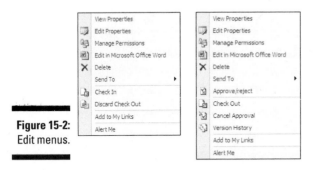

Figure 15-2:
Edit menus.

Table 15-1	Common Edit Menu Commands	
SharePoint Group	*Command*	*When You See It*
Site Visitor	View Properties	Default command
	Send To	Default command
	Version History	Content approval or versioning enabled
	Add to My Links	Site connected to a portal site
	Alert Me	Alerts enables for site collection

SharePoint Group	Command	When You See It
Site Member	Edit Properties	Default command
	Edit in Application	Depends on the file type
	Delete	Default command
	Check Out	Default command
	Discard Check Out	Visible for documents checked out by users
Approver	Approve/Reject	Content approval enabled
	Discard Check Out	Visible for documents checked out by another user
	Cancel Approval	Minor versions enabled with an approved major version
	Publish a Major Version	Minor versions enabled with no major version published
	Unpublish This Version	Minor versions enabled with major version published
Hierarchy Manager or Site Owner	Manage Permissions	Default command

The users of Office 2007 clients, such as Word 2007 and Excel 2007, can use the Office menu to check in or check out documents and view version history. Figure 15-3 shows the Word 2007 Office menu.

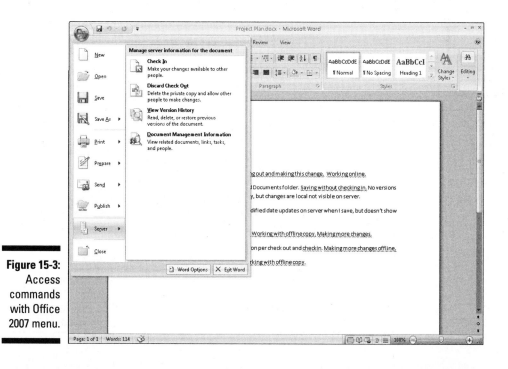

Figure 15-3: Access commands with Office 2007 menu.

Users of Office 2003 clients, such as Word 2003 and Excel 2003, can access commands on the File menu, such as Check Out and Version History. Office 2003 clients also display a Shared Workspace pane where users can view document information. Office 2007 (see Figure 15-4) has a similar version of the task pane.

Figure 15-4: Access commands in the Shared Workspace pane.

With so many document management features, knowing which to use can be challenging. Add to this the fact that you have to make these decisions for every document library you create, and you can see how such an embarrassment of riches might end up being a hassle. Here are a few rules to make the whole process a bit easier:

✔ **Require check out** to prevent confusion and conflict about who's editing a file. When contributors edit documents *without* first checking them out, they work with the actual online copy of the document. Checking out the document first downloads another copy of the document to the local SharePoint drafts folder in the My Documents folder. Requiring check out ensures that all contributors and library administrators know who's working with a document.

✔ **Enable major versions** if you want to maintain a history of all properties associated with a document. When authors edit documents in a library with major versions enabled without checking the document out first, they're editing the online version of the document. Each time the document is saved, a new major version is created. By requiring check out in a library with major versions enabled, a new major version is created at each check out.

✔ **Enable minor versions** if you want to save draft versions of documents. By requiring draft versions, authors have to explicitly publish a major version.

✔ **Enable draft item security** if you want to prevent readers from seeing draft (minor) versions of documents. By default, draft item security enables readers to see all versions. By setting draft item security so that only users with permissions to edit documents can see draft items, readers can see only the major versions that have been published in the library.

✔ **Enable content approval** if you want to require that published (major) versions are reviewed by a moderator before appearing in the library. Content approval prevents readers from seeing major versions until they're explicitly approved.

✔ **Enable content approval with draft item security** if you want to prevent readers and other contributors from seeing draft versions until they're published.

✔ **Implement Information Rights Management (IRM)** if you want to prevent users from performing certain actions, such as printing or e-mailing the documents in the library. Readers might not be able to edit or check out a document found in the library, but they can still download a read-only copy, edit a saved copy of the file, and distribute it. IRM prevents this from happening.

✔ **Associate workflows with a library** if you want to create an editorial process for the documents in a library.

✔ **Manage permissions in the library** or at the site level to control who has access to library content. For example, I often suggest that clients remove the Delete Items permission from the Contribute permission level. This prevents Site Members from deleting files from libraries.

Instead of allowing users to delete files, you can create an Expired column and advise users to flag any documents they wish to remove from the library. A library administrator can periodically review the Expired documents and delete files.

MOSS 2007 includes a Document Center site template that's intended for use with most of the preceding features enabled. The Document Center site template is deployed as part of the Collaboration Portal. The site template itself is pretty basic, with only one document library intended for use by many authors to store many different content types. The home page of the Document Center does display a useful Relevant Documents Web part, however, that lists all the documents uploaded and checked out by the current user.

If you don't need a site dedicated to a single document library, you can delete the Document Center. Alternatively, you can create a site based on the Document Center site template anywhere in your site hierarchy.

Using the Recycle Bin

WSS features a two-stage Recycle Bin that makes it easier for end users and administrators to manage file deletions. Each end user has his own Recycle Bin, which is considered the first-stage recycle bin. When documents are deleted, they're sent to this *(end user)* Recycle Bin. After a period of 30 days, the deleted documents are transferred to a *site collection* Recycle Bin, which is considered the second-stage Recycle Bin. End users can restore documents from their own Recycle Bins, whereas site collection administrators can restore documents from the site collection Recycle Bin.

Users must be a member of the *Site* Members SharePoint group or higher to access the site collection Recycle Bin. Users with read-only permissions, such as *Site* Visitors can't use this Recycle Bin because they don't have permission to delete anything.

End users access their Recycle Bin in the Quick Launch bar. The site collection Recycle Bin can be found by browsing to the Site Settings page for the top-level site in the site collection. The Recycle Bin link is in the Site Collection Administration section.

An administrator can access two views of the Site Collection Recycle Bin. More specifically, a site collection administrator can see all the items in the Recycle Bins of end users — these are the items that users have deleted from libraries and lists. An administrator can also see the items that have been deleted from the end user's Recycle Bin — these are the items that users have actually deleted from their Recycle Bin. From the end user's perspective, the item is gone. He can no longer see it in the Recycle Bin. An administrator can choose to restore or delete the items that appear in the first stage (end user's) or second stage (site collection's) Recycle Bins.

TIP

You can click any of the column headings in the Recycle Bin to sort the list by that column.

The Recycle Bin's settings are determined at the Web application level. You can access the Recycle Bin's settings by clicking the Web Application General Settings link on the Application Management page of the Central Administration site. As shown in Figure 15-5, you have the following options:

- ✔ Turn the Recycle Bin off.
- ✔ Specify how long to retain items in the Recycle Bin.
- ✔ Specify how much disk storage to allocate to the second stage Recycle Bin.
- ✔ Turn the second stage Recycle Bin off.

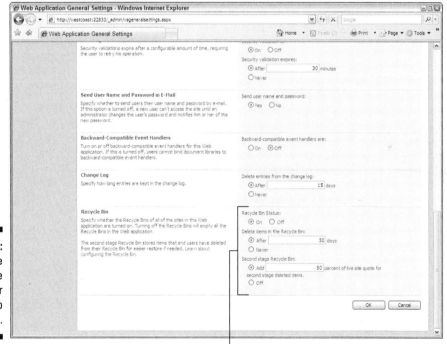

Figure 15-5: Configure the Recycle Bin for each Web application.

Recycle Bin settings

Controlling documents

MOSS 2007 lets you apply information management policy features to documents and list items. Information management policies bridge the SharePoint document management features with the physical world in which documents often circulate. You can create information management policies, such as these:

- **Auditing:** Create audit trails that record when an item is viewed, edited, checked out, moved, or deleted.

- **Barcodes:** When barcodes are enabled, MOSS 2007 automatically associates a unique barcode with each document. The barcode becomes a property of the document. You can optionally require that Office 2007 clients insert the barcode in the header of all documents. By inserting the barcode in a document, the barcode is printed out on all documents and can be scanned to retrieve the document's identifying properties.

- **Expiration:** Specify a document's retention period based on a period of time after the document's creation or last modified date. The expiration date can be set programmatically. The expiration policy can trigger an action, such as sending the document to the Recycle Bin or starting a workflow.

- **Labels:** Create a set of data that's visible in the header of all documents subject to the policy. The data can include property values. You can require that users insert the labels in the header of their documents by using Office 2007 clients.

Information management policies can be created at the site collection level, list or library level, or content type. Where you create the policy determines the policy's scope. For example, site collection policies are available to all content types, lists, and libraries in the site collection.

To create a site collection information policy, follow these steps:

1. **Browse to the Site Settings page for the top-level site in the site collection.**

   In a MOSS 2007 Collaboration Portal, click Site Actions⇨Site Settings⇨ Modify All Site Settings.

2. **Click the Site Collection Policies link in the Site Collection Administration section.**

   The Site Collection Policies page appears.

3. **Click the Create button.**

   The Edit Policy page appears.

You can import a policy from another site collection by clicking the Import button on the Site Collection Policies page. To export a policy, click an existing policy in the Site Collection Policies page and then click the Export button. This generates an .xml file that you can import to a different site collection.

4. **In the Name and Administrative Description section, enter a name and description for the policy.**

   This information appears when list and content type administrators associate information management policies with lists and content types. For example, you might create an information management policy that applies to contracts or financial spreadsheets.

5. **In the Policy Statement box, describe the policy in a way that's meaningful to end users who are trying to use the policy in their documents.**

   You can use the Policy Statement box to communicate information to user's about how the information is intended to be used. For example, you might indicate that the document is intended for internal distribution only.

6. **Select the Enable Labels check box to add labels to the policy.**

   Settings for labels appear in the Labels section.

7. **If you enable Labels, indicate whether users are prompted to display the labels, type a format for the labels, and configure the labels' appearance.**

   You can add text and column names in the Label Format textbox. Place curly braces ({}) around the column names. The names are replaced with values from the list or library. For example, to display values from the ExpireDate column you type **{ExpireDate}**.

8. **In the Auditing section, select the Enable Auditing check box and indicate the events you wish to audit.**

   You can opt to log activity any time the information is opened, viewed, downloaded, edited, checked out, moved, copied, or deleted.

9. **In the Expiration section, select the Enable Expiration check box and configure the retention period as well as the action that occurs upon expiration.**

10. **In the Barcodes section, select the Enable Barcodes check box and optionally, mark the check box to prompt users to insert the barcode before saving or printing.**

    This feature works only in Office 2007 clients.

11. **Click OK.**

    The policy is saved.

You can associate a site collection policy with a list or library:

1. **Browse to the list or library where you wish to use the site collection policy.**

2. **Choose Settings➪List Settings or Settings➪Document Library Settings.**

3. **Click the Information Management Policy Settings link.**

   The Information Management Policy Settings page appears.

4. **If you have content types enabled for your list or library, choose the content type you wish to apply the policy to.**

5. **Define a new policy or select the site collection policy from the list.**

You can define only one information policy per list or library; however, you can associate multiple content types with a list or library. Each content type can have only one information management policy.

End users can view a policy statement by using the Information Management Policy bar in an Office 2007 client, as shown in Figure 15-6.

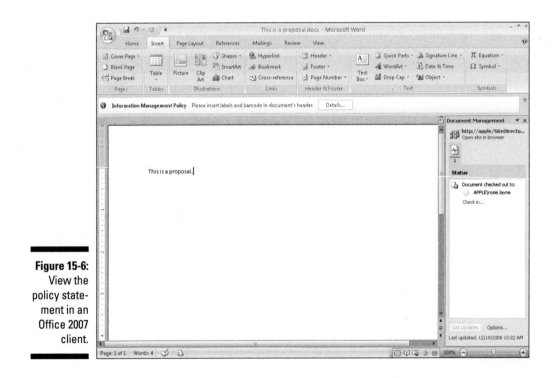

Figure 15-6:
View the policy state-ment in an Office 2007 client.

Users can also view policy information and exempt a document from a policy by viewing the document's properties. Figure 15-7 shows an example of a document with a policy that includes labels and a barcode. Users can click the Exempt from Policy link to exempt the document from the policy.

Users can search for a document using its barcode number. Users can either manually type the barcode number in the search box or scan the barcode. You can also display the barcode's value in the list or library's view.

Site collection administrators can view the results of audit reports created by information management policies. To view auditing reports, do the following:

1. **Browse to the top-level site in the site collection.**

2. **Click the Audit Log Reports link in the Site Collection Administration section.**

   The View Auditing Reports page appears.

3. **Select a report from the list.**

   The reports display data in eXtensible Markup Language (XML).

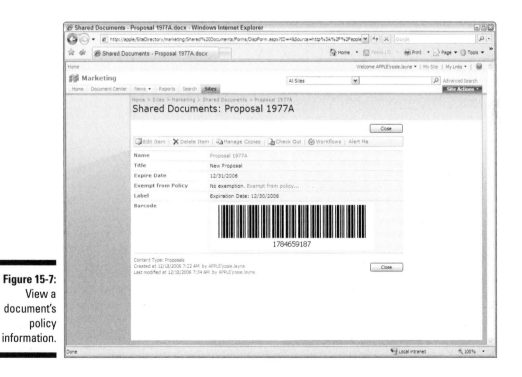

Figure 15-7:
View a document's policy information.

You can enable auditing for the entire site collection by clicking the Site Collection Audit settings on the top-level site's Site Settings page.

Managing Records

Records management is becoming more important in organizations of all sizes. Far too often, individual managers are responsible for determining how long to hold on to files and documents. It's also common for Information Technology (IT) departments to be charged with properly archiving and disposing of electronic documents. Good records management is a team effort that usually requires the input of IT, information workers, records managers, and compliance officers. Oh, and good software helps, too.

WSS version 3 provides the ability to submit files to a records repository using a Web service. A *records repository* is a storage location that's separate from where your active documents are stored. You can create your own custom records repository by using a SharePoint site or another storage medium. MOSS 2007 includes an implementation of a WSS-compatible records repository, the Records Center site template.

Microsoft recommends creating a new Web application to host the Records Center site template. The Web application should host only one site collection based on the Records Center site template. See Chapter 3 for more information on creating Web applications and site collections.

There are only four steps to configuring a Records Center, but a lot of planning is required to get to that point. For example, you have to decide which documents will be archived, how long they'll be archived, and who's responsible for monitoring the repository. To configure a Records Center, follow these steps:

1. **Create new information management policies.**

   As I describe in the preceding section, information management policies allow you to define expiration dates and auditing events for documents. You want to create policies that define how long to hold on to documents and what happens when the end of the retention period occurs.

2. **Set up document libraries for storing content and associate an information management policy with the library.**

   Set up one document library for each kind of content type you plan to store in the Records Center.

3. **Configure the routing table.**

   The routing table associates content types from your active SharePoint sites to the document libraries you create in Step 2. Use the routing table to determine how documents sent to the Records Center are moved to the document libraries. (I show you how to configure the routing table in the next section.)

4. **Test the Records Center by sending documents.**

   Test your information management policies and routing tables before deploying the site into production.

Setting up the routing table

The MOSS 2007 Records Center site template includes a special list — Record Routing — that's used to route documents to document libraries. The routing list (also known as a *routing table*) appears in the home page of the Records Center, or you can access it from the Quick Launch.

Here are the steps for adding a new record to the Record Routing table:

1. **Choose New⇨New Item in the Record Routing table that appears on the Record Center's home page.**

2. **In the Title field, type the name of the content type you wish to route.**

   For example, if you have a Proposals content type in your active SharePoint site, type **Proposals** in the Title field.

3. **Type a description of the record in the Description field.**

4. **In the Location field, type the name of the document library in the Records Center where you wish to store the record.**

   For example, if the name of the library is Purchasing, type that name in the Location field. Note that you don't have to have the document library created at this point. You can simply type the name you intend to use for the library and create the library later.

5. **In the Aliases field, type the name of any additional content types you wish routed to this document library.**

   For example, if you have a content type called RequestForInformation, type that in the Aliases field.

   The Aliases field makes it possible for you to retain friendly content types in your active SharePoint site.

6. **Deselect the Default field check box.**

   The Records Center provides a default content type to capture unrouted documents. The records manager will want to periodically review the Unclassified Records document library and manually move records to the appropriate document library.

7. **Click OK.**

Records submitted with the content types listed in the routing table are moved automatically to the specified document libraries.

Sending documents to the Records Center

Users must have some way of getting active documents to the Records Center for archiving. There are several options for sending documents to the Records Center. WSS provides the Send To command, which allows end users to manually send documents to a records repository, such as the Records Center.

Microsoft Exchange Server 2007 includes a Managed E-Mail Folders feature that allows users to send e-mail to the Records Center in MOSS 2007. When a user moves e-mail into a managed e-mail folder, Exchange sends the e-mail to the Records Center.

Alternatively, you can use a combination of information management policies and workflows to move content from active SharePoint sites to the Records Center. You can create an information management policy in a document library that defines a workflow to trigger when the document's expiration date is reached. The workflow would then move the document.

You have to create a custom workflow to handle this because MOSS 2007 doesn't provide any such workflows.

In order for users to send documents to the Records Center, you must grant users access to the site. The Records Center includes a special SharePoint group — Records Center Web Service Submitters. Add the application pool account for the Shared Services Provider (SSP) to this SharePoint group. See Chapter 2 for more information on finding the application pool account.

To configure SharePoint so users can manually send documents to the Records Center, do the following:

1. **Browse to the Application Management page in the Central Administration site.**

2. **Click the Records Center link in the External Service Connections section of the page.**

   The Configure Connection to Records Center page appears.

3. **Select the Connect to a Records Center radio button.**

4. **Type or paste the URL to the Records Center in the URL textbox.**

5. In the Display Name textbox, type the name of the Records Center.

The name you type here appears when a user manually sends the document to the Records Center.

6. Click OK.

Use these same steps to connect a WSS implementation to a records repository.

Users can see the Records Center when they use the Send To command to send the document to the Records Center, as shown in Figure 15-8.

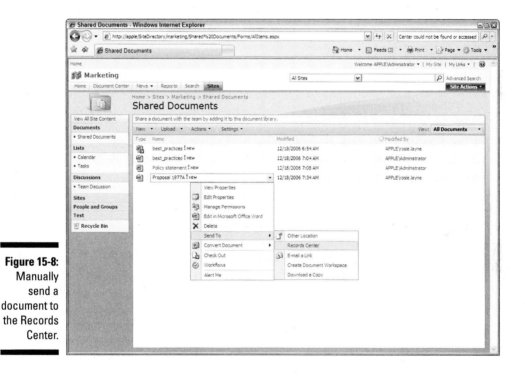

Figure 15-8:
Manually
send a
document to
the Records
Center.

Chapter 16

Publishing Web Content

· ·

In This Chapter

▶ Using the browser and Word to create Web pages

▶ Adding HTML and plain text to Web pages

▶ Understanding the Web content editorial process

▶ Customizing the Web content publishing experience

· ·

Many companies have started using Web sites as a means of distributing information inside and outside their organizations. In fact, many companies choose to implement Microsoft Office SharePoint Server (MOSS) 2007 precisely because they can use MOSS 2007 to create sites for sharing information, such as press releases and job listings.

Several organizations have trouble drawing the line between the roles of technical and non-technical employees in maintaining the freshness and relevancy of Web content. MOSS 2007 includes new publishing features that make it easy to manage publishing Web content.

MOSS 2007's Web content management features provide these features:

▶ **Authoring and publishing features** that allow non-technical users to create and manage content used in SharePoint sites.

▶ **Customizing frameworks** that allow technical users to change the look and feel of SharePoint pages and sites.

The key to these publishing features is the separation of content from presentation — a goal that many good Web designers strive to achieve. A Web page's *content* — the words and images that appear on the page — shouldn't be commingled with presentation commands that determine how the page is laid out. Separating content from presentation makes it possible for non-technical users to create the content, while technical people can focus strictly on the presentation issues.

In this chapter, I discuss the authoring feature and explain how to customize the authoring experience.

Authoring Web Content

The primary means for authoring and publishing managed Web content in MOSS 2007 is the Publishing page. Unlike plain, old HTML Web pages or even the Web Part pages used by Windows SharePoint Services (WSS), Publishing pages make it possible for anyone with a Web browser to add and maintain content on a Web site. Page authors don't need to know HyperText Markup Language (HTML) although they can use HTML in some instances.

The *Publishing page,* or just *Page,* is a site content type inherited from the System Page content type. The MOSS 2007 publishing features make extensive use of site content types. Authors aren't required to be familiar with content types; however, administrators need to understand content types in order to customize the authoring experience.

In order for a site to use publishing features, it must either have been created using a Publishing site template or have the publishing features enabled. You can choose a Publishing site template when you create a new SharePoint site. MOSS 2007 provides the following three Publishing site templates:

- ✔ **Publishing Site** creates a standard SharePoint site with publishing features enabled.

- ✔ **Publishing Site with Workflow** is similar to a Publishing Site except the Pages library uses an Approval workflow.

- ✔ **News Site** creates a site for publishing news articles. The Collaboration portal includes a News Site.

You can enable the Office SharePoint Server Publishing feature in any SharePoint site by clicking the Site Features link in the site's Site Settings page. See Chapter 5 for details on accessing a site's Site Settings page.

The Publishing feature adds a Pages library where the site's Publishing pages are centrally stored. The *Pages library* is a document library with support for major and minor versions enabled. The feature also adds libraries for storing images and documents used on pages.

The Publishing Site with Workflow site template adds content approval and a parallel approval workflow to the Pages library. This requires authors to submit their draft pages for review before they can be published.

One clue that a site is using Publishing pages is to check to see if `Pages` appears in the URL of the site's pages. For example, the News site in the Collaboration portal has the URL `http://server/News/Pages/Default.aspx`. The filename of the home page is `Default.aspx`, and it's located in the Pages library.

Creating pages

Creating new pages is a task frequently performed by page authors and site designers. In order to create a new Publishing page, the site must have the Publishing feature enabled. When an author creates a new Publishing page, SharePoint creates a new ASP.NET page and then saves it in the site's Pages library.

Here are three kinds of Publishing pages you can publish to SharePoint sites:

- ✔ **Article pages** are intended for publishing an article or story, such as a press release.

- ✔ **Redirect pages** take users to another URL. These are often used to route visitors to another site, such as an e-commerce site.

- ✔ **Welcome pages** are often used as the home page of a publishing-enabled site.

You can view a list of all the Article pages and Welcome pages in the Master Page gallery. Each site has its own Master Page gallery, but the Article and Welcome pages can be found in the Master Page gallery of the top-level site in the site collection. You can find a link to the Master Page gallery on the site's Site Settings page.

Article pages and Welcome pages aren't master pages, they're page layouts. *Page layouts* determine where content can be placed on the page. Each of these pages has a corresponding site content type that defines the page layout's properties. See the section, "Customizing Content Publishing," later in this chapter for details on page layouts.

The easiest way to create a new Publishing page is with the Site Actions menu. You can also create a new Publishing page with the Create page, which is the same way you create a Web Parts page.

To create a new Publishing page by using the Site Actions menu, follow these steps:

1. **Choose Site Actions➪Create Page.**

   The Create Page page appears.

2. **Type a title and description for the page.**

3. **Type a filename for the page in the URL Name field.**

   SharePoint automatically appends the file extension `.aspx` to the file because an ASP.NET page is created.

 4. **Select the kind of page you wish to create from the Page Layout list.**

    Again, your default categories here are Article pages, Redirect pages, and Welcome pages. You may also see custom page layouts added by an administrator.

 5. **Click the Create button.**

    The page is added to the site's Pages library and appears in the browser for editing.

You can also convert a Word 2007 document to a Publishing page. You might want to do this if you have content that you want to keep in a Word file but you need to display in a Web page. Follow these steps to convert a Word 2007 document to a Publishing page:

 1. **Browse to the document library where the Word 2007 file is saved.**

    The document library must be in a site with the Publishing feature enabled. You can enable publishing in the site using the Site Features link on the site's Site Settings page. However, I suggest you move the document to another site where publishing is already enabled. You shouldn't enable the Publishing feature unless you have a compelling reason to do so. It adds unnecessary complexity to the site.

 2. **Click the Edit menu for the document you wish to convert.**

 3. **Choose Convert Document⇨From Word Document to Web Page.**

    The Create Page from Document page appears.

 4. **Select a publishing-enabled location to publish the new page.**

 5. **Enter the title, description, and filename for the page.**

 6. **In the Processing section, indicate whether you want SharePoint to create the page now or send the page creation task to a job queue.**

    Queue the job during business hours to prevent consuming too many server resources.

 7. **Indicate whether you want SharePoint to send an e-mail when the page is created.**

 8. **Click the Create button.**

    SharePoint creates the page and adds it to the site's Pages library.

Document conversion is managed at the site content type level. In the case of a Word document stored in a standard document library, the content type is probably Document. See Chapter 7 for more about managing content types.

Editing pages

You can edit an existing Publishing page in two ways. You can browse to the page you wish to edit and choose Site Actions➪Edit Page, or you can browse to the Pages library and edit the page's properties. Your editing experience is very different, depending on the path you choose.

When you edit a page by browsing to the page, you see the content laid out on the page itself, as shown in Figure 16-1. You have access to the Page Editing toolbar, which makes it possible to add new Web Parts, associate workflows, and manage the page's publishing process. You can also edit any field controls that appear on the page. The image in Figure 16-1 shows two field controls — the Page Content and Page Image controls.

Page Editing toolbar

Figure 16-1:
Edit a
Publishing
page in the
browser.

Field Controls   Web Part zones

When you edit a page's properties in the Pages library, you're editing the fields associated with the page's content type. Field controls, such as Page Content and Page Image, are actually site columns that are associated with the Publishing page's content type. You can edit properties related to the page, such as the page's contact person (see Figure 16-2).

To edit a page's properties, do the following:

1. **Browse to the publishing site.**

2. **Click the View All Site Content link on the left side of the site.**

   The All Site Content page appears.

3. **In the Document Libraries section, click the Pages library.**

   The Pages library appears.

   Publishing pages are typically saved in the Pages library, but they could be saved in any library.

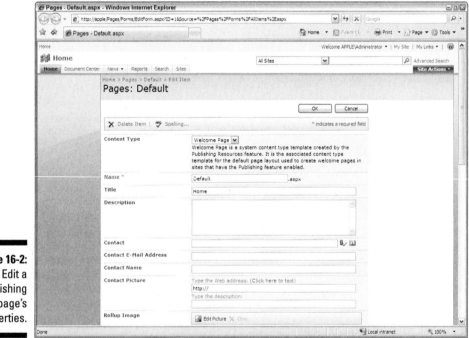

Figure 16-2:
Edit a
Publishing
page's
properties.

4. **Click the Edit menu for the page you wish to edit, such as**
   Default.aspx.

   A contextual menu appears.

5. **Click Edit Properties.**

   If the page is checked in, you're prompted to check out the page. The
   Edit page appears, as shown in Figure 16-3.

You can't add new Web Parts to a Publishing page by editing the page's properties, but you can access a Web Parts Maintenance page that allows you to
close unruly Web Parts or remove personal views of the page. To access the
Maintenance view, scroll to the bottom of the page's Edit Properties page and
click the Open Web Part Page in Maintenance View link. The Web Part Page
Maintenance page opens. The page lists all the Web Parts that appear on the
page, as shown in Figure 16-3. You can choose to close, reset, or delete any of
the Web Parts on the page. This is helpful if a page won't open because a Web
Part is broken.

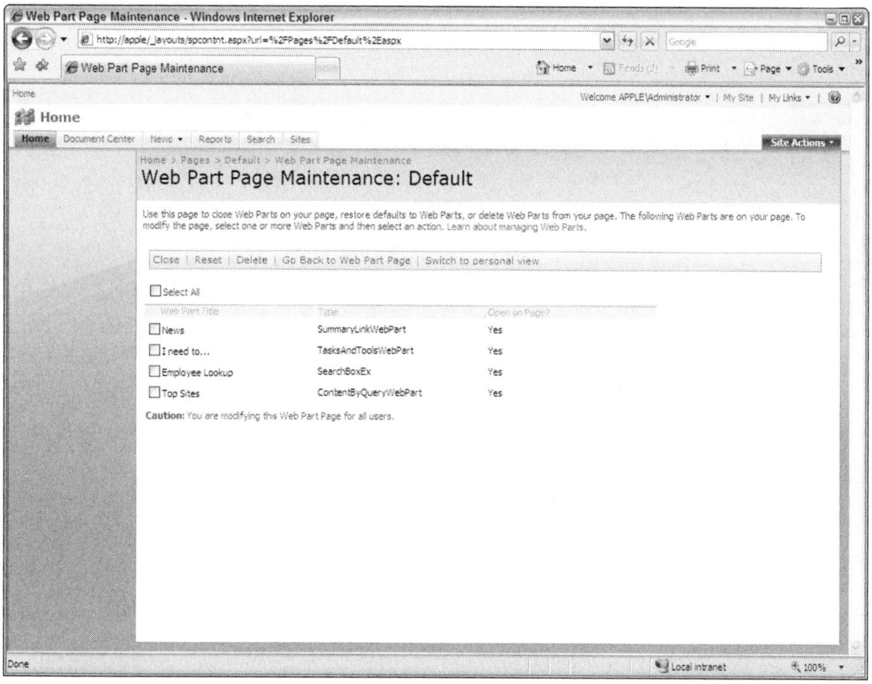

Figure 16-3:
Manage a
page's Web
Parts with
the Mainte-
nance page.

You can edit pages a third way. You can use SharePoint Designer 2007, the successor to Front Page 2003, to edit SharePoint sites and pages. To edit a page with SharePoint Designer, browse to the Pages library, select the page you wish to edit, and click Edit in Microsoft Office SharePoint Designer. You must have Designer installed on your machine. See my book, *SharePoint Designer 2007 For Dummies* (Wiley), for more information on using SharePoint Designer to edit pages.

Adding content to pages

You can add two kinds of content to Publishing pages. The primary vehicle for adding content to a Publishing page is the Web Part, which is also used in the Web Parts pages by WSS. Publishing pages also support the use of field controls, which are ASP.NET 2.0 controls.

I explain how to add and configure Web Parts in Chapter 4. Editing field content depends on the kind of control you're editing, but it usually involves clicking the Edit Content or Edit Picture link that you see on the page (refer to Figure 16-1).

The placeholders that you see on the Publishing page are made possible by the page layout associated with the page. Use the Pages library to see which page layout is associated with the page. For example, the default Home page (Pages/default.aspx) of a MOSS 2007 Collaboration Portal uses the DefaultLayout page layout.

Not all Publishing pages allow you to add Web Parts. Web Parts are added to Web Part Zones. In order for you to add a Web Part to the page, the page must have at least one Web Part Zone. See the section, "Customizing Content Publishing," later in this chapter for details on adding Web Part Zones to page layouts.

You can add any Web Part from the Web Parts gallery to a Web Part Zone in a Publishing page. If you want to add plain text or use HTML to add tables or other content, you can use the Content Editor Web Part. The Content Editor Web Part includes a Rich Text Editor and an HTML Source Editor that you can use to add free-form text or HTML to the page.

If the page has a Page Content field control, you can use it to add plain text as well. Figure 16-4 shows an example of the Page Content field control in an Article page.

You can also edit the contents of field controls by editing the page's properties.

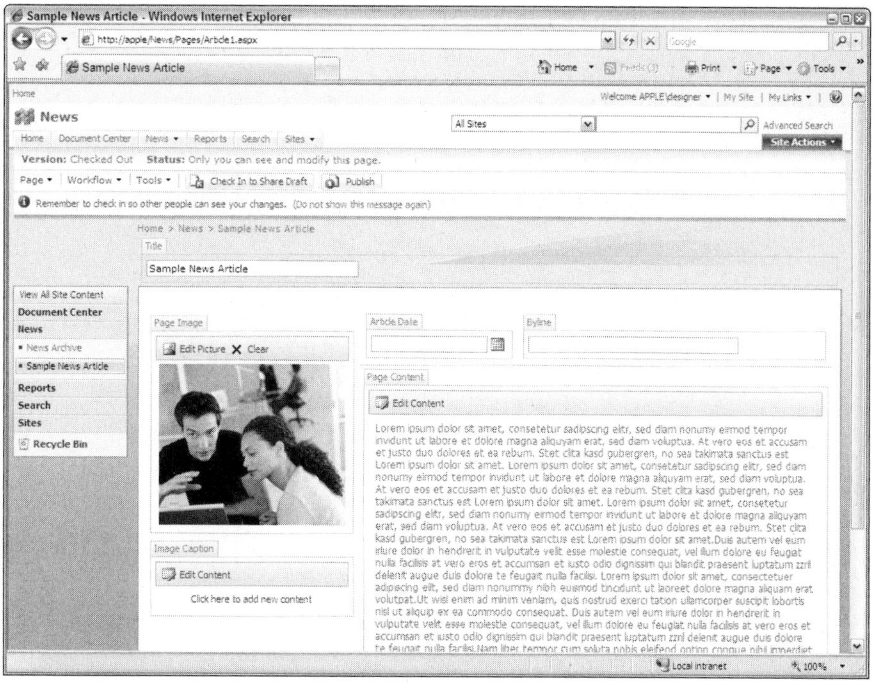

Figure 16-4:
Add text to
an Article
page.

Reusing text and HTML content

You also have the option to reuse content across Publishing pages that use
the Page Content field control. This makes it possible for you to create content, such as disclaimers and privacy policies. You only have to create the
content once and then you can reuse it in á Page Content field control.

You can find Page Content field controls in all Articles pages as well as the
Welcome Pages Intranet Home, Welcome page with Summary links, and
Welcome page with Table of Contents pages.

You can use SharePoint Designer 2007 to create additional page layouts that
use the Page Content field.

A publishing-enabled SharePoint site includes a special list — Reusable
Content — where you store the content you wish to reuse. There is a single
Reusable Content list per site collection, and it resides at the top-level site.
This enables you to define content once per site collection and reuse it
throughout your portal. You can create content as plain text or HTML.

Follow these steps to add reusable content to your site collection:

1. **Browse to the top-level site in your site collection.**

2. **Click the View All Site Content link in the left side of the page.**

   The All Site Content page appears.

3. **In the Lists section, click the Reusable Content list.**

   The Reusable Content list appears.

   If you don't see the Reusable Content list, it's probably because your site collection doesn't have publishing features enabled. You must use a publishing-enabled site to work with publishing features.

4. **Click the drop-down arrow on the New button.**

   The New menu item displays the option to create Reusable HTML or Reusable Text. Content created using the Reusable HTML option allows you to use HTML tags in the content.

   Reusable HTML and Reusable Text are examples of content types. In this case, these are hidden content types that you can't customize. See Chapter 7 for more details on content types.

5. **Select to create Reusable HTML or Reusable Text from the New menu.**

   The New Item page appears.

6. **Enter a title, such as Opinion Disclaimer, for the reusable content and any comments to describe the content.**

7. **Select a category for the content from the Content Category drop-down list.**

   By default, the Content Category drop-down doesn't include any choices other than None. You can add choices by customizing the Content Category list column. See Chapter 7 for details on working with list columns.

8. **Indicate whether the content should be updated automatically.**

   By choosing this option, the reusable content is automatically updated in the pages that it appears in when the content is updated.

9. **In the Reusable Text or Reusable HTML field, enter the content.**

10. **Click OK.**

    The content is saved as a list item in the Reusable Content list.

After you've added content items to your Reusable Content list, you can reuse this content in your Publishing pages.

To use reusable content in a publishing site, do the following:

1. **Browse to a page that uses a Page Content field control.**

   Any of the default article pages on the News site in a Collaboration Portal use Page Content field controls.

2. **Choose Site Actions⇨Edit Page.**

3. **Click the Edit Content link in the Page Content field control.**

   The HTML Editor opens.

4. **Click the Insert Reusable Content button — found next to the Insert Image button.**

   The Select Reusable Content window appears.

5. **Select the content you wish to reuse, as shown in Figure 16-5.**

6. **Click OK.**

   The reusable content appears in the Page Content field control.

If the reusable content is configured to update automatically, the content can't be changed. Otherwise, the reusable content is copied to the Page Content field control.

Figure 16-5:
Reuse
content
in a Page
Content field
control.

Adding navigational content

Publishing pages use the same navigational features of SharePoint Web Part pages. You may, however, wish to use the following three Web Parts to draw attention to site content:

- ✓ **Content Query Web Part** is a great way to display content from parent sites and sibling sites. You can specify the starting point for the query as any site within the site collection, identify the type of list to query, and select the content types to include. You can even apply additional filters based on column values and sort and group the results. For example, you could query the Project Tasks from a project team site and display the results on a Project portal. The Top Sites display that appears on the home page of the MOSS 2007 Collaboration portal is a Content Query Web Part.

- ✓ **Summary Link Web Part** displays a list of links to resources internal and external to your SharePoint site. You can also use the Web Part to link to people in the SharePoint User Profile Store.

- ✓ **Table of Contents Web Part** displays a site map on your site. The Web Part is configurable so you can control what gets displayed and how it looks.

Publishing Web content

Publishing pages are stored in the Pages library, which is a document library. Because pages use a document library, you have document management features similar to what's used for Excel spreadsheets or Word documents. Because there's no separate client interface like there is in Excel or Word, the management features of the Pages library appear in a special tool — the Page Editing toolbar.

You can see the Page Editing toolbar across the top of a Publishing page any time you edit the page, as shown in Figure 16-6. The toolbar displays the following information and actions:

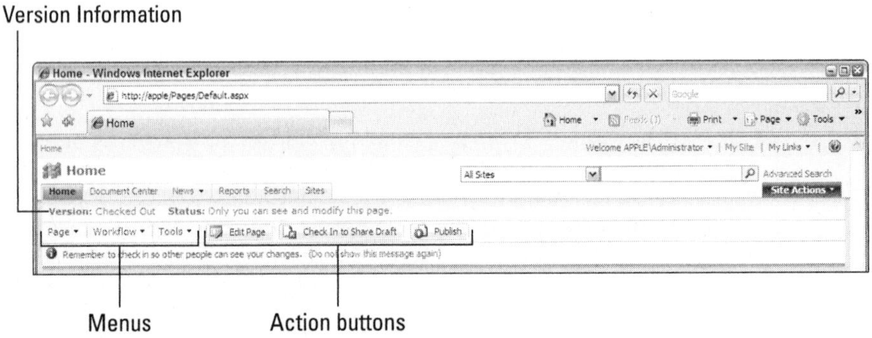

Version Information

Figure 16-6: Edit pages with the Page Editing toolbar.

Menus   Action buttons

✔ **Version and status information** allows you to easily see whether the page is checked out and who can see the page. As a Web page author, train yourself to look at this information.

✔ **Page menus** provide access to the page's editing commands, such as Save, Check In, and Delete Page. You can also use this menu to add Web Parts to the page.

✔ **Workflow menus** allow you to start a workflow for the page. You must have workflows enabled for the Pages library before you can start a workflow, however. See Chapter 8 for more on workflows.

✔ **Tools menus** provide access to commands, such as Spell Checking and Version History.

✔ **Action buttons,** such as Edit Page, Check In to Share Draft, and Publish, provide shortcuts to commonly-used menu commands.

You can show or hide the Page Editing toolbar using the Site Actions menu.

You aren't limited to using the Page Editing toolbar to manage the page's editorial process. You can access all the same menu commands from the Pages library.

One of the key features of publishing Web content in MOSS 2007 is the ability to use SharePoint's document management features with Publishing pages. Authors and content approvers can use the Page Editing toolbar and the Pages library to take care of many document management tasks, including the following:

✔ **Checking out pages** to ensure that only one person at a time is editing the page.

✔ **Checking in minor versions** enables multiple authors to contribute to a page. Minor versions aren't visible by the general public.

✔ **Publishing major versions** when authors are ready for the page to be viewed by others. By default, only authors with permissions to bypass the approval process can publish major versions. Usually major versions should be published by reviewers.

✔ **Submitting major versions** for approval ensures that pages go through a review process. Submitted items appear in the Pages library with a Pending status.

✔ **Approving or rejecting submitted pages** by using either the Pages library or Page Editing toolbar.

✔ **Scheduling items** for publishing via the Schedule Start Date and Schedule End Date fields. You must enable item scheduling in the Pages library to use this feature. You can choose Settings➪Document Library Settings➪ Manage Item Scheduling to enable item scheduling in a Pages library.

See Chapter 15 for more details on using SharePoint's document management features.

Publishing pages provide a Check for Unpublished Items feature that tests the validity of content contained on the page. The page may link to content that's not available or in the process of being updated. Using this tool highlights any content that has issues to be resolved. Follow these steps to use this feature:

1. **Browse to a page that's checked out but not in Edit mode.**

2. **Choose Site Actions⇨Show Page Editing Toolbar to display the Page Editing toolbar (if it's not visible).**

3. **Choose Tools⇨Check for Unpublished Items.**

   Any problems with the page are highlighted on the screen.

4. **Click the View the Full Report in a New Window link that appears in the Page Editing toolbar.**

   A list of issues and possible causes appears. Use the list to resolve any issues with the content.

For example, Figure 16-7 shows a page with dashes around the Home link. These dashes appear because the page that the Home link links to is checked out. The content from the published version of the page appears in the link, but it could change if I change the name of the home page.

Dashes

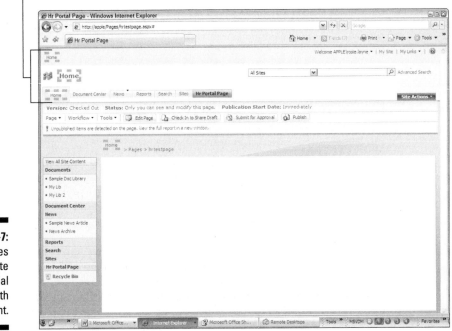

Figure 16-7:
Dashes indicate potential trouble with content.

Customizing Content Publishing

The Web content publishing features of MOSS 2007 make it possible for Information Technology (IT) administrators to delegate Web content maintenance to end users. If you've been the poor guy in IT responsible for updating the company's Frequently Asked Questions (FAQs) or maintaining the Contact Us page, you can appreciate how important it is to empower end users to take responsibility for these tasks.

However, end users can't do some tasks, such as customizing the look and feel of SharePoint sites. The same MOSS 2007 features that make managing Web content a breeze also provide a powerful framework for customizing the look and feel of your SharePoint sites.

To separate content from presentation, SharePoint uses a page model that uses two kinds of page templates to create a Publishing page:

✔ **Master pages define the reusable content** for a site, such as headers and navigation. Master pages also define the color schemes.

✔ **Page layouts define the kind of content** that can appear on the page and how it's laid out.

When a user creates a new Publishing page, the page's look and feel comes from a master page; the content that's available to be displayed and its layout comes from the page layout; and the actual content itself is saved in the Publishing page instance created by the author. In this way, master pages, page layouts, and page instances create a hierarchical page model that separates presentation from content.

Master pages and page layouts are stored in a special document library — the Master Page gallery. Each site collection has a single gallery for the entire site collection. You can access the gallery from the top-level site's Site Settings page.

MOSS 2007 includes several master pages and 15 page layouts. You may decide to create new master pages or page layouts for your content authors to use. You edit master pages or create new master pages any time you want to control content that appears on all the pages in a site. For example, you may decide to add a copyright or terms of use statement to a master page. You add new page layouts when you want to offer your page authors additional kinds of pages they can create.

In order to create new master pages and customize page layouts, you probably want to use some kind of visual editing software, such as SharePoint Designer 2007 or Visual Studio 2005. Master pages and page layouts are text pages, so you could edit them using a text editor such as Notepad.

Working with master pages

You can create a new master page from scratch or copy an existing page and then edit it. I suggest you start with an existing master page. Master pages use a combination of ASP.NET controls and HTML markup to create a reusable page template. Use a visual design tool, such as SharePoint Designer 2007 or Visual Studio 2005, to create and edit master pages.

If you don't have SharePoint Designer 2007 or Visual Studio 2005, you can use Visual Web Developer 2005 Express Edition to edit and create master pages. You can download the software free from Microsoft's Web site at

```
http://msdn.microsoft.com/vstudio/express/vwd
```

Master pages end with the file type extension .master. You can find nine master pages in the Master Page gallery. Because the Master Page gallery is a document library, you can check out a master page just like you would a Word document or other file. Similarly, you can use the Upload button to upload a new master page.

When you open a master page file, you see text that looks similar to HTML. The text is actually a combination of HTML and ASP.NET syntax. When you browse the file, you see a series of ASP.NET placeholders. These are used to display the navigation, search, and other controls that you see on every page. The PlaceHolderMain content placeholder is where content from the page layout is populated. The code looks like this:

```
<asp:ContentPlaceHolder id="PlaceHolderMain"
          runat="server" />
```

SharePoint's master pages uses the ASP.NET ContentPlaceHolder control for replaceable content, such as the page's content.

Master pages also link to Cascading Style Sheets (CSS), which control the look and feel of the page. CSS files used with master pages are stored in the Style library at the top-level site of the site collection. You can use master pages to determine how the styles are used and make changes to the style sheets.

You can change the master page associated with a site. Of the nine master pages provided with MOSS 2007, all the master pages except BlueVertical. master and BlackVertical.master work for internal SharePoint sites. Use these two master pages with Internet-facing sites.

To change the master page associated with a site, do the following:

1. **Browse to the Site Settings page for the site.**
2. **Click the Master Page link in the Look and Feel section.**

   The Site Master Page Settings page appears.

3. **In the Site Master Page section, select the master page to use for all Publishing pages in the site.**
4. **In the System Master Page section, select the master page to use for all forms and view pages in the site.**
5. **In the Alternate CSS URL, indicate whether the site should use default or custom CSS settings.**
6. **Click OK.**

   The master pages are applied to the site.

By applying different master pages to Publishing and System pages, you can have one look for Publishing pages while retaining the classic SharePoint look for default SharePoint pages, such as document libraries.

WSS supports the use of themes for changing the appearance of a Web site. Themes change the color scheme and fonts used by a site. The site's layout doesn't change. Follow these steps to change a site's theme:

1. **Browse to the Site Settings page for the site you wish to change.**
2. **Click the Site Theme link in the Look and Feel section.**

   The Site Theme page appears.

3. **Select a theme from the list of themes.**

   SharePoint displays a preview of the theme.

4. **Click the Apply button.**

   The site's colors and fonts are updated.

Themes don't have inheritance hierarchy like master pages do. As a result, you have to set the theme for each site in your site collection if you want them to have the same theme. You're better off to use themes for sites that you want to look different. You can create new themes with SharePoint Designer 2007.

Creating page layouts

SharePoint provides a number of page layouts that authors can use to create different kinds of welcome and detail pages. You aren't limited to the page layouts provided by SharePoint. You can create your own layouts or edit existing ones. When deciding how to approach page layout customization, you must consider whether you want to do the following:

- **Change the layout of the content:** If you only want to move content around on the page, you can edit an existing page layout or create a new layout based on an existing layout.

- **Display new kinds of content:** If you want to store new kinds of content on the page, you must create a new content type. For example, assume you want to create a custom page layout suited for authoring pages in a portal used to publish Human Resources content. You need to create a new content type to store the HR content.

Page layouts make extensive use of SharePoint's content type and site column model to provide a framework for publishing Web content. Page layout files are associated with a site content type. The content that can display in a page layout is defined by the site columns associated with the content type. Each site column you create has an associated field control used to display the site column on the page layout.

For example, the Page Content site column is used for storing HTML in several page layouts, including the Article page layout. In a page layout file, the corresponding Page Content field control looks like this:

```
<PublishingWebControls:RichHtmlField
        FieldName="PublishingPageContent"
        runat="server" id="RichHtmlField1">
</PublishingWebControls:RichHtmlField>
```

In addition to adding field controls, you can also add Web Part Zones to your page layouts. Web Part Zones make it possible for page authors to add Web Parts to the page. Many of the page layouts based on the Welcome content type include Web Part Zones like this one:

```
<WebPartPages:WebPartZone runat="server"
        AllowPersonalization="true" ID="TopColumnZone"
        FrameType="TitleBarOnly"
         Title="<%$Resources:cms,WebPartZoneTitle_Top%>"
        Orientation="Vertical"><ZoneTemplate></ZoneTemp
        late></WebPartPages:WebPartZone>
```

You can also add Web Parts to the page outside a Web Part Zone. By doing so, the Web Part's content appears on the page, but page authors can't move or configure the Web Part. Only Web Parts added to a Web Part Zone can be modified by page authors.

Your best bet is to use SharePoint Designer to drag and drop field controls, Web Parts, and Web Part Zones onto the page layout. However, you can also open existing page layouts from the Master Pages gallery to see examples of ASP.NET.

You need a basic understanding of HTML and CSS in order to work with master pages and page layouts. It also helps if you're familiar with ASP.NET.

Follow these steps to create a new page layout:

1. **Create site columns to store the content you wish to display in the page layout.**

   You can use any column type you wish for the site column. To display HTML content similar to a Page Content field control, use the type Full HTML content with formatting and constraints for publishing. The Site Column gallery displays site columns of this type as Publishing HTML. Alternatively, you can use the existing Page Content site column in a new content type. See Chapter 7 for more information on creating site columns.

   For example, assume you want to create a new kind of page layout for Human Resources portal pages. You want your page layout to have a place for page authors to add plain text. You need to create a new site column that uses the column type Multiple Lines of Text.

2. **Create a new site content type by using Page as the parent content type.**

   For example, create a new content type called HRPortalPage. See Chapter 7 for more information on creating site content types.

   Alternatively, instead of creating a new content type, you can reuse one of the existing page layout content types. For example, you could add your new site column to the Article Page page layout.

3. **Add site columns you create in Step 1 to the new site content type.**

   The site columns you add to the content type allow you to define any properties or field controls, such as Page Content, that you wish to use with the page layout. In the case of the HRPortalPage content type, add the site column you create in Step 1 for plain text.

4. Create a new page layout in the Master Page gallery.

To create a new page layout, choose New⇨Page Layout in the Master Page gallery. Select the content type you create in Step 2 to associate with the page layout. This steps creates the shell .aspx page that holds the new page layout.

The page layout appears in the list of available page layouts in the Create Page page. The page layout isn't prepared to accept content, however, until you complete the next step.

5. Use SharePoint Designer 2007 to add field controls, Web Parts, and Web Part Zones to the page layout.

In order for the site columns in the page layout's content types to appear in the page layout, you must add them to the page layout. The easiest way to do this is to open the page layout in SharePoint Designer 2007 and drag and drop the field controls from the toolbox. You can also open the page layout file and manually write the markup.

6. Create a new Publishing page based on the page layout.

Chapter 17

Providing Access to Business Intelligence

In This Chapter

▶ Displaying Excel workbooks in Web Parts

▶ Creating reports in Reports Center

▶ Storing data connections in libraries

▶ Connecting to back-end systems with the Business Data Catalog

Microsoft Office SharePoint Server (MOSS) 2007 provides a number of features that make it possible to create business intelligence (BI) reports and applications that are valuable and accessible to your organization. Some of these features are specific to BI, but others simply take advantage of other features in SharePoint. All the features that enable BI features in SharePoint are built on the Windows SharePoint Server (WSS) platform, so you can reuse what you already know about lists, libraries, and Web Parts.

In this chapter, I show you the building blocks for creating BI solutions in SharePoint. I also walk you through the *Reports Center,* which is an out-of-the-box BI application that you can customize to suit your business. And because connecting to external data sources is such an important feature of BI, I walk you through using data connection libraries and connecting to back-end databases with the Business Data Catalog.

You aren't limited to using the features I describe here to create BI reports and applications. As is the case with most SharePoint features, you can use these elements throughout your SharePoint implementation. Most of the features I explain in this chapter pertain strictly to MOSS 2007.

Using Excel Services

If your company is like most, tons of spreadsheets are probably in use. You'd be surprised, or maybe not, by the number of companies that have entire departments whose primary information system relies on spreadsheets. As you can imagine, trying to replicate the functionality provided in spreadsheets in a centralized information system is nearly impossible. To start with, many companies have no idea how many spreadsheets are being used in the first place.

Imagine being able to convert spreadsheets to ASP.NET Web applications complete with permissions management. MOSS 2007 introduces a feature — *Excel Services* — that makes it possible to display and interact with content from spreadsheets saved in Excel 2007.

No longer are spreadsheets just columns and rows of data. Many spreadsheets qualify as full-blown applications complete with intensive data calculations and connections to back-end databases. Using Excel Services to provide access to these resources moves calculations from the client PC to the server. SharePoint also has the ability to store data connections separate from the resources that use them.

The primary way that most users interact with Excel Services is through *Excel Web Access,* which is a Web Part that displays Excel 2007 spreadsheets in a SharePoint Web page. (See the section, "Displaying workbook content," later in this chapter, for more on practical uses of Excel Web Access.). Excel Services also exposes Excel Web Services as a means to provide programmatic access to Excel Services.

To take advantage of Excel Services, you have to have both Excel Web Access and Excel Web Services running on all Web servers in your SharePoint server farm. *Excel Calculation Services* is the back-end component responsible for loading workbooks and allowing users to interact with them. This service can run on back-end application servers in the SharePoint farm. Use the Services on Server page in Central Administration to enable or disable Excel Calculation Services.

Managing spreadsheets

Managing spreadsheets is a challenge for any organization. You can use simple SharePoint document libraries to provide document management features, such as versioning, check out, and content approval. However, document libraries don't begin to address some major issues with spreadsheets, including things like concurrent access or embedded data connections.

Excel Services solves many of these problems by bringing spreadsheet applications into a managed environment that includes the following:

✔ **Trusted file locations** that determine which spreadsheets are accessible through Excel Services.

✔ **Trusted data connection libraries** that limit the use of external data to data sources configured in the trusted data connection library.

By configuring trusted repositories in Excel Services, you can make spreadsheets accessible via the Excel Services presentation features. This makes it possible to create a managed environment for using and accessing spreadsheets.

A *trusted* file location is any location that you designate as trusted to Excel Services. By designating the location as trusted, Excel Services can access the workbooks found in the location. The obvious location choices are SharePoint document libraries. However, you don't have to use SharePoint libraries as trusted locations. You can also designate locations that are accessible via UNC and HTTP as trusted locations. For example, you can use a file share as an Excel Services trusted location.

Because Excel Services is a shared service, configure it using the Shared Services Administration site. Follow these steps to add new trusted file locations:

1. **Browse to the Shared Services Administration site.**

   You can access this site from the Central Administration site.

2. **Click the Trusted File Locations link in the Excel Services Settings section.**

   The Excel Services Trusted File Locations page appears.

3. **Click the Add Trusted File Location button.**

   The Excel Services Add Trusted File Location page appears.

4. **In the Location section, type the path of the document library where you wish to save spreadsheets for use with Excel Services.**

   For example, assume you have a team site used by financial personnel called Finance. You can add the location of a document library called Financial Documents as a trusted file location. The URL might look like `http://intranet/sites/finance/financialdocs`.

   You can also use spreadsheets stored in file shares and Web folders with Excel Services.

5. **Select Windows SharePoint Services as the location type.**

6. **Indicate whether child libraries should be trusted.**

   Trusting child libraries allows files from libraries below the address you specify in Step 4 to be used. Choosing to trust child libraries automatically trusts all libraries, even new libraries.

7. **Type a description for this location in the Description field.**

8. **Accept the defaults for Session Management.**

   These values determine how long Excel Services has before it times out. You can change these values if you're having problems, but if you're having problems with connecting to spreadsheets, try to find the underlying problem.

9. **In the Workbook Properties section, indicate the maximum sizes for workbooks and charts that can be opened with Excel Services.**

   If you're having trouble keeping your workbooks below the recommended 10MB limit, you might consider splitting the workbook into multiple spreadsheets and using Excel Web Access Web Parts to display each part. Requiring Excel Services to open large files consumes server resources.

10. **In the Calculation Behavior section, indicate how functions found in workbooks are calculated.**

    As the sizes of workbooks increase, it's important to take calculation behavior into consideration. In the Calculation Behavior section, you can indicate how long computed values are cached. You can enter **-1** to calculate values once, enter **0** to calculate every time a recalculation occurs, or specify a time frame to calculate formulas.

11. **In the External Data section, select the Trusted Data Connection Libraries Only radio button and then accept the remaining defaults.**

    Choosing to use trusted data connection libraries prohibits the use of embedded data connections in spreadsheets saved in the trusted file location. Users must use data connections from data connection libraries. See the section, "Using data connection libraries," later in this chapter.

12. **Indicate whether to allow user-defined functions.**

    User-defined functions are programs users create for use with their Excel workbooks. A user might use a user-defined function to perform a calculation that's too complex for Excel. The user can reference the user-defined function in his workbook to get the function's value. In order for user's workbooks to use user-defined functions in a trusted file location, you must enable its use.

    You must also register the user-defined function with Excel Services. To do so, click the User-Defined Function Assemblies link in the Excel Services Settings section of the Shared Services Administration site.

13. **Click OK.**

    The SharePoint document library appears in the list of trusted file locations.

You must add a data connection library to the list of trusted data connection libraries for Excel Services. You can use an existing data connection library or create a new one. A data connection library is a kind of library, similar to a document library. Instead of storing documents, you store data connection files. You create data connection libraries similar to how you create document libraries. Click the Trusted Data Connection Libraries link on the home page of the Shared Services Administration site to designate a data connection library as a trusted data connection library. See the section, "Using data connection libraries," later in this chapter, for more details.

Displaying workbook content

Excel Services provides the Excel Web Access Web Part to display content from Excel 2007 spreadsheets in SharePoint sites. Excel Web Access can display workbooks from any trusted location, including SharePoint libraries and network shares. Microsoft recommends that you create a designated document library to use as a trusted location. See Chapter 15 for more information on document management and saving files to document libraries.

Follow these steps to display an Excel workbook in an Excel Web Access Web Part:

1. **Upload an Excel 2007 workbook to a trusted file location.**

   See the preceding section for details on designating a document library or other address as a trusted file location.

2. **Browse to the page you wish to add the Excel Web Access Web Part to.**

   You may wish to add the Web part to an existing Web Part page or business intelligence dashboard. See the following section, "Exploring Reports Center," for details on working with dashboards.

3. **Choose Site Actions⇨Edit Page to add an Excel Web Access Web Part to the page.**

   You can find the Web Part in the Business Data section of the Add Web Parts dialog box. See Chapter 4 for details on working with Web parts.

4. **Open the Web Part Tool pane by clicking the Click Here to Open the Tool Pane link inside the Web Part.**

   You can also choose Edit⇨Modify Shared Web Part on the Web Part.

5. **Click the ellipsis button next to the Workbook field.**

   The Select a Link dialog box appears.

   Alternatively, you can paste or type a URL or UNC path to the workbook in the workbook field.

6. **Browse to the trusted location where the workbook is saved, select the workbook, and click OK.**

   For example, if your workbook is saved in the Financial Documents library in the Finance team site, you could browse to that site. Note that you don't have to use the Excel Web Access Web part in the Finance team site. You can browse to the Finance team site.

7. **If the workbook has named ranges, you can use the Named Item field to limit the workbook's display to the selected range.**

You can also use Named Items to create workbook parameters. Use the Defined Names group on the Formulas tab in Excel 2007 to create named items. Named items can be exposed as parameters that users can change or supply as connections for other Web Parts.

8. **In the Toolbar and Title Bar section, configure whether the Web Part automatically generates the title and configure the toolbar's menu commands.**

Use this section to determine which menu commands are available to users who interact with the workbook displayed in the Web Part.

9. **In the Navigation and Interactivity section, configure navigation options and specify the extent to which users can interact with the workbook in the Web Part.**

For example, you can enable sorting and filtering. Be aware that the more interactive your users are with the workbook, the more taxing the workbook might be on the server. If your servers are performing actions that cause values to recalculate, performance might slow.

10. **Specify configure settings for the Appearance, Layout, and Advanced sections.**

See Chapter 4 for details on configuring Web parts.

11. **Click the Apply button.**

The workbook appears in the Web Part, as shown in Figure 17-1.

Being able to display the contents of an Excel workbook in a SharePoint page is useful, but combining it with other SharePoint features makes it really powerful. You can do the following:

- **Create connections with other Web Parts,** such as Filter and List View, to customize what gets displayed in the Excel Access Web Part.

- **Use multiple Excel Access Web Parts** on a page to provide different views of data. For example, you could use three Web Parts to display the data as a list, pivot table, and chart on a single SharePoint Web Parts page.

- **Open the workbook in Excel** in order to print the workbook or perform what-if analysis. This feature can be disabled when the Web Part is configured.

- **Sort, filter, and outline data** that appears in the workbook.

- **Allow users to perform what-if scenarios** by using workbook parameters.

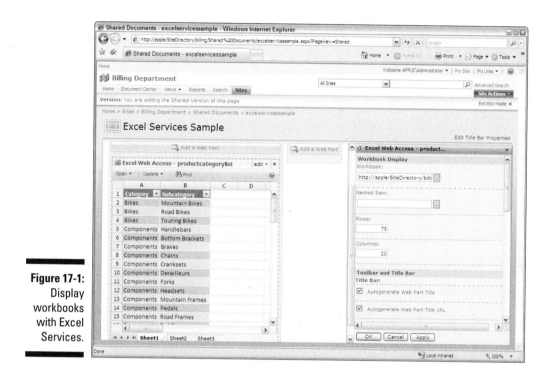

Figure 17-1:
Display
workbooks
with Excel
Services.

Exploring Reports Center

SharePoint provides the Reports Center site template as a site that's dedicated to storing reports. By default, a single Reports Center is created within Collaboration portals, as I describe in Chapter 11. You can add as many Reports Centers as you need to suit your organization. You may want Reports Centers that target a particular reporting area instead of trying to do all your reporting in a single site.

The Reports Center includes a Reports library for storing reports. I use the term report somewhat loosely because SharePoint defines report as a Web-based view of business data. In SharePoint, a *report* is essentially a collection of related Web Parts used to convey information.

Often, users find it useful to print reports. Consider providing links to printable versions of reports or some other means to access the report's underlying data.

The *Reports library* is a standard SharePoint library that has all the same features of document libraries. The Reports library is configured to store two content types:

- ✔ **Dashboard pages** create a Web Parts page optimized to display Reporting and Business Intelligence Web Parts.

- ✔ **Reports** create Excel workbooks that can be displayed using Excel Web Access Web Parts. When you create a new report using the Report content type, you're creating a blank Excel 2007 spreadsheet. You can open the file in Excel 2007 and create your workbook.

You can browse to the Reports library in the Reports Center and click the New button to create either kind of report. You can add a Reports library to any kind of site.

When you create a Dashboard page, you specify a Dashboard Layout, you specify whether to display the Dashboard in current navigation, and you specify whether to add Key Performance Indicators (KPIs).

Dashboard pages take advantage of all the Business Data Web Parts and Business Intelligence Web Parts to build a multi-summary Report page. Because a Dashboard page is a kind of Web Part page, you can use any Web Part on a Dashboard page. The Web Parts you're most likely to see include are these:

- ✔ **Business Data Web Parts** display summary and detail data from back-end databases. See the section, "Connecting to Data," later in this chapter.

- ✔ **Excel Web Access Web Parts** display data, charts, and pivot tables from Excel 2007 workbooks.

- ✔ **Filter Web Parts** make it possible to filter the data views that are displayed in the various Web Parts displayed on the Dashboard page. MOSS 2007 has ten filter Web Parts that can be used to automatically filter data or accept user data to create a filter. For example, the Date Filter Web Part allows users to select a date from a drop-down calendar. In most cases, filter Web Parts are connected to other Web Parts on the page to restrict the values displayed based on criteria provided by the filter Web Part.

- ✔ **Key Performance Indicator (KPI) Web Parts** display KPIs created in a KPI list. KPIs are used to display progress toward a goal, such as customer satisfaction or billing errors. A *KPI list* is a special kind of SharePoint list customized for storing KPIs. You can create KPIs based on data from other SharePoint lists, Excel workbooks, SQL Server 2005 Analysis Services, or manually entered information.

✔ **Reporting Services Web Parts** display reports from SQL Server 2005 Reporting Services (SSRS).

You aren't restricted to using these features in the Reports Center. You can use these Web Parts in any kind of SharePoint site.

The Reports Center includes a sample Dashboard page complete with sample data. The sample includes Filter, KPI, and Excel Web Access Web Parts. The Reports Center includes content to support these Web Parts, such as a KPI list and Excel workbooks. Click the View All Site Content link on the Quick Launch bar in Reports Center to view the supporting lists and libraries.

You can access the Sample Dashboard by clicking the Sample link in the Dashboards group on the Quick Launch bar. Figure 17-2 shows the Sample Dashboard.

Filter Web part

KPI Web part

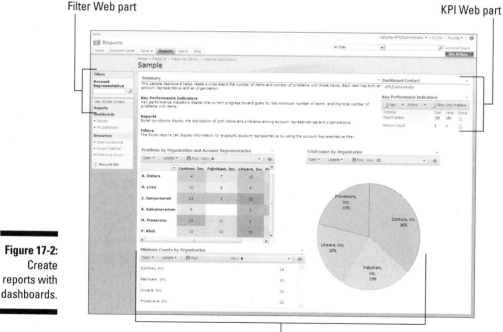

Figure 17-2: Create reports with dashboards.

Excel Web Access Web part

Connecting to Data

An important requirement of any reporting solution is the ability to connect to external data. MOSS 2007 provides extensive support for connecting to everything from Excel workbooks and Access databases to enterprise applications, such as SAP.

The features I describe in this section can be used with Dashboard pages and Excel Web Access, or they can be used to create custom applications with SharePoint. You're limited only by your imagination and your information technology infrastructure.

Using data connection libraries

Connecting to external data within Excel spreadsheets and Access databases is nothing new. Many companies use this feature to create impressive information systems. Office 2007 applications have many new features for managing these data connections, including saving the connection information in a separate file called a *data connection file*.

By default, these data connections are embedded in the file that uses the connection. Instead of embedding data connections inside Office 2007 files, SharePoint has Data Connection libraries that can be used to manage the data connections created by Office 2007 applications to access external data. See Chapter 4 for details on creating SharePoint libraries, such as data connection libraries.

With the Office 2007 application used to connect to external data, users can create data connection files and save the files in a data connection library. After these files are saved in the data connection library, other users can reuse these connections with their files. This is a great way for administrators to know which data sources people are accessing, along with controlling the data sources being used.

By creating a trusted data connection library, administrators can limit the data connections available to users of Excel Services. See the section, "Using Excel Services," earlier in this chapter.

To save a data connection in Excel 2007, follow these steps:

 1. **Open a workbook that uses an external data connection in Excel 2007.**

To connect to external data in Excel 2007, use the Get External Data section of the Data tab to create new data connections. See the topic, "Importing Data," at the Office Online Web site at `http://office.microsoft.com/ en-us/excel/CH100648471033.aspx` for more details.

2. Click the Existing Connections button on the Data tab.

The Existing Connections dialog box appears.

Alternatively, you can click the Connections button on the Data tab to access the Workbook Connections dialog box.

3. In the Show drop-down list, choose Connections in This Workbook.

A list of existing data connections appears. If you don't have any connections in the workbook, you can add a connection by using the link I provide in Step 1. Your connection can be simple. For example, you can connect to a table in an Access database.

4. Right-click the existing connection you wish to save and click Edit Connection Properties.

The Connection Properties dialog box appears.

5. Click the Definition tab.

6. Click the Export Connection File button.

The File Save dialog box appears.

If you can't click the Export Connection File button, the connection file can't be exported. However, you can get the name of the connection file from the Connection File field on the Definition tab. You can upload the connection file to a data connection library in the same way that you would upload a Word document to a document library.

7. Browse to the SharePoint data connection library where you wish to save the data connection file.

If you don't already have a data connection library, see Chapter 4 for details on creating one.

8. Click Save.

9. The Web File Properties dialog box appears.

The properties you see come from the Office Data Connection File content type used by the data connection library.

Because data connection libraries use content types, you can change the properties that are used to manage data connections. See Chapter 7 for details on working with content types.

10. **Type the title, description, and keywords for the data connection.**

11. **Select the connection's type from the Connection Type drop-down list.**

    The type you select indicates the data source for the connection type.

12. **Select the connection's purpose from the UDC Purpose drop-down list.**

    This property indicates the data connection file's intended purpose. Your options are ReadOnly, WriteOnly, ReadWrite. If the connection file is only used to read data, as is the case with Excel files, choose the ReadOnly options.

13. **Click OK to close the Web File Properties dialog box.**

    The data connection file is saved to the library.

Because the data connection library works like a document library, you can upload data connection files to the library in the same way you upload files to a document library. You can click the New button in the data connection library to access the upload page.

Users can use the Existing Connections dialog box to access the connections that are saved in data connection libraries in SharePoint.

Configuring the Business Data Catalog

The MOSS 2007 feature — the Business Data Catalog (BDC) — enables you to connect your back-end applications to SharePoint. You can establish a relationship between any kind of database or Web service. The applications you register with BDC are *enterprise applications*.

The BDC allows you to use enterprise application data in SharePoint in the following ways:

✔ **Add business data to lists and libraries:** SharePoint has a special business data column type that enables you to use data from enterprise applications. For example, you can use a business data column in a document library to provide metadata for a document or to provide a pick list of entries, such as states or zip codes.

✔ **Display business data in Web parts:** SharePoint provides five Web Parts that enable you to display lists of business data or individual data records. You can create connections between these Web parts and other Web parts to filter business data or create master/detail views of business data.

✔ **Associate a set of actions with each business data entity:** You can define actions — actions which then appear to the end user as a hyperlink — that extend the reach of the business data entity beyond SharePoint. For example, you could create an action that enables users to display a page to update values stored in a back-end database. Actions follow the business data entity everywhere. SharePoint defines the View Profile default action, which displays the business data entity on the page. You can customize the profile page by clicking the Edit Profile Page Template link in the Shared Services Administration site.

✔ **Index business data so it can be searched:** The Business Data Catalog is available to Office SharePoint Server Search as a content source. Users can use the Search Center to search business data sources. You can add business data entities as managed properties if you want users to be able to conduct advanced searches of enterprise applications. See Chapter 14 for more on advanced searches.

✔ **Import data into user profiles:** You can import data from enterprise applications into SharePoint's User Profile Store to supplement data provided by Active Directory (AD) or another directory service. After you configure the enterprise application in the Business Data Catalog, you can map the entities to user profile properties. Click the View Import Connections link in the User Profiles and Properties page to create a connection to an enterprise application. See Chapter 12.

You register applications with the BDC by describing the connection to the data source and the content you wish to access. You use *entities* to define the content you wish to access. Entities are analogous to tables in a database, but there need not be a one-to-one relationship between entities and tables. As part of the process of defining entities, you specify how the entity maps to the data source.

The entities and data connection you define is the *metadata model*. Unfortunately, MOSS 2007 doesn't include any user interface tools for creating metadata models. Instead, you have two options for creating the entities that describe your enterprise application:

✔ **An application definition file** is an eXtensible Markup Language (XML) file that conforms to the specification of the metadata model. The application definition file defines the entities that you wish to use from your enterprise application. For example, if your application has concepts, such as Customer and Order, you define the entities as Customer and Order in your application definition file along with the queries that retrieve the data from the enterprise application.

✔ **The Administration object model** allows you to create applications using .NET and Visual Studio that create, edit, and delete metadata from the Business Data Catalog. You can find the Administration object model in the `Microsoft.Office.Server.ApplicationRegistry.Administration` namespace in the `Microsoft.SharePoint.Portal.dll` file. SharePoint also provides the `Microsoft.Office.Server.ApplicationRegistry.MetadataModel` namespace to allow for fast queries of the BDC metadata models.

Of course, I'm grossly oversimplifying the rules for how metadata models are created. In reality, 13 objects are used to create metadata models, and each object has its own set of attributes. See the topic, "Business Data Catalog Metadata Model," in the MOSS 2007 SDK for specifics.

MOSS 2007 provides a set of administration pages for importing application definition files. If you don't like to write code, application definition files are a good alternative because you can create the files with a text editor.

I suggest you use an XML editor, such as Microsoft's XML Notepad, to work with application definition files. XML Notepad displays XML nodes in a tree that you can drill into.

To import an application definition file, follow these steps:

1. **Browse to the Shared Services Administration site.**

2. **Click the Import Application Definition link in the Business Data Catalog section.**

   The Import Application Definition page appears.

3. **Click the Browse button and browse to the application definition file you created.**

   The file doesn't need to have an XML file extension, but it does need to be a valid and well-formed XML document.

4. **Select the Model file type.**

   The BDC also has a specification for uploading resource files that set language-specific content.

5. **Click the Import button.**

   The Importing Application Definition page appears.

   SharePoint validates the definition file. If any errors occur, correct those errors and try again. After the file is validated, SharePoint creates the model in the SharePoint database, and the Application Definition Import Successful page appears.

6. **Click OK.**

   The View Application page appears.

The Business Data Catalog offers several choices for authenticating with enterprise applications. Many companies opt to implement the Single Sign-On (SSO) service to manage the storage and mapping of credentials from SharePoint to back-end systems.

For testing purposes, the easiest authentication choice is to use pass-through authentication. In this case, credentials are simply passed from SharePoint to the enterprise application.

Using business data in SharePoint

SharePoint includes a set of Web Parts that are used to display data from the Business Data Catalog. These Web Parts can be used to display a list of data or connected to other Web parts to create a complex business intelligence dashboard. The Web parts are as follows:

- **Business Data Actions,** which display a list of actions associated with an entity.

- **Business Data Item,** which displays details of single entity instance.

- **Business Data Item Builder,** which is used on Business Data profile pages to pass parameters to other Web Parts.

- **Business Data List,** which displays a list of data from the enterprise application.

- **Business Data Related List,** which displays a list of data that's associated with another business entity.

- **Business Data Catalog Filter,** which is used to filter the values in one Web Part by the values selected in this Web Part.

Using Business Data Web Parts is similar to using any other kind of Web Part. Each of these Web Parts allows you to select the business entity to display in the Web Part. Some parts, such as the List and Related List parts, allow you to customize the view to determine whether users can see all items or must enter criteria to query for items.

Figure 17-3 shows an example of a Web Parts page that displays four Business Data Web Parts. The data is queried from the Adventure Works Data Warehouse. Connections are created between the Web Parts so that they filter values. The page shows the following:

- **Actions Web Part** displays the list of actions for the Products entity. You can add custom actions to an entity with the View Entities link in the Shared Services Administration site.

- **List Web Part** displays a list of Product Subcategories.

- **Related List Web Part** displays a list of products that are associated with Product Subcategories. When a user clicks a Product Subcategory, a list of associated products appears in this Web Part. The association between the Product and Product Subcategories entities is defined in the metadata model.

- **Item Web Part** displays the detail record for the item selected in the Product List. This Web Part also displays the entity's actions across the top.

The display you see in Figure 17-3 uses out-of-the-box Web Parts. The only configuration required is to upload the metadata model to the Business Data Catalog. After the BDC knows your entities and how to connect to the data source, configuring Business Data Web Parts to display data is a piece of cake.

Actions Web part

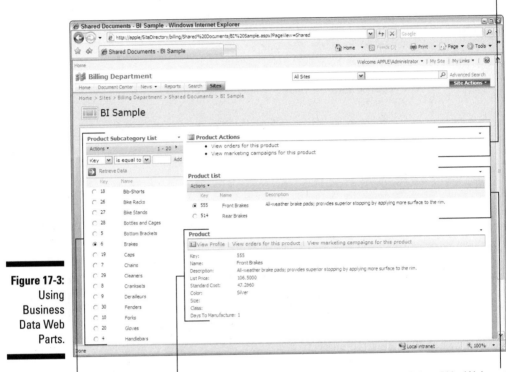

Figure 17-3:
Using
Business
Data Web
Parts.

List Web part   Item Web part   Related List Web part

Enabling Single Sign-On

In order to access back-end applications in SharePoint, SharePoint needs to know how to log into those applications. SharePoint uses a Single Sign-On (SSO) service that maps user credentials to back-end applications.

Before you can enable SSO in SharePoint, you must first start the Microsoft Single Sign-On Service on one of your SharePoint application servers. If you're only using one server, enable the service on that server.

It's important to start the service on an application server first because the first server started with the service becomes the Encryption-Key server for the other servers. Microsoft recommends starting the service first on the Index server.

After you start the SSO service on an application server, you must start the service on each of your Web servers. Then you can configure SSO for your server farm by following these steps:

1. **Browse to the Central Administration site.**

   You must be logged in to the physical console to perform this task. You can't use Remote Desktop or a client connection to configure SSO. You can, however, use the remote control client in Virtual Server 2005 to configure virtual servers.

2. **Click the Enable SSO in the Farm Administrative Task.**

   The task item appears. See Chapter 2 for details on working with Administrative Tasks.

   Alternatively, you can click the Manage Settings for Single Sign-On link on the Operations page.

   The Manage Settings for Single Sign-On page appears.

3. **Click the Manage Server Settings link.**

   The Manage Server Settings for Single Sign-On page appears.

4. **Type an account name in the Single Sign-On Administrator Account field.**

   This is the account used to manage SSO.

5. **Type an account name in the Enterprise Application Definition Administrator account.**

   This is the account used to manage settings for application definitions in MOSS 2007, which identify credentials used by the BDC.

6. **In the Database Settings section, type the name of the database server to use and database name.**

   SSO uses its own database to manage credentials You can accept the default values unless you want to use a different server and database.

7. **Specify values for the Time Out settings.**

   The Ticket Time Out settings determine how long an SSO ticket is valid in between the time it's received by a user's request and the time it's redeemed by an application. The ticket is issued by the SSO server and contains the encrypted domain name and username of the current user.

8. **Click OK.**

   SharePoint provisions the SSO database.

Use the links found on the Manage Settings for Single Sign-On page to map account credentials to enterprise applications defined in the BDC.

Part V
Administering SharePoint

The 5th Wave   By Rich Tennant

"It's a solid ID management and tracking system, Ted. Over 15 years on the Kalahari and we never lost a single lion."

In this part . . .

Keeping an eye on the health of your SharePoint environment doesn't require a medical license. In Chapter 18, I show you how to monitor SharePoint's usage and then I devote Chapter 19 to showing you how to get good backups.

Chapter 18

Administering and Monitoring SharePoint

In This Chapter

▶ Getting acquainted with SharePoint's administrative sites

▶ Keeping an eye on how sites are being used

▶ Setting limits on disk space usage

Even a simple SharePoint implementation is a complex beast to administer. SharePoint is set up so that you have a *layered* centralized administration, with each administration layer scoped to a specific set of activities. The layers allow higher-order administrators to delegate administrative tasks to others. The administrative layers you see in SharePoint are

✔ **Server level:** At the physical server level, Information Technology (IT) staff use tools, such as Event Viewer and IIS Manager, to monitor and administer the server.

IT may also use Microsoft Operations Manager (MOM) to monitor the health of servers within the IT infrastructure. You can find out more about using MOM and find a management pack for SharePoint at www.microsoft.com/mom.

✔ **Server farm:** IT administrators use SharePoint's Central Administration Web site to manage farm level resources. There's a single Central Administration site per farm that's used to create new Web applications and site collections as well as to set farm-wide settings.

✔ **Shared Services Provider (SSP):** MOSS 2007 implementations use an SSP to share services, such as Excel Services, across many sites. The SSP is managed through the Shared Services Administration site.

✔ **Site collection and site levels:** Each site collection and site within the site collection has its own dedicated administration page — the Site Settings page. Site owners use the Site Settings page to maintain and monitor the site. See Chapter 5 for more information on using the Site Settings page.

In this chapter, I discuss server farm and SSP administration. See Chapter 2 for more information on setting up the server farm.

 Administering SharePoint requires a complex and integrated set of technical skills, including networking and database administration skills. Most of the configuration settings I discuss in this chapter provide default values. Don't deviate from these settings unless you have a specific reason to do so. I suggest setting up a test environment if you want to play around with your configuration. Be sure to check out Chapter 20 for a list of resources you can use to beef up your skills on SharePoint and its supporting technologies.

Exploring Central Administration

Both Microsoft Office SharePoint Server (MOSS) 2007 and Windows SharePoint Services (WSS) version 3 provide a centralized location for accessing administration pages — the Central Administration site. This is one of the first sites you provision when you set up SharePoint, as I describe in Chapter 2.

The *Central Administration site* is a SharePoint site with all the features you expect to find in SharePoint sites, such as permissions, master pages, and libraries and lists. Although I don't recommend that you customize the Central Administration site, don't hesitate to add Tasks lists, calendars, and other resources that help you manage your SharePoint administration.

The Central Administration site (see Figure 18-1) has the following three pages:

✔ **The Home page** displays a list of tasks from the Administrator Tasks list along with a Farm Topology Web part. The Home page gives the administrator a bird's eye view of tasks that need to be completed as well as the servers that are in the farm. You can click any of the servers listed in the Farm Topology Web part to manage the services for that server.

The Home page is a Web Part Page that you can customize by adding Web Parts.

✔ **The Operations page** provides access to settings that affect the entire farm, such as configuring e-mail settings and performing backups.

✔ **The Application Management page** allows you to configure and maintain Web applications and site collections.

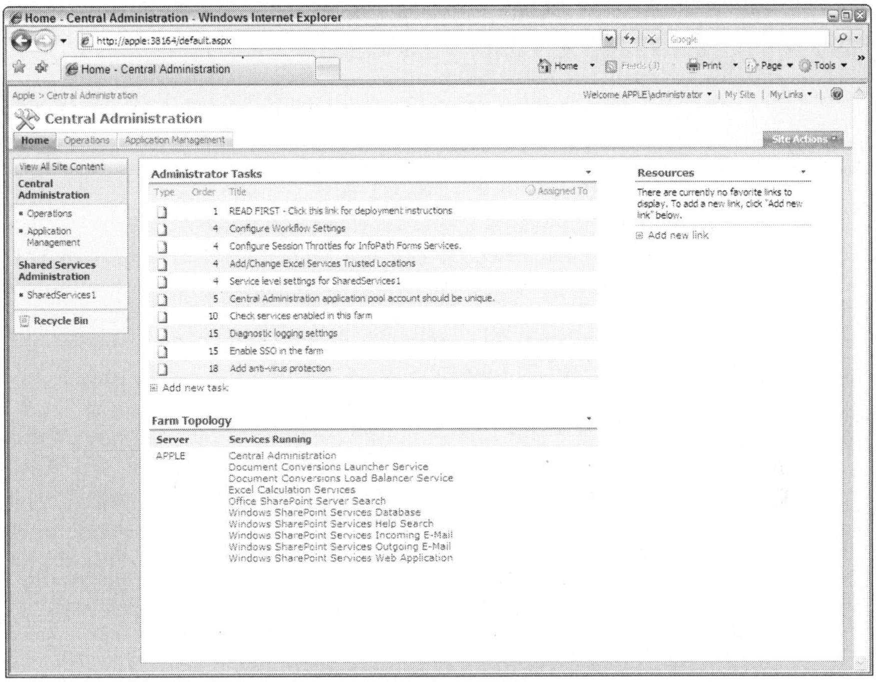

Figure 18-1:
Administer the server farm through the Central Administration site.

Because the Central Administration site is a Web site, you can access it using a browser on any computer in your network. You can find a link to the Central Administration site on any of your SharePoint Servers by choosing Start⇨Administrative Tools⇨SharePoint 3.0 Central Administration.

You use this link to access the Central Administration site for MOSS 2007, too. There's only one Central Administration site for a server farm.

Generally speaking, you should feel comfortable exploring these administrative pages without fear of breaking anything. All the links displayed take you to Settings pages, which you can cancel out of. The exact sections and links that you see in Central Administration vary, depending on whether you're using WSS or MOSS. The Central Administration site is extensible, so third-party applications can also add sections to the pages found in the site.

Configuring Shared Services

Shared Services Provider (SSP) is an important feature you configure in the Central Administration site. The SSP provides shared MOSS services across Web applications. Services provided by the SSP include personalization services and the Business Data Catalog.

You create an SSP when you deploy SharePoint, as I describe in Chapter 2. Most deployments have only one SSP per server farm; however, it is possible to have more than one. The most common reason to create additional SSPs is to isolate content. For example, you would create a second SSP if you wanted to create an Internet-facing portal.

You can create additional SSPs (or change the SSP associated with a Web application) by using the Application Management page of the Central Administration site. With the Office SharePoint Server Shared Services section, you can access the following links:

- ✔ **Create or Configure This Farm's Shared Services:** Use this link to create new SSPs, set the default SSP, or change associations between Web applications and SSPs. You can also use this link to edit the properties on an SSP so you can change its name as well as the credentials used by the SSP and SQL Server to access a particular SSP and search databases. You can also enable Secure Sockets Layer (SSL) communications for all SSP Web services.

- ✔ **Grant or Configure Shared Services between Farms:** Use this link to manage shared services across multiple farms. Use this link only if you want one server farm to consume the shared services of another farm.

- ✔ **Check Services Enabled in Farm:** Use this link to view issues with the server farm.

- ✔ **Configure Session State**: Use this link to temporarily disable session state for troubleshooting purposes. Session state is required to allow Web applications, like SharePoint, to remember the browser's state while a user interacts with the Web site. You can also adjust the session state's timeout duration.

SharePoint needs session state enabled to function properly.

Each SSP has its own administration site — the Shared Services Administration site. Use this site to configure the shared services of MOSS 2007, such as search and Excel Services. A hyperlink to the Shared Services Administration site appears in the Quick Launch bar of the Central Administration site. Figure 18-2 shows the Shared Services Administration site.

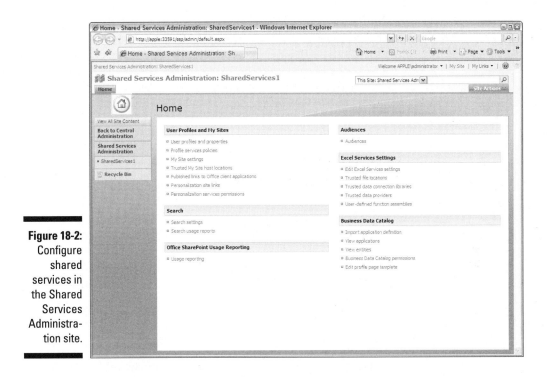

Figure 18-2:
Configure
shared
services in
the Shared
Services
Administra-
tion site.

Monitoring Site Usage

One of the frequent complaints I hear about SharePoint is that administrators have no idea how it's being used. SharePoint provides a number of tools for monitoring daily usage and capturing errors. Administrators can limit sites' disk storage use and configure sites to delete automatically after a specified period of inactivity.

WSS and MOSS 2007 provide extensive site usage monitoring reports. Reports are available at all levels of the server farm from the SSP to individual SharePoint sites.

Before administrators can start reviewing site usage reports, you must enable site usage reporting for the server farm. Usage reporting occurs in two distinct steps:

1. Web servers log activity to usage analysis logs.

2. SharePoint performs usage analysis processing, which reads the logs from all the Web servers in the farm and then saves the data to the content database.

Usage analysis processing is a scheduled job that runs once every 24 hours. As a result, it isn't possible to see up-to-the-minute usage reporting.

You don't have to use the usage reporting provided by SharePoint. You can use a third-party tool to analyze the usage analysis logs generated by SharePoint's Web servers.

Follow these steps to enable site usage reporting for WSS:

1. **Browse to the Operations page in the Central Administration site.**

   See the section, "Exploring Central Administration," earlier in this chapter for details on browsing to the Central Administration site.

2. **Click the Usage Analysis Processing link in the Logging and Reporting section.**

   The Usage Analysis Processing screen appears.

3. **Select the Enable Logging check box.**

4. **Enter the number of log files to create.**

   SharePoint can save up to 30 days of log files.

5. **Select the Enable Usage Analysis Processing check box.**

6. **Set the time of day you wish to run usage processing.**

   You can't control the exact time processing starts. The job is submitted during the time frame you specify.

7. **Click OK.**

By default, minimal usage reporting is enabled for the SSP. You must enable advanced reporting if you want to view more information, such as the results of search queries. Do the following to enable complete usage reporting:

1. **Browse to the Shared Services Administration site.**

2. **Click the Usage Reporting link in the Office SharePoint Usage Reporting section.**

   The Configure Advanced Usage Analysis Processing page appears.

3. **Select the Enable Advanced Usage Analysis Processing check box.**

4. **Select the Enable Search Query Logging check box.**

   Query logging is enabled by default.

5. **Click OK.**

Before you can view usage reports for a site collection, you must enable the Reports feature in the site collection. You need to perform these steps on every site collection that you want to view site usage reports on. This feature is available only in MOSS 2007. To enable the feature, follow these steps:

1. **Browse to the top-level site in the site collection.**

2. **Browse to the Site Settings page.**

   Choose Site Actions⇨Site Settings in a team site. Choose Site Actions⇨ Site Settings⇨Modify All Site Settings in a MOSS publishing site.

3. **Click the Site Collection Features link in the Site Collection Administration section.**

4. **Click the Activate button for the Reporting feature.**

Table 18-1 lists the various reports you can access to view usage reporting data you can access from the site or site collection's Site Settings page.

It takes 24 hours for usage data to be processed. Don't be surprised not to see any reports after enabling usage reports.

Table 18-1	**SharePoint Usage Reports**	
Level	*How to Access*	*What You See*
Site	Site Administration⇨ Site Usage Reports	Shows data on pages viewed in the site.
Site collection	Site Collection Administration⇨ Usage Summary	Lists storage, users, and activity summaries for the site collection; WSS only.
Site collection	Site Collection Administration⇨ Site Collection Usage Reports	A collection of reports, showing requests, users, referrers, destination pages, and other metrics; MOSS only.
SSP	Shared Services Administration site⇨ Search Usage Reports	Search queries and results.

SharePoint also includes diagnostic logging and event reporting that you can use to troubleshoot errors you may encounter in SharePoint. Follow these steps to enable diagnostic logging:

1. **Browse to the Operations page in the Central Administration site.**

2. **Click the Diagnostic Logging link in the Logging and Reporting section.**

   The Diagnostic Logging page appears.

3. **In the Customer Experience Improvement Program section, indicate whether you wish to participate in Microsoft's Customer Experience Improvement Program.**

   If you choose Yes, anonymous information about your server is sent periodically to Microsoft.

4. **In the Error Reports section, indicate whether SharePoint should collect error reports.**

   When an error is detected by SharePoint, a dialog box appears on the server, giving you the option to send an error report to Microsoft. Click the Help link listed in the Error Reports section to read Microsoft's information collection and privacy policy.

5. **In the Event Throttling section, select an event category (such as E-Mail) from the list of events.**

   A report detailing the severity of errors in the event category appears.

   Events recorded in the server's event log can be viewed via the Event Viewer. Events recorded in the server's trace log can be viewed in the trace log file. You can use the Event Throttling section to indicate the least severe events to record to the event log and trace log.

6. **In the Trace Log section, set a path for trace logs to be stored and indicate the number of log files to retain along with the number of minutes a single log file is used.**

   When the maximum log number is reached, the oldest log file is overwritten. If you're encountering a number of errors with SharePoint, you may wish to increase the number of log files retained while reducing the number of minutes traces are written to each log file. This allows you to view smaller snapshots of log entries.

 Log files are typically stored in `C:\Program Files\Common Files\ Microsoft Shared\Web Server Extensions\12\Logs`. You can go to that path to view trace logs and usage analysis logs. Viewing trace logs is a good way to get an understanding of the processes that are running on your servers.

7. **Click OK.**

Managing Site Collections

Managing site collections is an important administrative task that's often overlooked until it's too late. SharePoint provides several configuration settings that make it possible for administrators to limit disk storage use before it's a problem.

Administrators can define a quota template that limits the amount of disk storage a site collection can consume. MOSS 2007 includes a Personal Site template that limits the size of My Site personal sites to 100MB. Administrators can set up quota templates for each kind of site they need to manage, such as Team sites and Publishing portals.

Follow these steps to create a new quota template:

1. **Browse to the Application Management page in the Central Administration site.**

2. **Click the Quota Templates link in the SharePoint Site Management section.**

   The Quota Templates page appears.

3. **Select the Create a New Quota Template radio button.**

4. **Select an existing starting quota template from the Template to Start From drop-down list.**

   If you don't want to start from an existing template, you can choose [New Blank Template] from the drop-down list.

5. **Type a name for the template in the New Template Name field.**

6. **In the Storage Limit Values section, set the maximum amount of storage you wish to limit the site collection to.**

   Storage is measured in megabytes (MB).

7. **Set the storage amount threshold for sending a warning e-mail message to the collection administrator.**

8. **Click OK.**

See the TechNet library for more information on capacity planning at

```
http://technet2.microsoft.com/Office/f/?en-us/library/
        185da9e8-9ed1-4bf1-bfb5-2a5a874f2a191033.mspx
```

You can apply quotas to site collections and specify whether the content in a site collection is accessible. To apply quotas and locks to specific site collections, do the following:

1. **Browse to the Application Management page in the Central Administration site.**

2. **Click the Site Collection Quotas and Locks link.**

   The Site Collection Quotas and Locks page appears.

3. **Select the site collection you wish to administer in the Site Collection section.**

4. **In the Site Lock Information section, set the lock status for the site collection.**

   You can limit the site so that adding content is prevented, the site is read only, or the site can't be accessed at all. You might wish to use these options when you're migrating or archiving content from a site collection.

5. **In the Site Quota Information section, select an existing quota template.**

   You can apply a quota without selecting a quota template by selecting Individual Quota from the Current Quota Template drop-down list.

   The current storage used by the site collection appears in this section.

6. **Click OK.**

   Figure 18-3 shows the Site Collection Quotas and Locks page.

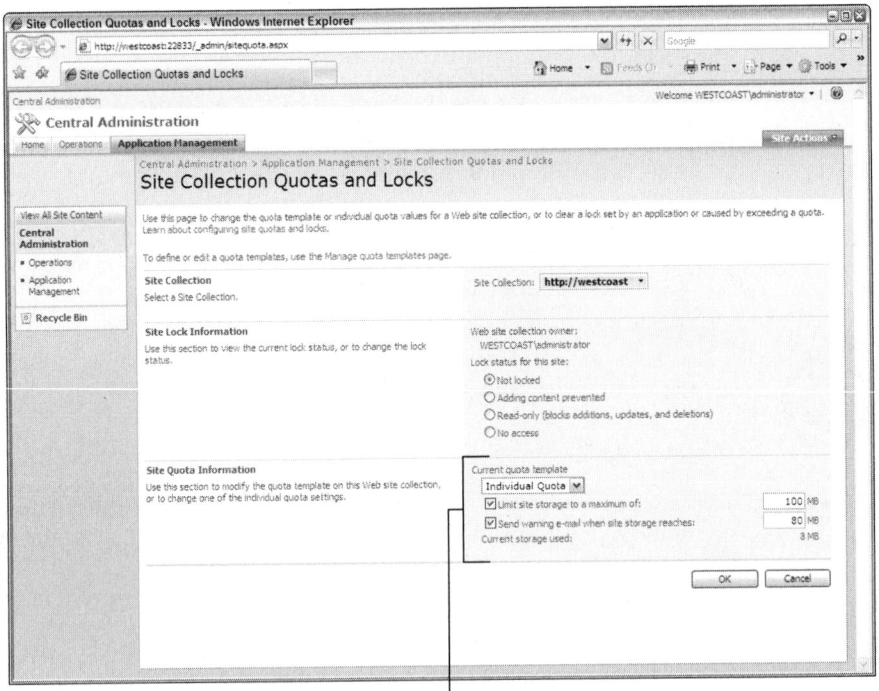

Figure 18-3:
Configure quotas and locks for site collections.

Current Storage used

After a quota is applied to a site collection, administrators can access the Storage Space Allocation page to see how much disk storage is used by document libraries, documents, lists, and the Recycle Bin. Do the following to access the Storage Space Allocation page:

1. **Browse to the top-level site in a site collection to which a quota is applied.**

2. **Choose Site Actions⇨Site Settings.**

   The Site Settings page appears.

3. **Click the Storage Space Allocation link in the Site Collection Administration section.**

   The Storage Space Allocation page appears.

The Storage Space Allocation page lists the contents of the site collection. You can use this page to delete content, such as documents and lists. The page includes a graphic that shows the amount of space used relative to the quota, as shown in Figure 18-4.

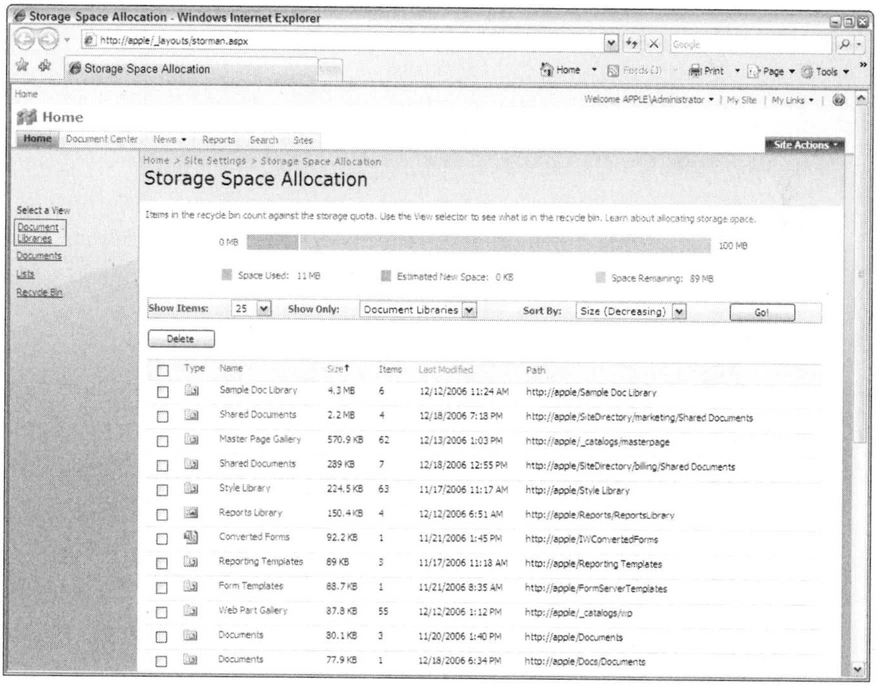

Figure 18-4: Use the Storage Space Allocation to view disk usage.

Administrators also have the option of sending e-mails to the administrators of site collections that aren't being used. Site collections can be configured to automatically delete themselves if they aren't being used. To configure site use confirmation and deletion, follow these steps:

1. **Browse to the Application Management page of the Central Administration site.**

2. **Click the Site Use Confirmation and Deletion link in the SharePoint Site Management section.**

   The Site Use Confirmation and Deletion page appears.

3. **In the Web Application section, select the Web application you wish to enable site use confirmation.**

4. **Select the Send E-Mail Notifications to Owners of Unused Site Collections check box.**

5. **Indicate how many days the site collection goes without use before sending e-mail notifications.**

6. **Select the frequency and time to check for site use.**

7. **Select the Automatically Delete the Site Collection if Use Is Not Confirmed check box.**

8. **Indicate how many notices are sent to the owner before the site collection is deleted.**

9. **Click OK.**

Enabling automatic deletion removes all content from the site collection and any subsites. Ensure that all site collections have a secondary site collection owner so you have two people receiving notifications.

Chapter 19

Backing Up the Server

*R*ecovering data involves more than nightly backups. Many times throughout the course of a day, data is deleted accidentally. Hardware isn't usually kind enough to fail right after a backup, which often leaves you faced with a day's worth of lost activity. When creating a backup strategy, you want a plan that gives you the ability to do the following:

✔ Recover data quickly and easily.

✔ Rebuild a server farm after a disaster, such as hardware failure.

Your solution must take into account the dual goals of incidental content recovery and catastrophic disaster recovery. SharePoint has several levels of backup and restore capabilities. In this chapter, I explore the options you have when crafting your SharePoint backup and restore strategy.

Recovering from End User Mishaps

As any help desk technician can tell you, end users commonly delete files by accident. You've probably done it yourself. SharePoint has several lines of defense to protect your end users' content from accidental deletion.

SharePoint has two out-of-the-box features that make it easy for end users to quickly recover from deletions:

✔ **Recycle Bin:** When a user deletes a document or list item, such as a task, it's moved automatically to the Recycle Bin. The end user or an administrator can restore the file from the Recycle Bin by using the browser. SharePoint features a second stage Recycle Bin that only administrators can access. Documents move to the second stage Recycle Bin after they've reached a retention quota in the Recycle Bin.

✔ **Version control:** SharePoint document libraries can save minor and major versions of documents. If a user realizes that he accidentally saved the wrong version of a file, he can restore a previous version.

See Chapter 15 for more information on using the Recycle Bin and version control.

Unfortunately, neither of these features works when a user deletes an entire site. Your best option then is to implement custom code that runs when the Web Delete Event fires. See the Windows SharePoint Services (WSS) Software Development Kit (SDK) for more information on responding to SharePoint events.

Migrating Sites and Site Collections

Commonly, administrators want to migrate sites or entire site collections to a different farm or content database. You can use the command line administrative tool `stsadm.exe` to migrate sites. Microsoft doesn't recommend using this as a full-time backup strategy, but it's helpful in a pinch.

Use the `import` and `export` operations of `stsadm.exe` to migrate sites. Use the `backup` operation to migrate site collections. See Chapter 18 for specifics on using `stsadm.exe`.

Recovering from Disaster

Realizing that a server has gone down makes for a bad day. Realizing that you don't have good backups is even worse. SharePoint provides backup solutions for recovering from a catastrophe. You should only use these solutions if you need to rebuild a server.

Backing up the server farm

SharePoint's Central Administration site is the place to go for administering your server farm. It makes sense that you also use this site to back up the server farm. You access the backup and restore commands in the Backup and Restore section of the Operations page in the Central Administration site, as shown in Figure 19-1.

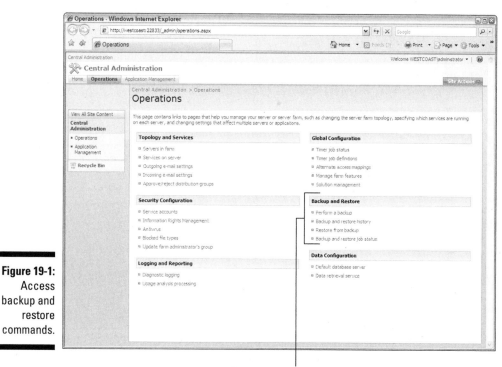

Figure 19-1:
Access
backup and
restore
commands.

Backup and Restore section

You use the Perform a Backup link to select what gets backed up in the server farm. You can elect to back up the following:

- ✔ **Entire server farm:** You can back up everything in the farm, including the Central Administration Web site.

- ✔ **Web applications:** You can back up the entire collection of Web applications or choose specific applications and content databases you wish to back up.

- ✔ **Shared Services:** You can back up the entire Shared Services application or just the content database.

- ✔ **Single Sign-On (SSO) database:** You can opt to back up the SSO database.

- ✔ **Search:** You can back up the indexes and databases that support search.

Like all Web sites, SharePoint's Web sites require a number of file resources to display pages in the browser. These file resources include image files, cascading style sheets, and eXtensible Markup Language (XML) configuration files. You must manually back up the files on the Web server with a third-party backup tool. You can use IIS Manager to determine the exact file location of the files you need to back up. By default, you at least need to back up at these two locations:

```
C:\Inetpub\wwwroot\wss\
C:\Program Files\Common Files\Microsoft Shared\web server
         extensions
```

Unless you've made significant customizations to SharePoint, you can rebuild your SharePoint Web server simply by reinstalling SharePoint on the server. All your content is stored in SQL Server databases, not on the Web server itself. It's generally best to avoid making changes to the files saved on the Web server because those files can be overwritten during an upgrade. However, if you do make customizations, such as creating your own graphics or style sheets, be sure to include those files in your backup plans.

Before you perform a backup, you must prepare your server for the backup. Here are the steps you perform to ensure your backup jobs run:

1. **Set up a file share to save the backup files to.**

   The backup process saves all the backup files to a directory or file share. You must use a third-party backup tool to back up the directory to a tape or other media.

2. **Make sure the Windows SharePoint Services Administrative Service is started on all servers in the farm.**

   This service isn't started on stand-alone servers. You can start the service by choosing Start➪Administrative Tools➪Services.

3. **Make sure the database server and the server being backed up can connect to one another.**

You must set up a remote file share to which the backup job can save files. Here are some rules pertaining to permissions and configuring the remote file share that you should adhere to:

1. **Make sure SQL Server 2005 services are using domain accounts.**

   Using domain accounts isn't required, but it is required if you want back up to a file share. You can view the accounts being used by SQL Server 2005 by choosing Start➪Administrative Tools➪Services on your database server. The default name for the database service for WSS is SQL Server 2005 Embedded Edition (MICROSOFT##SSEE). The default name for MOSS 2007 installations is SQL Server (OFFICESERVERS). Use the Log On tab to check the account used by the service.

   See the SQL Server 2005 Books Online for details on configuring SQL Server service accounts at:

```
www.microsoft.com/technet/prodtechnol/sql/2005/
         downloads/books.mspx.
```

2. **Create a file share on the backup server.**

This server doesn't have to be one of your SharePoint servers, but the farm servers and database server must be able to access the file share.

The share name can't end in a dollar sign ($). Shares that end in a dollar sign aren't visible from the network. SQL Server 2005 can't back up to those shares.

3. Grant the accounts listed in Table 19-1 rights to access the share using the Sharing and Security tabs of the file share's properties.

Share permissions determine who can access the share across the network. The rights granted in the Security tab determine who can access the contents inside the folder.

If you don't have a domain controller, you can't back up your files to a remote share. Instead, you can back up your files to the local hard drive of your server.

Table 19-1	Back Up Accounts and Rights	
Account	*Grant Rights on Sharing Tab*	*Grant Rights on Security Tab*
SQL Server Database Account	Change, Read	Read, Write
Central Administrator Pool Account	Change, Read	All except Full Control
Timer Service Account	Change, Read	All except Full Control

If you aren't using domain accounts for the accounts listed in Table 19-1, you can use the database server in place of the SQL Server account. For example, if your database server is named CLEO, you can grant CLEO rights in the Sharing tab.

Now that you have the environment set up, you can start a back up. Here are the steps:

1. Browse to the Operations page in the Central Administration site.

2. Click the Perform a Backup link in the Backup and Restore section.

The Perform a Backup page appears.

3. Select the components you wish to back up from the component tree.

The items you select are highlighted.

4. Click the Continue to Backup Options button.

The Start Backup page appears.

5. Indicate whether you wish to start a full or differential backup.

A *full backup* backs up everything, and a *differential backup* only backs up the content that's changed since the last full backup.

6. **Type the Universal Naming Convention (UNC) path to the file share you created in the Backup Location field.**

   The Backup File Location lists the estimated disk space required to perform the backup. Make sure you have adequate disk space before starting the backup. The Start Backup path shows an example of a UNC path.

7. **Click OK.**

   If there are no errors, the backup job is submitted, and the Backup and Restore Status page appears.

8. **Monitor the Backup and Restore Status page to see the progress of your backup job.**

When you configure a backup, you're actually configuring a one-time backup job. When you click OK in Step 7, SharePoint submits a job to the Job Timer service. You can't control the exact time the job starts. If the job fails, you can delete the job via the Timer Job Definitions link on the Operations page of the Central Administration site.

As shown in Figure 19-2, if SharePoint can't access your file share, error messages appear on the page.

You can always back up to a local file directory if you're having trouble accessing a file share. I don't recommend doing this permanently, but you can do it until you get your file share issues resolved.

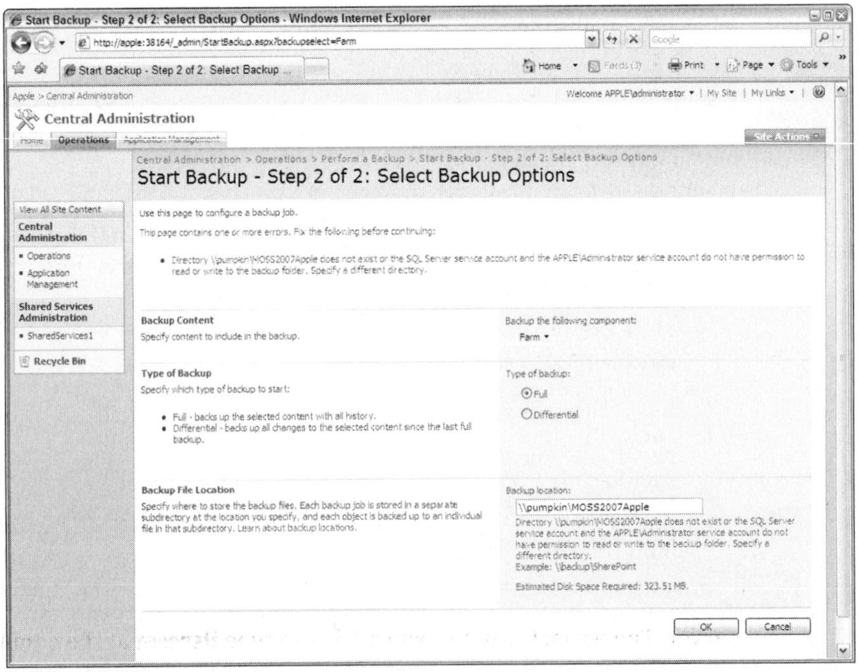

Figure 19-2:
Errors
appear in
the Start
Backup
page.

Restoring the server farm

You can use the backup created by Central Administration to overwrite a server farm or migrate content from one server farm to another. Before you restore from backup, you must make sure that the SharePoint software is installed on the server.

SharePoint's restore process restores all databases and hooks all your Web applications back up so your implementation is ready to go. Keep in mind that Restore creates a new Web application using a new application pool, which can degrade performance. If you'd rather avoid performance issues, you can create a new Web application that extends an existing application pool.

To restore from backup, do the following:

1. **Click the Restore from Backup link on the Operations page.**

   The Restore from Backup - Step 1 page appears.

2. **Enter the path to the backup files in the Backup location field.**

3. **Click OK.**

   The Restore from Backup - Step 2 page appears.

4. **Select a backup to restore and click the Continue Restore Process button.**

   The Restore from Backup - Step 3 page appears.

5. **Select the components you wish to restore.**

   If you can't select a component, it's because the component isn't in the backup. You can't restore the configuration database and Central Administration content database from this interface.

6. **Click the Continue Restore Process button.**

   The Restore from Backup - Step 4 page appears.

7. **In the Restore Options section, select the type of restore — New configuration or Same configuration.**

   If you select Same configuration, the backup files overwrite the existing content. If you select New configuration, you can specify a new URL and names for the restored content.

8. **Click OK.**

   The Backup and Restore Status page appears.

9. **Monitor the Backup and Restore Status page to ensure that the job completes successfully.**

After the restore finishes, restart the IIS (Internet Information Services) Web server. The easiest way to restart IIS is to type **iisreset** at the command line.

You can use the command line administrative tool `Stsadm.exe` to submit backup and restore jobs. Use the `backup` operation along with the `showtree` command to see a list of items you can back up, as shown here:

```
stsadm.exe -o backup -showtree
```

Here's the corresponding `restore` command:

```
stsadm.exe -o restore -directory \\backup -showtree
```

You can also use `Stsadm.exe` to back up and restore individual site collections. See Chapter 18 for more specifics on using `Stsadm.exe`.

You must use `Stsadm.exe` if you want to schedule a backup using the Windows Task Scheduler. SharePoint doesn't include any way to schedule backup jobs to start at a specific time.

Using SQL Server backup

Virtually everything that matters in SharePoint is stored in a database. So, the obvious question is why not use the existing SQL Server backup tools to back up SharePoint databases? This is a good option, especially if your company already has a backup and recovery plan for an existing SQL Server infrastructure.

The downside to this approach is that you must hook up everything after you do a restore. Also, you must use SharePoint backup to back up the search index.

SharePoint has the following databases that must be backed up:

- ✔ **Configuration Database (configdb):** There is only one configuration database per server farm. It stores data for sites, databases, servers, and Web applications.

- ✔ **Content Databases:** There is one content database per site collection. It stores all the site collection data, including site and structure details, end user content (such as lists and libraries, files, and security information). MOSS 2007 content databases also store InfoPath form templates and Excel Services data.

- ✔ **Shared Services Provider (SSP) Database:** There is one SSP database per SSP. The SSP database stores data for user profiles, audiences, Business Data Catalog, site usage data, and session state.

✔ **Office SharePoint Server Search Database:** There is one search database per SSP. The search database stores search data, history and search logs, and other search-related statistics. It isn't necessary to back up this database.

As you may have surmised, your user's data is stored in content databases. Backing up these databases on a regular basis is vitally important. See your database administrator for assistance with setting up SQL Server backups.

Click the Content Databases link in the Application Management page of the Central Administration site to configure content databases for Web applications.

Building redundancy into the system

In addition to using SQL Server's backup utilities, medium to larger companies often use sophisticated hardware and software configurations that make recovery faster. Both the SharePoint and SQL Server backup feature requires an administrator to rebuild the server and restore files from tape or some other medium. If you've ever had to do this, you know it's very time consuming.

Although it's essential to get good backups, you have other options that make it easier to recover from a failure without rebuilding everything:

✔ **Hardware redundancy:** There are many failure points in server hardware. One of the biggies is hard drive failure. Even if you have good backups, they're only as good as the last time they ran. So, if your hard drive fails at 4 p.m., you could lose a day's worth of work. This is unacceptable in most companies. Instead, you can configure your server with multiple hard drives so that if one fails, you have backups. Disk storage is cheap. Losing data isn't.

✔ **SQL Server clustering:** Instead of one database server, you can bind two or more servers to create a server cluster. Both servers are available to respond to requests. If one goes down, the other has to work harder. But it buys you some time until you can repair or replace the server.

✔ **SQL Server log shipping:** Databases use transaction logs to keep track of all the data that goes into the database. SQL Server can send these transaction logs to a backup server to create a secondary database server. If the primary server fails, you can manually fire up the secondary database server.

Creating Your Backup Plan

This chapter shows you the building blocks for creating a backup strategy for your organization. There is no one-size-fits-all recommendation for doing backups. You have to create a plan that best fits your organization, taking into consideration your company's tolerance for down time and lost data. See the sidebar, "Best practices for backup and restoration," later in this chapter, for more information on backup strategies.

Reading about backup solutions in a book is the first step in creating your backup plan. To create a good plan, you must try out the various options and see what works for you. I suggest you do the following:

1. **Create backups with each of the tools in this chapter.**

2. **Attempt a `restore` operation on a test server.**

    It's important that your test environment closely matches your production environment. Otherwise, you might be surprised at the complexity of a real life restore.

3. **Decide which tools best suit your organization's needs in terms of the following:**

    • How much data has to be backed up.

    • How frequently you need to back up (and restore).

    • How mission-critical your data is.

    • How much you've customized your implementation.

    • How many users are affected.

4. **Test, test, test your backups on a regular basis.**

    Restore your full backup to a test server at least once per month.

It's important that you match your backup solution to your restore need. For example, using Central Administration to restore a single file is like trying to get a drink of water from a fire hydrant. It isn't likely that just one backup solution provides everything you need. Instead, plan on creating a hybrid solution based on these recommendations:

> ✔ **Perform a full backup** using Central Administration or `stsadm.exe` once per week and perform a differential backup nightly for small- to medium-sized deployments.

✔ **Perform SQL Server backups** if your company already supports a SQL Server backup infrastructure. Your database administrator should also schedule monthly database defrags and consistency checks.

✔ **Implement hardware and server redundancy** to provide maximum up time.

✔ **Show end users how to use tools,** like Recycle Bin and Version Control.

✔ **Implement an event handler** for the Web Delete Event to back up deleted sites.

 SharePoint also implements a Volume Shadow Copy Service (VSS) writer service. If your company is using VSS as part of its backup strategy, you can use the VSS writer service to back up your server farm. VSS is often used by third parties to provide backup software. You can purchase third-party backup software that works with SharePoint.

Best practices for backup and restoration

Backing up mission-critical data is a vital element in every company's risk management and disaster recovery plans. Audit your policies and procedures to see how they measure up to these best practices:

✔ Check backup logs daily and resolve any errors or warnings.

✔ Build redundancy into mission-critical systems.

✔ Store physical backup media off-site, preferably in an off-site vault, NOT at your Information Technology (IT) manager's house.

✔ Have the media for your operating system and software applications available off-site; also, have tape drives (or whatever hardware is necessary for restoring data) available off-site in the event of disaster.

✔ Test your capability to restore the entire backup and smaller units of the backup.

✔ Have an overall disaster-recovery and risk management plan.

✔ Schedule backups to minimize downtime but make sure they have enough time to complete.

✔ Have a library for storing media and make sure media are labeled properly.

✔ Have a media pool but track reusable media so you can retire media when it reaches the end of its service life.

✔ Physically destroy all expired media; don't just throw them away.

✔ Have a monthly or quarterly restore-and-test schedule.

I can personally attest to the value of using a combination of approaches. I once had a server that failed over Christmas. When I came into work the morning before the Christmas holiday, I discovered that the database server wasn't running. It shut down because the nightly backup job failed. During that job, a consistency check on the database failed. I had to restore the database using the backup from the night before, which meant that I had lost an entire day's worth of transactions. Luckily, I had good backups of all the database's transaction logs. Unfortunately, one of the logs was corrupted. I had to send the log to an engineer at the database software company (Sybase) who fixed the file on Christmas Eve. I applied the logs and got the database up and running.

You can shift the burden of managing backups and restores to a third party by using a hosted SharePoint implementation.

Part VI
The Part of Tens

The 5th Wave   By Rich Tennant

"They can predict earthquakes and seizures,
why <u>not</u> server failures?"

In this part . . .

1 share with you ten of my favorite SharePoint-related resources. And just in case you don't have enough ideas for using SharePoint, I give you ten outcomes you can expect to achieve with SharePoint.

Chapter 20

Ten SharePoint Resources Worth Checking Out

*J*ust in case you had any doubt about the importance of SharePoint to Microsoft, I compiled this list of ten resources from Microsoft. Whether you're a power user or an eager developer, you'll find something here to help you dig deeper into SharePoint.

Microsoft's home page for SharePoint Products and Technologies is the jumping off place for finding all things related to SharePoint on Microsoft's site. You can navigate to most of the resources listed here from the site, which is aptly located at www.microsoft.com/sharepoint.

Something for everyone is in this list, from end users to Information Technology (IT) administrators. Be sure to look for RSS feeds that you can subscribe to so you can stay current.

You can create a Web Part page for your portal, team site, or even the Central Administration site that lists SharePoint resources using the sites listed here as a starting point. I suggest using a combination of links and RSS feeds to display content. You could add your own internal resources or possibly even create a SharePoint blog where you post all the tricks and tips you find.

Technically Speaking

If you're an IT professional, chances are you've used Microsoft's site — TechNet — dedicated to the technical aspects of their products. On TechNet, you find technical libraries and administrator guides for IT administrators for

SharePoint and every other Microsoft product. The library includes loads of information on planning and deploying your SharePoint implementation. You also find dozens of worksheets you can use to assist in your planning.

You can find the TechNet home page at `http://technet.microsoft.com`. Listed here are four SharePoint specific sites on TechNet you'll want to bookmark:

- ✔ **WSS TechNet Technical Library on TechNet:** Get planning and deployment information at

  ```
  http://technet2.microsoft.com/windowsserver/WSS/
          en/library/700c3d60-f394-4ca9-a6d8-
          ab597fc3c31b1033.mspx?mfr=true
  ```

- ✔ **MOSS 2007 Technical Library on TechNet:** At some point, you can download this whole document as an administrator's guide. As of this writing, it's only available via the Web at

  ```
  http://technet2.microsoft.com/Office/en-us/library/
          3e3b8737-c6a3-4e2c-a35f-f0095d952b781033.
          mspx?mfr=true
  ```

- ✔ **WSS home page on TechNet:** Here you can find links to all kinds of resources for WSS. You can download a copy of Windows SharePoint Services (WSS) version 3.0 and find site templates that you can use within your organization. Access the site at

  ```
  www.microsoft.com/technet/windowsserver/sharepoint
  ```

- ✔ **MOSS 2007 home page on TechNet:** Download a trial version and access featured technical resources at

  ```
  www.microsoft.com/technet/prodtechnol/office/sharepoint
  ```

Exploring MSDN

Microsoft's site dedicated to developers — the Microsoft Developer Network (MSDN) — features portals showcasing development-related articles and resources. You can find a Developer Center for both WSS and MOSS 2007, along with all of Microsoft's other products. The home page for MSDN is `http://msdn.microsoft.com`. Listed here are the links to the SharePoint Developers Centers:

- ✔ **MOSS 2007 Developer Center on MSDN:** Find downloads, articles, and videos on MOSS 2007 and related technologies at

  ```
  http://msdn2.microsoft.com/en-us/office/aa905503.aspx.
  ```

- ✔ **WSS Developer Center on MSDN:** Get resources that help you get the most out of using WSS as an application delivery platform at

  ```
  http://msdn2.microsoft.com/en-us/sharepoint.
  ```

Be sure to check out the latest edition of *MSDN Magazine,* the Microsoft Journal for Developers, while you're on MSDN. You'll find lots of detailed articles explaining how stuff works. Access *MSDN Magazine* at `http://msdn.microsoft.com/msdnmag`.

Digging Deeper with Software Development Kits

Software Development Kits (SDKs) are excellent resources for finding out how to develop custom SharePoint applications. Even if you never plan on writing one line of code, SDKs provide extensive documentation on product architecture. If you want to get your mind around what makes SharePoint work, poke your head into the SDK.

You can access the MOSS 2007 and WSS SDKs online via the Developer Centers on MSDN. You can also find links that download the SDKs on the MSDN Developer Centers. When you download an SDK, it usually includes sample applications to demonstrate developer opportunities.

Getting Acquainted with Office Online

One of the best resources for accessing end-user documentation is Office Online. You'll find walkthroughs of all sorts of tasks and resources for use with Office 2007 clients and servers. Access Office Online at `http://office.microsoft.com/en-us/sharepointserver`. Click the Products tab to see a list of all the products you can peruse on the site.

You can also find Discussion Groups for all the products in the Office 2007 suite, including SharePoint, at `www.microsoft.com/office/community/en-us/default.mspx`.

Downloading SharePoint Resources

The Microsoft Downloads Center is an excellent resource for finding all sorts of downloads. By conducting an advanced search, you can choose WSS or SharePoint Server from a list of products to see all relevant downloads. Sort by release date to see the most recent downloads first. Visit the Downloads Center at `www.microsoft.com/downloads`.

You can download a trial version of MOSS 2007 at

```
www.microsoft.com/downloads/details.aspx?FamilyID=2e6e5a9c-
        ebf6-4f7f-8467-f4de6bd6b831&displaylang=en
```

Anytime you download a file from Microsoft's Web site, be sure to scroll to the bottom of the page to see a list of related downloads.

Blogging SharePoint

Microsoft encourages their product teams and employees to blog about the products they're working on. These blogs give you an insider's track on announcements and tutorials that you can't get anywhere else:

- ✔ **SharePoint Team Blog:** This is the official blog of Microsoft's SharePoint Product Group. You can find SharePoint-related announcements at `http://blogs.msdn.com/sharepoint`.

- ✔ **Records Management Team Blog:** Read everything you ever wanted to know about records management in SharePoint at `http://blogs.msdn.com/recman`.

- ✔ **Enterprise Content Team Blog:** This blog covers the enterprise content management features of SharePoint. You'll find a little bit about document management, Web content management, and records management at `http://blogs.msdn.com/ecm`.

- ✔ **Knowledge Network Team Blog:** If you're interested in implementing knowledge networking features in your MOSS 2007 implementation, you must check out this blog at `http://blogs.msdn.com/kn`.

Discovering SharePoint

Microsoft provides an extensive set of online and in-person training opportunities on all its products. You can find training resources on SharePoint at the following sites:

- ✔ **Events and Webcasts:** Attend in-person events, participate in live Webcasts, or download pre-recorded Webcasts about SharePoint at `www.microsoft.com/events`. There are events and webcasts for all audiences from business professionals to IT executives.

✔ **Microsoft Learning:** Use self-paced clinics to get acquainted with SharePoint. Visit the Microsoft Office 2007 Learning portal at `www.microsoft.com/learning/office2007`.

✔ **Channel 9:** Watch videos shot inside Microsoft's campus, featuring the folks who work with SharePoint everyday at `http://channel9.msdn.com/tags/Sharepoint`.

Getting Support

I'm often surprised by the number of people who've never used Microsoft's knowledge base. In my opinion, such people really don't know what they've been missing. The knowledge base contains a truly exhaustive collection of support articles, so if you're having troubles with SharePoint, you'll more than likely find an article describing a fix in the knowledge base. You can access Microsoft's Help and Support home page at `http://support.microsoft.com`. Find SharePoint-specific support at the following:

✔ **WSS Support Center:** `http://support.microsoft.com/ph/12200`

✔ **MOSS 2007 Support Center:** `http://support.microsoft.com/ph/11373`

TIP

Be sure to use the Search Support text box that you find at these support centers to find knowledge base articles specific to SharePoint.

TIP

Microsoft doesn't have the market cornered on SharePoint support. You can find many resources on SharePoint on the Web. You can find a search engine of SharePoint-centric blogs and Web sites at `http://search.live.com/macros/lliu/spsearch`.

Finding SharePoint Hosting

Whether you're just looking to tinker with SharePoint or you've decided you don't want the overhead of one more server, you have your choice of service providers who sell hosted SharePoint services. Get a list of providers from Microsoft at

`www.microsoft.com/serviceproviders/directory/wssv3.mspx`

Getting a Head Start with Application Templates

Microsoft released 30 application templates for WSS version 2 that provided SharePoint sites geared for use as applications, such as help desk and project management. WSS version 3 has 40 application templates that are even more feature-rich. You can find templates for everything from timecard management to inventory tracking. You can run with these templates as-is or customize them to suit your business. Find more about these templates at

```
www.microsoft.com/technet/windowsserver/sharepoint/
            wssapps/v3templates.mspx
```

Bonus Resource

I've helped hundreds of readers and clients through my books on SharePoint. Be sure to check out my other books on SharePoint:

- ✔ *Microsoft SharePoint 2003 For Dummies* (Wiley)
- ✔ *Office 2007 and SharePoint Productivity For Dummies* (Wiley)
- ✔ *SharePoint Designer 2007 For Dummies* (Wiley)

You can find out more about these books or get in touch with me via my Web site at www.sharepointgrrl.com.

Chapter 21

Ten Positive Outcomes from Implementing SharePoint

In This Chapter

▶ Underscoring the importance of goal-setting

▶ Ideas for getting the most out of SharePoint

▶ Using SharePoint to improve relationships

*T*here are plenty of good reasons to implement SharePoint. Just 'cause, isn't one of them. In this chapter, I share with you ten positive outcomes that are reasonable to achieve by implementing SharePoint.

Think of these outcomes as goals or objectives. They don't happen simply by installing SharePoint. If you want to achieve these or similar results, you must identify these as desired outcomes of your implementation and make sure that users have the training, support, and tools they need to achieve the outcome.

What's more, you have to match the outcomes of your SharePoint project to the realities of your organization. Be sure your company has the right kind of culture and the right kind of people to achieve the goals you set for your project.

Increase User Productivity

Increasing user productivity is an obvious and attainable goal for implementing SharePoint. Don't expect to achieve this goal in the first month. In addition to providing adequate training and support, you must identify the specific ways you want to increase user productivity and target your training efforts. For example, you might want to do the following:

▶ Reduce time spent searching for information and people by using document management and people search.

▶ Minimize the number of calls to the help desk to restore documents by using versioning and the Recycle Bin.

✔ Aggregate research resources on your portal and limit the user's need to perform free-form search with tools like Google.

✔ Use SharePoint search to monitor user's search activity and get feedback on what users are searching on to improve the relevancy of SharePoint search.

✔ Implement SharePoint blogs to eliminate the use of free blogs on the Internet.

Reduce Calls to the Help Desk

By standardizing your company's document management in SharePoint, you create a single environment for all users to save and open documents. Instead of expecting employees to know how to use file shares, exchange public folders, and FTP sites, they only have one thing to know — SharePoint. Sure, they'll have questions about SharePoint, but they'll be the same questions about a single environment. Thanks to features like versioning and the Recycle Bin users can be more self-sufficient when files are deleted accidentally. All this adds up to fewer calls to the help desk and less diversity among the kinds of calls. For an added bonus, you can use SharePoint to track the kinds of calls you're receiving so you know where to target your training efforts.

Increase Opportunities for Knowledge Transfer

Your employees know a lot about running your business. Unfortunately, they don't always share that knowledge with each other. You can use SharePoint to create an environment that encourages knowledge sharing among employees in the following ways:

✔ Set up user profiles and encourage people to use the Colleague features in My Site.

✔ Expand People search by creating a knowledge network that enables them to search the contacts and other resources of their colleagues.

✔ Use the SharePoint Community Kit to create a forum for customers, partners, and employees to engage.

✔ Couple SharePoint with other server products, like Groove Server and Live Communications Server, to enable real-time collaboration.

Increase Employee Loyalty and Satisfaction

Most companies spend a not-so-small fortune on employee benefits and services. Quite often, employees have no idea what these benefits are or how to take advantage of them. To solve this problem, many companies have started sending annual compensation statements that inform employees of the total value of all payroll and benefits. Instead of sending static reports to your employees, use SharePoint to create a personalized portal that displays information to your employees in real time. Better yet, make the portal interactive so that employees can get more information about a benefit right away.

You can use SharePoint's survey feature to gauge your employees' satisfaction with their benefits and other aspects of their jobs.

Minimize Communication Barriers between Departments

Everybody knows that communication, or lack thereof, is a major issue in every company. Nowadays, it seems that companies rely solely on e-mail to communicate. You can use SharePoint to break out of the monotony and information overload of e-mail in these ways:

- ✔ Create a knowledge base, or *Wiki,* for sharing knowledge about customers or products.
- ✔ Publish announcements to each user's My Site personal portal instead of sending e-mails.
- ✔ Encourage workers, managers, and executives to share their insight on problems and opportunities with blogs.
- ✔ Display RSS feeds of content from your SharePoint sites and subscribe to RSS feeds of competitors, partners, and customers.
- ✔ Use featured search results and the site directory to highlight popular sites, pages, and resources.

Improve Relationships with Partners and Customers

How do you share information with partners and customers now? Do you have a monthly newsletter? A periodic e-mail blast? An out-of-date Web site? Chances are you have multiple channels for reaching partners and customers, and none of your activities are coordinated. You can use SharePoint to do the following:

✔ Create a public-facing Internet portal for publishing news releases and announcements.

✔ Coordinate projects that span across organizational boundaries with team sites.

✔ Use personalization features to make your partners and customers feel like they're your number one priority.

✔ Use lists and workflows to track and trigger periodic communications with partners and customers.

Mitigate the Risks of Software Development

You can use SharePoint to quickly generate application prototypes even if you don't plan to use SharePoint to host the final solution. You can use SharePoint to do the following:

✔ Dynamically generate New, Edit, and Display forms for content types, which are loosely analogous to objects in object-oriented programming. For example, you can create a Customer content type that allows users to enter a customer's name and contact information.

✔ Display master/detail views commonly found in most applications using folders and list items in lists.

✔ Create views to display filtered sets of data to specific groups of users.

✔ In addition, SharePoint provides permissions and a notification infrastructure. You don't have to provision a new Web site or design a database to get started with your application. You can start thinking in terms of the business entities involved in solving the business problem without being distracted by low-level technical issues.

Maximize ROI

Maximizing Return on Investment (ROI) is important for any organization, especially when it comes to getting the biggest bang for your buck from your existing reporting and business intelligence infrastructure. You can use SharePoint to provide users access to existing reports created with SQL Server and Crystal Reports. You can use SharePoint as a user interface to whatever business intelligence platforms you already have implemented. Instead of training users on using various third-party tools, they only need to know how to pull up a dashboard in SharePoint.

Reduce Merger/Acquisition Costs

Nowadays, it's common for companies to achieve growth through acquisition. Integrating new companies is not only expensive, it can dictate the extent to which the new employees are accepted within the organization. With SharePoint, you can keep employees abreast of news related to the acquisition and plans for integration. You can add the employees from the new organization into the company directory in a matter of hours. With Excel Services and Business Data Catalog, you can quickly integrate newly acquired businesses in a much shorter period of time than hand-rolling your own integration.

Build Bridges between Information Technology (IT) and Business Users

In many organizations, an adversarial relationship exists between IT and end users. IT staff are often backlogged with requests. End users are often overwhelmed with the seemingly never ending onslaught of upgrades and changes along with a perceived lack of support and training from IT. Unfortunately, the net effect is an uneasy truce where IT gets in the habit of saying no to all new requests (or requests that aren't high profile enough), and end users stop asking for anything.

I believe there are several reasons for this state of IT, and SharePoint can help. I think many end users feel powerless, and SharePoint can certainly help empower end users, but only if IT allows it. SharePoint has a number of monitoring and administration tools that enable IT to get their arms around what the users are doing. They can finally see how many spreadsheets,

Access databases, and Word documents are being used, what they're being used for, and by whom. They can start to see patterns in usage and take on the roles of advisor and partner in helping end users take control of managing their information environment.

IT has to be willing to let go of some of their control while realizing that they're gaining an opportunity to manage their information infrastructure. At the same time, end users have to be willing to accept this responsibility.

Index